SILVER BURDETT English

Betty G. Gray
Nancy N. Ragno
Marian Davies Toth

SILVER BURDETT COMPANY   MORRISTOWN, NJ

Atlanta, GA · Cincinnati, OH · Dallas, TX · Northfield, IL · San Carlos, CA · Agincourt, Ontario

Centennial Edition

Acknowledgments

Cover: Ted Spiegel/Black Star

Contributing Artists: Michael Adams; Robert Blake; Harry Borgman; Ray Burns; Pamela Ford-Johnson; Leigh Grant; Jane Kendall; Bob Marstall; Norma Rahn; Steven Schindler; William Schmidt; Herman Vestal; Daryl Urig.

Photographs: Unit 1 7: Glenn Short/Bruce Coleman. 35: Phil Schofield/West Stock. 51: Victoria Beller-Smith for Silver Burdett. **Unit 2** 75: © 1985 George Hall/Woodfin Camp & Associates. 107: S. Tselentis/Shostal Associates. 109: Jerry Wachter/Focus on Sports. **Unit 3** 135: Margot Conte/Animals Animals. 155: U.S. Postal Service. 157: Walter Hodges/West Stock. 173: Eddie Adams/Gamma Liaison. 175: Clyde Smith/Peter Arnold, Inc. 197: Edison National Historical Site. 199: Focus on Sports. **Unit 4** 223: Ted Spiegel/Black Star. 241: Jonathan Wright/Bruce Coleman. **Unit 5** 275: Michal Heron. 285: George M. Cassidy/Atoz Images. 291: Mike Malyszko/Stock, Boston. 298: Michael Philip Manheim/The Stock Shop. 305: Michal Heron for Silver Burdett. 320: Silver Burdett. 321: Lionel Atwill/Peter Arnold, Inc. 329: Michal Heron. 330—335: Silver Burdett. **Unit 6** 347: Dan De Wilde for Silver Burdett. 349: Dennis Brack/Black Star. 363: Dan De Wilde for Silver Burdett. 371: Silver Burdett. 374: Michal Heron. 393: Victoria Beller-Smith for Silver Burdett. 417: University of Texas at Austin. 439: Dan De Wilde for Silver Burdett. **Unit 7** 457: Dan De Wilde for Silver Burdett. 477: Michal Heron for Silver Burdett. **Unit 8** 491: Michal Heron for Silver Burdett. 496: Silver Burdett. 511, 531: Michal Heron for Silver Burdett.

Contributing Writers: Susan Banfield; Robert Bell; Bernard Brodsky; Judith Lechner; Duncan Searl

PERMISSIONS: We wish to thank the following authors, publishers, agents, corporations, and individuals for their permission to reprint copyrighted materials. Page 6: "Open Range" from *Cowboys and Indians* by Kathryn and Byron Jackson. Copyright © 1968, 1948 by Western Publishing Company, Inc. Reprinted by permission. Page 22: Excerpt from *The Story of Walt Disney* by Diane Disney Miller. Reprinted by permission of the author. Page 34: "A Horse Is a Horse" from *I Would Like to Be a Pony* by Dorothy W. Baruch. Reprinted by permission of Bertha Klausner International Literary Agency, Inc. Page 50: "Winter Circus" from *Young America World Parade* by Aileen Fisher. By permission of the author. Page 69: "Sight" by Cora Ball Moton from *Golden Slippers*, edited by Arna Bontemps. Copyright 1941 by Harper & Row, Publishers, Inc. Reprinted by permission of the publisher. Page 74: "Hard Questions" by Margaret Tsuda. Reprinted by permission of the author. Page 108: "Good Sportsmanship" from *All in Sport* by Richard Armour, published by McGraw-Hill, Inc. Reprinted by permission of the author. Page 134: "The Guppy" from *Verses from 1929 On* by Ogden Nash. Copyright 1944 by The Curtis Publishing Company. First appeared in *The Saturday Evening Post*. Reprinted by permission of Little, Brown and Company and Andre Deutsch. Page 156: "Velvet Shoes" from *Collected Poems of Elinor Wylie*. Copyright 1921 by Alfred A. Knopf, Inc.,

and renewed 1949 by William Rose Benet. Reprinted permission of Alfred A. Knopf, Inc. Page 174: "M sure Me, Sky!" from *Slow Wall: Poems* by Leon Speyer. Copyright 1939, 1946, 1951 by Leonora Spe and renewed 1967, 1974 by The Estate of Leon Speyer. Reprinted by permission of Alfred A. Kne Inc. Page 198: Robert Francis for "Skier," from *Transatlantic Review*, No. 2, Winter, 1959—(Copyright © 1960 by Robert Francis. Page 222: " ploring" from *There Is No Rhyme for Silver* by Eve N riam. Copyright © 1962 by Eve Merriam. Reprintec permission of the author. Page 240: "Comma in Sky" from *In the Woods, In the Meadow, In the Sk* Aileen Fisher, Scribner, NY, in 1965. Reprinted by mission of the author. Page 267: "The Night is Fre ing Fast?" from *The Collected Poems of A.E. Housm* Copyright 1922 by Holt, Rinehart and Winst Copyright 1950 by Barclays Bank Ltd. Reprinted permission of Holt, Rinehart and Winston, Publishe and The Society of Authors as the literary repres tatives of the Estate of A.E. Housman, and Jonatl Cape Ltd. Page 295: Excerpt from *A Wrinkle in T* by Madeleine L'Engle. Copyright © 1962 by Madele L'Engle Franklin. Reprinted by permission of Far Straus and Giroux, Inc. Page 348: The article "Le Carroll Materials Given to New York University Libra Reprinted by permission of The Associated Pre Page 362: Excerpt from *I Know Why the Caged Bird Si*

Acknowledgments continued on page

C O N T E N T S

Introduction   The Parts of a Book   **XV**

GRAMMAR, USAGE, MECHANICS

UNIT ONE
The Parts of Speech

Unit Preview   **2**
Using a Thesaurus   **4**

Chapter 1 *Nouns, Pronouns,*
             and Adjectives   **6**
   1 Nouns   **8**
   2 Kinds of Nouns   **10**
     Additional Exercises   **12**
     Application — Using Grammar in Writing   **13**
   3 Pronouns   **14**
   4 Antecedents of Pronouns   **16**
   5 Demonstrative and Reflexive Pronouns   **18**
   6 Interrogative and Indefinite Pronouns   **20**
     Additional Exercises   **22**
     Application — Using Grammar in Writing   **23**
   7 Adjectives   **24**
   8 Proper and Demonstrative Adjectives   **26**
   9 Words Used as Different Parts of Speech **28**
     Additional Exercises   **30**
     Application — Using Grammar in Writing   **31**
     Chapter Review and Challenge   **32**

Chapter 2   *Verbs and Adverbs*   34

    1 Verbs   36
    2 Verb Phrases   38
       Additional Exercises   40
       Application — Using Grammar in Writing   41
    3 Adverbs   42
    4 Facts About Adverbs   44
       Additional Exercises   46
       Application — Using Grammar in Writing   47

       Chapter Review and Challenge   48

Chapter 3   *Conjunctions, Prepositions, and Interjections*   50

    1 Conjunctions   52
    2 Prepositions   54
    3 Prepositional Phrases as Adjectives   58
    4 Prepositional Phrases as Adverbs   60
       Additional Exercises   62
       Application — Using Grammar in Writing   63
    5 Interjections   64

       Chapter Review and Challenge   66
       CUMULATIVE REVIEW: The Parts of Speech   68

UNIT TWO
Sentence Structure

Unit Preview   72

Chapter 4   *The Sentence*   **74**

1 Sentences   76
2 Four Kinds of Sentences   78
3 Complete and Simple Subjects   80
4 Complete and Simple Predicates   82
5 Subject and Verb Identification   84
6 Compound Subjects and Verbs   86
Additional Exercises   88
Application — Using Grammar in Writing   89
7 Direct Objects   90
8 Predicate Nominatives and
Predicate Adjectives   92
9 Indirect Objects   96
10 Verbals   98
Additional Exercises   104
Application — Using Grammar in Writing   105

Chapter Review and Challenge   106

Chapter 5   *Simple, Compound, and*
Complex Sentences   **108**

1 Simple and Compound Sentences   110
2 Clauses   112
3 Complex Sentences   114
4 Sentence Errors   116
Additional Exercises   118
Application — Using Grammar in Writing   119

Chapter Review and Challenge   120
CUMULATIVE REVIEW: Sentence Structure   122

UNIT THREE
Usage

Unit Preview   126
Words Often Confused   128

Chapter 6 *Noun and Pronoun Usage*   134
  1 Making Nouns Plural   136
  2 Nouns with Special Plural Forms   138
  3 Possessive Nouns   140
    Additional Exercises   142
    Application — Using Nouns in Writing   143
  4 Two Pronoun Cases   144
  5 Choosing Correct Pronouns   146
  6 Avoiding Pronoun Errors   148
  7 Rules for Three Kinds of Pronouns   150
    Additional Exercises   152
    Application — Using Pronouns in Writing   153

    Chapter Review and Challenge   154

Chapter 7 *Adjective and Adverb Usage*   156
  1 Degrees of Adjectives   158
  2 Using Comparatives and Superlatives   160
  3 Degrees of Adverbs   162
  4 Avoiding Double Negatives   164
  5 Correct Use of Adjectives and Adverbs   166
  6 Troublesome Adjectives and Adverbs   168
    Additional Exercises   170
    Application — Using Modifiers in Writing   171

    Chapter Review and Challenge   172

Chapter 8 *Verb Usage*   **174**
   1 Principal Parts of Verbs   **176**
   2 Tenses of Verbs   **178**
   3 Forms of *be, have,* and *do*   **182**
   4 Irregular Verbs   **186**
   Additional Exercises   **190**
   Application — Using Verbs in Writing   **191**
   5 Troublesome Verb Pairs   **192**
   6 Troublesome Verb Pairs   **194**
   Chapter Review and Challenge   **196**

Chapter 9 *Subject-Verb Agreement*   **198**
   1 Spelling Singular Verb Forms   **200**
   2 Three Verbs That Cause Problems   **202**
   3 Problems with Prepositional Phrases   **204**
   4 Agreement with Compound Subjects   **206**
   5 Problems with Inverted Sentences   **208**
   6 Problems with Indefinite Pronouns   **210**
   Additional Exercises   **212**
   Application — Using Agreement in Writing   **213**
   Chapter Review and Challenge   **214**
   CUMULATIVE REVIEW: Usage   **216**

UNIT FOUR
Mechanics

Unit Preview   **220**

Chapter 10   *Capitalization*   **222**

1 Capitalizing Names and Titles   **224**
2 Capitalizing Geographical Names   **226**
3 Capitalizing Other Names   **228**
4 Capitalizing First Words and Certain
   Parts of Speech   **230**
5 Capitalizing Other Titles   **232**
6 Writing Numbers   **234**
Additional Exercises   **236**
Application — Life Skills   **237**

Chapter Review and Challenge   **238**

Chapter 11   *Punctuation*   **240**

1 End Marks   **242**
2 Commas That Separate   **244**
3 Commas for Appositives and
   Nouns of Direct Address   **246**
4 Commas After Introductory Words and
   to Set Off Interrupters   **248**
5 Other Uses of Commas   **250**
6 Quotation Marks   **252**
7 Divided Quotations   **254**
8 Italics and Underlining   **256**
9 Semicolons and Colons   **258**
10 Apostrophes   **260**
Additional Exercises   **262**
Application — Life Skills   **263**

Chapter Review and Challenge   **264**
CUMULATIVE REVIEW: Mechanics   **266**

WRITING, SPEAKING and LISTENING, STUDY SKILLS

UNIT FIVE
The Basics of Writing

Unit Preview   272

Chapter 12 *Sentence Combining and Revising*   **274**
1 Combining Sentences
  with Repeated Ideas   **276**
2 Combining Compound Sentences   **278**
3 Expanding Sentences   **280**
4 Combining Sentences
  with Subordinate Ideas   **282**
5 Revising Windy Sentences   **284**
6 Revising Choppy Sentences   **286**

   Chapter Review and Writers at Work   **288**

Chapter 13 *Purpose and Audience in Writing*   **290**
1 Identifying a Purpose   **292**
2 Identifying an Audience   **294**
3 Writing for Different Audiences   **296**
4 Choosing a Form for Writing   **298**

   Chapter Review and Writers at Work   **302**

Chapter 14   *Organizing Ideas into Paragraphs*   **304**
   1 Paragraph Basics   **306**
   2 Selecting and Narrowing a Topic   **308**
   3 Main Ideas and Topic Sentences   **310**
   4 Developing Paragraphs by Examples   **312**
   5 Developing Paragraphs by Facts   **314**
   6 Developing Paragraphs by Reasons   **316**
   7 Paragraph Unity   **318**
   8 Order of Ideas In Paragraphs   **320**
   A Paragraph Checklist   **323**
   9 Using Transitions   **324**

   Chapter Review and Writers at Work   **326**

Chapter 15   *The Writing Process*   **328**
   1 A Photo Essay   **330**
   2 The Stages of the Writing Process   **336**
   Writer's Checklist   **340**

   Chapter Review and Writers at Work   **342**

UNIT SIX
Writing

Unit Preview   **344**

Chapter 16   *Informing and Describing*   **346**
1 Learning About Newspapers   **348**
2 Fact and Opinion   **350**
3 Conducting an Interview   **352**
4 Informing — A News Story   **354**
5 Writing Sensory Details   **358**
6 Writing Comparisons   **360**
7 Writing a Descriptive Paragraph   **362**
8 Describing — A Character Sketch   **364**

    Building Bridges to Computers   **368**

Chapter 17   *Narrating and Creating*   **370**
1 First Person in a Narrative Paragraph   **372**
2 Writing Dialogue   **374**
3 Narrating — A Personal Experience
   Narrative   **376**
4 Third Person in a Narrative Paragraph   **380**
5 Elements of the Short Story   **382**
6 Creating — A Mystery Story   **386**

    Building Bridges to Social Studies   **390**

Chapter 18   *Researching and Persuading*   **392**
1 Taking a Survey   **394**
2 Writing Survey Questions   **396**
3 Researching — A Survey Summary   **398**
4 Friendly Letters   **402**
5 Social Notes   **404**
6 Business Letters   **406**
7 Preparing Letters for Mailing   **408**
8 Persuading — A Letter of Opinion   **410**

    Building Bridges to Mathematics   **414**

Chapter 19   *Classifying and Reasoning*   **416**
1 The Media   **418**
2 Classifying Information   **420**
3 Classifying — A Media Review   **422**
4 Identifying Cause and Effect   **426**
5 Interpreting Data   **428**
6 Comparison/Contrast Paragraphs   **430**
7 Reasoning — A Consumer Report   **432**

Building Bridges to Science   **436**

Chapter 20   *Literature*   **438**
1 Plays   **440**
2 Myths   **446**
3 Poetry — Sound and Form   **450**

UNIT SEVEN
Speaking and Listening

Unit Preview   454

Chapter 21 **Speaking**   456
  1 Introductions   458
  2 Conversations   460
  3 Class Discussions   462
  4 Telephoning   464
  5 Giving Information   466
  6 Voice and Speech Techniques   468
  7 Giving a Talk   470

Chapter 22 **Listening**   476
  1 Listening   478
  2 Listening to Learn   480
    Memory Techniques
    Main Idea
    Details
    Taking Notes
    Context Clues
    Directions
  3 Critical Listening   486

UNIT EIGHT
Study Skills

Unit Preview   488

Chapter 23   *Library and Reporting Skills*   490
1 Using the Library   492
2 Using Reference Books   496
3 Taking Notes   500
4 Paraphrasing   502
5 Outlining   504
6 Structure of a Report   506
7 Writing a Book Report   508

Chapter 24   *Vocabulary and Word Study*   510
1 How to Study Vocabulary   512
2 The History of English   514
3 Using a Dictionary   518
4 A Dictionary as a Writing Aid   520
5 Prefixes and Suffixes   522
6 Denotation and Connotation   524
7 Using Context Clues   526

Chapter 25   *Reviewing and Taking Tests*   530
1 Taking Notes in Class   532
2 How to Review for a Test   534
3 How to Take a Test   536
4 Verbal Analogies   538

SPELLING   540
DIAGRAMING   546
THESAURUS   555
INDEX TO RULES   575
ACKNOWLEDGMENTS   580
INDEX   581

INTRODUCTION

The Parts of a Book

You use your textbook and other nonfiction books to find information for assignments and reports and to study for tests. Most textbooks and other nonfiction books have these four parts: a title page, a copyright page, a table of contents, and an index. Each part provides information that you will need or tells you where to find it.

The **title page** is often the first page of a book. It gives the title, author, publisher's name, and place of publication. The **copyright page** is on the back of the title page. It tells when and by whom the book was published. You should check the copyright date to make sure the book is up-to-date enough for your purpose. A recent book may be needed for topics such as science and current events.

Following the copyright page is the **table of contents.** Study the Table of Contents in the front of this textbook. It shows that this book is organized into units, chapters, and lessons. Note that the title of Unit 1, "The Parts of Speech," identifies a general area of study. The chapter titles focus on specific parts of speech such as "Verbs and Adverbs." Lesson titles then usually indicate very specific areas of study, such as "Verb Phrases" and "Facts About Adverbs."

If you are looking for a particular piece of information, the **index** is the place to look. The index, which is found in the back of most nonfiction books, lists in alphabetical order the most important topics covered in the book. Under some main topics, subtopics may also be listed. For example, under *sentence* in the Index of this book, you will find *simple, compound,* and *complex* as subtopics. Next to each topic and subtopic are the pages on which they are discussed. The index helps you find specific topics quickly.

This textbook also has a special index, the Index to Rules on pages 575–579. This index lists all of the rules concerning the English language that are covered by this textbook. The pages on which the rules appear are included for easy reference.

Exercises

A. Write the answers to the following questions.

1. Which part of a book tells you the name of the book as well as the book's author and publisher?
2. What is the copyright date of this textbook?
3. Which part of a book shows how the book is organized?
4. In which part of a book would you look to find a particular piece of information quickly?
5. What is the name of the special additional index that this textbook contains?

B. Use the Table of Contents of this textbook to answer the following questions.

6. How many units are in this textbook?
7. On what page does Chapter 12 begin?
8. In which lesson of Chapter 12 would you learn about revising windy sentences?
9. How many lessons are in Chapter 12?
10. What is the title of Lesson 3 in Chapter 12?

GRAMMAR,
USAGE,
MECHANICS

UNIT ONE

The Parts of Speech

In a sentence every word has a special job. Some words show action, some words name, some words describe, and some stand between other words and connect them. Just as all vehicles can be classified according to the job each one does, so all English words can be put into a few classifications.

Moving along a street are trucks, taxis, buses, limousines, and private cars. Each one is performing a special kind of transportation work. Working together in a sentence are *nouns, pronouns, adjectives, verbs, adverbs, conjunctions, prepositions*, and *interjections*. Each of these eight kinds of words performs a special kind of communication job.

These eight job classifications are called the *parts of speech*. Whenever you are asked to tell what part of speech a word is, you will tell to which of the eight classifications it belongs. Telling the part of speech of a word is not difficult if you first read and understand the entire sentence. Study the chart on the next page. It gives examples of each kind of word.

The Eight Parts of Speech

Nouns: Words that name
education   photographer   camera   studios

Pronouns: Words that take the place of nouns
it   they   he   you   she   ours

Adjectives: Words that describe
educational   proud   beautiful   difficult

Verbs: Words that express action or being
educate   bring   give   was   am

Adverbs: Words that also describe
educationally   almost   backward

Conjunctions: Words that join
and   or   but   yet

Prepositions: Words that relate
of   with   in   except

Interjections: Words that express emotion
ouch   oh   ugh   wow

On the next two pages is a lesson entitled "Using a Thesaurus." It will tell you what a thesaurus is, how to use it, and why it is important for good writing. In the back, pages 555–574, you will find a thesaurus developed especially for your English book. As you apply what you learn about grammar and usage to writing, you will be doing special exercises called "Using the Thesaurus" that require you to use the parts of speech in writing. You will be using the thesaurus in the back of the book to help you write better sentences and paragraphs.

Using a Thesaurus

- Use a **thesaurus** to help you write better.

A thesaurus is a book of synonyms and antonyms. **Synonyms** are words that have similar meanings. **Antonyms** are words that have opposite meanings. The entries of a thesaurus are in alphabetical order and contain many synonyms and antonyms. To find the right word when you write, turn to a thesaurus.

On pages 555–574 of this book, you will find a thesaurus. Below is a sample entry for the word *important.*

Part of speech   **Definition**

Entry word — **important** (adj)—marked by significant worth or value.

Example sentence — The <u>important</u> news bulletin was broadcast last night.

chief—of greatest importance or significance. The <u>chief</u> member of the crew on a plane is the pilot.

momentous—very important; consequential. The anniversary celebration was a <u>momentous</u> occasion.

noteworthy—worthy of attention because of special excellence. Her fine performance in the competition was <u>noteworthy</u>.

Synonyms — *paramount*—superior to all else. The final exams are of <u>paramount</u> significance.

Informal — *big-league* [informal]—something outstanding of its kind. Linda gave a <u>big-league</u> performance in the play.

Slang — *double-barreled* [slang]—important; having a dual purpose. The lawyer asked the witness a <u>double-barreled</u> question.

Idiom — *not to be sneezed at* [idiom]—of considerable importance. His chances in the race are <u>not to be sneezed at</u>.

Cross-reference — See also *urgent.*

Antonyms — ANTONYMS: inconsequential, insignificant, petty, superficial, trivial, unimportant, worthless

Exercises

A. Use the Thesaurus entry on the preceding page to write the answers to the following questions.

   1. What part of speech is the entry word *important*?
   2. How many synonyms are listed for the entry word?
   3. What are the antonyms of the entry word?
   4. What idiom is given for *important*?
   5. What other Thesaurus entry is given as a cross-reference for the entry word *important*?

B. Write each sentence. Complete it with a synonym for *important*. Use a different synonym for each sentence.

   6. It is _____ that you finish that assignment now.
   7. That piece of news is _____.
   8. The _____ reason for the collapse of the bridge was the heavy rain that caused the river to rise.
   9. The World Series is always a _____ event.
   10. Her speech was _____ because she explained all of the possible problems that could occur.

C. In each sentence below, replace the word *move* with an appropriate synonym. Turn to *move* in the Thesaurus for a list of synonyms. Write the new sentences.

   11. Does the river <u>move</u> over waterfalls?
   12. Because of the mountainous terrain, the construction of the new highway will <u>move</u> slowly.
   13. We saw a deer <u>move</u> through our backyard early yesterday morning.
   14. The passageway was so small that the workers could not <u>move</u> through it.
   15. Every autumn the birds <u>move</u> south.

1 Nouns, Pronouns, and Adjectives

Open Range

Prairie goes to the mountain,
  Mountain goes to the sky.
The sky sweeps across to the distant hills
And here, in the middle,
  Am I.

Hills crowd down to the river,
  River runs by the tree.
Tree throws its shadow on sunburnt grass
And here, in the shadow,
  Is me.

Shadows creep up the mountain,
  Mountain goes black on the sky,
The sky bursts out with a million stars
And here, by the campfire,
  Am I.

—Kathryn and Byron Jackson

1 — Nouns

- A **noun** names a person, place, thing, or idea.

Everyone and everything has a name. *Teacher* and *bicycle* are names. Something that cannot be seen, heard, or touched, such as *kindness,* also has a name. All these names are nouns.

Most nouns have a singular and a plural form. A word that refers to one is singular. A word that refers to more than one is plural. Some nouns are more than one word.

Examples of Nouns

Persons	**Places**
The students worked.	Visit those beaches.
They asked Marie Vega.	We sang in Nashville.

Things	**Ideas**
Do alligators smile?	I like his honesty.
Write an invitation.	We admire generosity.

Exercises

A. Write the noun in each sentence. Then write whether it names a *person, place, thing,* or *idea.*

EXAMPLE: The bridge shook.
ANSWER: bridge, thing

1. Photographers arrived.
2. Cameras clicked.
3. Develop this film.
4. Visit my neighborhood.
5. Notice its beauty.
6. The model laughed.
7. Show more patience.
8. Is the lens dirty?
9. Never lose hope.
10. Our town is quiet.

B. In this article about photography, there are twenty underlined words. Ten are nouns. Write each noun after its sentence number. Write *none* if the sentence has no underlined noun.

11. The first photographs were taken in the early years of the nineteenth century. 12. For a camera a photographer used a huge wood box. 13. Over a hole at one end was a large, thick lens. 14. The image was recorded on a heavy metal plate coated with chemicals. 15. The camera had no gears, levers, or shutter. 16. The photographer covered the lens with his hand. 17. When he wished to take a picture, he simply took his hand away from the lens. 18. The earliest photographs are views of buildings, statues, or streets without pedestrians or vehicles. 19. To make these pictures, the photographer left the lens uncovered for almost an hour. 20. Anything that moved looked like a smudge on these first photographs.

C. Write each sentence. Then underline the nouns.

21. The principal signed the certificate during the assembly in the auditorium.
22. A small lake is on the campus.
23. Many decorations were needed for the dance.
24. That table is decorated with blue stars.
25. Atlases, dictionaries, and almanacs can be found on those shelves.
26. Our superintendent never lacks enthusiasm for her work.
27. The gymnasts amazed the crowds.
28. Bill looked at the signature with delight.
29. Is your committee ready with its report?
30. At the entrance of the library was a large sign with a schedule of movies and lectures.

2 – Kinds of Nouns

- A **common noun** is the general name of a person, place, or thing.
- A **proper noun** names a particular person, place, or thing.

The word *city* is a common noun. The name *Little Rock* is a proper noun. It is the particular name of the capital city of Arkansas. All names of specific persons, animals, cities, states, countries, or things are called proper nouns. Many proper nouns such as *Maryann* or *Finland* are composed of single capitalized words. Some proper nouns are composed of two or more words. Each important word is capitalized.

Common Nouns	Proper Nouns
A great inventor	was Thomas A. Edison.
An important street	is Pennsylvania Avenue.
A famous landmark	is the Statue of Liberty.
My favorite story	is "To Build a Fire."
An exciting country	is France.

A **collective noun** is the general name of a group of persons, animals, or things. *Audience* is a collective noun referring to people. Examples of collective nouns referring to animals and things are *pack* and *convoy*.

Collective Nouns

A swarm of bees gathered near a herd of cattle.
At dawn a flock of geese flew over the fleet of ships at anchor in the calm bay waters.
The crowd cheers whenever our team wins.
That committee is a large group of people.

Exercises

A. Each set of words contains one proper noun. Write and capitalize it.

   1. state, avenue, colorado, river, mountains
   2. frankenstein, movie, book, story, doctor
   3. festival, holiday, dinner, thanksgiving
   4. coffee, forests, brazil, rivers, country
   5. city, harbor, boston, college, museums

B. Write the nouns in each sentence. Then label each noun *common* or *proper*.

   6. Paris is the capital of France.
   7. Alaska and Texas are our largest states.
   8. A holiday in September is Labor Day.
   9. The Amazon is a river in South America.
  10. Many people read magazines.
  11. Is Saturn the planet with rings?
  12. The success of our team is assured.
  13. Mark Twain was a famous American author.
  14. Mr. Kim is the principal of our school.
  15. Ms. Banks devotes much time to her work.

C. Write the collective noun in each sentence.

  16. Another squadron of jet fighters landed.
  17. A flock of ravens was inside the large cage.
  18. In the palace was a set of valuable dishes.
  19. A bunch of grapes slipped off the plate.
  20. The school of fish darted under the lily pads.
  21. Our volleyball team plays very well.
  22. The crew boarded the tanker yesterday.
  23. The orchestra is rehearsing on the stage.
  24. The entire family played a game together.
  25. A crowd of people poured out of the stadium.

Additional Exercises

A. In this article there are thirty underlined words. Fifteen are nouns. Write each noun after its sentence number. Write *none* if a sentence has no underlined noun.

1. Fear and <u>pain</u> can be <u>seen</u> in the <u>faces</u> of the <u>first</u> men and women to be <u>photographed</u>. 2. A session with a <u>photographer</u> was indeed a strenuous <u>experience</u>. 3. The <u>only</u> light in the dingy, <u>odorous</u> studio came from <u>windows</u>.

4. A <u>person</u> had to remain <u>completely</u> motionless before a huge, ugly <u>camera</u> for as long as five <u>minutes</u>. 5. Any <u>movement</u> ruined the <u>picture</u>. 6. Usually a large metal clamp was placed behind the head to <u>keep</u> it still. 7. <u>Nervous</u> <u>subjects</u> were sometimes tied in a chair. 8. Lips were <u>firmly</u> closed, and eyes were <u>kept</u> wide open. 9. Eventually <u>scientists</u> <u>developed</u> <u>chemicals</u> that <u>quickly</u> recorded an image on the metal plate <u>inside</u> the camera. 10. Then <u>portraits</u> of lively <u>children</u> and <u>frisky</u> pets could be made.

B. Write each proper noun in this article after its sentence number.

11. Few photographers have been as famous in America as Mathew B. Brady. 12. In 1849 he became the first photographer to make a portrait in the White House. 13. His photograph of President James Knox Polk is historic. 14. During the Civil War Brady had permission to take pictures of camps and battles, but he never gave military information to either side. 15. His portraits of General Ulysses S. Grant and other generals are famous.

Application USING GRAMMAR IN WRITING

Which sentence below provides more details?

1. The woman labored over her work.
2. The journalist labored over her article.

Except for the nouns, the two sentences are alike. The nouns in the second sentence, however, are more specific. Because they name things more precisely, specific nouns provide more details than do vague nouns.

Vague	Specific	Vague	Specific
stone	granite	bird	eagle
athlete	outfielder	building	barn
tree	maple	soldier	colonel

Writing with Nouns

A. Write each sentence, substituting a specific noun for each underlined vague noun.

1. Flowers grew near the water.
2. The dog likes to sleep in the room.
3. I left my book and stuff at Annie's place.
4. The sound of the animal broke the evening silence.
5. A large vehicle stopped, and people unloaded the food.

Using the Thesaurus

B. Find the entries for the vague noun *house* in the Thesaurus, pages 555–574. Then rewrite each sentence below, substituting a synonym for *house*.

6. Our *house* at the beach has only one room.
7. The millionaire's *house* has thirty-two rooms.
8. Some pioneers built their *houses* with logs.
9. There are fifty-six families living in my *house*.
10. A moat with a drawbridge surrounds the *house*.

3 — Pronouns

> - A **pronoun** takes the place of a noun or nouns.

Pronouns can be substitutes for any nouns.

He   it   them
Bryan made toast for Janet and Steve.

The **personal pronouns** are used most frequently.

Personal Pronouns

	Singular	Plural
First Person (the speaker)	I, me	we, us
Second Person (anyone addressed)	you	you
Third Person (anyone or anything discussed)	he, him she, her it	they, them

The **possessive pronouns** are a special kind of personal pronoun. They show ownership.

her   mine
I met Sara's parents. I introduced my parents.

Possessive Pronouns

	Singular	Plural
First Person	my, mine	our, ours
Second Person	your, yours	your, yours
Third Person	his, her, hers, its	their, theirs

My, your, his, her, its, our, and *their* are forms that are used with nouns. *Mine, yours, his, hers, ours,* and *theirs* are forms that can be used alone. *His* can be used either with nouns or alone.

Exercises

A. Write the personal pronoun in each sentence.

1. Did he arrive?
2. Has she left?
3. They fell.
4. Sam wrote it.
5. Call him.
6. She laughed.
7. Find them.
8. It broke.
9. Bill asked her.
10. He knows.

B. Write the possessive pronoun in each sentence.

11. Our pool is not very deep.
12. Have you ever swum in theirs?
13. Did everyone read her book report on *The Adventures of Tom Sawyer?*
14. Mine needs a catchy title like that one.
15. Cathy and Richard borrowed hers.
16. His nose is badly sunburned.
17. Their names are easy to spell.
18. Why was your dog barking?
19. Ours is either in the garage or in the attic.
20. Write her address on this envelope.

C. Ten of the twenty underlined words in this article are pronouns. Write each underlined pronoun after its sentence number.

21. If your hobby is photography, it could win you fame as well as great enjoyment. 22. In 1863, when she was forty-eight, Julia Margaret Cameron received her first camera as a gift from her husband. 23. With his encouragement she became skilled in its use. 24. They turned their home into a studio where she invited British celebrities to be photographed. 25. Her unusual close-up portraits were so exceptional that some became more famous than the people in them.

4 – Antecedents of Pronouns

> ● An **antecedent** is the word or words to which a pronoun refers.

You know that a pronoun takes the place of a noun. That noun is the antecedent of the pronoun. Sentences and paragraphs would be difficult to understand without antecedents.

Antecedents usually come before pronouns. Sometimes they follow. An antecedent is usually one word, but it can be a word group or several words. In the following chart the pronouns are underlined. Their antecedents are in italics.

One-Word Antecedents
Carlos said that <u>he</u> would go. *Carlos* believes the show will interest <u>him</u>. *Carlos* will take <u>his</u> brother.
Antecedents with More Than One Word
Marilyn and her friends think <u>they</u> see a comet. The *Dallas Cowboys* always thrill <u>their</u> fans.
Antecedents That Follow Pronouns
"<u>I</u> have some great news!" shouted the *coach*. If <u>she</u> wins, *Lisa Ames* will buy a new car.
Antecedents in Other Sentences
The *words* looked strange. <u>They</u> had no vowels. The *train* struggled up the hill. <u>It</u> was late.

Exercises

A. Write each underlined pronoun. Then write the word or word group that is its antecedent.

    1. The players said that <u>they</u> would practice.
    2. My cousin told a joke. No one understood <u>it</u>.
    3. Angela said, "<u>I</u> need more information."
    4. "<u>We</u> want dessert," chanted Pat and Mike.
    5. "What's following <u>me</u> now?" asked the driver.
    6. Parents and teachers have <u>their</u> cards.
    7. The plane is on <u>its</u> final approach.
    8. Sir, may I see <u>your</u> driver's license?
    9. <u>You</u> were the best speaker, Tanya.
    10. "No one can beat <u>us</u>!" roared the Raiders.

B. In this article ten pronouns are omitted. Write the article, using appropriate pronouns from the list. Use some pronouns more than once.

       he   his   it   they   their

    11. A treasured possession of some families is _____ collection of old photographs. **12.** _____ are the portraits of relatives who lived long ago. However, are all these pictures genuine? In the nineteenth century few people owned cameras. **13.** _____ were too costly. Not many people could go to photographers. **14.** _____ charged too much. **15.** Young soldiers wanted to be photographed in _____ uniforms. Some merchants knew this. **16.** _____ sold inexpensive copies of photos of soldiers. **17.** A private with little cash would buy a picture of someone whose face resembled _____ face. **18.** Then _____ sent this picture home. **19.** The soldier's parents were thrilled to receive a reminder of _____ son. **20.** _____ was then put in the family album.

5 — Demonstrative and Reflexive Pronouns

> - A **demonstrative pronoun** emphatically points out its antecedent.
> - A **reflexive pronoun** reflects action back to a noun or pronoun just named.

Demonstrative Pronouns *This, these, that,* and *those* are the demonstrative pronouns. They point out specific persons or things. *This* and *that* are singular. *These* and *those* are plural. In the following examples the demonstrative pronouns are underlined. Arrows point to their antecedents.

What a surprise this is! Are these my presents?

That was our principal.

Pick the berries. Those are ripe.

Reflexive Pronouns The reflexive pronouns end in *-self* or *-selves.* They reflect back or refer to nouns or pronouns used earlier in the same sentence. In the following examples the reflexive pronouns are underlined. The antecedents are in italics.

Singular	Plural
I understand <u>myself</u>.	*We* see <u>ourselves</u>.
You believe <u>yourself</u>.	*You* hear <u>yourselves</u>.
He taught <u>himself</u>.	*They* know <u>themselves</u>.
She helped <u>herself</u>.	
It can adjust <u>itself</u>.	

If the antecedent *you* refers to one person, *yourself* is used. If *you* refers to more than one, *yourselves* is used.

Exercises

A. Write each sentence. Underline each demonstrative pronoun and circle its antecedent.

1. These are your assignments.
2. Was that a dragonfly?
3. Whose gloves are these?
4. Those must be the new bookshelves.
5. What a strange signature this is!

B. Write each sentence. Underline each reflexive pronoun and circle its antecedent.

6. The camera focuses itself.
7. We should locate ourselves near the clearing.
8. The birds usually come here to feed themselves at this time of day.
9. You must keep yourself perfectly still so that we can get good pictures.
10. I will take the first photographs of the sparrows by myself.

C. Complete each sentence with the kind of pronoun indicated in parentheses. Use no pronoun more than once.

11. I almost cut (reflexive).
12. We can protect (reflexive) with these masks.
13. Is (demonstrative) your glass of milk?
14. Are (demonstrative) our new uniforms?
15. She always studies by (reflexive).
16. (Demonstrative) is the book you wanted.
17. Our refrigerator defrosts (reflexive).
18. Pierre, why did you go there by (reflexive)?
19. (Demonstrative) are my new gloves.
20. They discussed the game among (reflexive).

6 — Interrogative and Indefinite Pronouns

> • An **interrogative pronoun** asks a question.
> • An **indefinite pronoun** does not always indicate a definite person, place, or thing.

Interrogative Pronouns Interrogative pronouns are often used to begin questions. There are only five, and they all begin with *w: who, whose, whom, which,* and *what.* The interrogative pronouns are underlined in the sentences below.

<u>Who</u> has my camera?   <u>What</u> is a tripod?
<u>Whose</u> did you borrow?   <u>Which</u> is the lens?
       <u>Whom</u> did she photograph?

Indefinite Pronouns A pronoun that does not always indicate a definite person, place, or thing is called an indefinite pronoun. Many indefinite pronouns express the idea of quantity: *all, several, some.* Indefinite pronouns may or may not have antecedents.

With an antecedent: <u>All</u> of the *leaves* are dry.
Without an antecedent: <u>Somebody</u> lost a glove.

Indefinite Pronouns			
all	each	many	one
any	either	neither	several
anybody	everybody	nobody	some
anyone	everyone	none	somebody
anything	everything	no one	someone
both	few	nothing	something

Exercises

A. Write the pronoun in each sentence. Then identify it as *interrogative* or *indefinite*.

1. Who saw the sunrise today?
2. Will the music bother anybody?
3. What is a good solution to the problem?
4. Someone may develop a cure for the common cold.
5. William wanted neither of the gloves.
6. Whom did the chairperson finally appoint as the program director?
7. Which of the three is most nutritious?
8. Whose would the judges really prefer?
9. Wendy knows nothing about the accident.
10. Are both missing again?

B. Write each sentence, using an indefinite pronoun that completes it appropriately. Use no indefinite pronoun more than twice.

11. _____ was in the corridor.
12. Why were _____ dropped from the list?
13. That certainly is not good for _____.
14. _____ of it looks delicious.
15. We could not see _____ of them.
16. That dictionary defines almost _____.
17. _____ seems wrong with the photograph.
18. Have they seen _____ yet?
19. Certainly _____ must be there by now.
20. _____ of them are excellent actors.
21. _____ of the projectors are in use today.
22. A low calorie diet may not be good for _____.
23. _____ of us could have done more.
24. They might not use _____ of it.
25. _____ of the machines had been repaired.

Additional Exercises

A. Dianne Disney Miller, a daughter of Walt Disney, tells how Mickey Mouse was named in part of her book, *The Story of Walt Disney*. Ten of the underlined words are pronouns. Write each underlined pronoun after its sentence number. Write *none* if a sentence has no underlined pronoun.

1. Mice had been <u>used</u> in cartoons before, but until then they'd never been featured. **2.** "I think I've <u>got</u> <u>something</u>," Father told Mother. **3.** "It's a mouse. **4.** I'll call <u>him</u> Mortimer.... **5.** <u>I</u> like that, don't <u>you</u>?"
6. Mother thought it <u>over</u> and shook <u>her</u> head. **7.** "<u>I</u> like the mouse idea," she said, "<u>but</u> Mortimer sounds <u>wrong</u>...."
8. "What's wrong <u>with</u> <u>it</u>?" Father asked. **9.** "Mortimer Mouse, Mortimer Mouse. **10.** <u>It</u> swings, Lilly."
11. But Mother didn't <u>buy</u> it. **12.** <u>She</u> couldn't <u>explain</u> why "Mortimer" grated on her. **13.** <u>It</u> just did.
14. "All <u>right</u>," Father said, "How <u>about</u> Mickey? Mickey Mouse?"

B. Write each pronoun. Then label it *demonstrative, reflexive, interrogative,* or *indefinite.*

EXAMPLE: Someone left a sweater.
ANSWER: Someone, indefinite

15. Those are wild geese in the sky.
16. Did Ken weigh himself?
17. Who was inside the automobile?
18. Darlene wanted to congratulate herself.
19. Describe anything in the clearest manner.
20. Look at the geyser! That is spectacular!

Application USING GRAMMAR IN WRITING

By using pronouns, you can avoid using the same nouns over and over again. It is important, however, that every pronoun you use has a clear antecedent. Why are the following sentences unclear?

1. They claim the moon will be a source of minerals.
2. It says in this book that robots will run moon mines.
3. On a space station, you can have any climate you desire.

In the first two sentences, the pronouns *they* and *it* have no clear antecedents. In the third sentence, *you* is used as an indefinite pronoun. Avoid using *they*, *it*, and *you* as vague and unclear pronouns. Instead, rewrite the sentences using nouns.

1. Scientists claim the moon will be a source of minerals.
2. This author believes that robots will run moon mines.
3. On a space station, the residents can have any climate.

Writing with Pronouns

A. Rewrite each sentence, correcting the unclear pronoun.

1. They say the rain will continue for days.
2. In Yugoslavia you speak Serbo-Croatian.
3. At that company they never pick up the litter.
4. In the magazine it said pastel colors are popular.
5. In some classes you learn by computer.

Using the Thesaurus

B. Imagine you are writing a news story about a world leader and are using the pronoun *she* too often. You need to replace the pronoun with synonyms for *leader*. Find four synonyms for *leader* in the Thesaurus. Then use each in a sentence.

7 — Adjectives

> ● An **adjective** modifies a noun or pronoun.

Adjectives are words that modify. *Modify* means to "describe" or to "limit." Adjectives answer such questions as *What kind? Which one? How much?* and *How many?*

What kind?	<u>fresh</u> salad	<u>soggy</u> salads
	<u>green</u> salads	<u>small</u> salad
Which one?	<u>fourth</u> salad	<u>those</u> salads
	<u>last</u> salad	<u>every</u> salad
How much?	<u>no</u> salad	<u>some</u> salad
	<u>less</u> salad	<u>more</u> salad
How many?	<u>forty</u> salads	<u>fewer</u> salads
	<u>several</u> salads	<u>countless</u> salads

Adjectives usually stand before the words they modify. Sometimes they follow.

> <u>Tasty</u>, <u>nutritious</u> salads were served.
> Salads, <u>tasty</u> and <u>nutritious</u>, were served.
> They were <u>tasty</u> and <u>nutritious</u>.

The adjectives *tasty* and *nutritious* modify the noun *salads* and the pronoun *they.*

The adjectives *a, an,* and *the* are articles. They stand before the words they modify. *The* is called the **definite article** because it refers to specific persons, places, or things. *A* and *an* are called **indefinite articles** because they refer to any person, place, or thing in general.

> Catch <u>the</u> train on Track 2. (a specific train)
> Do you often ride <u>a</u> train? (any train)
> <u>An</u> umbrella is lying on the track. (any umbrella)

Exercises

A. Write the adjective in each sentence.

1. All fans rejoiced.
2. Happy times came.
3. Wheat is plentiful.
4. Spend the money.
5. Buy new clothes.
6. They seem anxious.
7. Good pupils study.
8. Do each lesson.
9. Learn many things.
10. Make wise choices.
11. Days can be rainy.
12. Brown leaves fell.

B. In this article about a photograph, there are twenty underlined words. Ten are adjectives. Write each adjective after its sentence number.

13. One <u>famous</u> photograph was used to make a <u>picture</u> most Americans know well. **14.** On February 9, 1864, Abraham Lincoln <u>walked</u> from the White House to the <u>photographic</u> studio of Mathew Brady. **15.** Lincoln had an <u>unusual</u> face that challenged every photographer. **16.** Some <u>pictures</u> showed an <u>ugly</u>, ordinary man. **17.** His <u>political</u> enemies even used <u>poor</u> photographs of him to <u>frighten</u> <u>voters</u>. **18.** On that <u>day</u> in 1864, Brady took <u>numerous</u> pictures of the illustrious <u>President</u>. **19.** <u>One</u> picture especially revealed Lincoln's <u>great</u> dignity, anxiety, and <u>tenderness</u>. **20.** Later an <u>engraver</u> used that <u>photograph</u> to make the picture of Lincoln that is on <u>every</u> five-dollar <u>bill</u>.

C. Write each sentence. Then underline the adjectives.

21. High winds and heavy seas delayed the ship.
22. Flowers, bright and fragrant, bloomed there.
23. It was easy, painless, and profitable.
24. She gave complete answers to both questions.
25. A warm welcome awaits another new customer.

8 – Proper and Demonstrative Adjectives

- A **proper adjective** is formed from a proper noun.
- A **demonstrative adjective** points out the noun it describes.

Proper Adjectives   When an adjective is formed from a proper noun, it is called a proper adjective. Like a proper noun, a proper adjective is always capitalized.

Proper Nouns	Proper Adjectives
Nigeria	a Nigerian freighter
Japan	a Japanese tanker
Iceland	an Icelandic trawler
Norway	a Norwegian cruise ship
Greece	a Greek liner
Peru	a Peruvian custom

Demonstrative Adjectives   When *this, these, that,* and *those* modify nouns, they are called demonstrative adjectives. They point out specific persons or things and are more specific than *a, an,* and *the. This* and *these* point out someone or something near. *That* and *those* point out someone or something farther away.

Singular	Plural
this tooth	these teeth
that cloud	those clouds

When *this, these, that,* and *those* are used alone, they are called demonstrative pronouns.

This is good.   Those are better.

Exercises

A. Write the proper adjective in each sentence.

1. The Hawaiian climate is usually delightful.
2. I once visited that Alaskan port.
3. The Australian wilderness is known as the outback.
4. That restaurant serves fine Italian food.
5. The Austrian slopes are favorites of skiers.

B. Write each proper adjective in this article after its sentence number. Write *none* if a sentence has no proper adjective.

6. Engravings of famous faces appear on the currency of many nations. 7. Portraits of Queen Elizabeth II are on Canadian dollars and British pounds. 8. Solemn faces of Norwegian, Swedish, and Danish monarchs can be seen on Scandinavian money. 9. A German hero may be found on a mark. 10. On the colorful money of France and Spain, pictures of French and Spanish authors have appeared.

C. Write each demonstrative adjective. Then write the noun it modifies.

11. These four dictionaries belong to my brother.
12. Did your father plant those trees?
13. This book is a Russian novel.
14. Her aunt made that shelf in one day.
15. That old red car belongs in a museum.
16. We discussed those political issues once.
17. Why is this old sweater so loose?
18. Be careful on that icy sidewalk.
19. I found these skates in our attic.
20. Those last tests were unusually easy.

9 — Words Used as Different Parts of Speech

> ● How a word is used in a sentence determines its part of speech.

Some words usually thought of as nouns can be used as adjectives. If a word names a person, place, thing, or idea, it is a noun. If a word answers the question *What kind? Which one? How much?* or *How many?*, it is used as an adjective.

Noun: The <u>computer</u> is on sale.
Adjective: The <u>computer</u> sale is today.

Noun: She manages this <u>restaurant</u>.
Adjective: Here is the <u>restaurant</u> manager.

You have learned about demonstrative pronouns and demonstrative adjectives. *This, these, that,* or *those* can be used as a pronoun in one sentence and as an adjective in another.

Pronoun: <u>These</u> are too small.
Adjective: <u>These</u> pennants are too small.

Many indefinite pronouns—such as *any, each, one, all, both,* and *few*—can also be adjectives. How a word is used in a sentence determines its part of speech. If a word *replaces* a noun, it is a pronoun. If a word *modifies* a noun, it is an adjective.

Pronoun: <u>Each</u> has been revised.
Adjective: <u>Each</u> report has been revised.

Pronoun: <u>Both</u> received awards.
Adjective: <u>Both</u> students received awards.

Exercises

A. Write each underlined word. Label it *adjective* if it modifies a noun. Label it *noun* if it is used as a noun.

  1. The <u>cafeteria</u> manager has another surprise.
  2. The <u>cafeteria</u> will be painted purple.
  3. There are no carrots in their <u>garden</u>.
  4. <u>Garden</u> magazines are on the green shelf.
  5. The coach revised the <u>basketball</u> schedule for the third time in a week.
  6. We played <u>basketball</u> yesterday.
  7. The <u>elevator</u> should be repaired soon.
  8. The <u>elevator</u> inspector is on the third floor.
  9. This <u>parakeet</u> food is expensive.
  10. This <u>parakeet</u> talks too much.

B. Write each underlined word. Label it *adjective* if it modifies a noun. Label it *pronoun* if it is used as a pronoun.

  11. Who taught you <u>that</u> trick?
  12. <u>That</u> amazed everyone.
  13. <u>These</u> are definitely the best bargains.
  14. Have you seen <u>those</u> towels?
  15. In <u>this</u> picture they look very young.
  16. How did <u>this</u> ever happen?
  17. <u>That</u> looks like a real emerald!
  18. Did the doctor examine <u>both</u> legs?
  19. <u>Both</u> should be examined carefully.
  20. <u>Each</u> teacher read the composition.
  21. <u>Each</u> was impressed with its excellence.
  22. <u>All</u> is well in the city tonight.
  23. Covers should be on <u>all</u> books.
  24. Do you have <u>any</u> transparent tape?
  25. I don't have <u>any</u> with me now.

Additional Exercises

A. Artist Francis Carpenter used the twenty-five adjectives in this article to describe Abraham Lincoln's face. Write each adjective after its sentence number. Do not write the article *the*.

1. The face of Lincoln was strange but powerful. **2.** Hair, coarse and unmanageable, spilled down his wide, high forehead. **3.** His thick eyebrows and heavy eyelids cast shadows over his gray eyes. **4.** Dark rings circled the sad, tender eyes. **5.** Long, deep wrinkles plowed across his large, hollow cheeks and into the short, rough beard on his sturdy chin. **6.** His nose was straight and prominent. **7.** His lips were thick yet delicate. **8.** His look revealed great thoughtfulness and much gentleness.

B. Write each sentence, completing it with the kind of adjective indicated in parentheses.

EXAMPLE: Who polished (demonstrative) surfboard?
ANSWER: Who polished that surfboard?

   9. (Demonstrative) knapsacks feel very light.
   10. Has anyone tried (demonstrative) sauerkraut?
   11. We sampled pieces of (proper) bread.
   12. (Proper) winters can be extremely cold.
   13. (Proper) artists made (demonstrative) rings.
   14. Who is (demonstrative) actor?
   15. I ate (proper) dinner at my grandmother's.
   16. Have you seen (demonstrative) sketch?
   17. A (proper) automobile just passed us.
   18. (Demonstrative) students are in the band.
   19. We are reading (proper) poetry.
   20. Take (demonstrative) microscopes to the lab on the second floor.

Application USING GRAMMAR IN WRITING

Adjectives can help give your writing sparkle and life. Using the same adjectives, however, can detract from the effectiveness of your writing. Knowing how to use a thesaurus will be especially useful when you are looking for vivid and exact adjectives when you write.

Writing with Adjectives

A. Look at an American one-dollar bill. Then write the paragraph, substituting adjectives for the blanks.

The one-dollar bill has a ____ portrait of George Washington. The President looks ____ and ____. He has ____ eyes, a ____ mouth, and a ____ jaw. His ____ clothes are ____. The portrait has an ____ shape and ____ leaves at the base.

Using the Thesaurus

B. Find the entries for the overworked adjectives *hard* and *strong* in the Thesaurus. Rewrite each sentence, using a synonym for *hard* or *strong* that best fits the meaning of the sentence. Use the synonym only once.

1. That *hard* look on his face frightened us.
2. The sergeant is a *hard* disciplinarian.
3. The science test seems unusually *hard.*
4. That entire cliff is composed of *hard* granite.
5. The trail covers some very *hard* territory.
6. This *strong* table will definitely not collapse.
7. The *strong* current capsized the new yacht.
8. Only a *strong* person could stand this cold.
9. Exercise developed that player's *strong* legs.
10. A *strong* person does things with enthusiasm.

Chapter Review

A. Write each sentence. Then underline the nouns.

   1. Your present is at the top of the stairs.
   2. Seth recited another version of his poem.
   3. Ten famous players were introduced.
   4. A quartet from Kansas showed great talent.
   5. Around the pier flew noisy pelicans.

B. Write each sentence. Then underline the pronouns.

   6. She placed them under a light.
   7. With whom did they travel on that journey?
   8. What can it do for me and for everyone?
   9. Will anybody do anything important tomorrow?
  10. This is the bike he taught himself to ride.

C. Write the pronoun in each sentence. Then write its antecedent.

  11. The engineers knew they would succeed.
  12. Laura asked, "May I use the abacus?"
  13. The record had once been mine.
  14. Yours was excellent, Stuart.
  15. "Are those tickets for us?" asked Amy and Vic.

D. Write each sentence. Then underline the adjectives.

  16. Clever ranchers outwitted those rustlers.
  17. This new recipe calls for Hungarian sausage, Belgian carrots, and Italian olives.
  18. The next two days will be warm but windy.
  19. Alone and helpless, it whimpered mournfully inside a hollow stump.
  20. The work gradually became easy and pleasant.

Chapter Review CHALLENGE

Read the article about five famous photographers. Using only the underlined words as answers, find and write these grammatical constructions:

A. one collective noun
B. two proper nouns
C. two articles
D. one personal pronoun (not a possessive one)
E. one possessive pronoun
F. one interrogative pronoun
G. one indefinite pronoun
H. one proper adjective
I. two demonstrative adjectives
J. two nouns used as adjectives

A **(1)** collection of photographs by Frances Benjamin Johnston is like **(2)** an exciting composition. Her pictures of the **(3)** activities of schoolchildren in Washington, D.C., won the highest awards at a **(4)** French exhibition in 1900. **(5)** She earned further praise for her photographs of students working and studying at **(6)** Tuskegee Institute in Alabama. **(7)** Nobody has made **(8)** school pictures as vivid as **(9)** hers. With her **(10)** photographs Chansonetta Emmons documented **(11)** village life in **(12)** Maine at the start of **(13)** this century. Dorothea Lange and Berenice Abbott made their cameras describe **(14)** the grief and **(15)** hardship of the Great Depression, in the 1930s. **(16)** Who took photographs of World War II **(17)** as remarkable as those by Margaret Bourke-White? The extraordinary success of **(18)** these documentary **(19)** photographers is the result of their dedication, enthusiasm, skill, and **(20)** hard work.

2 Verbs and Adverbs

A Horse is a Horse

I would like to be
A horse wild and free
Galloping with flying mane
Over miles of wide field,
Leaping fences and walls,
With the whistle of wind-sound
So strong in my ears
   That I
   Can simply not
   Certainly
   Not possibly
   Hear
      When anyone
      Calls.

—Dorothy W. Baruch

1 – Verbs

> ● A **verb** expresses action or being.

Every sentence has a verb. Some verbs show action. That action may be visible or invisible.

Visible Action	Invisible Action
She <u>ran</u> home quickly.	They never <u>worry</u>.
<u>Fasten</u> your seat belt.	<u>Memorize</u> the rule.
The plane <u>landed</u> early.	He <u>thinks</u> clearly.

Some verbs do not show action. Instead they show being. They state that a person or thing exists and are called state-of-being verbs. *Be, am, is, are, was,* and *were* are state-of-being verbs. Information about a person or thing often follows these verbs.

Here I <u>am</u>.   They <u>are</u> tall.   He <u>was</u> a friend.

Verbs such as *appear, become, feel, grow, look, remain, seem, smell, sound, stay, taste,* and *turn* can also express being. Each one can take the place of a form of the verb *be* in a sentence.

look	tastes	feel
They a̶r̶e good.	That i̶s sweet.	I a̶m fine.

Exercises

A. Write the verb in each sentence.

1. Go to the door.
2. Strangers enter.
3. Learn their names.
4. Water evaporates.
5. Is it a cloud?

6. Remain quiet.
7. Are you brave?
8. What looks new?
9. There were cinders.
10. The plot thickens.

B. Write the verb in each sentence. Then write *action verb* or *state-of-being verb* beside it.

EXAMPLE: Velma is a good student.
ANSWER: is, state-of-being verb

11. Brian brought the groceries home.
12. Please open that can of spinach.
13. Who is your science teacher?
14. The cat leaped over the fence.
15. Lee seems very busy today.
16. We played basketball all afternoon.
17. That song sounds familiar.
18. There were hardly any empty seats in the entire auditorium.
19. That giant sequoia tree is 2,000 years old.
20. Who stood in the rain all day?
21. Those clouds look ominous.
22. Juanita traveled for more than four hours.
23. Dad cooked his favorite dish, beef stew with potatoes, carrots, and onions.
24. Tammy became ill after dinner.
25. Be on your best behavior.

C. This article contains ten verbs. Write the article. Then underline the verbs.

26. Many successful people began their careers early in their lives. 27. Most great athletes and dancers practiced or rehearsed for many hours after school. 28. During school vacations the future business and political leaders often observed and learned about their fields of interest. 29. Wise students use spare time profitably. 30. They improve their athletic skills, enrich their minds, enhance their talents, and increase their chances for success in the future.

2 — Verb Phrases

> ● A **helping verb** works with the main verb to express action or being.

Sometimes a verb is just one word. Often a verb may consist of two or more words. This kind of verb is called a **verb phrase.**

> **Verb:** Dexter <u>painted</u> the walls.

> **Verb Phrases:** His sister <u>had painted</u> the cupboards.
> The ceiling <u>had been painted</u> earlier.
> The door <u>should have been painted</u>, too.

The most important verb in a verb phrase is the **main verb.** The other verbs are helping verbs.

Helping Verbs				
am	be	had	did	may
is	being	can	shall	might
are	been	could	should	must
was	has	do	will	
were	have	does	would	

Some helping verbs can also be used as main verbs in sentences.

> **Main Verb:** I <u>am</u> a painter. I <u>have</u> it now.
> **Helping Verb:** I <u>am</u> painting. I <u>have</u> seen it.

Words other than verbs can interrupt verb phrases. Notice in the following sentences that *not* and *n't* are not parts of the verb.

> <u>Haven</u>'t you or your sister ever <u>seen</u> our kitchen?
> We <u>did</u> not <u>go</u> because we <u>could</u> not <u>leave</u>.

Exercises

A. Write the verb phrase in each sentence. Underline the main verb.

1. Who could have written that story?
2. Jody must be the author.
3. It will be published soon.
4. Who might have informed him?
5. Everyone is asking questions.
6. Our library does need a new computer.
7. We should be having a paper sale.
8. Old telephone books can be contributed to the paper drive.
9. Do not bring loose papers or magazines.
10. Bundles should never be tied carelessly.

B. There is a verb or a verb phrase in each sentence in this article about Kurt Thomas. Write each verb or verb phrase.

11. Kurt Thomas is a great gymnast. **12.** He has made gymnastics popular in America. **13.** In 1978 he won a gold medal at a competition in France. **14.** An American had not placed first in an international gymnastics contest since 1932. **15.** Then in New York he defeated gymnasts from eighteen nations. **16.** In 1979 Kurt was honored with the James A. Sullivan Award. **17.** It is presented annually to America's best amateur athlete. **18.** No gymnast had ever been given that award. **19.** In 1980 at the age of twenty-four he turned professional. **20.** Kurt's career had its start in Miami, Florida. **21.** Each day he would train for hours. **22.** He could not attend many parties. **23.** He followed a strict diet. **24.** Kurt Thomas was rewarded for this discipline. **25.** Now he enjoys fame.

Additional Exercises

A. Write the sentences below. Underline each verb.

1. Move that boulder closer to that tree.
2. What trail is this?
3. The fog grew thick.
4. The river appears very deep here.
5. What was that very loud noise?

B. Write each verb or verb phrase in this article after its sentence number. Underline the main verb in each verb phrase.

6. Many people have never heard of Lillian Leitzel. 7. Her name does appear, however, in many books about famous athletes. 8. As a child she had joined a circus. 9. The acrobats and trapeze artists were her favorite performers. 10. In her spare time she would watch them in rehearsal. 11. She would then imitate their routines. 12. Eventually Leitzel became a skillful aerialist.

13. As an adult she was just four feet nine inches tall. 14. She weighed only ninety-five pounds. 15. She did have, though, great strength.

16. One day in 1918 Leitzel went to a gym in Philadelphia. 17. There at the age of thirty-six she broke the world's record for chin-ups with one hand. 18. An Englishman had held the record. 19. In 1878 he had done twelve chin-ups with one hand. 20. On that day Lillian Leitzel did twenty-seven chin-ups in a row with her right hand. 21. After a short rest she returned to the bar. 22. This time she was using her left hand. 23. She then did nineteen more chin-ups. 24. A world's record had been broken twice in the same day by Lillian Leitzel. 25. Achievements like hers will always be remembered by sports enthusiasts.

Application USING GRAMMAR IN WRITING

Good writers use both action and linking verbs. However, an action verb often states an idea more directly and clearly than a linking verb.

> **Linking Verb:** A young girl was the rescuer of the men.
> **Action Verb:** A young girl rescued the men.

Writing with Verbs

A. Rewrite the sentences below, substituting action verbs for linking verbs. Then make other necessary changes.

1. My mom is a math teacher at the university.
2. Jena's good grades are a pleasure to her parents.
3. Alan is the writer of many humorous tales.
4. The dry mountain air was of benefit to me.
5. That dog is a source of annoyance to everyone.

To describe actions clearly, select vivid verbs. The vivid verb *hobbled*, for example, describes the action better in the sentence than the overused verb *walked*.

> The injured athlete <u>walked</u> off the field.
> The injured athlete <u>hobbled</u> off the field.

Using the Thesaurus

B. Use the Thesaurus to find synonyms for *walk*. Then rewrite each sentence, using a synonym for *walk* that expresses the idea in parentheses.

6. The workers _____ down the road. (exhausted)
7. The ape _____ through the china shop. (clumsy)
8. The athletic club _____ through the woods. (long)
9. We _____ down near the river. (aimless)
10. The lawyer _____ back and forth in court. (nervous)

3 — Adverbs

> ● An **adverb** modifies a verb, an adjective, or another adverb.

An adverb is another part of speech that describes. It works with verbs, adjectives, and other adverbs to change their meanings.

<u>often</u> goes	<u>nearly</u> painless	<u>rather</u> slowly
adv. verb	adv. adj.	adv. adv.

Most adverbs answer a question about the word they modify: *How? When? Where? How often? To what extent?* The adverbs below all modify verbs.

How? They spoke <u>softly</u>.
When? We worked <u>yesterday</u>.
Where? The coin rolled <u>away</u>.
How often? It rained <u>twice</u>.
To what extent? I <u>hardly</u> noticed.

Four adverbs are commonly used to begin questions: *how, when, where,* and *why.*

<u>When</u> will the students write their reports?

An adverb can stand before or after the verb it modifies. It can separate parts of a verb phrase.

<u>Now</u> the students *are writing* their reports.

The students *are writing* their reports <u>now</u>.

The students *are* <u>now</u> *writing* their reports.

Do not confuse adverbs with adjectives. Remember that adjectives answer the questions *What kind? Which one? How much? How many?*

Exercises

A. Write the adverb in each sentence.

1. It rang once.
2. We rushed in.
3. Suddenly I stopped.
4. They quietly left.
5. It moved well.
6. How did you fix it?
7. He slowly withdrew.
8. Down it came.
9. She scarcely spoke.
10. When will you arrive?

B. In this article about Pablo Picasso, there are twenty underlined words. Ten are adverbs. Write each adverb after its sentence number.

11. Lolita Picasso may have <u>unintentionally</u> improved the <u>artistic</u> skill of her brother, Pablo. 12. As a child in <u>Spain</u>, Pablo always carried a pencil and <u>quietly</u> made sketches. 13. Lolita <u>often</u> <u>requested</u> pictures of birds. 14. She <u>usually</u> <u>challenged</u> him. 15. <u>Sometimes</u> she would ask <u>him</u> to begin a sketch with the wing. 16. Or she would ask for a picture with the <u>beak</u> drawn <u>first</u>. 17. He always accepted her <u>challenges</u> <u>eagerly</u>. 18. He <u>rarely</u> had trouble with <u>them</u>. 19. Pablo <u>soon</u> realized that he could make his own <u>rules</u> for art. 20. Picasso <u>eventually</u> became recognized as one of the <u>greatest</u> artists of the twentieth century.

C. Write the sentences below. Underline each adverb.

21. Andrea rushed downstairs and called my name twice.
22. The enormous crowd was shouting wildly and enthusiastically.
23. The diver leaped overboard and swam westward.
24. Everywhere the snow fell noiselessly.
25. Why are you worried now?

4 — Facts About Adverbs

- An adverb that modifies an adjective or another adverb usually comes directly before the word it modifies.
- Many adverbs end in *-ly*.

An adverb that modifies a verb can be found almost anywhere in a sentence. An adverb that modifies an adjective or another adverb usually comes directly before the word it modifies.

Adverbs Modifying Adjectives
<u>very</u> sweet   <u>totally</u> honest   <u>absolutely</u> true

Adverbs Modifying Other Adverbs
<u>very</u> proudly   <u>quite</u> smoothly   <u>only</u> once

Many adverbs end in *-ly*. Some adjectives also end in *-ly*. Do not confuse them.

        adv.   adj.

It arrives <u>daily</u>.   The <u>daily</u> paper has come.

The twenty underlined words in the sentences below are commonly used adverbs. They are sometimes not recognized because they do not end in *-ly*.

1. It is <u>almost</u> new.
2. We had <u>already</u> left.
3. They <u>also</u> serve.
4. She <u>always</u> wins.
5. Is it <u>ever</u> cold?
6. It will last <u>forever</u>.
7. I am waiting <u>here</u>.
8. They <u>just</u> left.
9. I like that <u>least</u>.
10. <u>Maybe</u> they called.
11. You should work <u>more</u>.
12. He <u>never</u> loses.
13. We may <u>not</u> come.
14. <u>Perhaps</u> he knew.
15. It <u>seldom</u> snows.
16. I am <u>so</u> happy.
17. She <u>still</u> runs.
18. Put it <u>there</u>.
19. It felt <u>too</u> dry.
20. Has it begun <u>yet</u>?

Exercises

A. Two words in each sentence end in *-ly*. One is an adverb. One is an adjective. Write the adverb.

1. Fog drifted soundlessly over the pebbly beach.
2. Stately pines swayed gently in the breeze.
3. Hourly the hall echoed with heavenly music.
4. The nightly news was temporarily interrupted.
5. Those oily rags are completely useless.

B. Write each underlined adverb. Then write the word or words each adverb modifies. Label the word or words *verb, adjective,* or *adverb.*

EXAMPLE: She had worked <u>strenuously</u>.
ANSWER: strenuously, had worked, verb

6. Women did <u>not</u> sell heavy industrial equipment until Kate Gleason of Rochester, New York, entered the field in 1885. **7.** She began her <u>highly</u> successful career <u>quite</u> early. **8.** Her father, an <u>unusually</u> clever inventor, had developed a machine that could make gears <u>faster</u> than any other. **9.** Kate worked in his factory, <u>very</u> carefully observed business procedures, and <u>afterward</u> studied mechanical engineering. **10.** With <u>so</u> much knowledge and experience, she could sell his machines <u>easily</u>.

C. Write each sentence. Complete it with an adverb from the examples on page 44.

11. My signature is _____ on this paper.
12. _____ the word was misspelled.
13. Have you corrected your paper _____?
14. Of all the skis, I like these _____.
15. This persimmon tastes _____ bitter.

Additional Exercises

A. Write the sentences below. Underline each adverb.

1. Our principal always visits each class twice during the school year.
2. They examined their monthly bills quickly.
3. Summer vacations usually go fast.
4. Turn left at the end of the hall.
5. The rain fell steadily in the evening.
6. Bill excitedly opened the package.
7. The little bird chirped merrily.
8. Walk slowly and listen carefully.
9. Betty rode swiftly on her bicycle.
10. The wind really lashed furiously.

B. Each sentence in this article contains an adverb. Write each adverb after its sentence number. Write the word or words that it modifies.

11. In 1983 Lieutenant Colonel Guion S. Bluford, Jr., zoomed skyward on the Space Shuttle. 12. America's first black astronaut conducted vitally important experiments aboard the *Challenger*. 13. Complicated problems have always fascinated him. 14. As a child he loved very difficult puzzles and games. 15. In school Guy did well in math. 16. He organized his junior high school's first math club and was an extremely active member. 17. At Pennsylvania State University in 1964, he successfully completed its aerospace engineering program. 18. He promptly joined the Air Force and won his wings at Williams Air Force Base in Arizona. 19. The Air Force Institute of Technology in Dayton, Ohio, later awarded him a doctorate. 20. Astronaut Bluford often reminds young people about the value of hard work.

Application USING GRAMMAR IN WRITING

By adding adverbs, you can include more information.

Dan was working. (where and when?)
Dan was working <u>downstairs</u> <u>today</u>. (to what extent and how?)
Dan was working <u>very</u> <u>hard</u> downstairs today.

Writing with Adverbs

A. Add adverbs to the sentences to answer the questions in parentheses. Write each sentence twice, placing the adverbs in different positions in each sentence.

1. Anna was swimming. (where and when?)
2. Aldo found the gold. (where, when, and how?)
3. The mail will be delivered. (when and how often?)
4. The employees worked. (to what extent and how?)
5. The bell always rings. (how and how often?)

A specific verb can often replace a vague verb and an adverb. For example, the vague verb *said* and the adverb *suddenly* can be replaced by the vivid verb *blurted*.

"What an ugly dress!" Lena <u>said</u> <u>suddenly</u>.
"What an ugly dress!" Lena <u>blurted</u>.

Using the Thesaurus

B. Use the Thesaurus to find synonyms for *say*. Then use one vivid verb to replace *said* and the underlined adverb in each sentence below.

6. "I refuse to go!" <u>said</u> Joe <u>boldly</u>.
7. "Don't let them hear you," Mona <u>said</u> <u>softly</u>.
8. "I'm up in the attic!" Mr. Ray <u>said</u> <u>loudly</u> to his son.
9. "I can't stand it here," Sue <u>said</u> <u>angrily</u> to herself.
10. The speaker <u>said</u> <u>forcefully</u>, "I am done for now."

Chapter Review

A. Write the sentences below. Underline each verb.

1. My father signed my report card.
2. They forgot the number of their locker.
3. Where were you yesterday?
4. Your notebook looks new.
5. Everyone had the right answer.

B. Write the sentences. Underline each verb phrase.

6. Dana is memorizing the definition.
7. Can you recommend another good story?
8. Did they do that lesson?
9. It should have been finished yesterday.
10. The counselor might not have ever seen the results of those tests.

C. Write each adverb in the sentences. Then write the word or words that each adverb modifies.

EXAMPLE: She was speaking very softly.
ANSWER: very, softly; softly, was speaking

11. The ship was moving quite slowly.
12. The eighth graders will arrive tomorrow.
13. Put all your packages there.
14. I almost fell on that sidewalk.
15. The carrots were unusually delicious.
16. Another huge truck roared away.
17. Study this very carefully.
18. He was extremely happy about it.
19. All the directions for the test were explained quite thoroughly.
20. They climbed ever closer to the peak.

Chapter Review CHALLENGE

Read the article about opportunities for young people. Using only the underlined words as answers, find and write these grammatical constructions.

A. one uninterrupted verb phrase
B. one main verb in a verb phrase
C. one helping verb in a verb phrase
D. one action verb with the action not visible
E. one state-of-being verb
F. one interrupted verb phrase
G. one adverb modifying a verb
H. one adverb modifying an adjective
I. one adverb modifying an adverb
J. one word ending in *-ly* that is not an adverb

Young people can **(1)** easily make valuable use of spare time. Opportunities **(2)** are everywhere. Adults need a **(3)** wide variety of services. **(4)** Anyone who is away from his or her home likes to know that it **(5)** is being watched by a trustworthy individual. The owner of a pet appreciates a **(6)** friendly person who **(7)** can conscientiously feed it every day. Many people also have **(8)** plants that need care. Some apartment dwellers need help in the **(9)** laundry room loading and unloading washers and dryers. Everyone needs calendars, but each year they are becoming **(10)** increasingly expensive. Attractive ones can be **(11)** drawn, reproduced, and then sold. By working with adults, young people **(12)** very soon develop skills and **(13)** learn responsibility. No business venture **(14)** should be started, however, without the advice and the **(15)** approval of a parent or guardian.

3

Conjunctions, Prepositions, and Interjections

Winter Circus

There's a circus in the sky;
clowns in frills of fluffy white
merrily come tumbling by,
turning cartwheels left and right.

Tiny dancers whirl about
dressed in white from head to toe,
back and forth and in and out
through the tent of sky they go.

White-clad acrobats flip by
in a daring, breathless way ...
there's a circus in the sky
every snowy winter day!

—Aileen Fisher

1 — Conjunctions

> ● A **conjunction** joins words or groups of words in a sentence.

Only a few words are used as conjunctions. The most common ones are *and, but, or,* and *nor.* These are called **coordinating conjunctions.** They connect words that do the same kind of work.

Coordinating Conjunctions

noun + noun	bread <u>and</u> water
pronoun + pronoun	you <u>or</u> they
noun + pronoun	Pamela <u>and</u> I
adjective + adjective	tall <u>and</u> handsome
verb + verb	laughed <u>or</u> cried
adverb + adverb	slowly <u>but</u> surely

Coordinating conjunctions can also be used to join groups of similar words.

They <u>have just arrived</u> <u>and</u> <u>will soon speak.</u>
We have <u>foggy mornings</u> <u>but</u> <u>sunny afternoons.</u>
It eats <u>very ripe seeds</u> <u>or</u> <u>very fresh leaves.</u>
They <u>did not see us,</u> <u>nor</u> <u>did we see them.</u>

Some conjunctions are made of pairs of words, such as *both ... and, either ... or, neither ... nor.* These pairs are called **correlative conjunctions.** Notice in the examples below that correlative conjunctions, like coordinating conjunctions, can join either individual words or groups of words.

Correlative Conjunctions

We toured <u>both</u> Virginia <u>and</u> West Virginia.
She <u>either</u> photographed <u>or</u> sketched trees.
The weather was <u>neither</u> hot <u>nor</u> humid.
They <u>either</u> <u>lost their way</u> <u>or</u> <u>forgot the time.</u>

Exercises

A. Write the coordinating conjunction or the correlative conjunctions in each sentence.

1. She and I left.
2. Was it you or he?
3. Be firm but kind.
4. Call Lou and me.
5. Buy or borrow ink.
6. It's dry but cold.
7. Go now or never.
8. Neither they nor we understood it.
9. In that park grow both oaks and elms.
10. Buy either corn or beets.

B. Write each coordinating conjunction or correlative conjunction after its sentence number. Underline the correlative conjunctions.

11. In prehistoric times people could neither read nor write. **12.** There were no alphabets or books, nor did paper or pens exist. **13.** The people were illiterate but imaginative. **14.** Men and women made the night sky both a library and a calendar. **15.** Many of their songs and stories about stars and planets became either myths or superstitions.

C. Write each coordinating and correlative conjunction. Then write the words joined by the conjunctions. Write their parts of speech.

EXAMPLE: Nick or I will come.
ANSWER: or; Nick, I (noun, pronoun)

16. That bird never sings or whistles.
17. She spoke softly and politely.
18. His story was long but funny.
19. The station wagon needed both oil and gas.
20. Neither Lida nor he revealed the secret.

2 — Prepositions

- A **preposition** relates a noun or pronoun to another word in the sentence.

Both a conjunction and a preposition join words, but a preposition joins them in a special way.

Conjunction: The actors <u>and</u> the parrot sang.
Preposition: The actors <u>near</u> the parrot sang.

The preposition *near* tells how the words *actors* and *parrot* are related.

The noun or pronoun that follows a preposition is called the **object of the preposition.** A preposition, its object, and any words that modify the object make up a **prepositional phrase.**

Prepositional Phrases

The actors (<u>near</u> the *parrot*) sang.
The actors (<u>in</u> blue *wigs*) sang.
The actors (<u>from</u> the new *school*) sang.

In the examples the prepositions are underlined. Their objects are in italics. Each prepositional phrase modifies the noun *actors.*

Some prepositions are made up of two or more words. In addition, a preposition may have two or more objects. These form a compound object. Prepositional phrases may also begin and end sentences.

(<u>Next to</u> *you* and *me*) stood the actors.
The actors sang (<u>next to</u> *them* and *us*).

Learn to recognize the commonly used prepositions in the chart on the next page.

Sixty Prepositions in Prepositional Phrases

1. aboard the plane
2. about midnight
3. above our house
4. according to her
5. across the sky
6. after any storm
7. against him or me
8. along the trail
9. among three dogs
10. around the school

11. at Pulaski School
12. because of him
13. before her or me
14. behind that wall
15. below Market Street
16. beneath one street
17. beside this desk
18. besides math and art
19. between two cars
20. beyond my dreams

21. but (except) them
22. by Margaret Mitchell
23. concerning a novel
24. despite difficulties
25. down this field
26. during that game
27. except these fans
28. for those players
29. from their city
30. in Kansas City

31. in front of me
32. in spite of pain
33. inside my tooth
34. instead of music
35. into Lake Tahoe
36. like these lakes
37. near everyone
38. of brass and tin
39. off a steamboat
40. on the Mississippi

41. out a porthole
42. out of the past
43. outside my tent
44. over the waves
45. past Labor Day
46. since that day
47. through a door
48. throughout time
49. till summer
50. to May or June

51. toward the gate
52. under a cloud
53. underneath a rug
54. until the end
55. unto us
56. up the Nile
57. upon its banks
58. with faith
59. within reason
60. without fear

Exercises

A. Write the preposition in each sentence.

1. Drive to Oregon.
2. Don't go past us.
3. We work near you.
4. Up a tree it flew.
5. Wait till Friday.

6. Stay off the raft.
7. Live without fear.
8. Down a lane I ran.
9. All of them study.
10. No one but me knew.

B. In this article about the Milky Way, there are ten prepositional phrases. Write each phrase after its sentence number. Underline each preposition. Circle each object or objects.

EXAMPLE: For centuries people have studied the stars.
ANSWER: For (centuries)

11. A great band of stars flows across the sky like a river. **12.** For us this is the Milky Way. **13.** In other countries and at other times, it has had different names and meanings. **14.** It has been called a mystical world without struggles, a silvery bridge between earth and heaven, and even a magic serpent with a shiny tail. **15.** One ancient writer thought that all trees and flowers were nourished by its light.

C. Write the prepositional phrases in these sentences. Underline each preposition. Circle each object.

16. Teresa dived into the lagoon.
17. Hans opened a book of poems.
18. A column of smoke curled from the chimney.
19. Before the next test we must review the lesson.
20. A passenger aboard the train to Denver knew my parents and me.

21. The latest results of the election appeared at the bottom of the television screen.
22. Despite the score the team from Allenville played with exceptional skill.
23. A large picture of an eagle with golden claws and silver feathers hung on the back wall.
24. In the greenhouse beside our school, the plants are growing rapidly.
25. Inside a locker on the second floor, the custodian found a pair of skates.
26. Everyone but you and me must have heard the announcement about the party for Ms. Russo.
27. Through the corridors of the school floated the wonderful aroma of freshly baked bread.
28. Underneath a stack of phonograph records were all of the notebooks with the lists of my homework assignments.
29. Many colonies of tiny ants lived under the damp leaves around the ancient sycamore trees in the park.
30. The good news about the harvest spread rapidly from the largest cities to the smallest towns and villages in the country.

D. Write each sentence, completing it with a prepositional phrase. Select prepositions from the following: *according to, because of, in front of, in spite of, instead of,* and *out of.* Underline your prepositional phrase.

31. We finished the assignment on time _____.
32. The game might be delayed _____.
33. A friendly crowd was gathering _____.
34. _____ we might study French.
35. _____ fell a ticket to the concert.

3 — Prepositional Phrases as Adjectives

> ● A prepositional phrase that modifies a noun or pronoun is an **adjective phrase.**

Like an adjective, a prepositional phrase can modify a noun or pronoun. It can also answer the same question an adjective answers: *What kind? Which one? How much?* or *How many?* This kind of prepositional phrase is called an adjective phrase. In the examples adjectives and adjective phrases are underlined. The words they modify are in italics. Notice that the adjectives and adjective phrases do the same work—they modify the nouns *room* and *flag.*

Adjectives	Adjective Phrases
I entered a <u>window-less</u> *room.*	I entered a *room* <u>without windows</u>.
The <u>Japanese</u> *flag* is red and white.	The *flag* <u>of Japan</u> is red and white.

An adjective phrase follows the noun or pronoun it modifies. A noun or pronoun can be modified by more than one adjective phrase.

This is the *road* (to Trenton).

This is the *road* (from Camden) (to Trenton).

Sometimes an adjective phrase modifies a noun used as an object of a preposition.

I have a *map* (of the *roads*) (in New Jersey).

Some (of the *roads*) (in the *state*) (of New Jersey) are very wide.

Exercises

A. Each sentence has one or two adjective phrases in parentheses. Write the noun that each adjective phrase modifies.

1. Win a certificate (for perfect attendance).
2. The literature books (without covers) are being replaced next semester.
3. Those people (in the hall) are visitors.
4. Find a key (to the door) (of the old shed).
5. Prepare a report (about craters) (on Mars).

B. This article about the zodiac has ten adjective phrases. Write each phrase after its sentence number. Then write the noun each phrase modifies.

6. Today we have a calendar with twelve months. 7. The zodiac, with its twelve signs, was a calendar for people in many ancient civilizations. 8. The zodiac is a band of stars. 9. The twelve signs of the zodiac are twelve constellations along a wide path in the sky. 10. The location of each constellation told the people the month of the year.

C. Change each underlined word to an adjective phrase. Write the noun and then your phrase.

EXAMPLE: wooden gates
ANSWER: gates of wood

11. cotton shirts
12. pearly teeth
13. colorless sky
14. horse barns
15. hilltop cabins
16. monster movies
17. seaside cottages
18. highway traffic
19. Oklahoma lakes
20. a dimpled chin

4 — Prepositional Phrases as Adverbs

> ● A prepositional phrase that modifies a verb, an adjective, or an adverb is an **adverb phrase.**

Like an adverb, a prepositional phrase can modify a verb, an adjective, or an adverb. It can also answer the same questions an adverb answers, such as *When?* and *Where?* This kind of prepositional phrase is called an **adverb phrase.** In the examples the adverb phrases are in parentheses. The words they modify are in italics.

> They *worked* (with enthusiasm). MODIFIES VERB
> We are *ready* (for the test). MODIFIES ADJECTIVE
> I left *early* (in the morning). MODIFIES ADVERB

Like an adverb, an adverb phrase may be located anywhere in a sentence.

> (In the spring) I *planted* seeds.
> I *watered* the garden (with a hose).

Sometimes a sentence contains both an adverb phrase and an adjective phrase.

> I *started* (on the first *day*) (of spring).
>   adverb   adjective

Preposition or Adverb? Some words can be either prepositions or adverbs.

> **Preposition:** I waited <u>inside</u> my house.
> **Adverb:**   I waited <u>inside</u>.

In the first example, *inside* has an object—*house.* Remember that a preposition always has an object. An adverb never does.

Exercises

A. Write the adverb phrase in each sentence. Then write the word that each phrase modifies.

1. The new research center is near Chicago.
2. Owls can be heard late at night.
3. Their names appear on this petition.
4. From the highest branch fell another leaf.
5. The leaves were wet with dew.

B. This article about the Milky Way has twenty adverb phrases. Write each phrase after its sentence number.

6. The Milky Way runs endlessly in the sky. 7. Often it rises over our heads. 8. Sometimes it rolls along the horizon. 9. During certain months it flows from east to west. 10. Occasionally it goes from north to south. 11. It varies in size and brightness. 12. Its route can easily be mapped by the constellations. 13. The Milky Way drifts out of Cassiopeia and curves under Perseus's feet. 14. It then moves near Taurus, between Orion and Gemini, past Sirius, and into Argo. 15. It dips around the Southern Cross, swings through Scorpius and Sagittarius, passes across Cygnus, and settles again at Cassiopeia.

C. Write the prepositional phrase in each sentence. Identify it as an adjective or adverb phrase.

EXAMPLE: Did you ride your bike to school?
ANSWER: to school, adverb phrase

16. Are those farmers without hats too warm?
17. They occasionally work without hats.
18. A mouse darted across the field.
19. My ring rolled under the couch again.
20. The ring under the couch is mine.

Additional Exercises

A. Write each underlined word. Label it *conjunction, preposition,* or *adverb.*

1. <u>Outside</u> their school are new tennis courts and a baseball field.
2. <u>Inside</u> is a circular swimming pool.
3. The freight train moved <u>along</u> slowly.
4. Everyone walked <u>around</u> during the reception on the sun-drenched lawn.
5. <u>Around</u> us were campers from every state.
6. Another empty barge was drifting <u>by</u>.
7. Dishes <u>like</u> these are collectors' items.
8. We have notified everybody <u>but</u> them.
9. The pearls were small <u>but</u> valuable.
10. Everything <u>but</u> the chairs is for sale.

B. This article has twenty prepositional phrases. Write each phrase after its sentence number and label it *adjective* or *adverb.*

11. One of the constellations in the zodiac is Andromeda. **12.** This chain of stars lies between the Milky Way and Pisces. **13.** Andromeda was a beautiful Ethiopian princess in Greek mythology. **14.** One day a monster from the sea stormed into Ethiopia and caused much damage throughout the land. **15.** The people needed an offering for the monster without delay. **16.** With sadness Andromeda was chosen and was chained to a huge rock near the sea. **17.** Perseus, a son of Jupiter, saved her life. **18.** With his sword he slew the monster and cut the chains from her. **19.** At that moment she selected Perseus for her husband. **20.** Her first son was Perses, the ancestor of the kings of Persia.

Application

Conjunctions are often used to combine two or more short sentences into one smoother-sounding sentence. Notice how conjunctions combine the sentences below.

> Jan likes to dive. Walt likes to dive. I like to swim.
> Jan <u>and</u> Walt like to dive, <u>but</u> I like to swim.

> I might swim in the bay. I might sail out to sea.
> I might swim in the bay <u>or</u> sail out to sea.

Writing with Conjunctions

A. Use a conjunction to combine each pair of sentences.

1. Willa swims well. Paul and Rita swim well.
2. You can fish here. You can fish in the harbor.
3. You can sunbathe here. You can't swim here.
4. Jay swims here. I sail here.
5. Don't go on the beach. Don't go in the water.

Writing with Prepositions

B. You can add variety to your writing if some of your sentences begin with prepositional phrases. Write sentences that begin with the phrases below.

6. In the water
7. After the summer
8. Without a complaint
9. For dinner
10. By this time next year

Using the Thesaurus

C. The prepositional phrases *by mistake* and *in fear* are often overused. Using the Thesaurus, find three synonyms each for *mistake* and *fear*. Then form a prepositional phrase with each synonym, and use it in a sentence. You will write six sentences.

5 — Interjections

> ● An **interjection** expresses feeling or emotion.

The seven parts of speech that have been presented are like gears in a machine. One works with another to make a sentence function. Each word in this sentence is a different part of speech:

> Write often to these people and me.

The verb *write* is modified by the adverb *often*. The preposition *to* begins a phrase modifying *write. These,* an adjective, modifies *people,* a noun. The conjunction *and* joins the pronoun *me* to *people.* All the words are related grammatically.

The words in one group have no grammatical relationship with any other word in a sentence. They are the interjections, the attention-getters. Interjections are used to express feeling or emotion.

Interjections				
Ah	Brr	Hey	Oh	Ugh
Aha	Goodness	Hooray	Oops	Whew
Bravo	Great	Hush	Phooey	Wow

Interjections are used to express many kinds of emotions or feelings. An interjection may express strong or sudden emotion. In that case it is followed by an exclamation mark (!). If an interjection expresses mild emotion, it is followed by a comma.

> <u>Ouch</u>! That lizard bit me!
> <u>Well</u>, I think I'll go to the library.

Exercises

A. Supply an appropriate interjection for each of the following sentences. Use no interjection more than once.

1. ____! Is that a filthy floor!
2. She whispered, "____, what a day."
3. "____!" the clown kept shouting.
4. ____! I dropped the dishes!
5. "____," Valerie said, "I doubt that."
6. ____! We won another game!
7. ____! It's cold outside!
8. Peter said softly, "____, don't cry."
9. "____!" screamed the enthusiastic audience.
10. ____! You can't go in there!
11. ____! This tastes terrible!
12. As the opera ended, everyone shouted "____!"
13. ____, that cool breeze feels good.
14. ____! What a storm this is!
15. ____! So that's where you were!

B. Select five of the emotions and situations listed. Write a sentence based on each one. Use an appropriate interjection in each sentence.

16. Thrill (A ride was taken on a roller coaster.)
17. Pain (An elbow has been bumped.)
18. Sorrow (A precious object has been lost.)
19. Impatience (A movie is long and boring.)
20. Disbelief (A strange prediction is made.)
21. Astonishment (Water in a pool is very cold.)
22. Pleasure (An award has been given.)
23. Disgust (The wrong assignment was done.)
24. Exhaustion (Many laps were run on a track.)
25. Happiness (A vacation has begun.)

Chapter Review

A. Write each sentence. Then underline the coordinating or correlative conjunction.

    1. Is this elevator going up or down?
    2. Divide the work between her and me.
    3. The tests seemed longer but easier.
    4. Supper was not ready nor was the table set.
    5. Both the sun and the moon were visible.

B. Write each sentence. Then underline the preposition.

    6. He stood beside the golden door.
    7. In twenty years everything will be different.
    8. The name of the constellation is Argo.
    9. Instead of marble they used granite.
    10. We had a conference about careers.

C. Write the prepositional phrase in each sentence.

    11. An unusual kite was flying over the city.
    12. A tunnel under the English Channel would benefit both Britain and France.
    13. After the conference the counselors and the students discussed careers.
    14. Tax rates were raised despite many objections.
    15. Along the coast we saw many sunny beaches.

D. Write each sentence. Then underline the interjection.

    16. Ouch! That spoon is hot!
    17. Good grief! The parking lot is full.
    18. She said, "Oh, don't worry about it."
    19. Yippee! The circus is coming!
    20. The dragon, alas, turned into a dandelion.

Chapter Review CHALLENGE

Read the article about the astronomer Maria Mitchell. Using only the underlined words as answers, find and write these grammatical constructions.

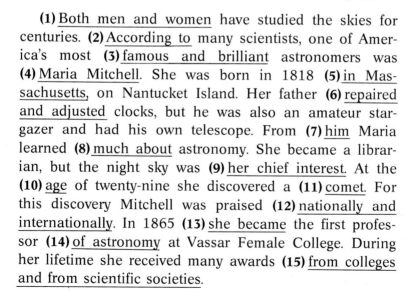

A. two verbs joined by a conjunction
B. two adjectives joined by a conjunction
C. two adverbs joined by a conjunction
D. two phrases joined by a conjunction
E. two nouns joined by a correlative conjunction
F. one adjective prepositional phrase
G. one adverb prepositional phrase
H. one noun used as an object of a preposition
I. one pronoun used as an object of a preposition
J. one preposition composed of two words

(1) <u>Both men and women</u> have studied the skies for centuries. (2) <u>According to</u> many scientists, one of America's most (3) <u>famous and brilliant</u> astronomers was (4) <u>Maria Mitchell.</u> She was born in 1818 (5) <u>in Massachusetts,</u> on Nantucket Island. Her father (6) <u>repaired and adjusted</u> clocks, but he was also an amateur stargazer and had his own telescope. From (7) <u>him</u> Maria learned (8) <u>much about</u> astronomy. She became a librarian, but the night sky was (9) <u>her chief interest.</u> At the (10) <u>age</u> of twenty-nine she discovered a (11) <u>comet.</u> For this discovery Mitchell was praised (12) <u>nationally and internationally.</u> In 1865 (13) <u>she became</u> the first professor (14) <u>of astronomy</u> at Vassar Female College. During her lifetime she received many awards (15) <u>from colleges and from scientific societies.</u>

Cumulative Review

The Parts of Speech	
Nouns (pp. 8–11)	Adverbs (pp. 42–45)
Pronouns (pp. 14–21)	Conjunctions (pp. 52–53)
Adjectives (pp. 24–27)	Prepositions (pp. 54–61)
Verbs (pp. 36–39)	Interjections (pp. 64–65)

A. Write the part of speech that answers each question. Do not repeat answers.

1. What expresses action or being?
2. What modifies a noun or pronoun?
3. What takes the place of a noun or nouns?
4. What expresses feeling or emotion?
5. What names a person, place, thing, or idea?
6. What modifies a verb, an adjective, or another adverb?
7. What relates a noun or pronoun to another word in the sentence?
8. What joins words or groups of words?

B. All the words in each group are examples of one part of speech. Write the part of speech of each group of words.

9. or, nor, but, and
10. now, twice, seldom, backward, extremely
11. did, had, could, build, operate, swim
12. we, she, him, them, whom, nothing, everyone
13. at, into, from, except, against, underneath
14. musicians, abilities, friendship, machine
15. big, small, careless, expensive, impossible

C. The lines in this poem by Cora Ball Moton are numbered 16–25. Write each underlined word and its part of speech after the line number.

Sight

16. I see <u>skies</u> more bright <u>and</u> blue
17. Than <u>any</u> skies beheld <u>by</u> you,
18. I see <u>trees</u> so <u>tall</u> and high
19. Their <u>green</u> leaves brush <u>against</u> the sky,
20. I see <u>birds</u> (and hear <u>them</u> sing)
21. Like <u>rainbows</u> that <u>have taken</u> wing;
22. <u>I</u> see <u>flowers</u> fairer far
23. Than <u>any</u> in your garden <u>are</u>,
24. <u>These</u> lovely sights you'll <u>never</u> find,
25. Because—my dear, you <u>*see*</u>; I'm <u>*blind.*</u>

D. Some words can be used as more than one part of speech. Write the part of speech of each underlined word.

26. The green bus will leave <u>last</u>.
27. Did the <u>last</u> chapter contain a summary?
28. Their lawn mower is <u>near</u> the shed.
29. Will the chipmunk come <u>near</u>?
30. <u>This</u> apple is crisp and juicy.
31. Can you read <u>this</u>?
32. We are going to the <u>library</u>.
33. I hope I can find my <u>library</u> card.
34. Look at <u>that</u> new skyscraper.
35. I wonder if <u>that</u> is enough food.
36. Write your name <u>below</u>.
37. There is little snow <u>below</u> the timberline.
38. At the next intersection turn <u>right</u>.
39. I made a <u>right</u> turn at the intersection.
40. Everybody has the <u>right</u> to an education.

E. A word or group of words is underlined in each sentence. Write the grammatical term that correctly describes that word or group of words.

41. We visited the waterfront in <u>Baltimore</u>.
    a. a common noun
    b. a proper noun

42. Did you order <u>anything</u> from this catalog?
    a. indefinite pronoun
    b. interrogative pronoun

43. She flung <u>herself</u> across the finish line.
    a. reflexive pronoun
    b. possessive pronoun

44. The announcer made <u>an</u> unusual offer.
    a. definite article
    b. indefinite article

45. Those workers <u>are</u> in the carport now.
    a. action verb
    b. state-of-being verb

46. Sonia might <u>have</u> the answer.
    a. helping verb
    b. main verb

47. The benches are old <u>but</u> sturdy.
    a. coordinating conjunction
    b. correlative conjunction

48. They celebrated <u>throughout the day</u>.
    a. adjective phrase
    b. adverb phrase

49. Leave <u>during the next intermission</u>.
    a. prepositional phrase
    b. verb phrase

50. Our <u>principal</u> said that he could come.
    a. antecedent of a pronoun
    b. object of a preposition

F. Rewrite the sentences according to the instructions in parentheses. Make any other necessary changes.

51. Everyone relaxed after the game.
(Write the prepositional phrase at the beginning of the sentence.)

52. The water began to boil suddenly.
(Write the adverb at the beginning of the sentence.)

53. My sisters photographed the players.
(Make one noun a collective noun.)

54. We looked at a small car.
(Change one adjective to a proper adjective.)

55. The Canadian flag is on that flagpole.
(Change one adjective to a prepositional phrase.)

56. She always drives carefully.
(Change one adverb to an adverb prepositional phrase.)

57. Those stamps belong to Bill.
(Make the object of the preposition a compound object.)

58. George discussed the news with Linda.
(Change both proper nouns to personal pronouns.)

59. A bad storm spoiled a pleasant afternoon.
(Add an adverb to modify one adjective.)

60. The bell is ringing.
(Begin the sentence with an interjection. Be sure to put either a comma or an exclamation mark after the interjection.)

UNIT TWO

Sentence Structure

The study of grammar may be divided into two units. The first is a study of the parts of speech. The second is a study of the parts of the sentence, or how sentences are constructed. The names of the units may sound similar, but the content of each is different.

The parts of speech, described in Unit 1, are like the materials used to build a house. They are the lumber, plasterboards, bricks, nails, tiles, and shingles.

The parts of the sentence, in Unit 2, are like the framework of a house. They can be arranged in different ways to build different kinds of sentences. With a knowledge of the rules of grammar that produce good sentence structure, a student can communicate effectively.

On the following page is a summary of many of the sentence parts and constructions you will be studying in this unit. The terms below are not included in the chart. Look them up in the Index to Rules in the back.

simple sentence	compound sentence
clause	complex sentence

Summary of Sentence Parts

1. A sentence expresses a complete thought.
   The students visited the media center.
2. A complete subject names the sentence topic.
   The films on that table may be borrowed.
3. A simple subject is the key subject word.
   The films on that table may be borrowed.
4. A complete predicate tells about the subject.
   The class examined all the new film catalogs.
5. A simple predicate is a verb.
   The class examined all the new film catalogs.
6. A direct object receives the verb's action.
   We wrote a review of a television movie.
7. A predicate nominative renames the subject.
   That machine is a splicer.
8. A predicate adjective modifies the subject.
   The lens was dirty.
9. An indirect object tells to or for whom.
   I handed the secretary my requests.
10. A verbal is a verb form used as a noun, an adjective, or an adverb.
    broken tapes   our taping   a tape to hear
11. A participle is a verbal adjective.
    The teacher speaking on the tape is Ms. Klein.
12. A gerund is a verbal noun.
    The media specialist discussed recording.
13. An infinitive is a verbal beginning with *to*.
    The phonograph to borrow has a green case.
14. A run-on sentence is a sentence error.
    The film fluttered then it broke.
15. A sentence fragment is a sentence error.
    Our club will meet. In the radio studio.

4 *The Sentence*

Hard Questions

Why not mark out the land
into neat rectangles
squares and clover leafs?

Put on them cubes of
varying sizes
according to use—
dwellings
    singles/multiples
complexes
    commercial/industrial.

Bale them together with
bands of roads.

What if a child shall cry
"I have never known spring!
I have never seen autumn!"

What if a man shall say
"I have never heard
silence fraught with living as
in swamp or forest!"
What if the eye shall never see
marsh birds and muskrats?

Does not the heart need
wildness?

—*Margaret Tsuda*

1 —Sentences

> ● A **sentence** is a group of words that expresses a complete thought.

A sentence is a group of words. The word group may be short or long. Each sentence begins with a capital letter and ends with a punctuation mark.

Shoppers laughed.
All the shoppers in the supermarket laughed at the unusual titles on some magazines.

A group of words is not a sentence unless it expresses a complete thought. First, it must name a topic—who or what the sentence is about. Second, it must tell something about the topic. If it fails to do either of these things, the result is an incomplete thought.

Incomplete Thoughts
Recognizes the face on that cover.
Many great authors.

Complete Thoughts
Everybody recognizes the face on that cover.
Many great authors have written for magazines.

Every sentence must have two parts. The subject part names the topic to be discussed. The predicate part tells what the subject is or does.

Subject Part	Predicate Part
Magazines	arrived.
Many popular magazines	are never thrown away.
The price of magazines	has risen steadily.

Exercises

A. The numbered groups are subject parts. The lettered groups are predicate parts. Write each subject part. Write the predicate that fits best.

1. Birds	**a.** has stolen the bait.
2. The sun	**b.** have been raked up.
3. These letters	**c.** are ticking loudly.
4. Ice on highways	**d.** need more postage.
5. The old clocks	**e.** has a rusty knob.
6. This heavy door	**f.** were announced.
7. Names of winners	**g.** causes accidents.
8. That sly catfish	**h.** was quite easy.
9. All of the leaves	**i.** is above us.
10. The test for today	**j.** fly.

B. Write the word group and add the missing subject part or predicate part to make a complete thought. Underline the part you add. Do not use any answer more than once.

EXAMPLE: has a colorful cover.

ANSWER: The magazine has a colorful cover.

11. Magazines
12. My favorite magazine
13. are usually kept longer than newspapers.
14. Many newsstands and bookstores
15. have weekly or monthly issues.
16. Beautiful color photography
17. Subscriptions for some magazines
18. have unforgettable photographs of animals, forests, and mountains.
19. is on the cover of that magazine.
20. had an article about bicycles.

—2—Four Kinds of Sentences

> ● The four kinds of sentences are **declarative, interrogative, imperative,** and **exclamatory**.

Sentences can express ideas in four ways. Every sentence must begin with a capital letter.

Declarative Sentences   A sentence that makes a statement is called a declarative sentence. This kind of sentence ends with a period.

> The news is good.   I discovered gold.

Interrogative Sentences   A sentence that asks a question is called an interrogative sentence. It ends with a question mark.

> Is the story true?   How do I know?

Imperative Sentences   A sentence that gives a command or makes a request is called an imperative sentence. It ends with a period.

> Do not believe it.   Please read this.

Exclamatory Sentences   A sentence that expresses strong feeling is called an exclamatory sentence. It ends with an exclamation mark.

> How short it is!   Do I feel happy!

Many declarative, interrogative, and imperative sentences can be made exclamatory by changing the period or question mark to an exclamation mark.

> The story is great.   The story is great!
> Did you write another? Did you write another!
> Read it now.   Read it now!

Exercises

A. Write whether each sentence is declarative, interrogative, or imperative. Then write the correct end punctuation mark in parentheses.

EXAMPLE: Who wrote that story
ANSWER: interrogative (?)

1. Where is the magazine
2. Did you leave it on your desk
3. Here it is
4. Look at the table of contents for this issue
5. Every article discusses a famous discovery
6. Notice the title of this article
7. Why are you interested in that article
8. I have always admired Marie Skłodowska Curie
9. Read about the discovery of gold in California
10. Gold was also mined in Georgia

B. Rewrite each sentence, changing it into the kind of sentence indicated in parentheses.

EXAMPLE: She doesn't watch TV. (imperative)
ANSWER: Don't watch TV.

11. I shall listen to the news. (imperative)
12. She saves important news stories. (imperative)
13. They write letters to editors. (imperative)
14. News magazines are popular. (interrogative)
15. A journalist writes news stories. (interrogative)
16. Are there newscasts on radio? (declarative)
17. Was Lowell Thomas a newscaster? (declarative)
18. Does TV cover special events? (declarative)
19. Was there an earthquake? (exclamatory)
20. The television reporters ran. (exclamatory)

3 — Complete and Simple Subjects

> • The **subject part** of a sentence names someone or something.

The Complete Subject The whole subject part of a sentence has a grammatical name. This part is called the complete subject. It contains the topic and any words or phrases that modify it. The complete subject is shown in blue in the following examples.

> The huge library is a busy place.
> A number of librarians work there.

The Simple Subject The main word in the complete subject is called the simple subject. A simple subject is usually a noun or pronoun. The simple subject may be found by removing any adjectives or any prepositional phrases from the complete subject. The simple subject is shown in dark blue.

> The huge library is a busy place.
> A number of librarians work there.

If the simple subject is a proper noun, it may consist of more than one word.

> The new Piedmont Library is on Faulkner Road.
> *Oahu Holiday* by Leilani Chan is a travel book.

Sometimes just one word is in the subject part of a sentence. It is usually a noun or pronoun. That one word is both the complete subject and the simple subject of the sentence.

> Luis was reading all day.
> We have been examining books by Willa Cather.

Exercises

A. Each word group is a complete subject. Write only the simple subject.

1. Colorful posters
2. An empty shelf
3. Many bulletins
4. Eager readers
5. Very loyal fans
6. Great excitement
7. Too much noise
8. The last minute
9. A big red sign
10. Something new
11. Pictures of an author
12. The name on the cover
13. Some gifts for friends
14. One of the almanacs
15. This new novel by him
16. The people with gifts
17. A cover without words
18. Books about football
19. A review of the novel
20. Everybody but me

B. Write the complete subject of each sentence. Then underline the simple subject.

21. Many reporters filled the press box.
22. An endless stream of fans entered the stadium.
23. The lines on the football field were sharp.
24. The greatest day of the season had come.
25. Everyone in the stadium was excited.
26. The Cactus City Coyotes were the home team.
27. They would face the Coronado Chargers.
28. A group of cheerleaders was shouting.
29. The bands from both schools were marching.
30. Both teams rushed out of the locker rooms.
31. The warm autumn air echoed with cheers.
32. "The Star-Spangled Banner" was movingly sung.
33. The moment for the kickoff was finally here.
34. The great football game would soon begin.
35. The sports pages of the local newspapers would feature the outcome tomorrow.

4 – Complete and Simple Predicates

> ● The **predicate part** of a sentence tells what the subject is or does.

Complete Predicate The whole predicate part of a sentence has a grammatical name. This part is called the complete predicate. Every complete predicate must have a verb. It may also have adverbs, prepositional phrases, and even nouns and pronouns. The complete predicate tells something about the subject. The complete predicate is shown in green.

> The new library is also a study hall.
> Many students were standing around a desk.

Simple Predicate The simple predicate is the main word or words in the complete predicate. The simple predicate is always a verb or verb phrase. It is shown in dark green.

> The new library is also a study hall.
> Many students were standing around a desk.

Sometimes an adverb interrupts a verb phrase. The adverb is not part of the simple predicate.

> The clock was quietly ticking.

The predicate part of a sentence may be one word, a verb. The verb is both the complete predicate and the simple predicate.

> The teacher of the seventh grade spoke.

Sentence Terms From now on, references to the *subject* will mean the "simple subject." References to the *verb* will mean the "simple predicate."

Exercises

A. Each word group is a complete predicate. Write only the verb.

1. wrote a report about the game.
2. carefully examined the canyon walls.
3. will make another request for service.
4. certainly does live near the new factory.
5. prepares long lists of unusual words.
6. has never been tardy in his life.
7. might not have ever seen her.
8. always is our favorite class.
9. sometimes can be placed under a broiler.
10. must have been studying.

B. Write and label the subject and the verb of each sentence.

EXAMPLE: The game finally ended.
ANSWER: game (subject), ended (verb)

11. The Chargers easily defeated the Coyotes.
12. The final score of the football game was 49–0.
13. Arlene Sanchez of the *Coronado Times* wrote an excellent article about the game.
14. She gave most of the credit for the Chargers' victory to their fine defensive play.
15. The linebackers on the Chargers tackled the Coyotes' quarterback seven times.
16. Five passes by the Coyotes were intercepted.
17. Their runners could not advance the ball.
18. Coach Tony Patero of the Chargers praised his entire team for the lopsided victory.
19. Last year the Coyotes had beaten them.
20. The coach of the Chargers will probably be featured in an article in a sports magazine.

5 — Subject and Verb Identification

> ● A subject may precede or follow a verb. It may interrupt a verb phrase or be understood.

Subjects and Verbs in Declarative Sentences In most declarative sentences the subject precedes the verb. This is called **normal word order**.

> A picture of the cheerleaders was on the cover.

In some sentences, especially those beginning with *here* or *there*, the subject follows the verb. This is called **inverted word order**.

> On the cover was a picture of the cheerleaders.
> Here come the cheerleaders.
> There is a picture of them.

Subjects and Verbs in Interrogative Sentences In many interrogative sentences the subject is between the parts of the verb phrase.

> Did the cheerleaders appear on the cover?
> Have their cheers been recorded?

Subjects and Verbs in Imperative Sentences The subject of an imperative sentence is the pronoun *you*. The word *you* is not usually stated. It is understood. In the sentences below, the subject is understood to be *you*.

> Read the caption under their picture, sir.
> Students, do not forget any cheers.

The words *sir* and *Students* are not subjects. They are nouns of direct address. A comma separates this kind of noun from the rest of the sentence.

Exercises

A. Write the subject and the verb of each declarative sentence. Underline the subject.

1. Some of these biscuits are still warm.
2. Soon came the sound of laughter.
3. In the center of the cake were two candles.
4. Here is another good recipe for rye bread.
5. There was not enough gravy in the bowl.

B. Write the subject and the verb of each interrogative sentence. Underline the subject.

6. Did the literary magazine staff meet yesterday?
7. Has anyone ever noticed that definition?
8. Would the editors understand it?
9. When should these letters be mailed?
10. Have the subscribers received their copies?

C. Write the verb of each imperative sentence. Put *you* in parentheses as the subject.

11. Revise your compositions now, students.
12. Be here early tomorrow, Carmen.
13. Never mix ammonia with bleach.
14. Do not forget the stamps for these letters.
15. Do give us the assignment now, sir.

D. Write the subject and the verb of each sentence. For imperatives, put *you* in parentheses.

16. Here are some lists of my favorite magazines.
17. Out of the box rolled one rusty thumbtack.
18. Did you fold these computer cards?
19. There are mysterious lights in the sky now.
20. Describe Ghana for our class, Dr. Otu.

6 — Compound Subjects and Verbs

- The word *compound* means composed of two or more parts.

Compound Subject Two or more simple subjects that have the same verb are called a compound subject. A conjunction such as *and* or *or* joins the simple subjects in a compound subject.

Newspapers or magazines arrived.
Newspapers, magazines, paperbacks, almanacs, calendars, and stationery arrived.

Compound Verb Two or more verbs that have the same subject are called a compound verb. A conjunction such as *and* or *or* joins the verbs. Sometimes adverbs, in addition to conjunctions, stand between the parts of compound verbs.

That title annoys or frightens.
That title does not annoy me and certainly should not frighten anyone.
That title has been used before and will be featured again.
Does that title bewilder or confuse them?

A sentence may have both a compound subject and a compound verb.

Both teachers and students have examined and will exchange these magazines.

An imperative sentence may have a compound verb. The subject is *you* understood.

Examine and exchange these magazines.

Exercises

A. Each sentence contains either a compound subject or a compound verb. Write and label only the compound subject or the compound verb.

1. She and I solved that problem by ourselves.
2. Everybody has arrived and is unpacking.
3. Read, review, and rewrite these stories.
4. Will all the walls be washed or repainted?
5. Inside were boxes of nails and cans of oil.

B. Write the subject and the verb of each sentence in this article about rare minerals. Underline the subject. If either the subject or the verb is a compound, write *compound* above it.

EXAMPLE: They located and collected minerals.

                            compound

ANSWER: They; located, collected

6. Many articles in magazines and stories in newspapers have become books. 7. Some chapters and sections of *In Suspect Terrain* by John McPhee first appeared in a magazine. 8. The facts about the location of minerals surprised and amazed readers. 9. In Indiana there are diamonds and gold. 10. These precious minerals can be seen and found among rocks in part of the state. 11. These valuable gems and stones were not always in Indiana. 12. The last great glacier of the Ice Age carried or dragged the diamonds and the gold into that state. 13. Either Ontario or Quebec may have been the original home of these minerals. 14. Geologists have studied and searched both of these Canadian provinces. 15. Neither the original gold field nor the main diamond bed in Canada has yet been found.

Additional Exercises

Write the subject and the verb of each sentence. Draw one line under each subject.

1. Is happiness or sorrow caused by gold?
2. Can the answer be found in a famous myth?
3. Into a stadium went men, women, and children.
4. The fastest runner in the world had been challenged to a race.
5. There were no reporters or photographers.
6. Would anybody cheer or applaud the winner?
7. The name of the great runner was Atalanta.
8. She had never been defeated on the track.
9. Her father had made the rules for the race.
10. A winner would become the husband of Atalanta.
11. Every loser would be executed.
12. Had one young man planned and trained enough for his race with the swift Atalanta?
13. The challenger was Hippomenes.
14. Then the race began.
15. Across the track rolled a golden apple.
16. Hippomenes knew of Atalanta's love for gold.
17. Atalanta stopped for that golden apple.
18. He ran ahead and dropped two more apples.
19. Three delays by Atalanta won for Hippomenes both the great race and Atalanta.
20. His coach and cheerleader had been Venus.
21. From her had come the three golden apples.
22. This clever goddess had planned the marriage of Atalanta and Hippomenes.
23. Do other unforgettable stories about athletic events and about gold exist in mythology?
24. Look in your library today.
25. Do not overlook articles in magazines.

Application USING GRAMMAR IN WRITING

Writers usually want to give their readers information. Therefore, most sentences are declarative sentences. Good writers, however, also use interrogative, imperative, and exclamatory sentences in their writing. These other kinds of sentences add variety and interest.

Imagine, for example, that you wanted to write about an outfielder making a game-winning catch in a baseball game. Notice how all four kinds of sentences could be used to tell about the experience.

> She'll be a hero if she catches this ball. (declarative)
> Should she catch it over her shoulder? (interrogative)
> Don't lose sight of the ball in the sun. (imperative)
> She just has to catch it! (exclamatory)

By occasionally including an interrogative, imperative, or exclamatory sentence, you can make your writing livelier and more interesting.

Writing with the Four Kinds of Sentences

A. Write a paragraph about one of the topics below. Include at least three of the four kinds of sentences in the paragraph.

1. Telling a joke
2. Buying a present
3. Cleaning the kitchen
4. The funniest sight I ever saw

Using the Thesaurus

B. Look over the paragraph you wrote above. Did you use the verbs *laugh, buy,* or *clean* in your paragraph? These verbs are often overused by writers. Using the Thesaurus, pages 555–574, find three synonyms for each verb. Then use each one in a sentence.

7 — Direct Objects

> ● The **direct object** receives the action of the verb.

Every sentence has two main parts, a subject and a verb. To express a complete thought, a sentence may need a third part, a direct object. Most direct objects are nouns or pronouns.

The subject answers the question *Who?* or *What?* before the verb. The direct object answers the question *Whom?* or *What?* after the verb.

Subject	Verb	Direct Object
California	attracted	John Sutter.
What attracted?		Attracted whom?
California		John Sutter

In a declarative or an imperative sentence, the direct object usually follows the verb. The direct object may not always follow the verb immediately. Other words may stand between the verb and the direct object.

Subject	Verb	Direct Object
Sutter	employed	many reliable workers.
Workers	saw	some gold.
(You)	Inform	all the newspapers.

If prepositional phrases are omitted, the subject, verb, and direct object stand out.

Sutter owned thousands (of acres) (of land).
Men (from cities) sought gold (on his ranch).

A sentence may have a compound direct object.

Sutter owned a home and many animals.
He lost it and them.

Exercises

A. Write the subject, the verb, and the direct object in each sentence. Underline each subject. Write *D.O.* above each direct object.

1. Their loyal fans showered them with praise at the end of the game.
2. Everyone must learn the words of this song before the next rehearsal.
3. We carefully read every notice on the board.
4. My mother and father repaired and repainted every chair and table in the family room.
5. The size of the faces of the four Presidents on Mount Rushmore always impresses each tourist or traveler in South Dakota.

B. Write this article about the discovery of gold in California. Underline the direct object in each sentence.

6. Good luck does not always bring happiness. 7. John Sutter owned a large ranch in the Sacramento Valley of California. 8. He had thousands of horses, cows, and sheep. 9. In January of 1848 his carpenter was building a sawmill. 10. In a river beside the mill, the carpenter discovered gold. 11. This discovery of gold on his land delighted Sutter. 12. Soon, however, his workers left their jobs. 13. The news of the gold quickly reached every town in California. 14. People abandoned their homes and businesses. 15. Sailors deserted their ships. 16. They began the rush to the Sacramento Valley. 17. Squatters gradually occupied Sutter's lands and streams. 18. No one could remove the people. 19. Soon thousands more from many distant places reached the ranch of John Sutter. 20. Eventually Sutter lost everything.

8 — Predicate Nominatives and Predicate Adjectives

> ● A **predicate nominative** is a noun or pronoun that follows a linking verb and renames or identifies the subject of the sentence.
>
> ● A **predicate adjective** follows a linking verb and describes the subject of the sentence.

Predicate Nominatives Some nouns and pronouns that follow verbs are direct objects. Some are predicate nominatives.

> Direct Object: He discovered <u>gold</u>.
> Predicate Nominative: He was a <u>carpenter</u>.

A predicate nominative renames or identifies the subject of the sentence.

Subject	Verb	Predicate Nominative
John Sutter	was	a <u>rancher</u>.
The rancher	was	<u>he</u>.
This	is	his <u>portrait</u>.

A predicate nominative follows a linking verb. This kind of verb shows being, not action. It is like an equal sign (=) between the subject and the predicate nominative. The most common linking verb is *be*. This verb has many forms. Some of them are *am, are, is, was, were, shall be, will be, have been, has been*, and *had been*.

If prepositional phrases are omitted, the subject, verb, and predicate nominative stand out.

> He was the <u>man</u> (with the plans) (for the mill).
> These are <u>some</u> (of the largest gold nuggets).
> This is a <u>piece</u> (from that nugget).

A sentence may have a compound predicate nominative.

> James Marshall was a <u>carpenter</u> and a <u>farmer</u>.
> The lucky miners might have been <u>you</u> and <u>I</u>.

Predicate Adjectives Like a direct object and a predicate nominative, a predicate adjective is an important part of a sentence. It completes the meaning of the sentence.

Subject	Verb	Predicate Adjective
John Sutter	was	ambitious.
His businesses	were	profitable.

A predicate adjective follows a linking verb. In addition to *be*, other verbs that may be linking verbs are *appear, become, feel, grow, look, remain, seem, smell, sound, stay, taste,* and *turn*.

> She appears <u>unhappy</u>. It sounds <u>correct</u>.
> We felt <u>lucky</u>. They taste <u>bitter</u>.
> It looks <u>valuable</u>. It turned <u>purple</u>.

A sentence may have a compound predicate adjective.

> His land was <u>rich</u>, <u>fertile</u>, and <u>peaceful</u>.
> John Sutter seemed <u>proud</u> and <u>courageous</u>.

Three Kinds of Verbs A verb that is followed by a predicate nominative or a predicate adjective is called a **linking verb**.

> Gold <u>is</u> a metal. It <u>stays</u> shiny.

A verb that is followed by a direct object is called a **transitive verb**.

> Sutter <u>had</u> problems. They <u>wanted</u> gold.

A verb that is not followed by a direct object is called an **intransitive verb**.

> Water <u>flowed</u>. Gold <u>appeared</u> suddenly.

Exercises

A. Write each sentence that has a predicate nominative or a predicate adjective.

1. **a.** Her father was a successful rancher.
   b. Her father met a successful rancher.
2. **a.** The winner of the prize was you.
   b. The winner of the prize saw you.
3. **a.** I tasted the orange.
   b. The orange tasted sour.
4. **a.** She became a famous author of short stories.
   b. She helped a famous author of short stories.
5. **a.** They interviewed scientists.
   b. They will be scientists.
6. **a.** That pleases me very much.
   b. That must have been he.
7. **a.** We are not experts in oceanography.
   b. We know an expert in oceanography.
8. **a.** Photographers took pictures.
   b. They are photographers.
9. **a.** The leaves on that shrub turned orange.
   b. They usually eat oranges.
10. **a.** Pollution has become a problem.
    b. No one has solved the problem.
11. **a.** Tennis is their favorite sport.
    b. They attended the tennis match.
12. **a.** The monitor sounded an alarm.
    b. The monitor sounded nervous.
13. **a.** I began a difficult journey.
    b. The journey looked difficult.
14. **a.** The cover of the magazine impressed us.
    b. The cover of the magazine was beautiful.
15. **a.** The writers of that article were she and I.
    b. The readers of that article will smile.

B. Write the subject and the verb of each sentence in this article about John Sutter. If a sentence has a predicate nominative or a predicate adjective, write it after the verb.

16. John Sutter was a pioneer. **17.** He came to America from Switzerland at the age of thirty-one. **18.** His original name was Johann Suter. **19.** In 1834 he changed his name. **20.** He worked briefly in St. Louis. **21.** But the Pacific Ocean fascinated him. **22.** He had read much about it. **23.** Finally he went to Oregon. **24.** He became a successful trader. **25.** Sutter also visited Alaska. **26.** In 1839 he moved to California. **27.** He settled in the Sacramento Valley. **28.** Here he established a ranch. **29.** He even built a fort. **30.** Sutter became rich and powerful. **31.** But he was also kind. **32.** Newcomers received much help from him. **33.** Settlers were grateful. **34.** Valuable timber grew on his land. **35.** A sawmill became a necessity. **36.** James Marshall built a sawmill for him. **37.** Marshall found gold on the site of the excavation for the sawmill. **38.** News of the gold spread rapidly. **39.** Squatters soon destroyed Sutter's land and cattle. **40.** The sawmill was a complete failure. **41.** Further attempts were unsuccessful. **42.** He requested aid from Congress without success. **43.** Later the state of California granted him a small pension. **44.** In 1873 he moved to Pennsylvania. **45.** At his death in 1880, John Sutter was almost penniless.

C. Write a sentence using each verb below as indicated in parentheses.

46. remember (transitive) **49.** turn (linking)
47. taste (linking) **50.** paint (intransitive)
48. turn (transitive)

9 — Indirect Objects

> ● The **indirect object** comes before the direct object. It tells to whom or for whom the action of the verb is done.

Some sentences have two different kinds of objects after the verb. A direct object receives the action of the verb. An indirect object does not. It tells to whom or for whom something is done. In the example below, *pay* is the direct object and *workers*, the indirect object.

> Sutter offered his <u>workers</u> extra pay.

A word used as an indirect object can also be used as an object of a preposition in a prepositional phrase beginning with *to* or *for*.

> Sutter offered extra pay to his <u>workers</u>.

The word *workers* after *to* is an object of a preposition, not an indirect object.

Indirect objects are usually nouns or pronouns.

> The gold brought <u>Sutter</u> no happiness.
> The squatters gave <u>him</u> many problems.

Two or more indirect objects form a compound indirect object.

> They showed <u>him</u> and <u>me</u> a gold coin.

Indirect objects are often found after such verbs as these: *bring, buy, give, lend, offer, owe, sell, send, show, teach, tell, write.*

> Sutter gave <u>them</u> help.
> Sutter wrote <u>Congress</u> a letter.

Exercises

A. Rewrite each sentence, using each prepositional phrase in parentheses to make an indirect object. Underline the indirect object.

1. They gave a magazine (to me).
2. I mailed another letter (to them).
3. Bake some bread (for us).
4. You must tell that story (to everyone).
5. We bought a catcher's mitt (for Lolinda).

B. Write and label the subject, verb, indirect object, and direct object of each sentence.

6. Other languages have given the English language many important words.
7. A dictionary can teach a reader the history of some especially colorful words.
8. The English language owes the Arabic language thanks for one common but valuable word.
9. Arabic lent English its word for "storehouses," *makhāzin.*
10. That word offered publishers inspiration for a name for a special publication, the magazine.
11. A tour of Arabian storehouses gives a visitor hours of excitement and surprises.
12. Merchants in storehouses could sell shoppers almost anything from gold to goldfish.
13. A magazine can tell its subscribers many interesting and surprising things.
14. It provides them numerous articles on almost any subject from mythology to modern sports.
15. People often buy their friends subscriptions to magazines for birthdays and holidays.

10 –Verbals

- A **verbal** is a verb form used as a different part of speech.
- A **participle** is a verb form used as an adjective.

Verbals Verb forms that do the work of adjectives, adverbs, and nouns are called verbals. There are three kinds of verbals: participles, gerunds, and infinitives.

Participles A verb has a present participle and a past participle. The present participle is formed by adding *-ing* to the verb. The past participle is usually formed by adding *-ed* or *-d* to the verb.

Verb	Present Participle	Past Participle
walk	walking	walked
prepare	preparing	prepared

Participles can be used in two ways. Sometimes a participle is the main verb in a verb phrase.

I was <u>walking</u> to school.   I have <u>walked</u> there.

Sometimes a participle does the work of an adjective. It modifies a noun or pronoun.

<u>flickering</u> lights   <u>canceled</u> stamps

A participle can stand before or after the noun or pronoun it modifies.

The <u>smiling</u> athlete received an award.

The people <u>standing</u> are my friends.

<u>Spilled</u> coffee stained the rug.

The people, <u>fascinated</u>, stared in wonder.

Exercises

A. Write the present participle in each sentence. Then write the noun it modifies.

   1. I photographed the rising sun.
   2. Unlock the sliding door carefully.
   3. The drifting dunes covered the trails.
   4. We have heard some exciting news.
   5. Wash these rags in boiling water.

B. Write the past participle in each sentence. Then write the noun it modifies.

   6. My uncle may purchase a used car.
   7. He knows a recipe for fried rice.
   8. Collect all of the unopened boxes.
   9. That composition does not have one misspelled word.
  10. Return the damaged merchandise.

C. Two participles are underlined. Write the participle used as an adjective.

  11. Beaming, my father was unwrapping my gift.
  12. The exhausted jogger has returned.
  13. The thrilling game was televised locally.
  14. The startled chipmunk has scampered away.
  15. Were they fighting a losing battle?

D. Write the participle used as an adjective.

  16. A loaded truck had entered the yard.
  17. I was drenched by the driving rain.
  18. We were hiking through the swirling snow.
  19. The shaking bridge was finally closed.
  20. Vida was telling us an amazing story.

> ● A **gerund** is a verb form ending in *-ing* used as a noun.

Like a verb form, a gerund ends in *-ing*. Like a noun, it can be a subject, direct object, predicate nominative, or object of a preposition.

> **Subject:** <u>Reading</u> is an important skill.
> **Direct Object:** They preferred silent <u>reading</u>.
> **Predicate Nominative:** Your hobby must be <u>reading</u>.
> **Object of a Preposition:** We learn by <u>reading</u>.

All gerunds and some participles end in *-ing*. A gerund is used as a noun. A participle modifies a noun or pronoun. Study the following examples.

> **Gerund:** <u>Winning</u> games requires skill.
> **Participle:** The <u>winning</u> student is Pat.

In order to determine whether an *-ing* word is a verb, a participle, or a gerund, it is necessary to determine how it is used in the sentence.

> **Verb:** We are <u>running</u> home.
> **Participle:** A <u>running</u> total is being kept.
> **Gerund:** <u>Running</u> in good weather is fun.

Exercises

A. Two *-ing* words are underlined. Write the word that is a gerund.

1. The <u>concluding</u> act has much <u>dancing</u>.
2. We are <u>learning</u> about <u>writing</u>.
3. The player was <u>concentrating</u> on <u>batting</u>.
4. Pam was <u>enjoying</u> <u>eating</u> the grapes.
5. You are <u>showing</u> your joy by your constant <u>smiling</u>.

6. Flooding is causing much damage in the part of town near the river.
7. Typing is difficult on a moving train.
8. They were preparing the rocket for testing.
9. The blinding light continued its blinking.
10. Swimming has been taking most of my spare time.

B. Write the gerund in each sentence below. Then label it *subject, direct object, predicate nominative,* or *object of a preposition.*

EXAMPLE: Skiing is a popular winter sport.
ANSWER: Skiing, subject

11. Fishing provides many hours of relaxation.
12. My favorite sport is swimming.
13. We saw a filmstrip about mining.
14. Running strengthens the leg muscles.
15. Nobody enjoys losing.
16. The importance of memorizing was discussed.
17. My counselor suggested a course in typing.
18. That artist also does printing.
19. Their only occupation was farming.
20. Dancing made them famous.

C. Write the gerund in each sentence.

21. Discovering gold can have a striking effect upon the growth of a region.
22. Prospecting for gold began in the sparsely populated soaring mountains of Colorado.
23. In 1858 the searching was becoming fruitful.
24. News of the finding of gold was spreading.
25. By 1859 about 100,000 persons were engaging in prospecting in Colorado.

> • An **infinitive** is the basic form of the verb
>   preceded by *to*. It can be used as a noun,
>   adjective, or adverb.

An infinitive used as a noun can be a subject, direct object, or predicate nominative.

> **Subject:** <u>To win</u> is our goal.
> **Direct Object:** Everybody wanted <u>to win</u> the game.
> **Predicate Nominative:** Her ambition was <u>to win</u>.

An infinitive used as an adjective modifies a noun or a pronoun.

> A person <u>to study</u> is John Sutter.
>
> We need something <u>to study</u> now.

An infinitive used as an adverb modifies a verb or an adjective.

> We came <u>to join</u>.
>
> We are eager <u>to join</u>.

An infinitive is *to* plus a verb. It should not be confused with a prepositional phrase beginning with *to*.

> **Infinitive:** They hurried <u>to finish.</u>
> **Prepositional Phrase:** They hurried <u>to class.</u>

Exercises

A. Write the underlined words in each sentence, and label them *infinitive* or *prepositional phrase*.

1. Gold was the first metal known <u>to humans</u>.
2. The interest in it seems <u>to remain</u> universal.

3. For centuries people tried <u>to turn</u> base metals into gold in a process called alchemy.
4. Many alchemists spent their lives searching for an easy way <u>to make</u> gold from cheap metals, such as mercury and lead.
5. An interest in alchemy spread from the Greeks and Arabs <u>to the western Europeans.</u>
6. Alchemists in laboratories toiled over smoking pots, or crucibles, hoping <u>to uncover</u> the great secret.
7. <u>To prove</u> their beliefs, they tested nearly every substance known <u>to them.</u>
8. The credit for uncovering basic knowledge about the properties of many important chemicals and compounds belongs <u>to the alchemists.</u>
9. The study of alchemy was not scientific, but it led <u>to the discovery</u> of valuable information.
10. It proved <u>to be</u> the forerunner of chemistry.

B. Each infinitive is used as a noun. Write the infinitive. Label it *subject, direct object,* or *predicate nominative.*

EXAMPLE: My duty is to return.
ANSWER: to return, predicate nominative

11. Everyone started to write.
12. To write is the dream of many people.
13. All of us need to review.
14. The purpose of this class is to review.
15. To stop would be impossible now.
16. They had not planned to stop.
17. The guests at the reception want to leave.
18. Their recommendation is to leave.
19. To relax is not easy for some people.
20. Their immediate goal was to relax.

Additional Exercises

A. Write each sentence, completing it with the kind of verbal named in parentheses.

1. We like (gerund).
2. Nobody really wanted (infinitive).
3. (Participle), I stood before the class.
4. They were having a talk about (gerund).
5. The audience left (participle).
6. This is a good magazine (infinitive).
7. (Infinitive), they should practice more.
8. (Gerund) is a popular activity.
9. We stood around the fire (participle).
10. That orange juice looks too good (infinitive).

B. Write the verbal in each sentence and label it *participle, gerund,* or *infinitive.*

11. The people in ancient Greece and Rome always enjoyed the telling of stories about gold.
12. The traveling storytellers often repeated the legend of King Midas.
13. Midas had received a gift for helping Bacchus.
14. Midas was granted the power to turn anything into gold.
15. Laughing, the king touched everything.
16. The greedy king, singing with joy, turned objects into shiny gold in his huge palace.
17. At his golden dinner table, Midas began to notice a serious problem.
18. Eating was now impossible for him.
19. Any food touched turned into gold.
20. Bacchus mercifully prescribed bathing as a cure for Midas's harmful golden touch.

Application USING GRAMMAR IN WRITING

Sentences can be improved with participles. Students use such words as *and, or,* and *then* unnecessarily in their sentences. One way to eliminate many unnecessary words is to use participles instead. Use the following method. First, find the first verb in the sentence. Then change it to a participle. Next, write the participle with a comma after it at the beginning of the sentence. Other words in the sentence may also have to be rearranged. Study the example below.

> We were shivering, so we went inside.
> Shivering, we went inside.

Writing with Participles

A. Rewrite the sentences below, using participles. Follow the method described above.

1. The astronaut was smiling and then stood up.
2. Susan was dissatisfied, so she returned the radio.
3. The lion was snarling and clawing the tree.
4. I was excited, so I raised my hand.
5. The fullback was injured, so he left the game.
6. John yawned and began to read another article.
7. The car was sputtering, and then it stopped.
8. I was embarrassed, so I hid my face from view.
9. The workers complained, so they called the boss.
10. The teacher squinted and studied the ad carefully.

Using the Thesaurus

B. The words *rich* and *poor* are often used in writing. Using the Thesaurus, pages 555–574, find four synonyms for each word and use each in a sentence. You will write eight sentences.

Chapter Review

A. Write each sentence and label it *declarative, interrogative, imperative,* or *exclamatory.* Use correct end punctuation.

1. Check the oil and the battery
2. Pine cones covered the lawn
3. Do you have any carbon paper
4. How sweet these peaches are
5. Do not misspell those names

B. Write the subject and verb of each sentence.

6. Across the stage walked the candidates.
7. One of my favorite shows will be canceled.
8. Here are the answers to those questions.
9. Always have an extra pen or pencil.
10. Will the new curtains arrive soon?

C. Write each underlined word and label it *direct object* or *predicate nominative.*

11. Turn the <u>pages</u> carefully.
12. They will deliver the <u>package</u>.
13. A fresh apple is my favorite <u>snack</u>.
14. That is his <u>ticket</u>.
15. Who folded these <u>towels</u>?

D. Write the verbal in each sentence and label it *participle, gerund,* or *infinitive.*

16. When do they wish to leave?
17. Leave the driving to the driver.
18. I picked up a box wrapped in velvet.
19. Blinking, I looked into the sky.
20. The writing in the book is in Latin.

Chapter Review

Read the article about Athena. Using only the underlined words as answers, find and write these grammatical constructions.

A. a compound subject
B. a compound verb
C. two direct objects
D. a predicate nominative
E. a predicate adjective
F. a linking verb
G. an indirect object
H. a participle (adjective)
I. a gerund
J. an infinitive

The ancient Greeks **(1)** had many mythological **(2)** gods. Perhaps the most remarkable one was **(3)** Athena. Much Greek **(4)** poetry and art deals with her. Athena **(5)** possessed and shared unusual wisdom and strength. Facing defeat in a battle with giants, Zeus requested her help. **(6)** She promptly overpowered Enceladus, the strongest giant of all. Athena was **(7)** skillful in peace, too. The people of Athens loved her. She gave **(8)** them the olive tree and the flute. She also taught them the art of **(9)** weaving. To honor her, they built the **(10)** Parthenon. Inside, the gold and ivory statue of her **(11)** was magnificent. That **(12)** treasured statue **(13)** vanished long ago. The temple is now in ruins. Today a **(14)** reproduction of the original Parthenon can be seen in Nashville, Tennessee. **(15)** To erect a copy of the famous lost statue someday is the hope of a committee of Tennessee citizens.

5

Simple, Compound, and Complex Sentences

Good Sportsmanship

Good sportsmanship we hail, we sing.
It's always pleasant when you spot it.
There's only one unhappy thing:
You have to lose to prove you've got it.

—Richard Armour

1 — Simple and Compound Sentences

> - A **simple sentence** has one subject and one predicate.
> - A **compound sentence** consists of two or more simple sentences.

Simple Sentences A simple sentence may have a one-word subject and a one-word predicate. Each of these words may be modified.

> Reporters write.
> The reporters on the staff of our school
>   newspaper write clearly and accurately.

A simple sentence may have a compound subject or a compound predicate or both.

> Students and teachers came and looked.
> Nila or I will print the title or write it.

Compound Sentences A compound sentence is a sentence that contains two or more simple sentences often joined by the conjunction *and, or, but,* or *nor.* A comma usually precedes the conjunction. Sometimes a semicolon joins the simple sentences.

> Reporters may interview many people, or they
>   may search a library for information.
> Reporters write; students read.

Each part of a compound sentence has its own subject and its own predicate.

> Rafael and Rena brought the papers, but we
>   counted and distributed them.

Exercises ————————————————————

A. Write each pair of simple sentences as one compound sentence. Join each pair with a comma and the conjunction *and*, *but*, or *or*.

   1. They draw cartoons. We write captions.
   2. We have bake sales. We have auctions.
   3. Your writing is good. It could be better.
   4. I told a joke. No one understood it.
   5. Tara found paint. Archie borrowed brushes.

B. Write the sentence and underline each subject once and each verb twice. Label the sentence *simple* or *compound*.

   6. Benjamin Franklin once owned a newspaper, but not everyone knows this.
   7. Franklin corresponded with other journalists, and they shared their news with him.
   8. He often lent them money; he also gave them practical suggestions and good advice.
   9. The owner of a newspaper in South Carolina received great praise from Benjamin Franklin.
  10. Elizabeth Timothy owned and edited the *South Carolina Gazette* in the city of Charleston.
  11. Her husband had founded the paper, but she had learned business methods in her native Holland.
  12. She did not sell the paper after his death in 1738, nor did she stop writing articles.
  13. The *South Carolina Gazette* featured news; it sometimes carried reprints of famous poems.
  14. Elizabeth Timothy encouraged many writers and published their work in her newspaper.
  15. She successfully managed the newspaper and her family of seven children.

2 – Clauses

> • A **clause** is a group of words that has a subject and a verb.

Phrases and Clauses Phrases and clauses both are groups of words. But they differ in one important way. A phrase does not have both a subject and a verb. A clause does have a subject and a verb.

Phrases	**Clauses**
at night	we know
before the class	before she left
must have been seen	when she saw them

Independent and Subordinate Clauses Every clause has a subject and a verb. An independent, or main, clause expresses a complete thought. It can be a sentence by itself. A subordinate, or dependent, clause does not express a complete thought. It can be only a part of a sentence.

Independent Clauses	**Subordinate Clauses**
I ran	because I was late.
We washed the windows	until they sparkled.
Josh buys stamps	if he has money.

Words, Phrases, and Clauses A phrase and a subordinate clause are not sentences by themselves. Within a sentence they do the same kind of work that a part of speech does.

I went yesterday. (adverb)

I went after supper. (prepositional phrase)

I went after I had eaten. (subordinate clause)

Exercises

A. Write *phrase* if the word group is a phrase. Write *clause* if it is a clause.

1. during the spring
2. when I see rain
3. until help comes
4. should have been reconstructed
5. someone needs us

B. Write the clause in parentheses. Underline the subject once and the verb twice. Label each clause *independent* or *subordinate*.

EXAMPLE: (They walk) (after they eat.)
ANSWER: (They walk) independent, (after they eat.) subordinate

6. (If you can write well now,) (you may become a successful journalist in the future.)
7. (Eliza Poitevent of Pearlington, Mississippi, began her career in journalism) (when she sold some poems to a newspaper in the 1860s.)
8. (She became a literary editor) (after she was hired by the New Orleans *Daily Picayune*.)
9. (While she was employed there,) (she married the publisher of that Louisiana newspaper.)
10. (It became her paper) (when he died in 1876.)
11. (Eliza Poitevent had a serious problem) (because the paper owed money to many people.)
12. (If she could attract more readers,) (the *Daily Picayune* might become profitable.)
13. (Before she went home each day,) (Poitevent wrote the society column for the newspaper.)
14. (Nothing appeared in print) (until it met her high standards for quality and accuracy.)
15. (As the *Daily Picayune* improved,) (the number of its readers grew rapidly.)

3 — Complex Sentences

> ● A **complex sentence** has one independent clause and at least one subordinate clause.

Sentences may be classified by their clauses. One independent clause forms a simple sentence. Two or more independent clauses form a compound sentence. One independent clause and one or more subordinate clauses form a complex sentence.

Simple Sentence: They listened.
Compound Sentence: They listened, and we spoke.
Complex Sentence: They listened when we spoke.

A subordinate clause may precede, interrupt, or follow an independent clause. Most subordinate clauses at the beginning or in the middle of sentences are set off by commas.

While he spoke, my cousin held a sign.
My cousin, while he spoke, held a sign.
My cousin held a sign while he spoke.

Many subordinate clauses begin with a special kind of word called a **subordinating conjunction**.

after you left	since we arrived
as they played	until I was called
because she works	when she studies
before it rang	where they lived
if anyone wins	while you wait

Some words can be used either as prepositions or as subordinating conjunctions.

after our test (prep.)	after our test began (conj.)
before lunch (prep.)	before we ate lunch (conj.)

Exercises

A. Identify each sentence as *simple* or *complex.*

1. Everything has grown rapidly since the rain.
2. Everything has grown rapidly since our town had two inches of rain.
3. We celebrated after we counted the ballots.
4. We had a big party after the last election.
5. They always go where the food is tasty.

B. Write each sentence. Underline the subject once and the verb twice in each clause. Label the sentence *simple, compound,* or *complex.*

6. Elizabeth Cochrane was born in Pennsylvania in 1867, but she became world famous as Nellie Bly.
7. She was hired by the Pittsburgh *Dispatch* in 1885 and became one of its best reporters.
8. The title of a popular song by Stephen Foster inspired her unforgettable pen name.
9. Nellie Bly, while she worked for the Pittsburgh newspaper, wrote a variety of articles.
10. Some articles described conditions in factories, and others were reviews of plays.
11. When she was only twenty, she was hired by the New York *World.*
12. One of her first assignments was an investigation of a public hospital in New York City.
13. Before she wrote an article on that assignment, Nellie Bly became a patient in that hospital.
14. Because her stories were so vivid and accurate, conditions in the hospital began to improve.
15. As her career with the *World* continued, Nellie Bly wrote many articles about urban problems.

4 — Sentence Errors

> ● **Run-on sentences** and **sentence fragments** should not appear in written work.

A sentence that should be broken into two or more sentences is called a **run-on sentence**. The second part of a run-on sentence is often a sentence beginning with one of the following pronouns or adverbs: *he, she, it, they, now, then, soon,* and *later.*

> **Run-on:** The car stopped it was out of gas.
> **Correct:** The car stopped. It was out of gas.

> **Run-on:** The sun is rising now we can start.
> **Correct:** The sun is rising. Now we can start.

A group of words that begins with a capital letter and ends with a period but does not express a complete thought is called a **sentence fragment.** Prepositional phrases, compound verbs, verbals, and subordinate clauses are *parts* of sentences. They should not be written as sentences.

> **Fragment:** She bought them. At the fair.
> **Correct:**   She bought them at the fair.

> **Fragment:** We stood up. And sang the song.
> **Correct:**   We stood up and sang the song.

> **Fragment:** Find that dog. Whimpering softly.
> **Correct:**   Find that dog whimpering softly.

> **Fragment:** Everyone came inside. To keep warm.
> **Correct:**   Everyone came inside to keep warm.

> **Fragment:** If you arrive early. (What must be done?)
> **Correct:**   If you arrive early, go to Room 101.

> **Fragment:** When we returned. (What happened?)
> **Correct:**   When we returned, we wrote letters.

Exercises

A. Each word group is a run-on sentence. Write each one as two sentences. Add a period and change one small letter to a capital letter.

1. Mr. Adams is our librarian he is always busy.
2. His youngest daughter is in my earth science class her name is Lee.
3. These stories are short you will like them.
4. Those magazines have finally been returned I can now finish my report for social studies.
5. Our class studied the card catalog later we examined the collections of reference books.

B. This article about Nellie Bly contains ten sentences. Write each sentence. Capitalize the first word and put a period at the end. Underline words in italics.

a popular novel in Nellie Bly's time was *Around the World in Eighty Days* by Jules Verne this book amazed and thrilled people because such a trip in so very few days seemed impossible hoping for more readers, the publisher of the New York *World* planned and arranged an unusual publicity stunt he carefully studied timetables of American and foreign steamships and railroads then he purchased tickets for Nellie Bly and on November 14, 1889, sent her on a trip around the world she would complete the journey in less than eighty days if all the ships and trains were on schedule the newspaper put her lively reports from Europe and Asia on its front page a special train was waiting for her when she reached San Francisco it whisked her to New York on the last lap of her journey Nellie Bly completed her trip around the world in seventy-two days and became nationally known

Additional Exercises

A. Each word group is a sentence fragment. Make each one a sentence by adding your own words. Write sentences about a vacation trip.

1. The vacation of my dreams.
2. Because it looks so wonderful on television.
3. Have ever been there.
4. After buying new suitcases.
5. With everyone in my family.
6. Traveling in comfort on a plane.
7. To stay in a hotel with a large pool.
8. Dining in a colorful restaurant.
9. Would write something every day.
10. About all the unusual sights.

B. The ten sentences in this article lack capital letters and periods. Write each sentence. Capitalize the first word and put a period at the end. Underline the words in italics.

as she rushed around the world, Nellie Bly was in a race with another reporter the publisher of the San Francisco *Examiner* also wished to gain publicity he chose Elizabeth Bisland to make the globe-circling race she had worked for the New Orleans *Times-Democrat* before being hired by the *Examiner* while Bly was traveling east, Bisland went west everything went well until she reached Europe there Elizabeth Bisland missed her ship to America she finally completed her journey in seventy-six days in the 1930s, globe-circling races became popular again Dorothy Kilgallen of the New York *Evening Journal* made headlines in 1936 when she traveled around the world by plane in twenty-four days

Application USING GRAMMAR IN WRITING

When writing, do not use too many short, or simple, sentences. Writing can often be improved by combining two simple sentences into one complex sentence. First, look for two sentences whose ideas are closely related. Then use a word such as *after, since,* or *when* to combine them. Remember that in complex sentences one idea is subordinate to another. When combining simple sentences into a complex sentence, one idea must be made subordinate to the other. Study the example below.

> The candle flickered. He whistled.
> The candle flickered as he whistled.

Writing with Complex Sentences

A. Combine each pair of simple sentences into a complex sentence. Make the second a subordinate clause.

1. The lights went out. The movie began.
2. We set the table. Dad made the salad.
3. Val found my Frisbee. I had gone home.
4. We were hiking. The trails were easy to see.
5. The lake changed colors. The sun slowly set.
6. I will lend you my coat tomorrow. I can find it tonight.
7. The astronauts waited inside the spacecraft. They received orders to leave.
8. The number of accidents has declined. New traffic lights have been installed.

Using the Thesaurus

B. Reporters often use the adjectives *brave* and *weak* in their stories. Using the Thesaurus, find four synonyms for each word and write each in a sentence.

Chapter Review

A. Identify each sentence as *simple* or *compound.*

1. Close that door, or we will freeze.
2. Potatoes are grown in Idaho, Maine, and Texas.
3. Everybody but you ordered fish.
4. They prepared the food, and I served it.
5. A tree fell, but no one heard it.

B. Identify each word group as a *phrase* or *clause.*

6. without any further delay
7. when they were delayed
8. too many tickets have been sold
9. could have been leaving
10. before the next session begins

C. Identify each sentence as *simple* or *complex.*

11. The store has not opened since the fire.
12. We have not gone there since the new supermarket was built nearby.
13. The flowers bloomed until the snow came.
14. The plants grew until the first frost.
15. We may go if the weather improves.

D. Identify each incorrect word group as a *run-on sentence* or *sentence fragment.*

16. I finished my work then I played chess.
17. Cary was shivering uncontrollably it was cold in his room.
18. During the first act of the comedy.
19. And recited the names of the states.
20. Because we needed that information.

Chapter Review CHALLENGE

Read the article about newspapers. Using only the under-lined words or word groups as answers, find and write these grammatical constructions. Do not use any answer more than once.

A. one simple sentence
B. one compound sentence
C. one complex sentence
D. one independent clause
  in a complex sentence
E. one subordinate clause
F. one prepositional phrase
G. one compound subject
H. one compound verb
I. one subordinating conjunction
J. one preposition

Julius Caesar may have invented the newspaper. **(1)** Notices were posted daily in public places by his order when he ruled Rome. **(2)** Those notices informed the citizens about new laws and current events. **(3)** Before Caesar's time people could hear the news, but they could not read it. A newspaper **(4)** was printed and distributed in China in the eighth century. In the fifteenth century, **(5)** newspapers or newsletters were published in a few German cities, but each one was written by hand. The first printed newspaper in Europe appeared in Venice about 1556. If Venetians wished a subscription, **(6)** they paid a small fee. The Italian word **(7)** for the small fee was *gazetta*. There were no newspapers **(8)** in America **(9)** until one was published in Boston in 1690. Royal authorities promptly stopped it **(10)** because it criticized the government.

Cumulative Review

Sentence Structure

Four Kinds of Sentences (pp. 76–79)
Subjects and Predicates (pp. 80–85)
Compound Subjects and Verbs (pp. 86–87)
Direct Objects (pp. 90–91)
Predicate Nominatives and Predicate Adjectives
   (pp. 92–95)
Indirect Objects (pp. 96–97)
Verbals (pp. 98–103)
Simple and Compound Sentences (pp. 110–111)
Clauses (pp. 112–113)
Complex Sentences (pp. 114–115)

A. Write the name for the sentence part or the sentence type that answers each question.

1. What sentence type asks a question?
2. What sentence type makes a statement?
3. What sentence type gives a command?
4. What sentence type has two or more simple sentences?
5. What sentence type has one subject and one verb?
6. What is the main word in the complete predicate?
7. What is the main word in the complete subject?
8. What sentence part renames the subject?
9. What sentence part describes the subject?
10. What sentence part receives the action of the verb?
11. What is a verb form used as another part of speech?
12. What sentence part lacks both a subject and verb?
13. What sentence part has a subject and a verb?
14. What kind of clause is a complete thought?
15. What kind of clause is not a complete thought?

B. Write the name of the sentence part for each numbered word in the article below. Use the following words as answers: *subject, verb, direct object, predicate nominative, predicate adjective, indirect object,* and *object of a preposition.*

Old newspapers are not **(16)** worthless. Some organizations collect **(17)** them. **(18)** They are sold to recycling plants. Many people give scout **(19)** groups their **(20)** bundles of old newspapers. In dry regions **(21)** gardeners often **(22)** cover the soil around their vegetables with newspapers. The soil then stays **(23)** moist and cool. A wad of **(24)** newspaper can be an excellent **(25)** material to shine windows and mirrors. Crumpled newspaper **(26)** protects breakable **(27)** items in packages. **(28)** Newspaper can even absorb odors in freezers and **(29)** refrigerators. Every newspaper is a doubly good **(30)** investment.

C. Write how the word *treasurer* is used in each sentence. Use the italicized words in the directions for Exercise **B** above as answers.

31. Shannon met the treasurer of the club.
32. Lisa is the treasurer of the club.
33. They gave the treasurer some money to take to the local bank.
34. Here comes the treasurer of our club.
35. Here is another bill for the treasurer.
36. Did the treasurer give a report on the financial situation of our club?
37. Send the treasurer your statement.
38. Leslie will be the new treasurer.
39. Into the bank walked the treasurer.
40. The treasurer of the bank took the deposit and put it in our club account.

D. A word or group of words is underlined in each sentence. Write the grammatical term that correctly describes that word or group of words.

41. The workers replaced the <u>dented</u> fenders.
    a. participle
    b. infinitive

42. <u>Hoping</u> for a letter, I rushed to the mailbox.
    a. gerund
    b. participle

43. <u>Dancing</u> is a good form of exercise.
    a. infinitive
    b. gerund

44. These stamps are good for <u>collecting</u>.
    a. gerund
    b. participle

45. Everyone wishes <u>to succeed</u>.
    a. participle
    b. infinitive

46. <u>Down the hill rolled a large log</u>.
    a. normal word order
    b. inverted word order

47. <u>Some of the coins were missing</u>.
    a. declarative sentence
    b. exclamatory sentence

48. <u>We had left</u> before the tide came in.
    a. independent clause
    b. subordinate clause

49. They cleaned the carpets. <u>And waxed floors</u>.
    a. run-on sentence
    b. sentence fragment

50. <u>I reviewed everything now I will pass</u>.
    a. run-on sentence
    b. sentence fragment

E. Rewrite the following sentence according to the instructions listed below it.

Pat writes often.

EXAMPLE: Make the sentence negative.
ANSWER: Pat does not write often.

51. Make the sentence interrogative.
52. Make the sentence imperative.
53. Make the sentence exclamatory.
54. Add a pronoun so that the sentence will have a compound subject.
55. Add a verb so that the sentence will have a compound verb.
56. Add a direct object.
57. Add a compound direct object.
58. Add an indirect object and a direct object.
59. Add a present participle to modify the subject.
60. Add an infinitive to modify the verb.
61. Add a prepositional phrase that has a gerund as its object.
62. Add an independent clause so that the sentence will be a compound sentence.
63. Add a subordinate clause so that the sentence will be a complex sentence. (Be sure to place a comma after the subordinate clause if it begins the sentence.)
64. Change the verb *writes* to *is*, and add a predicate nominative.
65. Change the verb *writes* to *is*, and add a predicate adjective.

UNIT THREE

Usage

A carpenter uses many different kinds of tools. Each tool must be used at the right time and for the right purpose. By using tools correctly, a carpenter is able to take wood and turn it into a table, a wagon, or even a house.

A writer also uses many tools. The most important are the pen and the paper. These are the only tools needed by someone who writes something that no one else will read.

Most writing, however, is intended for an audience, or for others to read. When a final copy is being prepared for a reader, a good writer has a dictionary and a thesaurus at hand. All words should be spelled correctly, and the appropriate words should be selected to make a message clear, fresh, and forceful.

Every writer still needs one more tool, a dictionary of usage rules. Errors in usage can weaken writing. Words should be used correctly. A writer should know what is correct and what is incorrect. For example, which word group in each pair on the following page is correct?

women's names	womens' names
near you and me	near you and I
the oldest city	the most oldest city
could have come	could of came
different from ours	different than ours
to whom it may concern	to who it may concern

A writer who knows usage rules would choose the first word group in each pair. The second word group breaks a usage rule.

The most important usage rules for American English have been assembled in this unit. It is a usage dictionary. It is an important tool for every writer. It can be used in every class, not just in English class. The rules have been organized according to the parts of speech and subject-verb agreement. The Index to Rules at the back of this book lists the rules in the order in which they appear. It then gives the number of the page on which a rule is found.

On the next few pages are lists of words that can be troublesome for writers of all ages. They should be learned now. Some words like *to, too,* and *two* cause no difficulties in speech because they are **homophones,** or words that sound alike but have different meanings and spellings. If the meaning and spelling of each word is learned, then these three words will cause no problems in written work.

Prepositions are used with great frequency in English. In fact, English has more prepositions than any other language. Some are carelessly used. The wrong preposition can seriously alter the meaning of a sentence. The ones that require special attention are listed and explained on page 132. Be certain to study them carefully.

Six Troublesome Words

their, there, they're

their	Possessive form of the pronoun *they* They held up <u>their</u> hands. <u>Their</u> answers are correct.
there	An adverb that tells where Please put the damaged boxes <u>there</u>. A word that begins a sentence in which the verb comes before the subject <u>There</u> is a letter on your desk.
they're	Contraction of *they are* <u>They're</u> coming for supper tonight. <u>They're</u> going with us.

A **contraction** is a shortened form of two words. An apostrophe is placed where a letter or letters have been dropped.

to, too, two

to	A preposition meaning "toward" We walked <u>to</u> the gate with them. A word that is used to begin an infinitive The gate began <u>to</u> open.
too	An adverb meaning "also" Will she come, <u>too</u>? An adverb meaning "very" or "excessively" The room was <u>too</u> cold.
two	The number 2 Everyone asked <u>two</u> questions.

Exercises

A. Write *their, there,* or *they're* to complete each sentence.

1. _____ goes my father.
2. Are _____ tests easy?
3. _____ in the basket.
4. _____ is your locker.
5. _____ new lockers.

6. Did she go _____?
7. Do you see _____ car?
8. _____ always working.
9. What is _____ story?
10. _____ son knows me.

B. Write these sentences, completing them with *their, there,* and *they're.*

11. _____ dog is _____ best friend.
12. _____ always on time when they must go _____.
13. _____ singing _____ favorite song now.
14. _____ were very few errors in _____ book reports this month.
15. Have _____ parents seen _____ report cards?

C. Write *to, too,* or *two* to complete each sentence.

16. I saw _____ mice.
17. They saw me, _____.
18. I wanted _____ run.
19. I was _____ nervous.
20. I have _____ legs.

21. We went _____ Georgia.
22. I hope _____ see you.
23. The title is _____ long.
24. They said _____ much.
25. Try _____ say less.

D. Add *to, too,* or *two* to each of these words. Write a complete sentence using your answer.

26. floors
27. expensive
28. understand
29. quickly
30. sandwiches

31. listen
32. lazy
33. quietly
34. prepare
35. school

Pronouns and Contractions

	its, it's	
its	Possessive form of the pronoun *it* Everything is in <u>its</u> place.	
it's	Contraction of *it is* No, <u>it's</u> not raining now.	
	whose, who's	
whose	Possessive form of the pronoun *who* Do you know <u>whose</u> pen this is?	
who's	Contraction of *who is* and *who has* Do you know <u>who's</u> at the door?	
	your, you're	
your	Possessive form of the pronoun *you* Where are <u>your</u> skates?	
you're	Contraction of *you are* Yes, <u>you're</u> the new secretary of the club.	
	yours, hers, ours, theirs	
yours	Possessive pronoun made from *your* I see my book. Where is <u>yours</u>?	
hers	Possessive pronoun made from *her* It's my book. It's not <u>hers</u>.	
ours	Possessive pronoun made from *our* Your books are blue. <u>Ours</u> are red.	
theirs	Possessive pronoun made from *their* Our book is new. <u>Theirs</u> is old.	

Your's, her's, our's, and *their's* are never correct.

Exercises

A. Write *its* or *it's* to complete each sentence.

1. _____ a new bike.
2. I like _____ color.
3. Dad liked _____ price.
4. Yes, _____ a moth.
5. I see _____ wings.

6. _____ not harmful.
7. _____ cage is small.
8. What is _____ size?
9. Note _____ features.
10. _____ not cheap.

B. Write *whose* or *who's* to complete each sentence.

11. _____ a good speller?
12. _____ card is this?
13. _____ using it now?
14. _____ letter came?
15. I know _____ it is.

16. _____ watching us?
17. _____ been talking?
18. _____ towel fell?
19. _____ very reliable?
20. _____ car arrived?

C. Write *your* or *you're* to complete each sentence.

21. I found _____ ring.
22. I know _____ happy.
23. _____ a lucky person.
24. Here is _____ reward.
25. I hope _____ winning.

26. We like _____ music.
27. Bring _____ friends.
28. _____ doing well.
29. Is this _____ note?
30. Where is _____ home?

D. Each sentence has at least one error. Write the sentence correctly.

31. Did you compare our compositions for the writing contest with their's?
32. Our's are not as good as your's.
33. Did her's win as many prizes as his?
34. Theirs are probably as good as our's.
35. Mine is very much like her's and yours, but it's organized differently.

Preposition Problems

at, to	
at	Indicates presence in a place We were <u>at</u> a meeting.
to	Indicates motion toward a place We went <u>to</u> a meeting.

beside, besides	
beside	Means "next to" or "at the side of" The principal sat <u>beside</u> me.
besides	Means "in addition to" <u>Besides</u> French, I will study Latin.

between, among	
between	Used in discussing two people or objects Divide the food <u>between</u> her and him.
among	Used in discussing three or more Divide it <u>among</u> her, him, and them.

different from	
different from	Always *different from*, never *different than* My signature is <u>different from</u> hers.

in, into	
in	Indicates location within one place When it rains, I stay <u>in</u> the house.
into	Indicates motion or change of location If it rains, I run <u>into</u> the house.

Exercises

A. Write the correct preposition.

1. He was (at, to) a concert yesterday.
2. Why were you (at, to) the library?
3. They have gone (at, to) their uncle's house.
4. Are they (at, to) his house now?
5. Stand (beside, besides) the flagpole.
6. What do you have (beside, besides) coffee?
7. Please sit (beside, besides) that door.
8. What did she teach (beside, besides) algebra?
9. Walk (between, among) the barn and the shed.
10. Let's divide all of this work (between, among) the three of us.
11. He walked (between, among) all those statues.
12. The two students are friends, but there is great rivalry (between, among) them.
13. Is your book different (from, than) ours?
14. Were their grades different (from, than) mine?
15. San Antonio is different (from, than) Dallas.
16. Emeralds appear quite different (from, than) rubies and sapphires.
17. Did a stone fall (in, into) the well?
18. We were (in, into) three cities yesterday.
19. We went (in, into) three museums.
20. I left the principal's office and walked (in, into) our school library.

B. Write a sentence using each word group correctly.

21. strolled into
22. strolled in
23. divided between
24. divided among
25. beside his house
26. besides her house
27. was at
28. went to
29. were at
30. different from

6 *Noun and Pronoun Usage*

The Guppy

Whales have calves.
Cats have kittens.
Bears have cubs.
Bats have bittens.
Swans have cygnets.
Seals have puppies.
But guppies just have little guppies.

—Ogden Nash

1 — Making Nouns Plural

> ● Most nouns are made plural by adding -*s* or
> -*es* to the singular form.

A **singular noun** names one person, place, thing, or
idea. A **plural noun** names more than one person, place,
thing, or idea. Basic rules for correctly spelling plural
nouns follow.

■ Add -*s* to most singular nouns.

friend	house	onion	idea
friends	houses	onions	ideas

■ Add -*es* to nouns ending in *ch, s, sh, x,* or *z.*

arch	class	dish	fox
arches	classes	dishes	foxes

■ Add -*s* to nouns ending in a vowel and *y.* Change *y* to
i and add -*es* to nouns ending in a consonant and *y.*

key	toy	sky	hobby
keys	toys	skies	hobbies

■ Add -*s* to nouns ending in a vowel and *o* and to musical terms ending in *o.*

radio	zoo	cello	solo
radios	zoos	cellos	solos

■ The correct spelling of nouns ending in a consonant
and *o* should be learned. Many such nouns have two
acceptable spellings. Consult your dictionary.

echo	hero	potato	tomato
echoes	heroes	potatoes	tomatoes

auto	zero	motto
autos	zeros, zeroes	mottoes, mottos

Exercises

A. Write each singular noun. Under it, write its plural form.

1. bank	**6.** witness	**11.** cameo
2. tax	**7.** play	**12.** piano
3. donkey	**8.** echo	**13.** toe
4. factory	**9.** action	**14.** crutch
5. melon	**10.** brush	**15.** copy

B. Write each sentence. Use the plural form of each singular noun in parentheses.

16. Those (pencil) are not broken.

17. Your (reaction) seem to be normal.

18. Do you paint your (fence) yearly?

19. These (sandwich) certainly taste delicious.

20. There are new (dish) in the cupboard.

21. Do those (box) contain workbooks or textbooks?

22. Are the new (overpass) closed today?

23. These (turkey) are still quite small.

24. Not one of the (library) has that book.

25. Their (ally) have surrendered.

26. Those dark (alley) lead nowhere.

27. The (display) of new books impress everyone.

28. These (community) need more bike paths.

29. Are the art (studio) on the fourth floor?

30. Sweet (potato) grow rapidly.

31. Do the (alto) know their parts?

32. Do any (auto) use kerosene?

33. Are the (hero) receiving any medals?

34. There are green (tomato) on the windowsill.

35. There have never been (mosquito) on this side of their farm.

2 — Nouns with Special Plural Forms

> ● Some nouns have special plural forms.

■ Add *-s* to many nouns ending in *f, fe,* or *ff.*

roof	belief	safe	cliff
roofs	beliefs	safes	cliffs

■ For some nouns, drop the *f* or *fe* and add *-ves*.

calf	thief	leaf	self	life
calves	thieves	leaves	selves	lives

■ A few nouns have irregular plural forms.

man	woman	child	ox
men	women	children	oxen

tooth	foot	goose	mouse
teeth	feet	geese	mice

■ Some nouns have identical singular and plural forms.

deer	salmon	series	Iroquois
deer	salmon	series	Iroquois

■ For compound nouns, usually make the most important word plural.

eyelid	son-in-law	board of health
eyelids	sons-in-law	boards of health

A **compound** is a word formed from two or more words.

■ Add *-s* to compound nouns ending in *ful.*

cupful	spoonful	mouthful
cupfuls	spoonfuls	mouthfuls

■ Add an apostrophe and *s* (*'s*) to form the plural of a letter or numeral used as a noun.

A	*i*	*s*	*2*	*75*	*100*
A's	*i*'s	*s*'s	*2*'s	*75*'s	*100*'s

Exercises

A. Write each singular noun. Under it, write its plural form.

1. cuff
2. calf
3. foot
4. woman
5. mouse
6. series
7. Iroquois
8. notebook
9. capful
10. *U*

11. belief
12. thief
13. tooth
14. child
15. louse
16. goose
17. deer
18. teacup
19. bucketful
20. *12*

21. daughter-in-law
22. department of recreation
23. assistant manager
24. committee for civic pride
25. lieutenant governor

B. One noun in each sentence is misspelled. Write each misspelled word correctly.

26. The children filled boxes with leafs and twigs.
27. On those ranches were oxes, horses, and mules.
28. His sister-in-laws work in factories or stores.
29. The antlers of reindeers are quite large.
30. Friends, think about yourselfs for two minutes.
31. The jewelry and money are in those saves.
32. Put two handsful of stones in that terrarium.
33. Always dot your *i*s when writing addresses.
34. The mouses were kept in large cages.
35. Scientists examined the fins, jaws, and tooths of the salmon.
36. That license plate has three *7*s.
37. They taped the two halfs of the paper together.
38. We built those shelves by ourselfs.
39. I bruised both my kneescap during the game.
40. All board of trades are closed on holidays.

3 — Possessive Nouns

● A **possessive noun** shows ownership.

Many nouns have four different forms.

Singular noun:	writer
Singular possessive noun:	writer's
Plural noun:	writers
Plural possessive noun:	writers'

Here are three rules for writing possessive nouns.

■ To write the possessive form of a singular noun, add an apostrophe and *s* (*'s*).

a girl	Larry	a boss
a girl's card	Larry's stamps	a boss's pen

■ To write the possessive form of a plural noun that ends in *s*, add only an apostrophe (*'*).

many girls	all bosses
many girls' letters	all bosses' stationery

■ To write the possessive form of *men, women, children,* and any other plural noun that does not end in *s*, add an apostrophe and *s* (*'s*).

both men	five children
both men's mailboxes	five children's notes

The possessive forms of a noun should not be confused with its plural form. A possessive noun shows ownership. It is usually followed by the name of the thing owned.

Plural:	Those writers impress us.
Possessive:	One writer's letter was read.
Possessive:	Many writers' notes are long.

Exercises

A. Write each noun. Label it *singular, singular possessive, plural,* or *plural possessive.*

1. cousins	**6.** servants	**11.** children's
2. cousin's	**7.** servants'	**12.** Nicholas's
3. cousin	**8.** servant's	**13.** women's
4. cousins'	**9.** Lois	**14.** witness's
5. servant	**10.** Lois's	**15.** witnesses'

B. Write the appropriate possessive form of the noun in the prepositional phrase.

EXAMPLE: names of the chiefs   (chief's, chiefs') names
ANSWER: chiefs'

16. uncle of the boy   (boy's, boys') uncle
17. wing of a bird   (bird's, birds') wing
18. faces of the girls   (girl's, girls') faces
19. hats of those men   (men's, mens') hats
20. pace of a snail   (snail's, snails') pace

C. Write the possessive form of each underlined noun.

21. The students heard the <u>custodians</u> voice.
22. We met <u>Anns</u> parents and <u>Jims</u> grandparents.
23. I always enjoy hearing her <u>fathers</u> stories about his various jobs.
24. Many <u>farmers</u> sons and daughters have left the farm to live in cities.
25. Experts examined those <u>artists</u> paintings.
26. The <u>childrens</u> questions amazed the librarians.
27. Crowded parks spoil many <u>families</u> picnics.
28. These <u>students</u> desks were in that <u>teachers</u> room.
29. <u>Nurses</u> uniforms are made in this factory.
30. The <u>womens</u> club discussed the <u>nations</u> future.

Additional Exercises

A. Write each underlined noun in its plural form or in one of its possessive forms as needed.

EXAMPLE: two <u>teacher</u> classrooms
ANSWER: teachers'

1. two <u>coach</u>
2. one <u>coach</u> cap
3. all <u>coach</u> jackets
4. ten <u>pony</u> lives
5. a <u>pony</u> hooves
6. a <u>child</u> tongue
7. all <u>child</u>
8. few <u>child</u> hearts
9. many <u>thief</u> faces
10. the <u>thief</u> mouth

B. Write each underlined noun in its plural form or in one of its possessive forms as needed.

11. Some busy <u>adult</u> have little time to write long <u>letter</u>. **12.** They do, however, send cards to <u>friend</u> and <u>relative</u>. **13.** Greeting cards, in fact, have become one of <u>America</u> important <u>business</u>. **14.** <u>Million</u> of <u>box</u> of cards are printed annually in huge <u>factory</u> in Kansas City and Cleveland. **15.** With their <u>photo</u> and <u>poem</u>, greeting cards fill <u>shelf</u> in many <u>store</u>. **16.** These <u>display</u> reveal many <u>artist</u> skills and many <u>writer</u> talents.

17. Cards now satisfy most <u>customer</u> needs because there are cards for all <u>member</u> of <u>family</u> and even for many <u>occupation</u>. **18.** Special greetings may be sent to <u>grandparent</u>, <u>aunt</u>, <u>cousin</u>, <u>niece</u>, <u>brother-in-law</u>, <u>teacher</u>, <u>secretary</u>, <u>attorney</u>, and <u>sheriff</u>. **19.** With a card one can acknowledge a <u>baby</u> birthday, a <u>stepbrother</u> graduation, a <u>wife</u> or a <u>husband</u> anniversary, a <u>boss</u> promotion, or a <u>grandparent</u> retirement. **20.** A few eccentric people use <u>boxful</u> of cards just to send greetings to <u>themself</u>.

Application USING NOUNS IN WRITING

Many people use the plural form of their last name on greeting cards. To spell the plural form of a proper noun, add either -s or -es to the singular form. A last name is not made plural by adding 's.

Writing with Plural Nouns

A. Study the examples. Then write your last name in the plural and the last names of nine other people.

1. (Lincoln) Greetings from the Lincolns
2. (Adams) Get-well wishes from the Adamses
3. (McKinley) Happy holidays from the McKinleys
4. (Kennedy) Regards from the Kennedys
5. (Truman) Congratulations from the Trumans
6. (Picasso) Good luck to the Picassos
7. (Pulaski) Best wishes to the Pulaskis
8. (Wolf) More success to the Wolfs
9. (Bush) Best of everything to the Bushes
10. (Cortez) Bravo to the Cortezes

B. Write a paragraph describing the contents of one of the items below. Use plural and possessive nouns.

11. a locker
12. a desk drawer
13. a scrapbook
14. a purse or wallet
15. a trunk or suitcase
16. a glove compartment

Using the Thesaurus

C. A large number of people is a *crowd.* A small number is a *group.* Using the Thesaurus, find three synonyms for each word. Write each one in a sentence. In some sentences use the plural or possessive noun form.

4 – Two Pronoun Cases

> ● Pronouns change form to show case.

Personal pronouns have three cases: nominative, objective, and possessive. The way a pronoun is used in a sentence determines its case. Many pronoun usage problems occur with the nominative and the objective cases. Study the rules and examples below.

Subject pronouns are in the **nominative case.**

Use	I you he she it we they who	as	**a Subject of a Verb** Lee and <u>I</u> want mail. <u>We</u> sent letters. <u>Who</u> has a pen pal?
		or as	**a Predicate Nominative** It was <u>I</u> who phoned. Could it have been <u>she</u>? The operators are <u>they</u>.

Object pronouns are in the **objective case.**

Use	me you him her it us them whom	as	**a Direct Object** Dana called Lee and <u>me</u>. They invited <u>us</u>.
		or as	**an Indirect Object** Sell <u>him</u> some envelopes.
		or as	**an Object of a Preposition** The telegram was for <u>her</u>. To <u>whom</u> did you reply?

The pronouns *you* and *it* are the same in both the nominative and the objective cases.

Exercises

A. Write each pronoun. Then label it *nominative case* or *objective case.*

1. Do they know me?
2. She spoke with us.
3. We gave them food.
4. Di saw her and him.
5. The typists will be he and I.

B. Write a nominative case pronoun to replace each group of words in parentheses.

6. The secretary and (my father) read the letter.
7. I receive more mail than (your sister) does.
8. How did (the pioneers) mail letters?
9. Ken and (his friends) wrote invitations.
10. A great writer of letters was (Abigail Adams).

C. Write an objective case pronoun to replace each group of words in parentheses.

11. No one but (my mother) had bought stamps.
12. Who sent Mary and (her brothers) this parcel?
13. Has anyone found (the addresses) yet?
14. Who telephoned (my grandfather) and me?
15. Their postcard surprised me more than it surprised (my aunt).

D. Write the correct pronoun. Then label it *nominative case* or *objective case.*

16. Willie or (I, me) might receive a phone call.
17. Did anyone notify the principal or (they, them)?
18. Who told your cousin and (she, her) the news?
19. Will (we, us) receive an award?
20. The winners of the typing contest should be Paula and (he, him).

5 – Choosing Correct Pronouns

> ● Many pronoun errors can be avoided by using simple tests.

■ If a noun follows a pronoun in a sentence, test for the correct pronoun by leaving out the noun.

To choose the correct pronoun in each sentence below, omit the underlined noun after (*we, us*). Then read each sentence without the noun.

> An author sent (we, us) <u>students</u> his photograph.
> Where can (we, us) <u>reporters</u> find his biography?

In the first sentence the correct choice is *us*, the indirect object in the objective case. In the second sentence the correct choice is *we*, the subject in the nominative case.

■ If a pronoun is joined to either a noun or another pronoun by *and* or *or*, test for the correct pronoun by leaving out the other elements.

To choose the correct pronoun in each sentence below, omit the underlined words. Then read each sentence without those words.

> <u>My friends and</u> (I, me) collect autographs.
> Are those autographs for <u>them or</u> (I, me)?

In the first sentence the correct choice is *I*, a subject. In the second sentence the correct choice is *me*, an object of a preposition.

If two pronouns are joined by *and* or *or*, both must be in either the nominative or the objective case.

Correct: They and I prefer autographed photographs.
Incorrect: Them and I prefer autographed photographs.

Exercises

A. Test for the correct pronoun in parentheses by omitting the underlined words. Write the correct pronoun.

1. (We, Us) <u>the people</u> need more information.
2. It was good news for (we, us) <u>football fans</u>.
3. Why are (we, us) <u>club members</u> proud today?
4. Describe the job to (we, us) <u>volunteers</u>.
5. How can (we, us) <u>teenagers</u> help our city?
6. Everyone talked about (we, us) <u>gardeners</u>.
7. Watch for (we, us) <u>runners</u> in the big race.
8. Who told (we, us) <u>altos</u> to sing softly?
9. Should (we, us) <u>players</u> wear our uniforms?
10. Where can (we, us) <u>swimmers</u> practice tomorrow?

B. Write the correct pronoun in each sentence.

11. Dad and (I, me) studied the recipes.
12. Grandmother told Jamie and (I, me) another joke.
13. Will Fred or (she, her) correct the papers?
14. Are these plants for his aunt or (he, him)?
15. The teachers and (they, them) will advise us.
16. The senator greeted them and (we, us) yesterday.
17. Each answer was checked by her and (I, me).
18. Will they or (we, us) be assigned the job?
19. He or (I, me) can select the vegetable seeds.
20. How much did they and (she, her) prepare?

C. Write the correct pair of pronouns in each sentence.

21. They hired (she and I, her and me).
22. (Him and I, He and I) admired her paintings.
23. When may (they and I, them and I) visit you?
24. Is the card for (her or him, she or him)?
25. Will (she or me, her or me, she or I) be the projectionist at the next assembly?

6 — Avoiding Pronoun Errors

> ● Three rules can help you avoid many common pronoun errors.

■ Use objective case pronouns after prepositions.

Sometimes nominative case pronouns seem to sound correct after the prepositions *between, but,* and *except.* However, only objective case pronouns should be used as objects of prepositions.

> Between you and <u>me</u> (not <u>I</u>) was a mailbox.
> No one but her and <u>me</u> (not <u>I</u>) noticed it.
> Everyone except <u>me</u> (not <u>I</u>) had forgotten it.

■ Supply the missing words after *than* or *as* to learn which kind of pronoun to use.

When a pronoun follows *than* or *as,* the writer usually omits some words. The missing words may come either before or after the pronoun. Add these words. The correct pronoun will immediately appear.

> He sends more letters than (I, me).
> He sends more letters than <u>I</u> **send.**
>
> The reply pleased them as much as (we, us).
> The reply pleased them as much as **it pleased** <u>us</u>.

■ Do not put a needless pronoun after a noun.

The pronouns in parentheses are unnecessary. Personal pronouns used that way are incorrect.

> My sister (she) buys pens with fine points.
> Our neighbors (they) sell stationery.
> His brother (he) went to the tennis matches.
> Those boxes (they) are very heavy.

Exercises

A. Write the correct pronoun in each sentence.

1. Stand between him and (she, her).
2. Nobody could solve it but (she, her).
3. All the members except Pam and (I, me) have voted.
4. It was very easy for everyone but (I, me).
5. Divide these labels between them and (we, us).
6. No one but you or (I, me) will be allowed to go.
7. Everybody except (he, him) has left.
8. Just between you and (I, me), that room was cold.
9. They knew every student except (she, her).
10. Nobody but (he, him) had completed the test.

B. Write the correct pronoun in each sentence.

11. Clifford is as tall as (she, her).
12. They can run as fast as (we, us).
13. That joke amused them more than (we, us).
14. We liked that breakfast more than (they, them).
15. The game was played by them better than (we, us).
16. That squeak annoyed him as much as (I, me).
17. I will sell as many subscriptions as (he, him).
18. All the voters admired her as much as (he, him).
19. They hiked farther than (I, me).
20. It will help him less than (she, her).

C. Each sentence contains one error. Write each sentence correctly.

21. My uncle he lives in Oklahoma now.
22. Yes, volleyball it is a great sport.
23. Those facts about African rivers they are amazing.
24. My sister and I we received a telegram.
25. Our old desk upstairs it has two secret drawers.

—7— Rules for Three Kinds of Pronouns

- Interrogative, indefinite, and reflexive pronouns have special usage rules.

■ Use the interrogative pronoun *who* as a subject.
Use the interrogative pronoun *whom* as an object.

The choice of *who* or *whom* in a question depends on the use of the word in the question.

Subject:	Who answered the phone?
Direct Object:	Whom did they want?
Object of a Preposition:	With whom did she speak?

One way to find the correct pronoun is to write an answer using *he* or *him*. If the answer is *he*, then *who* is correct. If the answer is *him*, then *whom* is correct.

(Who, Whom) has a pen? He has it. (Use who.)
(Who, Whom) do you see? You see him. (Use whom.)

■ A singular indefinite pronoun used as an antecedent should be followed by a singular pronoun.

Anybody, anyone, everybody, everyone, nobody, no one, somebody, and *someone* are singular. Used as antecedents, they are followed by singular pronouns, such as *he, him, his, himself, she, her, hers,* and *herself.*

Incorrect: Everybody has their pen.
  Correct: Everybody has his or her pen.
    Everybody has his pen. (Men are discussed.)
    Everybody has her pen. (Women are discussed.)

■ Use a reflexive pronoun only when the person it refers to has been mentioned earlier in the same sentence.

Incorrect: The note was written by myself.
  Correct: I wrote the note by myself.

Exercises

A. Write the correct pronoun in each sentence.

1. (Who, Whom) is playing the piano?
2. (Who, Whom) do you suspect?
3. To (who, whom) did they complain?
4. (Who, Whom) asked that question?
5. (Who, Whom) will they call?
6. For (who, whom) was it written?
7. (Who, Whom) invented the radio?
8. By (who, whom) was radium discovered?
9. (Who, Whom) have we forgotten?
10. (Who, Whom) could have forgotten us?

B. Rewrite each sentence. The revised sentences have been started.

11. People use handwriting to record their ideas.
    Everyone uses ...
12. Many adults write letters to their friends.
    Somebody writes ...
13. Students write their homework assignments.
    Someone writes ...
14. Businesswomen may write their important memos.
    Anybody may write ...
15. Some men could improve their handwriting.
    Anyone could improve ...

C. Three of the following sentences are incorrect. Write the incorrect sentences correctly.

16. She built this outdoor grill by herself.
17. This chart was prepared for themselves.
18. These sandwiches were made by myself.
19. We shall introduce ourselves to the guests.
20. The closet will be cleaned by himself.

Additional Exercises

A. Write each pronoun. Then write its case and its use in the sentence.

EXAMPLE: I heard the thunder.
ANSWER: I (nominative) (subject)

1. We raked the leaves.
2. The new title will please her.
3. The kindest people are always they.
4. Sally sent him a birthday card.
5. Bill will practice with us tomorrow.
6. Where can I find another dictionary?
7. Could the artist have been she?
8. Who was that person on the stage?
9. Whom did the guard identify?
10. For whom was this jacket made?

B. Each sentence in this invitation has one error in pronoun usage. Write the invitation correctly.

Dear Shawn,

    11. My mother and father they have asked me to invite you to our Labor Day picnic. **12.** Them and I hope you will come. **13.** As you know, us three can make memorable meals. **14.** Whom can forget that last Thanksgiving dinner? **15.** I am sure you will remember it as long as us. **16.** Everyone left some food on their plate. **17.** Nobody but you and I had room for dessert. **18.** Yes, it was me who made that pumpkin pie. **19.** Mom, Dad, and me are planning another great feast. **20.** Your presence at the picnic will make they and me happy.

Sincerely,
Heather

Application USING PRONOUNS IN WRITING

A. Write an original sentence for each word group. Use all pronouns correctly. Underline the word group in each sentence.

EXAMPLE: them and us
ANSWER: Who stood between <u>them and us</u>?

1. you and me
2. you or I
3. she and he
4. they and you
5. you or us
6. than she
7. than us
8. Does everyone have …?
9. Will they or I …?
10. the new president and she
11. Who …?
12. Whom …?
13. will be she and I
14. as much as him
15. between her and …
16. us football fans
17. his parents and him
18. we young people
19. Has anybody lost …?
20. by herself

B. Write a letter inviting someone you know well to a surprise party for a friend or relative. Mention the time and place of the party. Tell who will also be invited. Make some gift suggestions. Ask for ideas to help make the party a success. Be especially careful not to make errors in pronoun usage.

Using the Thesaurus

C. When people communicate by letter or telephone, the words *write* and *talk* are often used. Find the entries for *write* and *talk* in the Thesaurus, pages 555–574. Select four synonyms for each word. Then use each synonym in a sentence. You will write eight sentences in all.

Chapter Review

A. Write the correct plural form of each noun.

1. a waltz   many (waltzs, waltzes)
2. a life   many (lifes, lives)
3. a donkey   many (donkeys, donkies)
4. a tomato   many (tomatos, tomatoes)
5. a spoonful   many (spoonfuls, spoonsful)

B. Write the correct possessive form of each underlined noun.

6. arm of a <u>hero</u>   a (hero's, heroes') arm
7. names of <u>friends</u>   (friend's, friends') names
8. pen of my <u>aunt</u>   my (aunt's, aunts') pen
9. homes of <u>men</u>   (men's, mens') homes
10. sons of <u>Zeus</u>   (Zeus', Zeus's) sons

C. Write the correct pronoun in parentheses.

11. (He, Him) or I will stuff the envelopes.
12. The post office notified Tara and (I, me).
13. Did you give (they, them) our ZIP code?
14. It was (she, her) who designed that stamp.
15. Everyone but (we, us) used a typewriter.

D. Write the correct pronoun or correct sentence in parentheses.

16. No one made more calls than (I, me).
17. (Who, Whom) invented the telegraph?
18. To (who, whom) was the cablegram sent?
19. Did everyone have (their, his or her) card?
20. (I composed that letter by myself.)
     (That letter was composed by myself.)

Chapter Review CHALLENGE

A. Write each underlined noun. Label it *singular, plural, singular possessive,* or *plural possessive.*

Sometimes the best part of a letter is the **(1)** stamp on the envelope. My **(2)** brother and I collect **(3)** stamps, especially those with **(4)** faces. In my album are pages with **(5)** authors', **(6)** heroes', and even **(7)** children's faces. In my **(8)** brother's album are pages with faces of animals in the **(9)** wilderness. Here we can safely look into the **(10)** eyes of **(11)** wolves and **(12)** tigers or enjoy seeing a **(13)** reindeer's antlers or a **(14)** lion's mane. Yes, stamp collecting is the best of all **(15)** hobbies.

B. Write each underlined pronoun. Label it *nominative* or *objective.* Then write how it is used in the sentence: *subject, predicate nominative, direct object, indirect object,* or *object of a preposition.*

My twin sister and **(16)** I belong to a large family. On our birthday, cards from relatives in almost every state come to **(17)** her and **(18)** me. Uncle Lacey in Tulsa always remembers **(19)** us two in special ways. This year everybody but **(20)** him had sent a card. He mailed **(21)** us a cassette. On it **(22)** he and Cousin Marla sang "Happy Birthday" and a few choruses of "Oklahoma." Then **(23)** they read **(24)** us one of her poems. In verse, Uncle Lacey and my cousin invited us to beautiful Oklahoma. Our most unforgettable relatives are **(25)** he and Cousin Marla.

7 Adjective and Adverb Usage

Velvet Shoes

Let us walk in the white snow
  In a soundless space;
With footsteps quiet and slow,
  At a tranquil pace,
  Under veils of white lace.

I shall go shod in silk,
  And you in wool,
White as a white cow's milk,
  More beautiful
  Than the breast of a gull.

We shall walk through the still town
  In a windless peace;
We shall step upon white down,
  Upon silver fleece,
  Upon softer than these.

We shall walk in velvet shoes:
  Wherever we go
Silence will fall like dews
  On white silence below.
  We shall walk in the snow.

—*Elinor Wylie*

1 — Degrees of Adjectives

● Many adjectives have three forms.

Three special forms of adjectives are called the **degrees of comparison.** The adjective *small* has three forms, or degrees.

Positive Degree:	Venus is a <u>small</u> planet.
Comparative Degree:	Mars is <u>smaller</u> than Venus.
Superlative Degree:	Mercury is the <u>smallest</u> of all the planets.

There are three rules for writing the comparative and superlative degrees of adjectives.

■ Add *-er* or *-est* to the positive form. This rule is for most one-syllable and many two-syllable adjectives. Sometimes spelling changes occur. Notice the comparative and superlative forms of *big* and *busy* below.

sharp	brave	big	busy
sharper	braver	bigger	busier
sharpest	bravest	biggest	busiest

■ Put *more* or *most* before the positive form. This rule is for some two-syllable adjectives and almost all adjectives with three syllables or more.

careful	generous	obedient
more careful	more generous	more obedient
most careful	most generous	most obedient

■ Learn which adjectives have irregular forms in the comparative and superlative degrees.

good	bad, ill	much, many	little
better	worse	more	less
best	worst	most	least

Exercises

A. Write each adjective. Label it *comparative* or *super-lative*. Then write its positive form(s) under it.

EXAMPLE: safest
ANSWER: safest (superlative)
              safe

1. richest	**6.** riper	**11.** driest
2. newest	**7.** simplest	**12.** better
3. quicker	**8.** thinnest	**13.** worse
4. colder	**9.** hotter	**14.** most
5. greatest	**10.** merrier	**15.** less

B. Write each adjective. Then write its comparative form and its superlative form.

16. short	**21.** helpful	**26.** difficult
17. sweet	**22.** careless	**27.** important
18. quick	**23.** jealous	**28.** delicate
19. dusty	**24.** happy	**29.** bad
20. noble	**25.** strange	**30.** many

C. Write each sentence, using the comparative form of each adjective in parentheses.

31. Letters are usually (long) than telegrams.
32. Of the two stamps, this one is (valuable).
33. Our stationery is (colorful) than theirs.
34. Of the two signatures, yours is (legible).
35. I have (much) mail than you have.
36. This is the (funny) of the two get-well cards.
37. The new telephone is (pretty) than the old one.
38. *E.T.* was the (good) half of the double feature.
39. Was E.T. (intelligent) than the scientists?
40. E.T.'s planet might be (friendly) than ours.

2 Using Comparatives and Superlatives

> ● Use the comparative degree for two.
> ● Use the superlative degree for more than two.

There are four rules for using the comparative and superlative degrees correctly.

■ Use the comparative degree of an adjective when two persons, places, or things are compared.

> Lincoln was <u>taller</u> than Washington.
> Is North Carolina <u>larger</u> than South Carolina?
> Diamonds are <u>more valuable</u> than rubies.

■ Use the superlative degree of an adjective when more than two persons, places, or things are compared.

> Lincoln was the <u>tallest</u> of all the presidents.
> Charlotte is the <u>largest</u> city in North Carolina.
> Of all the diamonds on the table, this one is the <u>most valuable</u>.

■ Never use double comparatives or superlatives nor incorrect comparatives or superlatives.

> I hope you feel <u>better</u> (not <u>more better</u>) soon.
> Which is the <u>smallest</u> (not <u>most smallest</u>) state?
> Be <u>more cordial</u> (not <u>cordialer</u>) with the guests.
> It was the <u>worst</u> (not <u>worstest</u>) storm in history.

■ Use *than,* not *then,* when making comparisons. *Then* is an adverb that tells *when.*

> Harvard is older <u>than</u> (not <u>then</u>) Yale.
> Open the can and <u>then</u> (tells when) heat the beans.
> His notebook is more expensive <u>than</u> (not <u>then</u>) mine.
> After we had cleared the table, we <u>then</u> (tells when) washed the dishes.

Exercises

A. Write the correct form.

1. That car is the (older, oldest) of the two.
2. That car is the (older, oldest) of the three.
3. Barbara is the (more, most) dependable twin.
4. Keep the (smaller, smallest) of the two pieces.
5. Of the five books, which one is (better, best)?
6. Who is (younger, youngest), Allison or Kelly?
7. Which is (better, best), the book or the movie?
8. I am the (luckier, luckiest) student in America.
9. We are (busier, busiest) today than they are.
10. Both stalks are large, but this is (larger, largest).

B. Write the correct comparative or superlative form of each adjective in parentheses.

11. Noreen has the (bright) eyes we have ever seen.
12. Tear it in two, and give me the (large) piece.
13. Both hats are small, but the red one is (small).
14. Which report is (interesting), hers or his?
15. This is the (expensive) of the two tractors.
16. I have had many bad colds, but this one is the (bad).
17. Of the three birds, the blue one is the (noisy).
18. I feel (cheerful) today than I did last night.
19. It is the (humorous) story I have ever read.
20. My flashlight is dim, but yours is even (dim).

C. Write each sentence, using either *than* or *then*.

21. Our cat is cleaner _____ theirs.
22. His paintings are larger _____ her paintings.
23. They studied intensively and _____ took the test.
24. It is now later _____ you think.
25. Proofread your letter and _____ mail it.

3 — Degrees of Adverbs

> ● Many adverbs have three forms.

Like adjectives, adverbs also have three degrees of comparison. The adverb *fast* has three forms, or degrees.

Positive Degree:	I work *fast.*
Comparative Degree:	He works *faster.*
Superlative Degree:	She works the *fastest* of all.

There are four rules for writing and using the comparative and superlative degrees of adverbs.

■ Add *-er* or *-est* to the positive form of most one-syllable adverbs.

soon	near	close
sooner	nearer	closer
soonest	nearest	closest

■ Put *more* or *most* before the positive form of most adverbs of two or more syllables.

easily	clearly
more easily	more clearly
most easily	most clearly

■ Learn which adverbs have irregular forms in the comparative and superlative degrees.

well	badly	much	little
better	worse	more	less
best	worst	most	least

■ Use the comparative when two persons or things are compared. Use the superlative when three or more are compared.

Comparative:	Did she or he arrive <u>earlier</u>?
Superlative:	Did you, she, or he arrive <u>earliest</u>?

Exercises

A. Write each sentence, using the comparative form of each adverb in parentheses.

1. A jet plane can fly (high) than a propeller plane.
2. Which of the two mayors spoke (confidently)?
3. The new doorbell rings (loud) than the old one.
4. Which do you like (much), rice or potatoes?
5. Both secretaries are excellent typists, but Carlton types (well).

B. Write each sentence, using the superlative form of each adverb in parentheses.

6. Of all the snacks, I like the almonds (little).
7. Which animal in the jungle can run the (fast)?
8. Of all the contestants, Bryan spoke (clearly).
9. Which of the three phonographs played (badly)?
10. Of the three cats, the gray one came (close) to me.

C. Write the correct comparative or superlative form of each adverb in parentheses.

EXAMPLE: Is February (cold) than January?
ANSWER: colder

11. Which of those two dogs barks (loud)?
12. Does a submarine travel (smoothly) than a plane?
13. We are now (close) to our goal than ever before.
14. Of all the actors, the villain performed (well).
15. The band plays western music (often) than polkas.
16. Did Jill, Michelle, or Linda work the (hard)?
17. Of all the chairs, we liked that one (little).
18. The rain fell (heavily) than we had expected.
19. Why do they write (frequently) than you?
20. The movie ended (soon) than I thought it would.

4 — Avoiding Double Negatives

> ● A **double negative** is the incorrect use of two or more negative words in a sentence.

Affirmative sentences are made negative in different ways with just one negative word. If an extra negative word is added, the result is an error called a double negative.

Affirmative (right):	I made a phone call.
Negative (right):	I made <u>no</u> phone call.
Negative (right):	I did <u>not</u> make a phone call.
Double Negative (wrong):	I did <u>not</u> make <u>no</u> phone call.

Any one of the following twelve negative terms makes a sentence negative.

1. neither	4. nobody	7. not (n't)	10. barely
2. never	5. none	8. nothing	11. hardly
3. no	6. no one	9. nowhere	12. scarcely

Errors may occur with the last three words above. Other negative words should not be used with them.

Negative (right):	I could <u>hardly</u> hear you.
Double Negative (wrong):	I could <u>not hardly</u> hear you.

Contractions that include *n't*, for *not*, are often overlooked as negatives. They require special attention.

Negative (right):	Why <u>don't</u> you ever call?
Double Negative (wrong):	Why <u>don't</u> you <u>never</u> call?

When the word *no* is used as an answer to a question, it is separated from the rest of the sentence with a comma. That *no* does not count as a negative word in a sentence.

<u>No</u>, I made <u>no</u> long-distance calls.

Exercises

A. Write the negative word in each sentence.

1. Hardly anyone appreciates the telephone directory more than my parents and I. 2. We can scarcely survive without it. 3. None of us read it for entertainment. 4. It has no stories or poems. 5. It does not have an expensive binding. 6. It barely fits in our bookcase. 7. Nowhere, however, is there so much valuable information. 8. The directory never fails us. 9. Besides addresses and phone numbers, it gives first-aid facts, ZIP codes, and lists of places in our city that nobody should fail to visit. 10. In my opinion, nothing is more useful than a telephone directory.

B. Answer each question below with a complete sentence. Use a negative word in each sentence.

11. Do you have some coins? No, we have …
12. Did Andy do anything? No, he did …
13. Did she call either of you? No, she called …
14. Did it land anywhere near us? No, it landed …
15. Did they buy some? No, they bought …

C. Write the correct word in parentheses.

16. They don't wish to speak with (anyone, no one).
17. From our seats we (could, couldn't) hardly see.
18. They never go (anywhere, nowhere).
19. We did not select (neither, either) of them.
20. No one wears that kind of hat (no, any) more.
21. Haven't you (ever, never) tasted a mango?
22. Speak louder. We (can't, can) barely hear you.
23. I served carrots, but no one ate (any, none).
24. No, there aren't (any, no) pigeons in that park.
25. No, it makes (any, no) difference to us.

5 – Correct Use of Adjectives and Adverbs

> ● Verbs are modified by adverbs. Nouns and pronouns are modified by adjectives.

Many adjectives can be made into adverbs by adding the suffix *-ly* to them.

Adjectives:	silent	brave	rapid	easy
Adverbs:	silently	bravely	rapidly	easily

Because both words of each pair above are similar in sound and appearance, it is easy to misuse them. Follow these two rules when using adjectives and adverbs.

■ Modify a verb with an adverb.

In the sentences below, *worked* and *did smile* are verbs. They must be modified by adverbs.

> The inventor worked carefully. (not careful)
> Why did she smile so proudly? (not proud)

■ After a linking verb, use an adjective to modify the subject.

After a linking verb, an adjective instead of an adverb is usually needed. This adjective is called a predicate adjective. The subject is being modified, not the verb.

> The inventor was proud. (not proudly)
> The inventor seemed proud. (not proudly)
> The inventor looked proud. (not proudly)

In each sentence the noun *inventor* is being modified, not the verb. The most common linking verbs are forms of *be (am, are, is, was, were)*. Other linking verbs that are often followed by predicate adjectives are *appear, become, feel, look, remain, seem, smell, sound,* and *taste*.

Exercises

A. Write an adverb ending in *ly* to complete each sentence. The verb is underlined.

   1. The new announcer <u>speaks</u> ____.
   2. They <u>skated</u> ____ around the rink.
   3. <u>Seal</u> those envelopes ____.
   4. Those young trees <u>are growing</u> ____.
   5. He <u>was approaching</u> us ____.

B. Write an adjective to complete each sentence. The subject is underlined.

   6. Did that <u>pineapple</u> taste ____?
   7. Those huge <u>pillows</u> felt ____.
   8. <u>Everyone</u> seemed very ____ yesterday.
   9. Their <u>stories</u> always sound ____.
  10. Today the <u>sky</u> looks ____.

C. Write the correct adjective or adverb in each sentence.

  11. The operator replied (courteous, courteously).
  12. Those new clerks seem (courteous, courteously).
  13. The test looked (easy, easily).
  14. I answered every question (easy, easily).
  15. Who said that we played (bad, badly)?
  16. When we saw the film, we felt (bad, badly).
  17. Everyone remained (silent, silently) for an hour.
  18. They moved (silent, silently) down the stairs.
  19. That food tasted (bitter, bitterly).
  20. Why did they complain so (bitter, bitterly)?
  21. The dogs barked (angry, angrily).
  22. The owners became (angry, angrily).
  23. Huge clouds floated (calm, calmly) in the sky.
  24. The lake appears (calm, calmly) today.
  25. Our principal always speaks (calm, calmly).

6 — Troublesome Adjectives and Adverbs

> ● Do not replace an adverb with an adjective.

■ Good, Well

Good is an adjective. It modifies a noun or a pronoun.

> What kind of letter is it? It is a good letter.

Well is an adverb. It modifies a verb.

> How does she write? She writes well. (not good)

Well is an adjective if it refers to a person's health. It means "in good health."

> I was quite ill, but I am well now.

■ Real, Really

Real is an adjective. It means "genuine."

> The collector showed us a real inkwell.

Really is an adverb. It means "very."

> This ink is really (not real) thick.

■ Sure, Surely

Sure is an adjective. It means "certain."

> Are you sure about the postage?

Surely is an adverb. It means "certainly."

> You surely (not sure) need more stamps.

■ Most, Almost

Most used as an adjective means "the majority of."

> Most post offices close at five o'clock.

Almost is an adverb. It means "nearly."

> I sent letters to almost (not most) everyone.

Exercises

A. Write each sentence, using *good* and *well* where needed.

1. She is a _____ writer, and she speaks _____, too.
2. He likes _____ workers, and he treats them _____.
3. I always work _____ if I rest _____.
4. My voice is _____, but it isn't as _____ as hers.
5. How _____ can a really _____ chef cook?
6. We prepare _____ food, and we serve it _____.
7. The report is _____ because it is written _____.
8. If you study _____, you will do _____ tomorrow.
9. _____ students usually work _____ together.
10. Many _____ athletes do _____ in school.

B. Write the correct adjective or adverb in each sentence.

11. Todd (sure, surely) appreciated my gift.
12. (Most, Almost) all the crackers were stale.
13. I was never (real, really) frightened.
14. Why did (most, almost) everybody leave early?
15. You (sure, surely) must have seen it.
16. He showed us some (real, really) Swiss watches.
17. I will (sure, surely) have the answer tomorrow.
18. We (most, almost) fainted when we won.
19. (Most, Almost) new buses are air-conditioned.
20. A (real, really) good report card pleases me.

C. Each sentence has one error. Write each sentence correctly.

21. How good did everyone do on the last test?
22. Most everybody had a high grade.
23. Our parents will be real proud.
24. It sure is wise to study for a test.
25. Most all the students studied really well.

Additional Exercises

A. Write the correct comparative or superlative form of each adjective or adverb in parentheses.

1. These apples look (bad) than those apples.
2. Of all the bands, that one played (well).
3. They swim (well) than they skate.
4. Of the two rusty locks, this one works (badly).
5. Trees need (much) food in summer than in winter.
6. Of all words, which one has the (many) letters?
7. This is the (bad) pen that I have ever had.
8. Our new car uses (little) gasoline than yours.
9. Today I feel (ill) than I did yesterday.
10. The (good) movie of the year will win awards.

B. Each sentence in this letter has one error in usage. Rewrite the letter correctly.

Dear Heather,

11. We just watched a real old movie starring Don Ameche and Loretta Young. 12. They both performed very good. 13. The movie told the story of Alexander Graham Bell, the inventor of the telephone—a most importantest device. 14. Bell wished to invent something more easier to use than the telegraph. 15. Most everyone thought he would fail. 16. Bell and his assistant, Thomas Watson, worked endless. 17. At first they did not have no success. 18. One day Watson sat quiet beside an untested telephone. 19. In another room Bell burned himself bad with an acid and shouted through his new phone, "Mr. Watson, come here! I want you!" 20. It was sure fortunate that Watson heard that message.

Sincerely,
Shawn

Application USING MODIFIERS IN WRITING

A. Write each word correctly in a sentence. Follow the instruction in parentheses after each word.

1. good (Use it after a linking verb.)
2. well (Use it as an adverb to modify a verb.)
3. well (Use it to describe someone's health.)
4. almost (Use it to modify either *every* or *all.*)
5. real (Use it as an adjective.)
6. really (Use it to modify an adjective.)
7. happier (Use it to describe two people.)
8. happiest (Use it to describe how you felt once.)
9. careful (Use it after a linking verb.)
10. carefully (Use it to modify a verb.)

B. Some people prefer to send a message in a letter. Others prefer to use the telephone. Write a paragraph that tells which form of communication you think is better. Give several reasons for your choice. You might mention the cost, time, and importance of each. You could tell about a letter or telephone call that will never be forgotten by you or by someone you know. Be sure to use comparatives and superlatives correctly in your paragraph.

Using the Thesaurus

C. Everyone welcomes a letter or telephone call, whether it comes from a next-door neighbor or from a friend in another country. When these two forms of communication are discussed, the adjectives *far* and *near* are often needed. Using the Thesaurus, pages 555–574, find three synonyms for each word. Then write each synonym in a sentence. You will write six sentences.

Chapter Review

A. Write the correct comparative or superlative form of each adjective or adverb in parentheses.

1. Of the two old typewriters, this one is (old).
2. Is the Empire State Building the (tall) building in New York City?
3. Are orchids (beautiful) than roses?
4. Dino uses a camera (skillfully) than I.
5. Of all the employees in this company, Margarita always arrives the (early).

B. Write the correct word to avoid a double negative.

6. They don't want (no, any) weeds in their lawn.
7. The doctor cannot speak with (anyone, no one) now.
8. I (couldn't, could) barely read the fine print.
9. We won't go (anywhere, nowhere) without a map.
10. Aren't you (never, ever) going to finish that game?

C. Write the correct adjective or adverb in parentheses.

11. Look (careful, carefully) before crossing roads.
12. The patient seems quite (cheerful, cheerfully).
13. My clock still ticks too (noisy, noisily).
14. He played the organ very (soft, softly).
15. This fabric certainly feels (smooth, smoothly).

D. Write the correct word in parentheses.

16. It was a (real, really) valuable stamp.
17. You (sure, surely) must be eager to see it.
18. The child recited the alphabet (good, well).
19. (Most, Almost) all the theaters had been closed.
20. Did (most, almost) everyone solve the problem?

Chapter Review CHALLENGE

Using only the underlined words or word groups as answers, find and write these grammatical constructions.

A. four adjectives or adverbs in the positive degree

B. six adjectives or adverbs in the comparative degree

C. five adjectives or adverbs in the superlative degree

D. two negative words

E. three linking verbs

The characters in the movie *Star Wars* **(1)** are **(2)** famous. The character E.T. has probably become **(3)** more famous. Three different actors played E.T. The **(4)** most famous one was Michael Patrick Bilon. Only thirty-four inches tall and weighing forty-five pounds, he was one of Hollywood's **(5)** smallest actors.

Michael **(6)** never grew **(7)** tall because of a bone defect at birth. During his life **(8)** nobody tried **(9)** harder or did **(10)** better than he. As a child, Michael loved singing and dancing **(11)** more than anything else. With his parents' encouragement, he performed before **(12)** many groups.

In 1972, Bilon graduated from Youngstown State University in Ohio. Although he was **(13)** shorter than **(14)** most other people, he was surely **(15)** busier. He worked as a police radio dispatcher. **(16)** Proud of his ethnic heritage, Michael **(17)** was an announcer for a radio program of Ukrainian music. Michael also **(18)** became one of Youngstown's **(19)** best volunteers. He even coached a basketball team and won the respect of its **(20)** tallest players.

On January 27, 1983, Michael Patrick Bilon died of pneumonia at the age of thirty-five.

8 Verb Usage

Measure Me, Sky

Measure me, sky!
   Tell me I reach by a song
Nearer the stars;
   I have been little so long.

Weigh me, high wind!
   What will your wild scales record?
Profit of pain,
   Joy by the weight of a word.

Horizon, reach out!
   Catch at my hands, stretch me taut,
Rim of the world:
   Widen my eyes by a thought.

Sky, be my depth,
   Wind, be my width and my height,
World, my heart's span;
   Loveliness, wings for my flight.

—Leonora Speyer

1 — Principal Parts of Verbs

> • The **principal parts** of a verb are its basic forms. They are the present, the past, the past participle, and the present participle.

In most dictionaries the following words are printed in dark type after the verb *speak*: *spoke, spoken, speaking*. Together these four forms are called the principal parts of the verb. Each form has a grammatical name.

Present:	Machines <u>speak</u>.
Past:	Machines <u>spoke</u>.
Past Participle:	Machines have <u>spoken</u>.
Present Participle:	Machines are <u>speaking</u>.

In most dictionaries no principal parts are listed after the verb *listen*. This omission in a dictionary indicates that the principal parts of *listen* end in *ed* and *ing*.

Present:	People <u>listen</u>.
Past:	People <u>listened</u>.
Past Participle:	People have <u>listened</u>.
Present Participle:	People are <u>listening</u>.

Most English verbs, including *listen*, are called **regular verbs**. The past and the past participle are the same. Both are formed by adding *-ed* or *-d* to the present.

About 130 verbs, including *speak*, are called **irregular verbs**. They do not form the past and the past participle by adding *-ed* or *-d* to the present.

The past participle is used with a form of the helping verb *have*: for example, <u>have</u> listened. The present participle is formed by adding *-ing* to the present. It is used with a form of the helping verb *be*, such as <u>are</u> listening.

Some regular verbs require spelling changes when *-ed* or *-d* and *-ing* are added to the present.

arrive	shop	reply
arrived	shopped	replied
arriving	shopping	replying

Exercises

A. Each word below is either the past participle or the present participle of a regular verb. Write the word. Above it write the present form.

EXAMPLE: turned

ANSWER: turn
        turned

1. talked	**11.** followed	**21.** hoping
2. lived	**12.** carried	**22.** hopping
3. cried	**13.** studied	**23.** happening
4. tapped	**14.** delayed	**24.** snowing
5. smiled	**15.** laughed	**25.** humming
6. joked	**16.** walking	**26.** spilling
7. jogged	**17.** saving	**27.** creating
8. opened	**18.** trying	**28.** copying
9. rained	**19.** dotting	**29.** playing
10. grinned	**20.** closing	**30.** coughing

B. Write the four principal parts of each verb. All are regular verbs.

31. ask	**36.** drown	**41.** attack
32. use	**37.** sneak	**42.** suppose
33. skid	**38.** climb	**43.** hurry
34. obey	**39.** raise	**44.** roast
35. flow	**40.** treat	**45.** misspell

2—Tenses of Verbs

> ● The **tense** of a verb shows time.

The time expressed by a verb is called its tense. All the tenses are formed from the principal parts.

■ The **present tense** expresses an action taking place now.

> These electronic calculators <u>talk</u> to their users.

■ The **past tense** expresses an action that took place in the past.

> That thermometer <u>talked</u> to the nurse.

■ The **future tense** expresses an action that will occur in the future. It is formed by adding the helping verb *will* or *shall* to the present.

> Soon many automobiles <u>will talk</u> to their drivers.

■ The **present perfect tense** expresses an action that occurred at an indefinite time in the past. The action may still be going on. It is formed with the helping verb *have* or *has* and the past participle.

> Your watch <u>has talked</u> again.

■ The **past perfect tense** expresses an action that happened before another past action. It is formed with the helping verb *had* and the past participle.

> The elevator <u>had talked</u> before it moved.

■ The **future perfect tense** expresses an action that will be finished before a stated time in the future. It is formed with *will have* or *shall have* and the past participle.

> The clock <u>will have talked</u> eleven times before noon.

Study the table below, which lists the tenses of *talk*. A list of all the forms of a verb is a **conjugation**. To give such a list is to conjugate a verb.

Conjugation of the Verb *Talk*

Principal Parts: talk, talked, (have) talked, talking

Present Tense

	Singular	*Plural*
First Person	I talk	we talk
Second Person	you talk	you talk
Third Person	he, she, it talks	they talk

Past Tense

First Person	I talked	we talked
Second Person	you talked	you talked
Third Person	he, she, it talked	they talked

Future Tense

First Person	I shall talk	we shall talk
Second Person	you will talk	you will talk
Third Person	he, she, it will talk	they will talk

Present Perfect Tense

First Person	I have talked	we have talked
Second Person	you have talked	you have talked
Third Person	he, she, it has talked	they have talked

Past Perfect Tense

First Person	I had talked	we had talked
Second Person	you had talked	you had talked
Third Person	he, she, it had talked	they had talked

Future Perfect Tense

First Person	I shall have talked	we shall have talked
Second Person	you will have talked	you will have talked
Third Person	he, she, it will have talked	they will have talked

Exercises

A. Write the underlined verb and its tense: *present*, *past*, or *future*.

1. The doors slowly open.
2. Neil opened the four boxes of costumes.
3. Who will open that jar of pickles?
4. I shall close the letter with a funny story.
5. The state fair closes today.
6. We closed the show with a song.
7. Your book covers look new.
8. Everyone looked through the new telescope.
9. It looks cold outside now.
10. The search team will look everywhere.
11. We shall look happier tomorrow.
12. The sherbet quickly melted.
13. Ruthanne will answer the next question.
14. My little sister reads very well.
15. These shoes need new heels already.

B. Write the underlined verb and its tense: *present perfect*, *past perfect*, or *future perfect*.

16. His answers have surprised us again.
17. The letter had arrived before we left.
18. We shall have finished it before midnight.
19. Robyn said that her brother had studied Portuguese for three years.
20. Who will have memorized it by June 3?
21. She has defined all the words in the lesson.
22. No one had noticed the new chair until today.
23. We have lived in this state for five years.
24. The librarians have moved the magazine rack.
25. Soon he will have visited every national park in the United States.

C. Write each underlined verb and its tense.

26. A customer in a supermarket approaches the checkout counter. **27.** Soon the cash register will communicate with the customer. **28.** Many of the new cash registers seem almost human. **29.** They scan the price codes on boxes and cans. **30.** They display on a monitor the name of the product and its price. **31.** Finally they thank the customer for his or her business. **32.** These cash registers have appeared in many stores. **33.** Not many years ago, however, engineers had dreamed of such machines. **34.** They experimented with many different kinds of models. **35.** Perhaps by the year 2000, engineers will have designed a cash register that also will wrap the customer's purchases.

D. Write each underlined verb in the tense indicated in parentheses.

EXAMPLE: We smile. (past)
ANSWER: smiled

36. We skate. (past)
37. They worry. (present perfect)
38. Players practice. (future)
39. You qualify. (past perfect)
40. The teacher translate. (present)
41. Frisbees vanish. (future perfect)
42. The choir rehearse. (present)
43. Everything hum. (past)
44. We exaggerate. (future)
45. People hurry. (past)
46. Students ask. (present perfect)
47. The meetings end. (future)
48. They satisfy. (past perfect)
49. It quench. (present)
50. The guests chat. (future perfect)

3 — Forms of *be*, *have*, and *do*

> ● The verbs *be*, *have*, and *do* are irregular.

No other verbs are used more frequently in English than *be*, *have*, and *do*. Each one can be either the main verb in a sentence or a helping verb.

Main Verb	Helping Verb
I <u>am</u> a student.	I <u>am</u> studying English.
I <u>have</u> my book.	I <u>have</u> studied my book.
I <u>do</u> the lessons.	I <u>do</u> study the lessons.

Be, *have*, and *do* are irregular because they do not form the past and past participle by adding *-ed* or *-d* to the present. Study the conjugations of all their tenses on the next page. The rules below summarize the way *be*, *have*, and *do* should be used.

■ In the present tense, use the third-person form of the verb ending in *s* after *he*, *she*, *it*, or a singular noun. Remember that *singular* means "one."

> He <u>is</u> (not *be*) a student.
> She <u>has</u> (not *have*) my book.
> It <u>does</u> (not *do*) my work for me.
> The computer <u>does</u> (not *do*) my work for me.

■ The past participle always has a helping verb, but the past never does.

> We <u>did</u> (not *have did*) that lesson.
> We <u>have done</u> (not *done*) many lessons.

■ The present participle should be spelled correctly. It also has a helping verb.

> We are <u>having</u> (not *haveing*) a test today.
> We are <u>doing</u> (not *doeing*) well this year.

Conjugation of the Verb *Be*

Principal Parts: be, was, (have) been, being

Present	Past	Future
I am	was	shall be
she, he, it is	was	will be
we, you, they are	were	shall, will be

Present Perfect	Past Perfect	Future Perfect
I have been	had been	shall have been
she, he, it has been	had been	will have been
we, you, they have been	had been	shall, will have been

Conjugation of the Verb *Have*

Principal Parts: have, had, (have) had, having

Present	Past	Future
I, we, you, they have	had	shall, will have
she, he, it has	had	will have

Present Perfect	Past Perfect	Future Perfect
I, we, you, they have had	had had	shall, will have had
she, he, it has had	had had	will have had

Conjugation of the Verb *Do*

Principal Parts: do, did, (have) done, doing

Present	Past	Future
I, we, you, they do	did	shall, will do
she, he, it does	did	will do

Present Perfect	Past Perfect	Future Perfect
I, we, you, they have done	had done	shall, will have done
she, he, it has done	had done	will have done

Exercises ―――――――――――――――――――

A. Write each sentence, completing it with the correct present tense of the verb in parentheses.

1. We (be) the hall guards now.
2. I (be) in my English class at this moment.
3. She (be) taller than her sisters are.
4. It (do) not work well in damp weather.
5. He (have) the tickets today.

B. Write each sentence, completing it with the correct past tense of the verb in parentheses.

6. We (be) at the art museum last week.
7. I (be) in my math class an hour ago.
8. She (be) very small in kindergarten.
9. It (do) not make any strange noises yesterday.
10. He (have) measles when he was a child.

C. Write the present perfect tense of each verb in parentheses. (Use *have* or *has* and the past participle.)

11. We (be) neighbors for many years.
12. I (be) in this school for only one month.
13. She (be) our principal since 1980.
14. It (do) very poor work since its installation.
15. He (have) three colds since November.

D. Write each sentence, completing it with the present participle of the verb in parentheses.

16. We are (be) awarded a prize at this assembly.
17. I was (be) bothered by a mosquito.
18. She is (do) her best in the competition.
19. It was (do) everything wrong when it broke.
20. He is (have) his report duplicated for us.

E. Write the correct form of the verb in parentheses.

The idea for the first communications satellite **(21)** (was, were) conceived by Arthur C. Clarke, a British scientist and author of science fiction. In the October 1945 issue of *Wireless World* **(22)** (was, will be) an article by Clarke stating that radio and television communications over long distances could **(23)** (be, being) tremendously improved. He had **(24)** (did, done) much thinking about using satellites for receiving and relaying signals transmitted from one area of the earth to another. According to his article, such satellites would orbit the earth from a 22,000 mile-high orbit, rotating once every twenty-four hours, as the earth **(25)** (do, does). Satellites, however, would appear to be in the same position above the earth. The development of solar energy for fuel, he wrote, would **(26)** (be, been) a limitless source of power.

When Clarke **(27)** (have, had) this idea in 1945, satellites were still considered science fiction. However, in 1958 his look into the future became reality when the first communications satellite **(28)** (is, was) launched. This event began a revolution in the telephone, television, and data transmission industries. Many of Clarke's predictions, such as the height of the orbit and the use of solar energy, **(29)** (have been, will have been) strikingly accurate for later satellites. For what he **(30)** (did, done) to bring about this remarkable success, Clarke received only the payment of $40.00 for his article in *Wireless World.*

F. Write each verb and its tense.

31. did	**36.** am	**41.** had done
32. shall be	**37.** did	**42.** has been
33. is	**38.** shall do	**43.** does
34. has	**39.** was	**44.** were
35. had had	**40.** have	**45.** will have been

4 —Irregular Verbs

> ● Some irregular verbs follow patterns when forming their principal parts. Others do not.

Although irregular verbs do not form their principal parts by adding -d or -ed, many do follow other patterns.

Some form the past participle by adding -n to the past.

Present	Past	Past Participle	Present Participle
break	broke	(have) broken	breaking
choose	chose	(have) chosen	choosing
freeze	froze	(have) frozen	freezing
tear	tore	(have) torn	tearing

Some have the same present and past participle.

| come | came | (have) come | coming |
| run | ran | (have) run | running |

Some have the same past and past participle.

bring	brought	(have) brought	bringing
feel	felt	(have) felt	feeling
find	found	(have) found	finding
sell	sold	(have) sold	selling

Some have the same present, past, and past participle.

burst	burst	(have) burst	bursting
cost	cost	(have) cost	costing
hurt	hurt	(have) hurt	hurting
put	put	(have) put	putting

Learn the principal parts of the irregular verbs in the chart on the next page. Some follow the patterns listed above. Some follow no pattern at all.

Irregular Verbs			
Present	Past	Past Participle	Present Participle
become	became	(have) become	becoming
begin	began	(have) begun	beginning
bite	bit	(have) bitten	biting
blow	blew	(have) blown	blowing
catch	caught	(have) caught	catching
draw	drew	(have) drawn	drawing
drink	drank	(have) drunk	drinking
drive	drove	(have) driven	driving
eat	ate	(have) eaten	eating
fall	fell	(have) fallen	falling
fly	flew	(have) flown	flying
get	got	(have) gotten (got)	getting
give	gave	(have) given	giving
go	went	(have) gone	going
grow	grew	(have) grown	growing
know	knew	(have) known	knowing
ride	rode	(have) ridden	riding
ring	rang	(have) rung	ringing
say	said	(have) said	saying
see	saw	(have) seen	seeing
shake	shook	(have) shaken	shaking
sing	sang	(have) sung	singing
sink	sank	(have) sunk	sinking
steal	stole	(have) stolen	stealing
swim	swam	(have) swum	swimming
take	took	(have) taken	taking
teach	taught	(have) taught	teaching
think	thought	(have) thought	thinking
throw	threw	(have) thrown	throwing
wear	wore	(have) worn	wearing
write	wrote	(have) written	writing

Exercises

A. Write the correct form of the verb in parentheses.

1. The game has (began, begun).
2. Has the wind (blew, blown) down any trees?
3. One of the pipes has (burst, bursted).
4. Has the bus from Mobile (came, come) yet?
5. How many items have you (chose, chosen)?
6. Have they (drank, drunk) the lemonade?
7. Where have we been (drove, driven)?
8. Who (ate, eaten) all the pears?
9. How many records have (fell, fallen) this year?
10. Where had those birds (flew, flown)?
11. We (gave, given) our reports yesterday.
12. Everyone (went, gone) to the park.
13. They (grew, grown) corn and tomatoes last year.
14. My tooth has not (hurt, hurted) much since it was capped last week.
15. They have (knew, known) us for many years.
16. Where have you (put, putted) the forks?
17. We (rode, ridden) our bicycles downtown.
18. Have you (ran, run) in a marathon before?
19. Has the bell (rang, rung) yet?
20. What could they have (saw, seen)?
21. How many times have you (sang, sung) that song?
22. The logs (sank, sunk) in the mud.
23. The dog (shook, shaken) its tail vigorously.
24. How many bases were (stole, stolen) in the game?
25. We (swam, swum) to the other side of the lake.
26. I (taught, teached) survival skills at camp.
27. How many photos have you (took, taken)?
28. The ball was (threw, thrown) to the shortstop.
29. This sweater has never been (wore, worn).
30. We (wrote, written) many letters last week.

B. Complete the answers to these questions. Use only the past or past participle in your answers.

EXAMPLE: Did you <u>ride</u> on that roller coaster?
ANSWER: Yes, we <u>rode</u> on it several times.

31. Did he <u>throw</u> it away?
Yes, he _____ it away at once.
32. Did you <u>give</u> them anything?
Yes, we _____ them food and clothes.
33. Did she <u>drive</u> that car?
Yes, she _____ it several times.
34. Did they <u>steal</u> it?
No, someone else must have _____ it.
35. Did Stella <u>write</u> it?
No, Ann had _____ it before Stella arrived.
36. Have you <u>worn</u> that?
Yes, I have often _____ it.
37. Has the show <u>begun</u>?
No, it has not yet _____.
38. Has the balloon <u>burst</u>?
Yes, I am afraid that it has _____.
39. Have the guests <u>gone</u>?
No, they have not _____ yet.
40. Have they <u>taken</u> the medicine?
No, they have not _____ it.
41. Did he <u>freeze</u> any of the fish he caught?
Yes, he _____ twenty-two pounds.
42. Has anyone <u>seen</u> my notebook?
No, we have not _____ it.
43. Did the temperature <u>fall</u>?
Yes, it _____ quite suddenly an hour ago.
44. Has anybody <u>drunk</u> the cranberry juice?
Yes, everybody has _____ some of it.
45. Did anybody <u>eat</u> the salad?
Yes, everybody _____ the salad.

Additional Exercises

A. Write the principal parts of each verb.

1. do   3. eat   5. have   7. sing   9. steal
2. go   4. hurt   6. take   8. wear   10. sneak

B. Write each sentence, completing it with the correct form (the past or the past participle) of the verb in parentheses.

11. Just before midnight the storm (begin). **12.** The moon had just (sink) behind the craggy hills. **13.** The wind (blow) fiercely. **14.** Many ancient trees (fall). **15.** Broken branches with jagged ends were (throw) about wildly. **16.** The old stone dam had (burst) a short time earlier. **17.** The swirling river had (reach) the edge of the haunted village. **18.** Snakes had (swim) into flooded cellars. **19.** Bats had (fly) into broken windows in many houses. **20.** Frightened animals had been (drive) from the forest into the village streets. **21.** The howling wind (ring) the bell in the clock tower. **22.** In a noisy old automobile, a newspaper reporter (ride) into the village. **23.** She had (come) because of a mysterious telephone call. **24.** If she had (know) what lay ahead, would she have left the city?

25. Many programs on radio once (begin) with a scene like this one. **26.** People (use) to listen to such shows for hours. **27.** Their imaginations were (give) opportunities to grow. **28.** Helped by clever sound-effects technicians, listeners (see) in their minds what they heard. **29.** Using many gadgets, the technicians created the noises that had been (write) in the script. **30.** Of all the machines that talked, the radio (be) the most popular with people of all ages.

Application ▐ USING VERBS IN WRITING

A. Write original sentences that include the following word groups. Use each verb form correctly.

1. did the job slowly
2. swum in the new reservoir
3. sung with the adult chorus in the theater
4. took the wrong bus to work again
5. went inside the office with the principal
6. seen with the new neighbors across the street
7. gave us a real surprise last week
8. written the publisher another letter
9. drunk a pint of fresh milk from the dairy
10. sneaked away from the group without a sound
11. done many extremely difficult assignments
12. have had no major illnesses in ten years
13. came across the meadow with the visitors
14. were very happy with the news about the baby
15. has been in many different countries

B. On many trains and buses, taped messages are played automatically, announcing the stations and giving safety suggestions. Write a paragraph giving suggestions for other messages that might be played for the passengers. Some passengers are aboard a train or bus for over an hour. They might wish to hear a variety of announcements. Your suggestions could include items that are educational, entertaining, or inspirational.

Using the Thesaurus

C. The verbs *win* and *lose* are often overused in writing. Using the Thesaurus, find four synonyms for each verb. Then write each one in a sentence.

5 — Troublesome Verb Pairs

> ● Some verb pairs are often confused.

Do not use *leave* when *let* is needed.

■ The verb *leave* means "to place," "to go away from," or "to allow to remain." Its principal parts are *leave, left, left, leaving*. It may have a direct object.

> <u>Leave</u> the calculator with me.
> She often <u>leaves</u> her dessert untouched.
> They <u>left</u> Italy in 1971.
> The farmer has <u>left</u> the barn unpainted.

■ The verb *let* means "to permit." Its principal parts are *let, let, let, letting*.

> <u>Let</u> me add those numbers.
> He <u>lets</u> me borrow his skates each Wednesday.
> They <u>let</u> us go to Puerto Rico.

Do not use *set* when *sit* should be used.

■ The verb *set* means "to put or place something." Its principal parts are *set, set, set, setting*. It usually has a direct object.

> <u>Set</u> the dish on the counter.
> I <u>set</u> the microscope on the table.
> What have you <u>set</u> there?

■ The verb *sit* means "to move into a seat" or "to be in a place." Its principal parts are *sit, sat, sat, sitting*. It rarely has a direct object.

> <u>Sit</u> down on this bench.
> She often <u>sits</u> in that chair.
> A microscope <u>sat</u> on the table.
> Why have you <u>sat</u> there so long?

Exercises

A. Write the correct form of the verb in parentheses.

1. (Leave, Let) me operate that cash register.
2. (Leave, Let) your bicycle on the rack.
3. (Leave, Let) a friend help you with that task.
4. Please (leave, let) me paint this fence, Tom.
5. (Leave, Let) me borrow your brush for a minute.
6. The coach of our swimming team always (leaves, lets) me distribute the towels.
7. Does she ever (leave, let) you dive from the high board at the pool?
8. Children, never (leave, let) thunder frighten you.
9. Who (left, let) this dictionary on my desk?
10. (Leave, Let) this room as it is now.

B. Write the correct form of the verb in parentheses.

11. Where did you (set, sit) the ice cubes?
12. An emperor once (set, sat) on that throne.
13. (Set, Sit) here and tell me another good story.
14. Don't (set, sit) the dessert on the table yet.
15. (Set, Sit) it there, please.
16. Don't let the dog (set, sit) on the couch.
17. I heard nothing because I (set, sat) too far away from the speaker.
18. Never (set, sit) too close to a fire.
19. (Set, Sit) the typewriter on that table.
20. If you (set, sit) a heavy machine on this table, it might collapse.
21. I have never (set, sat) so long in one place.
22. (Set, Sit) this plant in a shady place.
23. They told us not to (set, sit) on that balcony.
24. The elephant (set, sat) on a tiny stool.
25. She (set, sat) her package on that rack.

6 — Troublesome Verb Pairs

> ● Similar verbs often cause usage errors.

Do not use *raise* when *rise* is called for.

■ The verb *rise* means "to get up" or "to go up." Its principal parts are *rise, rose, risen, rising*. It never has a direct object.

> You should <u>rise</u> fifteen minutes earlier.
> The temperature <u>rises</u> when the sun shines.
> The theater curtain slowly <u>rose</u>.
> The children have <u>risen</u> early again.

■ The verb *raise* means "to lift" or "to move something higher." It is a regular verb. Its principal parts are *raise, raised, raised, raising*. It may have a direct object.

> Our band will <u>raise</u> money for new uniforms.
> They <u>raised</u> the shades and looked out.
> They have <u>raised</u> their hands often today.

Do not use *lay* when *lie* is needed.

■ The verb *lie* means "to rest" or "to recline." Its principal parts are *lie, lay, lain, lying*. It never has a direct object. Note that *lay* is its past form.

> The dog always <u>lies</u> on Dad's recliner.
> Exhausted, she <u>lay</u> down and quickly fell asleep.
> That rock must have <u>lain</u> there for a century.

■ The verb *lay* means "to put something down" or "to place." Its principal parts are *lay, laid, laid, laying*. It may have a direct object.

> <u>Lay</u> that pencil down and use this one instead.
> Where are the books that I <u>laid</u> here yesterday?
> You might have <u>laid</u> them somewhere else.

Exercises

A. Write the correct form of the verb in parentheses.

1. Don't (raise, rise) the lid on that trunk.
2. The prices have (raised, risen) again.
3. Why did the club (raise, rise) its dues?
4. If I study more, my grades should (raise, rise).
5. The teacher has (raised, risen) my grade.
6. Has the sun (raised, risen) yet?
7. Salute when the flag (raises, rises).
8. They (raised, rose) the flag at dawn.
9. Why did Nick (raise, rise) that question?
10. She (raised, rose) to her feet and spoke.

B. Write the correct form of *lie* to complete each sentence below.

11. Those tigers _____ down after they eat.
12. The cat has been _____ there for an hour.
13. The sunbather _____ on the beach and dozes.
14. The fawn _____ motionless in the underbrush and waited.
15. How long has that photograph _____ there?

C. Write the correct form of the verb in parentheses.

16. (Lay, Lie) those packages on the counter.
17. If you are tired, (lay, lie) down and rest.
18. In which pile do we (lay, lie) these ribbons?
19. Whose cap is (laying, lying) on that box?
20. Yesterday I (laid, lay) in the hammock.
21. Millions of leaves (laid, lay) on our lawn.
22. We (laid, lay) our money on the table last night.
23. They (laid, lay) their gifts there a week ago.
24. How long has the book (laid, lain) here?
25. No one has (laid, lain) a hand on it.

Chapter Review

A. Write the present form of each verb in parentheses.

1. They (be) aboard a cruise ship now.
2. He (be) very happy with his grade.
3. I (be) the president of the club this year.
4. She (have) another new tennis racket.
5. It (do) not begin until seven o'clock.

B. Write the past form of each verb in parentheses.

6. The raccoons (eat) and (drink) almost everything.
7. The rocket (rise) and (fall) quickly.
8. When the bell (ring), everybody (sing).
9. He (put) on a blue cap and (wear) it all day.
10. She (know) who (come) on Fridays.

C. Write the past participle of each verb in parentheses.

11. Have you (see) what I have (write)?
12. She has (fly) planes and has (drive) tractors.
13. I have (give) away most of the food that I have (grow) in my small garden.
14. It was (steal) when it was (take) there.
15. He has (go) where we have always (swim).

D. Each sentence has one error. Write the correct form of the incorrect verb.

16. How long have those logs laid there?
17. Your scarf is laying on the stair.
18. How high has the temperature rose today?
19. Everyone set down and waited quietly.
20. Please leave me read this letter from my pen pal in France to the class.

Chapter Review `CHALLENGE`

Using only the underlined verbs as answers, find and write the verbs in the tenses listed below. Do not repeat any answers.

A. Two verbs in the present tense
B. Five verbs in the past tense
C. Four verbs in the future tense
D. Two verbs in the present perfect tense
E. One verb in the past perfect tense
F. One verb in the future perfect tense

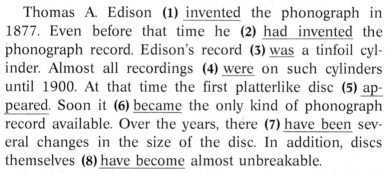

Thomas A. Edison **(1)** <u>invented</u> the phonograph in 1877. Even before that time he **(2)** <u>had invented</u> the phonograph record. Edison's record **(3)** <u>was</u> a tinfoil cylinder. Almost all recordings **(4)** <u>were</u> on such cylinders until 1900. At that time the first platterlike disc **(5)** <u>appeared</u>. Soon it **(6)** <u>became</u> the only kind of phonograph record available. Over the years, there **(7)** <u>have been</u> several changes in the size of the disc. In addition, discs themselves **(8)** <u>have become</u> almost unbreakable.

It **(9)** <u>is</u> possible that the phonograph record **(10)** <u>will undergo</u> another major change in shape. Some audio technicians **(11)** <u>believe</u> that phonograph records of the future **(12)** <u>will be</u> plastic cards about the size of postcards. A computer **(13)** <u>will print</u> music on a card in a special digital code for the phonograph. By the year 2000, according to some predictions, plastic cards **(14)** <u>will have replaced</u> discs in stores. Discs eventually **(15)** <u>will become</u> obsolete, like Edison's cylinders, and the talking machine he invented will have another new voice.

9

Subject-Verb Agreement

Skier

He swings down like the flourish of a pen
Signing a signature in white on white.

The silence of his skis reciprocates
The silence of the world around him.

Wind is his one competitor
In the cool winding and unwinding down.

On incandescent feet he falls
Unfalling, trailing white foam, white fire.

—*Robert Francis*

1 — Spelling Singular Verb Forms

● A verb must agree with its subject in number.

Number means a word is either singular or plural. A subject and verb are said to agree in number when they are both singular or both plural.

Singular: The dog barks.   The car stops.
Plural: The dogs bark.   The cars stop.

Nouns ending in *s* are usually plural. Verbs, however, ending in *s* are usually singular. Study the singular and plural verbs in the present tense below.

	Singular	*Plural*
First Person	I swim	we swim
Second Person	you swim	you swim
Third Person	he, she, it swims	they swim

The form of the verb *swim* used with the singular pronouns *I* and *you* is the same as the plural form. Rules for spelling present-tense verbs when the subject is a singular noun or *he, she,* or *it* follow.

■ To make verbs ending in *ch, s, sh, x,* or *z* singular, add *-es.*

Plural: they watch   we splash   the bees buzz
Singular: he watches   she splashes   the bee buzzes

■ To make verbs ending in a consonant and *y* singular, change *y* to *i* and add *-es.*

Plural: they hurry   we spy   the babies cry
Singular: he hurries   she spies   the baby cries

■ To make verbs ending in *o* singular, add *-es.*

Plural: they go   we echo   the ranchers lasso
Singular: he goes   she echoes   the rancher lassoes

Exercises

A. Write the present-tense verb form that would agree with a third-person singular subject.

1. write	**6.** carry	**11.** undergo
2. hiss	**7.** cultivate	**12.** construct
3. study	**8.** fix	**13.** rush
4. leave	**9.** paint	**14.** hatch
5. wash	**10.** echo	**15.** worry

B. Write each sentence, using the present-tense form of the verb in parentheses.

16. A large cloud (block) the sun.

17. A bell (signify) the end of the lecture.

18. The little boy (scratch) his mosquito bites.

19. Our new fan (blow) cool air into the living room.

20. The cautious man always (latch) his door.

21. The light (flash) on and off sixty times a second.

22. Warm soda (fizz) more than cold soda.

23. A large maple tree (shade) our house.

24. The airplane (fly) to the east coast every day.

25. The train (move) slowly through the mountains.

26. The catcher (miss) the ball every time.

27. The restaurant (supply) the waiters with uniforms.

28. She (walk) several miles around the lake every day before breakfast.

29. The door (open) by itself.

30. The flower (fill) the room with a beautiful scent.

31. The seal (splash) water at the crowd.

32. Each car (undergo) a series of qualifying laps.

33. The customer (pay) his bill with a check.

34. The painter (mix) her colors carefully.

35. He (play) the guitar, the violin, and the piano like a professional.

2—Three Verbs That Cause Problems

> ● The verbs *be, have,* and *do* have special singular and plural forms.

■ When using forms of the verb *be* in the third person, remember that the verbs *is* and *was* are singular and the verbs *are* and *were* are plural.

> **Singular:** the play <u>is</u>   the actor <u>was</u>
> **Plural:**   the plays <u>are</u>   the actors <u>were</u>

■ When using forms of the verb *have* in the third person, remember that the verb *has* is singular and the verb *have* is plural.

> **Singular:** the television <u>has</u>   it <u>has</u>
> **Plural:**   the televisions <u>have</u>   they <u>have</u>

■ When using forms of the verb *do* in the third person, remember that the verb *does* is singular and the verb *do* is plural.

> **Singular:** the computer <u>does</u>   it <u>does</u>
> **Plural:**   the computers <u>do</u>   they <u>do</u>

■ Use the following forms of the verbs *be, have,* and *do* with the pronoun *I.*

> I <u>am</u>   I <u>was</u>   I <u>have</u>   I <u>do</u>

■ Use the following forms of the verbs *be, have,* and *do* with the pronoun *you.*

> you <u>are</u>   you <u>were</u>   you <u>have</u>   you <u>do</u>

■ When the verbs *be, have,* and *do* are combined with the contraction *n't,* their forms do not change.

> **Singular:** it <u>isn't</u>   it <u>hasn't</u>   he <u>doesn't</u>
> **Plural:**   they <u>aren't</u>   they <u>haven't</u>   they <u>don't</u>

Exercises

A. Write the correct verb in parentheses. Beside it, write whether it is plural or singular.

1. the dog (has, have)
2. we (is are)
3. the radio (was, were)
4. the cars (does, do)
5. the games (is, are)
6. they (was, were)
7. the clouds (isn't, aren't)
8. the book (does, do)
9. the pen (is, are)
10. the people (has, have)

B. Write each sentence, using the correct verb in parentheses.

11. The heavy trucks (was, were) in the right lane.
12. The television (does, do) not keep me from doing my homework.
13. Your letter (has, have) arrived with the check in it.
14. I (was, were) going to ask you a favor.
15. Two telephones (is, are) enough for this house.
16. You (doesn't, don't) sound like yourself.
17. My friends (has, have) a part-time job.
18. A bad storm (is, are) about to break.
19. The computer (doesn't, don't) make many mistakes.
20. You (do, does) write interesting letters.
21. The key (was, were) misplaced by my neighbor.
22. I (doesn't, don't) know what time the train arrives.
23. The taxi driver (was, were) very helpful.
24. The kittens (has, have) all been fed.
25. Six different people (has, have) told me the show is the best they have seen.
26. It (isn't, aren't) warm enough to eat outside.
27. The runners (was, were) exhausted.
28. The trees (does, do) help conceal the house.
29. The water (wasn't, weren't) clean.
30. The car (has, have) been in the repair shop.

3 – Problems with Prepositional Phrases

> ● A prepositional phrase following the subject does not affect agreement.

The subject and verb of a sentence must agree in number. When the subject and verb are next to each other, agreement is usually easy to figure out.

> The dinner (smells, ~~smell~~) delicious.
> One (is, ~~are~~) missing.

The singular verb in each sentence above agrees with the singular subject. However, it can be difficult to determine correct agreement if a prepositional phrase comes between the subject and verb.

> The dinner <u>for the runners</u> smells delicious.
> One <u>of my books</u> is missing.

The noun in each prepositional phrase above is plural. However, each verb agrees with the singular subject, not with the noun in the prepositional phrase.

A plural subject may be followed by a prepositional phrase with a singular noun. The verb again agrees with the subject of the sentence.

> The flowers <u>on that bush</u> are beautiful.
> The musicians <u>at the dance</u> were great!

An easy way to avoid agreement errors in sentences with prepositional phrases is to drop the prepositional phrase. Then look at the subject and verb by themselves.

> **Sentence:** The records <u>on the table</u> (is, are) mine.
> **Drop the Phrase:** The records (is, are) mine.
> **Subject and Verb:** records <u>are</u>

Exercises

A. If the subject in the phrase is singular, write *is*. If it is plural, write *are*.

1. Dark clouds in the sky _____
2. The kittens under the chair _____
3. The paint on the walls _____
4. Several horses in the field _____
5. The choice of the judges _____
6. Our costumes for the play _____
7. The color of the flowers _____
8. The heat from the flames _____
9. Many trees on my block _____
10. The noise from the streets _____

B. Write each sentence, using the correct verb in parentheses.

11. Computers of every kind (is, are) useful for communication.
12. Information from computers (makes, make) life easier.
13. Computers in a car can (tells, tell) whether anything is wrong.
14. A car with computers even (has, have) the ability to talk.
15. Games of every type (utilizes, utilize) computers.
16. Rides in an amusement park may (operates, operate) with the help of computers.
17. Many appliances in your kitchen may be (runs, run) by computers.
18. An airplane with several computers (is, are) easier to fly.
19. Computers in every way (affects, affect) our life.
20. The age of computers (has, have) just begun.

4 — Agreement with Compound Subjects

> ● Compound subjects joined by *and* use the plural form of the verb.
>
> ● Compound subjects joined by *or, either/or,* or *neither/nor* sometimes use the singular form of the verb and sometimes the plural.

Compound subjects share the same verb. Agreement between a compound subject and its verb requires special attention. Three rules follow.

■ When two subjects are joined by *and,* they take a plural verb. It does not matter if the subjects are both singular, both plural, or singular and plural.

> Your <u>pen</u> and <u>paper</u> are on the table.
> The <u>cups</u> and <u>saucers</u> belong on that shelf.
> The <u>perfume</u> and <u>slippers</u> were nice gifts.

■ When two singular subjects are joined by *or* or *nor,* the verb is singular. When two plural subjects are joined by *or* or *nor,* the verb is plural.

> Either <u>sleet</u> or <u>snow</u> is predicted for today.
> Neither <u>apples</u> nor <u>oranges</u> grow here.

■ If a singular subject and a plural subject are joined by *or* or *nor,* the verb agrees with the closer subject.

> The students or the <u>teacher</u> knows the schedule.
> The teacher or the <u>students</u> know the schedule.
> Neither two nickels nor a <u>dime</u> is enough.
> Neither a dime nor two <u>nickels</u> are enough.

Exercises

A. Write the correct verb in parentheses.

1. Milk and juice (is, are)
2. The plates or saucers (needs, need)
3. A pen or pencil (writes, write)
4. Neither a taxi nor a bus (goes, go)
5. One man and two women (sings, sing)
6. Either two suitcases or a trunk (is, are)
7. The trains and buses (has, have)
8. My mother and father (arrives, arrive)
9. Neither the television nor the radios (was, were)
10. Two dogs and a cat (chases, chase)

B. Write the verb in parentheses that agrees with the subject of the sentence.

11. Knowledge and information (travels, travel) in a variety of ways.
12. A signal or a wave (sends, send) information.
13. Wires or cables (carries, carry) information.
14. Laser beams and other light sources (is, are) also message carriers.
15. Waves or electrical signals (creates, create) your television picture.
16. A telephone or a teletype machine (receives, receive) messages through wires.
17. Sounds and pictures (is, are) picked up by laser beam from video discs.
18. Radios or television sets (provides, provide) most people with their information.
19. Neither magazines nor books (reaches, reach) as many people as television does.
20. Entertainment or information (comes, come) into many homes by way of a computer.

5 — Problems with Inverted Sentences

> ● The subject and verb must agree, even if the subject follows the verb.

Usually the subject comes before the verb in a sentence. When this order is reversed, the sentence is called an **inverted sentence.** The subject and verb must still agree.

> **Normal Word Order:** The cat sits under the chair.
> **Inverted Word Order:** Under the chair sits the cat.

In both sentences *cat* is the subject and *sits* is the verb. Notice in the inverted sentence that the verb *sits* comes before the subject *cat.*

Sentences that begin with the words *here, there,* and *where* are almost always inverted sentences.

> Here is the box.   Here are the boxes.
> There is the pencil.   There are the pencils.

Agreement errors often occur when the contraction for the verb *is* (*'s*) is used with the words *here, there,* and *where.*

> **Wrong:** Here's the books.   Where's my keys?
> **Right:** Here are the books. Where are my keys?

The subjects *books* and *keys* are both plural. They must be used with the plural verb *are* in both sentences.

In interrogative sentences verbs almost always come before subjects. Reverse the word order, and then look at the subject and verb by themselves.

> **Sentence:**   Where (is, are) my bicycle?
> **Reverse the Order:** My bicycle (is, are) where?
> **Subject and Verb:** bicycle <u>is</u>

Exercises

A. Write *is* if the subject is singular. Write *are* if the subject is plural.

1. Where _____ the cups and saucers?
2. On the table _____ a large red bowl.
3. Here _____ a book for you to read.
4. There _____ two people waiting for you.
5. In the mountain _____ a large cave.
6. What _____ the children's names?
7. Which way _____ they going?
8. Under the tree _____ a beautiful flower.
9. _____ your pet snake loose?
10. Here _____ five more letters to sign.
11. Where _____ the books for me to read?
12. In the building _____ several broken windows.
13. There _____ still a few people in line.
14. _____ the windows clean yet?
15. Here _____ some sandwiches for the picnic.

B. Write the sentence, using the correct verb in parentheses.

16. On the roof (sits, sit) several large birds.
17. There (flows, flow) a river through the town.
18. Where (does, do) the others want to go?
19. Under the porch (is, are) a rake.
20. What (was, were) the teacher saying?
21. Here (is, are) the papers you asked for.
22. On the bush (hangs, hang) several lovely flowers.
23. How (does, do) the music sound from across the street?
24. When (has, have) the train ever been on time from Chicago?
25. In the sky (floats, float) several large balloons.

6 — Problems with Indefinite Pronouns

> ● When an indefinite pronoun is the subject of a sentence, the pronoun and verb must agree.

Indefinite pronouns are sometimes used as subjects of sentences. Here are three rules for verb agreement with indefinite pronouns.

■ The following indefinite pronouns are always singular: *each, either, neither, anyone, anybody, anything, someone, somebody, something, one, everyone, everybody, everything, nobody, nothing, no one.* They are always used with singular verbs.

> Each of us wants to run in the race.
> Nobody laughs at a bad joke.

■ The following indefinite pronouns are always plural: *few, many, several, both.* Use plural verbs with them.

> Few of the campers leave early.
> Many of the flowers are in bloom.

■ The following indefinite pronouns are either singular or plural: *all, any, most, none, some.* You can tell whether the indefinite pronoun is singular or plural by looking at the word it refers to.

> **Singular:** Most of the street is closed.
> **Plural:**　 Most of the streets are closed.

In the first sentence, the indefinite pronoun *most* refers to the singular noun *street.* It takes the singular verb *is.* In the second sentence, *most* refers to the plural noun *streets* and takes the plural verb *are.*

Exercises

A. Write the correct verb for each of the following sentences.

1. Both of the tires (looks, look) flat.
2. Most of the road (goes, go) through the hills.
3. All of the birds (sings, sing) in the morning.
4. Someone (writes, write) very long letters.
5. Nobody (wants, want) to be the first to speak.
6. Each of the cars (looks, look) new to me.
7. None of the fruit (was, were) ripe.
8. Something (smells, smell) good enough to eat.
9. Nothing (feels, feel) as good as a cool breeze.
10. Most of the food (is, are) gone.

B. Write each of the sentences, using the correct verb in parentheses. Underline each subject.

EXAMPLE: Anyone (is, are) welcome to come along.
ANSWER: <u>Anyone</u> is welcome to come along.

11. Everyone (is, are) going to the theater.
12. Each of us (wants, want) a computer.
13. One in the crowd always (yells, yell) loudly.
14. Some of the books (is, are) in the library.
15. Most of my friends (has, have) two radios.
16. Few in the class (takes, take) notes.
17. Several of the houses (has, have) nice lawns.
18. Somebody (leaves, leave) a newspaper on my desk.
19. Both of the films (sounds, sound) interesting.
20. Neither of my television sets (is, are) working.
21. Anything with red (attracts, attract) hummingbirds.
22. All of the park (is, are) open at dawn.
23. Many in our group (has, have) cameras with them.
24. Someone over there (sees, see) me waving.
25. None of the house (is, are) painted yet.

Additional Exercises

A. Write the correct verb in parentheses.

1. The movie on television (runs, run) for two hours.
2. Video cassettes (includes, include) sound and picture.
3. Film and video tape (is, are) used in my class.
4. Some of my friends (carries, carry) radios.
5. A computer (needs, need) instructions.
6. The instructions (tells, tell) a computer what to do.
7. The instructions (is, are) called programs.
8. Here (is, are) the cans for the film.
9. Almost everyone (likes, like) computer games.
10. Where (does, do) Bill keep his tape recorder and his earphones?

B. Write the correct verb in parentheses.

11. A friend of mine (is, are) putting together her own computer system. 12. The computer (calculates, calculate) the answers to many kinds of problems. 13. The keyboard (looks, look) like a typewriter keyboard. 14. The memory unit of a computer (stores, store) information.

15. The personal computer and the monitor (forms, form) part of the system. 16. A monitor (is, are) a display screen. 17. Disk drives (reads, read) floppy disks. 18. Information (is, are) stored on and retrieved from floppy disks. 19. Disks (is, are) easy to use. 20. Janell's computer system (has, have) a printer. 21. The printer (performs, perform) like a typewriter. 22. Letters or reports (is, are) typed very quickly. 23. Her computer also (hooks, hook) up to a telephone. 24. It (communicates, communicate) with other computers this way. 25. More people (is, are) using computers every day.

Application USING AGREEMENT IN WRITING

A. Each sentence below consists of just one subject and one verb. Expand each sentence so that it has at least ten words. Add adjectives, adverbs, and prepositional phrases.

1. Telephone rings.
2. Vacation ends.
3. Choir rehearses.
4. State is growing.
5. Styles change.
6. Discussions continue.
7. Boats are sailing.
8. Popularity is increasing.
9. Plants wilted.
10. Diseases have disappeared.

B. Write complete sentences by adding to the word groups below. Make certain the subjects and verbs agree. Write the sentences in the present tense only.

11. A radio or television …
12. The clowns in the parade …
13. Some of the people …
14. The air conditioner …
15. Several of your bookcases …
16. Here on the table …
17. The airplanes in the hangars …
18. The red telephone on the desk …
19. Neither my sisters nor my brother …
20. Either the police officer or the detectives …

Using the Thesaurus

C. No machine lasts forever, including a computer. All need repairs. When you write about a manufactured item, you may often use the words *break* and *fix.* Using the Thesaurus, find three synonyms for each verb. Then write each one in a sentence. Be certain all your subjects and verbs agree.

Chapter Review

A. Write each sentence, using the correct verb.

   1. The horses (gallops, gallop) around the track.
   2. My briefcase (was, were) on the table yesterday.
   3. The roof (leaks, leak) whenever it rains.
   4. Our fans (cheers, cheer) every time our team scores.
   5. It (takes, take) two people to carry this trunk.

B. Write the correct verb in parentheses.

   6. The flower among the weeds (is, are) beautiful.
   7. Animals of every kind (lives, live) in the zoo.
   8. The clouds in the sky (moves, move) quickly.
   9. Cake with ice cream (tastes, taste) delicious.
   10. The magazine on the table (looks, look) colorful.

C. Write the correct verb in parentheses.

   11. On the porch (is, are) several chairs.
   12. Here (sits, sit) the cat on the chair.
   13. In its den (hides, hide) the scared fox.
   14. Through the sky (streaks, streak) a meteor.
   15. Where (does, do) your grandparents live?

D. Write each sentence, using the correct verb.

   16. Everyone here (likes, like) to swim.
   17. Some of the houses (is, are) empty.
   18. Few in the city (wants, want) higher property or state taxes.
   19. Each of the children (looks, look) happy.
   20. Most of the street (remains, remain) unpaved in that section of town.

Chapter Review CHALLENGE

A. There are ten errors in subject-verb agreement in the paragraph below. Write the paragraph correctly.

1. There is audiovisual centers in many schools. **2.** These centers contains many kinds of equipment. **3.** Filmstrips and cassettes is common items in audiovisual centers. **4.** Educational games also attracts much attention. **5.** Film projectors or recording equipment are often requested by the students. **6.** Some of the schools has small television studios as part of their centers. **7.** Students makes their own television programs. **8.** They broadcasts them to the classrooms. **9.** A computer, of course, keep track of it all. **10.** What do your school have in its audiovisual center?

B. Write the letter, using correct agreement.

Dear Uncle Bob,

11. Tomorrow Julie and I plans to see a multimedia show. **12.** It are being held at the new City Center building. **13.** There is three gigantic movie screens. **14.** One reflect slide projections. **15.** Another show filmstrips. **16.** The third one have moving pictures. **17.** All of them is coordinated by a computer. **18.** The taped music and narration for the show runs on twelve different tracks. **19.** During the intermission there appears some laser effects, too. **20.** It promise to be a great show.

Sincerely,

Judy

Cumulative Review

Usage

Noun Usage (pp. 136–141)
Pronoun Usage (pp. 144–151)
Adjective and Adverb Usage (pp. 158–169)
Verb Usage (pp. 176–195)
Subject-Verb Agreement (pp. 200–211)

A. Write the correct plural form of each noun.

1. one ax   two (axs, axes)
2. one radio   two (radios, radioes)
3. one son-in-law   two (son-in-laws, sons-in-law)
4. one monkey   two (monkies, monkeys)
5. one *A*   two (*A*s, *A*'s)
6. one glass   two (glass's, glasses)
7. one community   two (communitys, communities)
8. one rash   two (rashes, rashs)
9. one handful   two (handfuls, handsful)
10. one series   two (series, serieses)

B. Write each underlined noun. Label each one *singular, singular possessive, plural,* or *plural possessive.*

11. The pages of the book had turned yellow.
12. Do you think that cartoonist's comics are funny?
13. Cass's suitcases are up in the attic.
14. The women's group gave its report.
15. Bess's *o*'s are not round enough.
16. Were Mrs. Santos's replies correct?
17. Who sat on the men's hats?
18. The blades of the axes were quite dull.
19. That novelist's endings don't satisfy readers.
20. Did the Joneses see the herd of deer?

C. Write the correct pronoun in parentheses.

21. Dan and (I, me) visited the trolley museum.
22. Will you show Mother and (I, me) the puzzle?
23. It was (she, her) who wrote the poems.
24. Helen and (she, her) raise many sheep.
25. Mr. Fitz gave the oars to Donna and (I, me).
26. No one but (he, him) knew about the gold.
27. Deep in the forest labored Willie and (he, him).
28. The girls in the picture are Deidre and (I, me).
29. Make copies of it for Rebecca and (I, me).
30. Mrs. Grimaldi and (they, them) visited Dublin.
31. Both Rod and (he, him) collect old coins.
32. Give Anna and (he, him) a ride in the balloon.
33. Al went to Mexico with Harry and (they, them).
34. Terri and (we, us) refuse to believe that story.
35. Will (he and I, him and we) work at the fair, too?
36. Between you and (I, me), he doesn't work hard.
37. Jake received more applause than (she, her).
38. Success pleased Dad as much as it did (I, me).
39. Everyone except (I, me) got the question wrong.
40. It came as a surprise to all (we, us) athletes.

D. Write the correct comparative or superlative form of each adjective or adverb in parentheses.

41. This is the (unusual) house in town.
42. Tad drives (carefully) than Elliott.
43. Who is (short)—Guy, Peter, or Margaret?
44. Of the six cousins, Frances acts (friendly).
45. Wendy is the (happy) of the twins.
46. Now Arthur is (tall) than Douglas.
47. Of the track stars, Leah trains (diligently).
48. Sonia writes (persuasively) than I do.
49. Our climate is the (pleasant) in the state.
50. Of all the reports, this one is the (good).

E. Write the correct word in parentheses.

51. Your garden looks (pretty, prettily) this summer.
52. At this rate we won't (ever, never) finish.
53. The bark of this tree feels (rough, roughly).
54. Can't (nobody, anybody) solve this problem?
55. At first I (could, couldn't) hardly run a mile.
56. (Almost, Most) everyone is excited about our winning the trophy.
57. Water the flowers (thorough, thoroughly), please.
58. This has been a (real, really) fine summer.
59. He (sure, surely) must be hungry by now.
60. Have you noticed how (good, well) she draws?

F. Write the past and past participle of each verb.

61. speak	66. ride	71. know
62. talk	67. drink	72. listen
63. choose	68. write	73. throw
64. burst	69. wear	74. become
65. freeze	70. see	75. fall

G. Write the correct form of the verb in parentheses.

76. I (laid, lay) the book there yesterday.
77. Whose shoes are (laying, lying) on my bed?
78. When the people had (sat, set) down, he began.
79. Has the baby's temperature (risen, rose) higher?
80. Have they been (raising, rising) their prices?

H. Write the correct form of the verb in parentheses.

81. Everyone (knows, know) the secret code now.
82. In the iron mine (is, are) many workers.
83. Each of the girls (runs, run) quite fast.
84. Neither of the windows (is, are) open.
85. There (is, are) a golden key in the box.

86. Neither lions nor tigers (live, lives) there.
87. One box or two bagfuls (costs, cost) the same.
88. The plates and bowl (remains, remain) unwashed.
89. The flowers in the garden (smells, smell) sweet.
90. The bird in the bushes (has, have) a broken wing.

I. Each sentence has one error in usage. Write each sentence correctly.

91. Its warm enough there for the monkeys.
92. Stand between the two trees besides the wall.
93. Seven cupsful of berries are in Ross's pie.
94. The invitation was sent to there sister and me.
95. Our neighbors they own a farm in the valley.
96. The boy with all the comic books were he.
97. No one can't cook better than Jody and I.
98. Doesn't anyone have their report finished yet?
99. With whom did you see a wolves paw print?
100. Does Gus's cake or his pie taste gooder?
101. Either you or she has drank all the grape juice.
102. No one but her has seen the childrens' playthings.
103. Three communitys have already chosen the plan.
104. For whom had the old bell rang the loudest?
105. Everyone in our class's show performed good.
106. This room is sure too warm for Jason and me.
107. Have you ever heard of a more stupider plan?
108. Father looked up quick and stared at me.
109. It was lying on the desk just where you lay it.
110. A student or teacher have laid the papers here.
111. Here's the girls who can swim really well.
112. Behind the china closet hides some mice.
113. Every student in these classes have been tested.
114. He don't know anything about Ms. Wells's offer.
115. There wasn't enough apples for the members of the team to share among themselves.

UNIT FOUR

Mechanics

——— UNIT PREVIEW ———
Are Capitalization and Punctuation Important?

Capitalization and punctuation are important to your final written work. An error in capitalization or punctuation can create a poor impression and hurt the overall impact of what you have written. Capitalization and punctuation are mechanical skills. They are tools that a writer uses to communicate effectively. You should study the rules for capitalization and punctuation in this unit carefully.

Punctuation marks provide guideposts for the reader. The comma, for example, is used mostly to assist the reader, but a misplaced comma can cause writing to be misread.

Capital letters are also guideposts. They often show the reader which words in a sentence name particular persons, places, or things. Do you know which words in these sentences should be capitalized? You need to supply eight capital letters.

1. fifth avenue was the scene of the thanksgiving day parade.
2. The grand canyon is located in arizona.

Everyone is required to fill out forms. Some are short, one-page items; others are longer and more complicated, two-page or three-page forms. Schools, businesses, and organizations need information about you. You fill out forms when you apply for a driver's license, a library card, or a checking account.

Here is an example of a form you might fill out to enroll in a summer recreation program.

```
APPLICATION FOR SUMMER RECREATION PROGRAM
Full Name_____Date_____
Address_____
                   (number and street)
_____
 (city)                              (state)    (ZIP)
Telephone number (     )_____
             (area code)
Date of birth ___/___/___          Sex _____  _____
             mo   da   yr                   m        f
School now attending _____
_____ Grade _____
Parent or guardian _____
Type of recreation preferred ._____
_____
```

1. Do you know how to punctuate dates correctly? (See Chapter 11, Lesson 5.)
2. Do you know the capitalization and punctuation rules for addresses? (See Chapter 10, Lesson 2; and Chapter 11, Lesson 5.)
3. Do you know how to capitalize the name of your school? (See Chapter 10, Lesson 3.)
4. Do you know how to capitalize your parent's or guardian's name? (See Chapter 10, Lesson 1.)

After you complete this unit, you will know many of the rules for capitalization and punctuation. If you forget a rule while you are writing, you can always return to this unit for reference.

CHAPTER

10 *Capitalization*

Exploring

If I could go exploring,
Boldly I'd set forth
With Ponce de Leon in Florida,
With Lewis and Clark in the North.

I might go with Magellan
And sail around the Straits,
Or with Marco Polo to Asia
And the Chinese gates.

With Hannibal I'd cross the Alps,
With Caesar into Gaul,
With Lief Erickson to Greenland;
But I'd like best of all

To be on the Santa Maria
Or Nina or Pinta that day
When Christopher C. came sailing
Into the New World bay.

—Eve Merriam

222

1 — Capitalizing Names and Titles

A proper noun names a particular person, place, or thing. It is always capitalized. A common noun is the general name of a person, place, or thing. A common noun is not capitalized.

Capitalizing Proper Nouns

Capitalize the names of people.
> **Rosa Nogales**   **Alfred P. Wilson, Jr.**

Middle initials and the abbreviations *Jr.* and *Sr.* should be capitalized.

Capitalize titles or abbreviations that come before the names of people.
> **Dr. Sarah M. Frost**   **Doctor Sarah M. Frost**
> **Mr. Jason Randolph**   **Mrs. Helen McNeal**

Capitalize A.D. and B.C. Capitalize A.M. and P.M.
> Julius Caesar was born in 100 B.C.
> We begin at 9:00 A.M. and end at 5:00 P.M.

Capitalize the titles President and Vice-President when used alone.
> The **P**resident signed the treaty.
> The **V**ice-**P**resident entered the room.

Do not capitalize other titles unless they appear before a person's name.
> The <u>mayor</u> of Chicago will be there.

Capitalize words showing family relationships when used as titles or as substitutes for a name.
> **U**ncle **F**red and **A**unt **M**arcia moved to **B**altimore.
> I asked **M**other to come.

Do not capitalize these words if they are preceded by a possessive noun or pronoun.
> My <u>aunt</u> and <u>uncle</u> moved to Baltimore.

Exercises

A. Write the word groups with correct capitals.

1. thomas malley, jr.
2. 8:00 a.m.
3. aunt rose
4. gov. pauline smith
5. professor perry
6. uncle dominick
7. mrs. nina showner
8. 28 b.c.
9. mr. j. k. louis
10. president harding

B. Write each sentence with correct capitals.

11. Our neighbors are mr. and mrs. arnold craig.
12. Their children are arnold, jr., and joan.
13. The letter was dated a.d. 1860.
14. Did mother come to the party?
15. They set the alarm for 6:00 a.m.
16. The meeting was addressed by senator lund.
17. In 44 b.c. julius caesar was slain.
18. Does uncle arthur still live in Vermont?
19. Our family physician is dr. martin driscol.
20. She met president johnson in Miami.

C. After each sentence number in the paragraph, write the words that should be capitalized.

21. arnold craig and his family took an automobile trip. 22. Before leaving, mrs. frances craig packed clothes, their son arnie purchased film, and his sister joan bought stamps for sending postcards. 23. At 7:00 a.m. they drove to Philadelphia to see historic sites. 24. The craigs visited the University of Pennsylvania, which was founded in a.d. 1756. 25. Later joan sent a postcard to her aunt, and arnie sent one to their neighbors, dr. sarah m. frost and derrick g. frost, sr.

—2— Capitalizing Geographical Names

Capitalizing Proper Nouns
Capitalize names of cities, states, countries, and continents.

Cities:	Tel Aviv, Boston, Juneau, Los Angeles
States:	North Dakota, Minnesota, Vermont, Ohio
Countries:	Dominican Republic, Belgium, Egypt
Continents:	South America, Africa, Asia

Capitalize names of bodies of water and other names found on maps.

| *Bodies of Water:* | Lake Erie, Red Sea, Amazon River, Gulf of Mexico, Atlantic Ocean |
| *Other Map Features:* | Mammoth Cave, Cape Horn, Iberian Peninsula, Rock Creek Park, Mount Everest |

Do not capitalize unimportant words such as *of* or *on* with proper nouns.

Great Wall of China, Croton-on-Hudson

Capitalize names of buildings, monuments, and bridges.

Buildings:	World Trade Center, Sears Tower
Monuments:	Taj Mahal, Grant's Tomb, Fort Sumter
Bridges:	Golden Gate Bridge, Walt Whitman Bridge

Capitalize names of streets and highways.

| *Streets:* | Memorial Drive, Madison Avenue, Ely Place |
| *Highways:* | Pennsylvania Turnpike, Route 44, Santa Ana Freeway, Garden State Parkway |

Capitalize names of sections of the United States.

Mona was born in the Midwest.

Do not capitalize directions of the compass.

The Craigs headed <u>south</u> on their trip.

Exercises

A. Write each sentence with correct capitals.

EXAMPLE: Is mount kilimanjaro in kenya or somalia?
ANSWER: Is Mount Kilimanjaro in Kenya or Somalia?

1. In new mexico we visited carlsbad caverns.
2. Beyond the rocky mountains is the pacific ocean.
3. Civilizations grew in the nile delta.
4. Is peru east or west of the andes mountains?
5. Rainfall is precious in the southwest.
6. The sprague hotel is on north street.
7. In london she visited the british museum and st. paul's cathedral.
8. Much of his art work is in paris.
9. The city of pittsburgh is west of scranton.
10. The statue of liberty came from france.
11. The gobi desert touches china and mongolia.
12. When did she visit independence hall?
13. The virgin islands lie in the caribbean sea.
14. Major Powell explored the colorado river.
15. He left ellesmere island for the north pole.

B. After each sentence number in the paragraph, write the words that should be capitalized.

16. Having left philadelphia, the Craigs crossed both the brandywine river and the susquehanna river on their way to baltimore, maryland. 17. First they visited fort mchenry, which lies on the patapsco river, an inlet of chesapeake bay. 18. Later they went to the baltimore streetcar museum and the national aquarium. 19. The next morning they went to the flag house. 20. In the afternoon they drove on the baltimore–washington expressway on their way to washington, d.c.

3 — Capitalizing Other Names

Capitalizing Proper Nouns

Capitalize names of clubs, organizations, businesses, and institutions.

Clubs:	Elks, Rotary, Springfield Glee Club
Organizations:	American Bar Association
Businesses:	Acme Food Co., Don's Gas Service
Institutions:	Williams College, Tulane University

Do not capitalize words such as *school, college,* or *theater* unless they are used as names.

After high school I entered Colby College.

Capitalize brand names but not the products.

Clearall soap, Ford automobiles, Pledge polish

Capitalize the names of days, months, and holidays.

Days:	Tuesday, Friday, Thursday
Months:	October, June, February
Holidays:	Thanksgiving Day, Veteran's Day

Do not capitalize the names of seasons.

In the autumn the foliage is quite beautiful.

Capitalize names of languages, races, and nationalities.

Languages:	French, German, Chinese
Races:	Asian, Polynesian
Nationalities:	Greek, Italian, Bolivian

Do not capitalize names of school subjects except languages or those followed by a number.

She took history, Spanish, and Algebra II.

Capitalize names of historical events, periods, or documents.

Events:	Revolutionary War, Louisiana Purchase
Periods:	Renaissance, Bronze Age
Documents:	Bill of Rights, Magna Charta

Exercises

A. Write the word groups with correct capitals.

1. declaration of independence
2. french II and english history
3. harlem renaissance
4. age of enlightenment
5. ivory soap
6. massachusetts institute of technology
7. girl scouts of america
8. cherry microcomputers, inc.
9. smith college
10. thursday, april 1
11. mother's day
12. latin, greek, and early egyptian
13. league of women voters
14. american wax and dye company
15. boston tea party

B. After each sentence number in the paragraph, write the words that should be capitalized.

16. On tuesday, the day before the fourth of july, the Craigs visited the smithsonian institution in Washington, D.C. **17.** That afternoon, in the library of congress, they saw the constitution of the united states and the bill of rights. **18.** "We studied these documents in our american history class," said Arnie. **19.** In the evening the Craigs heard the gonzaga high school band, the howard university glee club, and a pianist from american university at the john f. kennedy center for the performing arts. **20.** Before they went to sleep, Arnie and Joan each drank a glass of cold schweppes ginger ale.

4 – Capitalizing First Words and Certain Parts of Speech

Capitalizing First Words

Capitalize the first word of a sentence.
      At night the city lights shone brightly.
      Too many cooks spoil the broth.

Capitalize the first word in a line of poetry.
      By the rude bridge that arched the flood,
      Their flag to April's breeze unfurled,
      Here once the embattled farmers stood
      And fired the shot heard round the world.
Not all poets use capital letters to begin lines of poetry. This is particularly true of modern poets.

Capitalize the first word of a direct quotation.
      Marcia said, "**P**lease serve the potatoes first."
Do not capitalize the first word of an indirect quotation.
      John said that <u>he</u> would do as Marcia had asked.

Capitalize the first word, words such as *Sir*, and names of people addressed in letter salutations.   Dear **H**enry, Dear **S**ir, Dear **M**adam,
Capitalize only the first word in letter closings.   **L**ove, **Y**ours truly, **S**incerely yours,

Capitalizing Certain Parts of Speech
Capitalize the pronoun *I*.   "What a sight **I** saw!" exclaimed Miriam.
Capitalize proper adjectives.   We met the **N**orwegian ambassador.

Exercises

A. Write the sentences, using capital letters. Some are lines of poetry.

EXAMPLE: he took a final test in english prose.
ANSWER: He took a final test in English prose.

1. the farmer's son was stuck in the mud.
2. a few people in my class know russian history.
3. o friends!
   with whom my feet have trod.
4. "where are the car keys?" asked Maria.
5. "true ease in writing comes from art, not chance
   as those move easiest who have learned to dance."
6. this french cheese is delicious.
7. earlier this year i visited my british cousin.
8. the grocery store sells kenyan coffee, swiss choco-
   late, and hawaiian pineapples.
9. "dear sir," began the applicant's letter.
10. hector said, "i will try out for the track team and
    the football team."

B. Joan Craig sent a postcard to her Aunt Doris. Write her message using correct capitals.

dear aunt doris,
   we are now in Williamsburg, Virginia. mother took us
to see many of the old houses. dad said, "i would like to
go, but i really don't feel well."
   in one house we met the british ambassador who quoted
some lines by the poet Longfellow:
       "all houses wherein men have lived and died
       are haunted houses."
                    your niece,
                    Joan

5 – Capitalizing Other Titles

The titles of written works, movies, and works of art are capitalized in writing. Certain religious terms are also capitalized.

Capitalizing Other Titles

Capitalize the first word and all important words in titles.

Books:	The Yearling, A Tale of Two Cities
Stories:	"The Cask of Amontillado"
Articles:	"The Reluctant Dragon"
Poems:	"The Skeleton in Armor," "Annabel Lee"
Magazines:	Popular Mechanics, Time
Plays:	The Skin of Our Teeth, Hamlet
Newspapers:	St. Louis Post-Dispatch
Movies:	Gone with the Wind
Paintings:	Mona Lisa, American Gothic
Works of Music:	Aida, "Yesterday"

Unimportant words, such as articles, coordinating conjunctions, and prepositions, are usually not capitalized unless they are the first word in the title.

Capitalizing Certain Religious Terms

Capitalize words referring to the Deity, the holy books, religions, and denominations.

Deity:	God, Allah, the Father
Holy Books:	the Bible, the Torah
Religions:	Christianity, Islam
Denominations:	Roman Catholic, Baptist

Do not capitalize the word *god* when referring to deities in ancient mythologies.

> Odin was the chief god in Norse mythology.

Exercises

A. Write the word groups with correct capitals.

1. *to sir with love* (movie)
2. "the rime of the ancient mariner" (poem)
3. *washington post* (newspaper)
4. *all quiet on the western front* (book)
5. *carmen* (work of music)
6. *christina's world* (painting)
7. "sea cucumbers are not a menace" (article)
8. *journal of medicine* (magazine)
9. "the most dangerous game" (story)
10. *you can't take it with you* (play)

B. Write each sentence with correct capitals.

11. The ecumenical society meets here on Sunday.
12. We watched *i love lucy* on TV last night.
13. Angie played the lead part in *a doll's house.*
14. In some religions god is called jehovah.
15. His article, called "how the mind works," was printed in *science* magazine.
16. We read an excerpt from her story "south of the border" in *newsweek* magazine.
17. There was an article in *time* about the bible.
18. Maria loves the song the "st. louis blues."
19. I'm reading the book *johnny tremaine.*
20. The koran is the holy book of islam.
21. The class saw *the sound of music* yesterday at Radio City Music Hall.
22. Longfellow wrote "the wreck of the hesperus."
23. He stood and sang "the star-spangled banner."
24. *"the lion, the witch, and the wardrobe* is an exciting book," said Mrs. Barker.
25. Winslow Homer painted the *herring net.*

6 — Writing Numbers

Writing Out Numbers

Write out numbers that are made up of fewer than three words.

> Out of **one hundred** stamps **ninety-four** were left.
> The workers counted **437** new job applications.

Write out a number that begins a sentence or rewrite the sentence.

> **Three hundred fifty** sheep grazed nearby.
> In the meadow grazed **350** sheep.

Write out ordinal numbers. Ordinal numbers are the names for numbers such as *first, tenth*, and *fifth*.

> The **third** person to arrive received a prize.

Write out approximate times of day.

> We'll meet at **quarter past** or **half past three.**

Express exact times as numerals.

> The red alert signal sounded at **3:51** A.M.

In dialogue write out all numbers except dates.

> Minerva said, "All **seven hundred two** students graduated on May **30, 1981.**"

Writing Numbers as Arabic Numerals

Write dates as numerals.

> The Martians landed on October **12, 1999.**

Write divisions of written material as numerals.

> Chapter **4**   lesson **19**   line **12**   item **42**

Write house numbers and room numbers as numerals.

> Raul lives at **41** Walnut Street in Room **301.**

Exercises

A. Write each sentence, using correct number forms.

1. 75 couples attended the dance.
2. On July sixth we ate salmon and fresh peas.
3. Mrs. Argent lives at ten Mulberry Street.
4. Did you find any errors on page nine?
5. Wilmer asked, "Will 7 of you come with me?"
6. Every 3rd student raised a hand.
7. Chapter four is the shortest in the book, and Chapter twenty is the longest.
8. Our meeting is scheduled for June tenth.
9. Is Room sixty-five or Room sixty-seven yours for the conference?
10. Item six on page fourteen is incomplete.
11. Spring arrives officially at two seventeen A.M.
12. Nikki dated her letter May ninth, 1983.
13. Alexander the Great lived in the 4th century.
14. All 32 scouts earned their 15 merit badges before leaving for summer camp.
15. We should be there by 4 o'clock on January twenty-third, nineteen hundred eighty-five.

B. In the paragraph write the correct number forms after each sentence number.

16. The Craigs left at 2 o'clock on July third, 1983. **17.** 1st they drove to Philadelphia, then to Baltimore, and 3rd to Washington, D.C. **18.** They had to fill the car with 20 gallons of gasoline, and they refilled it 2 more times on the way. **19.** In Washington the Craigs visited old friends at forty-eight Tyson Street. **20.** Chapter 3 of the Williamsburg guide book pointed out three hundred seventy-eight places of interest to visit.

Additional Exercises

A. Write each sentence, using correct capitals.

1. "the tell-tale heart" was written by edgar allan poe.
2. abraham lincoln delivered the gettysburg address on november 19, 1863.
3. break, break, break,
   on thy cold gray stones, O sea.
4. try carpet fresh cleaner on that carpet.
5. on march 20 spring will finally come.
6. we all take biology, american history, and art I at arden high school.
7. gil speaks spanish as well as rosa ortiz does.
8. these english muffins are for breakfast.
9. just east of here is the st. lawrence river.
10. gutzon borglum worked high on mt. rushmore.

B. After each sentence number in the paragraph, write the words that should be capitalized.

11. the craigs spent five days at the williamsburg inn. 12. they drove on the colonial parkway to the information center. 13. the colonial williamsburg foundation was set up to preserve the city, which was once the capital of virginia. 14. next they visited the robert carter house, where governor dinwiddie had once lived. 15. they also went to market square to see the courthouse. 16. the declaration of independence was once proclaimed from the courthouse. 17. the craigs walked east on duke of gloucester street to see other sites. 18. then they had lunch at the king's arms tavern. 19. at the college of william and mary, uncle bob was a professor of literature. 20. joan said, "i think williamsburg shows what life was like in the american colonial period."

Application

Have you ever received a check, perhaps on your birthday or on some other occasion? If you have, you know that when you cashed the check, you received money in return. A check that is correctly made out and signed is just the same as money. Therefore it is important to make out checks carefully. Study the sample check below.

```
                    SAMPLE—NOT VALID              101
                           (1) May 5,    19 86
(2)
PAY TO THE   The Shoe Tree        $ 45.00  (3)
ORDER OF
(4) Forty-five and 00/100 ~~~~~~  DOLLARS
             Biddle Savings Bank
(5)
MEMO  Shoes        (6) Teresa Blake
```

Notice the places that are filled in on the check.
1. The date is written on line 1.
2. The name of the person or business to whom you are writing the check is written on line 2.
3. The amount of the check in Arabic numerals is written on line 3.
4. The amount of the check in words is written on line 4. It should be the same amount as in item 3. Notice that the amount in cents is written in numerals.
5. The reason for writing the check is written on line 5.
6. The check writer's signature is written on line 6.

Exercise

Copy the sample check above but without the six items that are handwritten. Write the check to the Austin Department Store to pay for a radio you bought for $79.00. Use today's date.

Chapter Review

A. Write each sentence, capitalizing the proper nouns that need capitals.

1. On saturday agnes m. cloud finished her job.
2. The senator spoke with president roosevelt.
3. My mother and aunt aggie did all the catering.
4. Here is a message for dr. millicent barnes.
5. philip, try to be here by 8:00 P.M. tomorrow.
6. The capital of india is new delhi.
7. The bosphorus is a strait between the black sea and the sea of marmara.
8. The pyramid of cheops is in giza, egypt.
9. We visited san francisco's golden gate park.
10. The white house is on pennsylvania avenue.

B. Write each sentence, capitalizing the proper nouns.

11. One canadian holiday is dominion day.
12. A famous president was shot in ford's theater.
13. I use dove soap, made by lever brothers.
14. Enid took ancient history, french III, and geometry this year.
15. The magna charta is in the british museum.

C. Write each title, capitalizing the words that need capitals.

16. *the bridge of san luis rey*
17. *news of the week* magazine
18. *the kid from tompkinsville*
19. "introducing a computer and its language"
20. *peter and the wolf*

Chapter Review CHALLENGE

Write Joan's letter, using correct capitalization.

august 20, 1983

dear aunt elena,

for my graduation present my father took us to see atlanta. we left july 3. it was a beautiful day for driving over the george washington bridge. we drove on the new jersey turnpike first, and then we drove south on other highways. crossing all those rivers, such as the susquehanna and the potomac, and seeing the appalachian mountains in the distance gave us an idea of how vast and impressive america is. indeed, it's hard to believe that europe or asia are as beautiful.

in washington, d.c., we visited the washington monument, the senate office building, and the supreme court. among other documents, we saw the constitution and the bill of rights. at the library of congress, famous books were displayed, such as walt whitman's book of poems *leaves of grass.*

in atlanta we saw that famous painting the cyclorama of the *battle of atlanta.* we visited the birthplaces of presidents. while driving back, we stopped at cape hatteras, at roanoke island (where we saw the musical play *the lost colony*), and at natural bridge in virginia.

now we're home again at 171 shoreham road. i start at sarah lawrence college just before labor day. arnie, of course, has one more year in high school. father is back at diggs brothers, inc., and mother is doing her work for the presbyterian church. i had time to visit all my friends at the booster's club. arnie says, "hello."

much love,
Joan L. Craig

11 *Punctuation*

Comma in the Sky

A comma hung above the park,
a shiny punctuation mark;
we saw it curving in the dark
the night the moon was new.

A period hung above the bay,
immense though it was far away;
we saw it at the end of day
the night the moon was full.

—*Aileen Fisher*

1 – **End Marks** ─────────────────

> • **End marks** are punctuation marks that show where a sentence ends.

Periods   Use a period at the end of a declarative sentence. A declarative sentence makes a statement.

> Bismarck is the capital of North Dakota.

Use a period at the end of an imperative sentence. An imperative sentence makes a command or request.

> Don't pull the dog's tail. (a command)
> Please open the window. (a request)

Use a period after abbreviations and initials. Use periods with A.M. and P.M.

> Dr. Mary M. Clarke lives in Blakestown.
> Jill met me at 3:15 P.M. on Hillside Avenue.

Question Marks   Use a question mark at the end of an interrogative sentence. An interrogative sentence asks a question.

> When was Thomas Edison born?
> Who won the World Series in 1964?

Exclamation Marks   Use an exclamation mark at the end of an exclamatory sentence. An exclamatory sentence expresses strong feeling.

> My books are falling!
> He won first prize in the contest!

Use an exclamation mark at the end of an imperative sentence that expresses strong feeling.

> Watch out for the puddle!

Exercises

A. Write the sentences with the correct end marks.

1. Mom used to collect matchbook covers
2. How long ago was that
3. She was a teenager
4. Wow! That was a long time ago
5. Don't be rude
6. The matchbook covers had flowers printed on them
7. Mom organized them by type of flower
8. She also arranged them by color
9. How many did she finally collect
10. She collected a few hundred
11. You've got to be kidding
12. How did she get so many
13. She found some She traded with friends, too
14. Please tell me how I can start a collection
15. It's easy You have enough records to open a store

B. Write the paragraph with the correct end marks.

Do you know anything about stamp collecting In the first place, the study and collection of stamps is called philately It probably was started in Great Britain in 1840 In that year the British government produced the first official postage stamp Imagine owning one of those original stamps It would be worth thousands and thousands of dollars Stamp collecting is an enjoyable hobby, even if your stamps are not worth a fortune There are so many different stamps that it is probably best to limit the ones you collect For example, you might choose to collect the stamps of just one country Which country would you choose

2 — Commas That Separate

> ● Use a **comma** to separate items in a series and to separate the parts of a compound sentence.

Commas in a Series Unlike an end mark, a comma stands for a pause in a writer's thought. If you read without pausing, you will be confused. A comma makes writing easier to understand.

Use a comma to separate items in a series. A series is made up of three or more items. The items may be single words or groups of words.

> Dan is allergic to strawberries, fish, and oranges.
> I ate my lunch, rode my bike, and walked two miles.

Do not use a comma after the last item in a series.

> Lori, Brad, and Dale were at home today.

Commas in Compound Sentences Use a comma before the conjunction that joins the parts of a compound sentence.

> The magician performed many dazzling tricks, and her daughter assisted her.
> We wanted to go to the ball game, but the game was canceled because of the storm.

Do not use a comma before a conjunction in a short compound sentence.

> The dog barked and it yelped.
> They sang and they danced.

Do not use a comma to separate a compound verb.

> The singer bowed to the audience and sang again.
> The tennis player jumped and hit the ball.

Exercises

A. Write each sentence, adding commas where necessary. If a sentence needs no commas, write *correct.*

1. Many people collect stamps, coins, or autographs.
2. Others collect cans strings or ticket stubs.
3. Amy collects and sells mugs.
4. She also collects thimbles spoons and music boxes.
5. She wants to start more collections but she has run out of shelf space.
6. Tia collects statues of glass china wood and metal.
7. Animal statues are very popular and she adores them.
8. Mr. Burke collects and repairs owl statues.
9. He likes owls but he cannot collect real ones.
10. Plastic, clay, and crystal owls appear on his shelf.

B. Write each paragraph, adding commas where needed.

11. Many people collect magazines and they don't throw them out. 12. Collectors of *National Geographic* magazine have issues from the sixties fifties and even the forties! 13. Old issues turn up in doctors' dentists' and lawyers' offices. 14. Old copies have outdated information but collectors do not care. 15. Collectors compete for these old copies and they try to find the oldest copies. 16. They advertise for these old issues and they attend conventions. 17. Very old issues are valuable but what real collector would want to sell?

18. Probably no one will want to collect *Pet Rock News Fly-Fishing Weekly* or *Great Sardine Recipes.* 19. Some people believe computers may turn printed matter into antiques and they save *any* magazine. 20. Magazines books and newspapers may soon become items of the past.

3 — Commas for Appositives and Nouns of Direct Address

> ● Use commas to set off appositives and nouns of direct address.

Appositives Use commas to set off most appositives. Appositives explain the meaning of nouns that directly precede them. Appositives often include prepositional phrases.

> Ed, my friend, lives upstairs.
> Juneau, the capital of Alaska, is by the water.
> The Pauls, our neighbors, are moving.

Do not use commas with an appositive when it is part of a proper name or when it is needed to identify the noun it follows.

> Richard the Lion-Hearted   his friend Tony

Nouns of Direct Address Use commas to set off nouns of direct address. You often use a person's name when you speak. The person's name is called a noun of direct address. It may appear anywhere in a sentence.

> Mr. Diaz, may we go to the beach tomorrow?
> I do not know, Sue, if I can come to the party.
> Is something on your mind, Barry?

A noun of direct address may also be a nonspecific name that refers to a person.

> Excuse me, Sir, but could you tell me what time it is?
> Waiter, may we have a menu.

When a noun of direct address appears in the middle of a sentence, it is both preceded and followed by commas.

Exercises

A. Write each sentence, adding commas where necessary. If a sentence needs no commas, write *correct.*

1. Class this is Mrs. Helen Parker our guest speaker.
2. She has brought a package with her.
3. It contains an unusual collection boys and girls.
4. Class it is nice to be here.
5. Jill my niece first started this collection.
6. She once asked me, "Aunt Helen only boys have cards to collect."
7. "What do you mean Jill?" I asked.
8. "Baseball cards are collected mostly by boys."
9. "Jill girls collect baseball cards, too."
10. "Girls want cards about female athletes."

B. Write the paragraph, adding commas where necessary. Underline each appositive.

11. Some U.S. Treasury Department medallions for 1982 have Louis Armstrong the jazz musician on them. 12. Numismatists coin collectors will enjoy them. 13. Medallions are like coins but are larger. 14. Another difference is that medallions are made of gold a precious metal. 15. United States coins metal money are not made of gold. 16. The places that make coins mints are forbidden to make coins from gold. 17. The Bureau of the Mint an agency of the Treasury Department is in charge of producing money and medals. 18. There are mints in San Francisco, Philadelphia, and Denver three of America's largest cities. 19. Gold bullion gold in the shape of bars is kept at Fort Knox in Kentucky. 20. The Secretary of the Treasury a member of the President's Cabinet is director of the bureau.

4 — **Commas After Introductory Words and to Set Off Interrupters**

> ● Use a comma after introductory words and to set off words or expressions that interrupt the sentence.

Introductory Words   Use a comma after words such as *yes, no, well,* and *why* at the beginning of a sentence.

> Yes, I think you're right.
> Why, I didn't recognize him!

Interrupters   Parenthetical expressions are interrupting words that are added to a sentence for extra emphasis or clarity. Some parenthetical expressions are listed below.

of course	by the way	I suppose (guess, hope,
after all	to be fair	think)
however	for example	to tell the truth
in fact	in addition	in my opinion
indeed	furthermore	to say the least
therefore	besides	on the other hand

Parenthetical expressions may appear anywhere in a sentence.

> On the other hand, you are hardworking.
> That movie, in my opinion, was wonderful.

Parenthetical expressions can be dropped from a sentence without changing its meaning.

> Kyle, after all, won the election fairly.
> Kyle won the election fairly.

When a parenthetical expression is in the middle of a sentence, it is both preceded and followed by commas.

Exercises

A. Write each sentence, adding commas where necessary.

1. Yes there are people who collect old school books.
2. Many such collectors by the way are not teachers.
3. In fact many collectors do not keep old texts for their educational value.
4. Old textbooks after all have much to offer.
5. Of course we can learn about people in the past.
6. In addition I like the old-fashioned printing.
7. In fact some of the subjects are the same as ours.
8. Many things have changed however.
9. Well textbooks are no longer illustrated with woodcuts.
10. In my opinion these textbooks are valuable.

B. Write the paragraph, adding commas where necessary. Some sentences are correct.

11. Well I didn't know that old comic books can be valuable, or I wouldn't have thrown mine out! 12. My brother and I kept our *Classics Illustrated* and *Superman* comics for many years. 13. Our mother on the other hand was not interested. 14. In fact she could not wait for us to get rid of them. 15. She did not enjoy reading comics very much. 16. She was we guessed not thrilled about dusting piles of comics. 17. To tell the truth we did have too many. 18. Yes the day came when even we thought we had too many. 19. There was a question of age after all. 20. I mean the age of the comics as well as our ages. 21. Many comics had yellowed for example. 22. In addition many pages were torn or loose. 23. We could not have kept all of them of course. 24. We should have held on to some of them. 25. To be honest I sometimes still get the urge to read them.

5 — Other Uses of Commas

- Use a comma to separate items in dates and addresses.
- Use a comma with certain letter parts.

Commas in Dates and Addresses Use a comma to separate items in dates and addresses.

> Sunday, April 17, 1983   March 17, 1977
> 24 West Elm Street, Brockton, MA   02401

Notice that you do not use a comma between the state and the ZIP code in an address. The ZIP code number should be written a few spaces after the state unless it is included in a sentence.

Use a comma after the last part of a date or an address when they are included in a sentence.

> April 23, 1616, was the day William Shakespeare died.
> A bill from 44 Yale Avenue, Tulsa, OK 74136,
>   came today in the mail.

Do not use a comma between the month and the year if no specific day is given.

> December 1985   May 1957

Commas with Letter Parts Commas are used with certain parts of a letter. Use a comma after the salutation of a friendly letter.

> Dear José,   Dear Justin,

Use a comma after the closing of a friendly or a business letter.

> Love,   Yours truly,   Sincerely yours,

Exercises

A. Write each sentence, adding commas where necessary.

1. On February 9 1964 Mom was one of the thousands who welcomed the Beatles to New York New York.
2. Mom was born on June 27 1946 in the Bronx New York.
3. She lived at 840 Grand Concourse Bronx NY.
4. Paul McCartney was born on June 18 1942.
5. He was born in Liverpool England.
6. Ringo Starr was born in July 1940 and John Lennon was born in October 1940.
7. George Harrison's birthdate is February 23 1943.
8. Mom and some friends went to Atlantic City New Jersey to see the Beatles in August 1964.
9. On June 4 1968 and September 7 1970 Mom went to St. John's Wood London England to look for Paul McCartney.
10. John Lennon died December 8 1980 in New York.

B. Write Randi's letter, adding commas where needed.

September 14 1984

Dear Shawn

The reason I did not answer your letter earlier is that you sent your letter to my old address. We do not live at 212 Hill Road Reading PA 19610 anymore. Our new address is 8422 Lyons Place Philadelphia PA 19142.

Thanks very much for the beautiful stamps from the Caribbean. Did you get them in San Juan Puerto Rico or in the West Indies? They're already in my album.

Affectionately yours

Randi

6 – Quotation Marks

> ● Use **quotation marks** to enclose a person's exact words.

Direct Quotations   A direct quotation is enclosed within quotation marks. It is often separated from the rest of the sentence by a comma. Use a comma *after* a quotation and *inside* the quotation marks if the quotation begins a sentence. Do not use a comma if the quotation ends with a question or an exclamation mark.

> "The library is closed today," said Andy's mother.
> "Are you sure of that?" asked Andy.

A direct quotation begins with a capital letter. Use a comma *before* a quotation and *outside* the quotation marks if the quotation ends a sentence. Periods should be placed inside closing quotation marks.

> Toni said, "My report card is in my book."

Place a question mark or an exclamation mark inside the closing quotation marks of a quotation that is a question or an exclamation. Otherwise place it outside.

> Alicia exclaimed, "What a beautiful baby!"
> Did you say, "I am too tired to go out"?

Do not use quotation marks with an indirect quotation.

> **Indirect:** Marc suggested that we raise money.
> **Direct:** Marc said, "Let's raise money."

Quotation Marks with Titles   Use quotation marks to enclose titles of works like those listed below.

> **Short stories:** "The Car"   **Songs:** "Yesterday"
> **Poems:** "The Road Not Taken"   **Chapters:** "First Fear"

Exercises ————————————————————————

A. Write each sentence, adding quotation marks where necessary.

1. What's in your collection of strange but true facts today? asked Wendy.
2. Paul said, Try the world's worst tongue twister.
3. I'd like to hear that, Wendy remarked.
4. The sixth sick sheik's sixth sheep's sick, Paul said.
5. Wendy exclaimed, I can't even say it slowly!
6. Here are some more facts, Paul went on.
7. The *Apollo 9* astronauts sang a song in space on March 8, 1969, Paul said.
8. This chapter in the book is called Unique Facts.
9. Happy Birthday is sung frequently in English.
10. He said, Of course, Thomas Jefferson had red hair.

B. Write each sentence, adding quotation marks and commas where necessary.

11. Paul read the short story Wonderful Words.
12. Paul said that *apple* is one of the oldest words in the English language.
13. Wendy said Yes, and Mandarin is spoken by at least 660 million people, more than any other language.
14. That's right, and English is next Paul continued.
15. Paul said that millions of people speak English.
16. Wendy added English contains about 490,000 words.
17. Did you like the word with twenty-nine letters, which is one of the longest words in English? Wendy asked.
18. Quick, pronounce it for me teased Paul.
19. She laughed Pick one of the other 489,999 words.
20. I prefer floccipaucinihilipilification Paul said.

7 — Divided Quotations

> ● Sometimes a direct quotation is divided into two or more parts.

Divided Quotations A speaker's words may be divided into parts by other words. If the second part of the divided quotation is a separate sentence, begin it with a capital letter, and enclose it with quotation marks.

> "It is warm outside," said Lou. "I do not need a coat."

Do not begin the second part of a divided quotation with a capital letter if that part is not a separate sentence. Put a comma after the first part of the quotation, and enclose that part with quotation marks. Begin the second part of the quotation with a small letter, and enclose that part with quotation marks also.

> "He is," said Lynn, "at the bus stop in the morning."
> "Well," Terry said, "it is about time you came."

Dialogue A conversation between two people is a dialogue. Start a new paragraph each time another speaker begins talking.

> "*Deltiologist* is the word for today," said Sue.
> "I know what that means," replied Chad. "You are talking about a place to buy sandwiches, right?"

Do not put quotation marks around every sentence spoken by the same person. Put quotation marks around the entire uninterrupted speech.

> Sue laughed and said, "You are funny, Chad. That is a delicatessen! A deltiologist collects postcards!"

Exercises

A. Write each sentence, adding quotation marks, commas, and capital letters where necessary.

1. Then said José there is a man in California who owns more than 1,000 different credit cards.
2. He must exclaimed Stacy have a large wallet!
3. Never mind that José responded. can you imagine the size of his monthly bills?
4. Actually Stacy said it is an inexpensive collection.
5. Just how José questioned do you figure that?
6. After all Stacy explained it costs only the yearly fee for each card, if a card has one.
7. That is true José agreed but it is expensive if you buy things.
8. Plastic cards said Stacy do not seem like money.
9. You are right José said. paper money is special.
10. Actually, what I would miss replied Stacy would be seeing the presidents on the bills.

B. In the following dialogue, write each quotation as a divided quotation.

"Did you hear about the dentist who kept all the teeth he had pulled for thirty-six years?" asked José.

"Why did he do that? Was he going to make a necklace?" asked Stacy.

"Once he pulled them, I guess he thought they were his," replied José.

Stacy remarked, "Maybe that is true. After all, what could the patients do with the teeth?"

"What could he do with more than two million teeth?" questioned José.

"Well, I am sure he made a world record," said Stacy.

8 — Italics and Underlining

> ● **Italics** are letters that lean to the right in printed material—*italics.* In writing, these words are underlined.

The titles of books, magazines, newspapers, movies, plays, paintings, and operas should be underlined in handwriting or in typing. This is true also for names of planes, trains, ships, and spacecraft. In printed materials these titles and names appear in *italics.*

Books: *The Phantom Tollbooth*

Newspapers: *The New York Times*

Magazines: *Newsweek*

Operas: *The Magic Flute*

Plays: *Othello*

Movies: *Star Wars*

Paintings: *The Starry Night*

Ships: the *Delta*

Exercises

A. Write the following titles and names. Use underlining for italics or quotation marks.

1. The Outsiders (book)
2. E.T.: The Extra-Terrestrial (movie)
3. Boston Globe (newspaper)
4. Family Reunion (chapter)
5. Sports Illustrated (magazine)
6. Amahl and the Night Visitors (opera)
7. The Pit and the Pendulum (story)
8. Old Ironsides (ship)
9. Romeo and Juliet (play)
10. Ribbon in the Sky (song)
11. Roots (book)
12. Sunflowers (painting)
13. The Elephant Man (play)
14. Jabberwocky (poem)
15. Lady Sings the Blues (movie)

B. After each sentence number in the paragraph, write the words that should be printed in italics. Then underline them.

16. I walked to the Louvre Museum in Paris, France, carrying my copy of the International Herald Tribune. 17. I saw the famous painting Arrangement in Gray and Black No. 1: Portrait of the Painter's Mother, commonly called Whistler's Mother, by James Whistler, an American. 18. Later I saw Bizet's opera Carmen at the Paris Opera House, a world-famous theater. 19. The only thing I saw that did not need translation was the Marx Brothers' film A Night at the Opera. 20. Someday I would like to return to Europe and cruise on the Mediterranean in a ship such as the Golden Odyssey.

9 — Semicolons and Colons

- Use a **semicolon** to join the parts of a compound sentence when conjunctions are not used.

- Use a **colon** between the hour and the minute in time, after the salutation of a business letter, and before a list of items.

Semicolons Use a semicolon to join independent clauses in a compound sentence when the clauses are not joined by a conjunction such as *and, but, or,* or *nor.*

> Leslie read a book; then she visited her friend Sam.
> It was raining; Taro didn't take his umbrella.

Colons Use a colon as shown below for time, after salutations, and before lists.

> **Time:** 10:45 P.M. 6:17 A.M. 4:00 P.M.
> **Salutation:** Gentlemen: Dear Ms. Goldman:
> **List:** To operate the elevator proceed as follows: press button labeled Close Door, press button for your floor, press Start button.

When you write a list of items in a sentence, try to use a phrase such as *the following* or *as follows.* This phrase will help you use colons correctly.

> Use the following items: pens, ink, and paper.

Do not use a colon immediately after a verb or a preposition. Either leave out the colon or reword the sentence.

> **Wrong:** According to his horoscope, Chris's lucky days are: Tuesday, Friday, and Saturday.
> **Right:** According to his horoscope, Chris's lucky days are Tuesday, Friday, and Saturday.
> **Right:** According to his horoscope, Chris's lucky days are as follows: Tuesday, Friday, and Saturday.

Exercises

A. Write the sentences, adding semicolons where needed.

1. Dr. John Chung spoke he told of his collection.
2. The valuable collection of antique children's books was guarded no one could touch them.
3. Few children's books existed before 1650 even one century later not many were printed.
4. Early children's books did not entertain they simply preached.
5. Today that is not true children's books are fun.

B. Write the sentences, adding colons where necessary.

6. Dr. Chung began at exactly 3 30 this afternoon.
7. He talked about several things nursery rhymes, jokes and riddles, and educational books.
8. Authors of children's books included the following the brothers Grimm, Hans Christian Andersen, and Andrew Lang.
9. Dr. Chung left at 6 15 on his way to his next talk.
10. He will be in these cities Tulsa, Boston, and Reno.

C. These sentences are incorrectly punctuated. Write them and punctuate them correctly.

11. Many early children's books were printed in: New York, London, and Boston.
12. The early books were often instructional; and they consisted of the alphabet, spelling, or arithmetic.
13. Some of these books were: *Jack Jingle, The Good Child's Illustrated Alphabet,* and *The Tragical Death of an Apple Pie,* an alphabet book.
14. *American Pictorial Primer,* of about 1825, helped children learn: reading, spelling, and character.
15. These books weren't fun; but they were needed.

10—Apostrophes

> • **Apostrophes** show ownership and the omission of letters in contractions.

Use an apostrophe with the possessive form of a noun. The possessive form of a noun shows ownership.

1. To write the possessive form of a singular noun, add an apostrophe and s (*'s*).

boy	person	Maria	Mrs. Simmons
boy's	person's	Maria's	Mrs. Simmons's

2. To write the possessive form of a plural noun that ends in *s*, add only an apostrophe (*'*).

workers	babies	runners	bees
workers'	babies'	runners'	bees'

3. To write the possessive form of a plural noun that does not end in *s*, add an apostrophe and s (*'s*).

women	people	mice	children
women's	people's	mice's	children's

Use an apostrophe with a contraction. Some letters are left out when the two words are combined. The apostrophe takes the place of those letters.

1. Some contractions are formed by combining verbs with the word *not.*

is not (isn't)	has not (hasn't)	do not (don't)

2. Contractions are also formed by combining nouns or pronouns with verbs such as *am, is,* or *will.*

I am (I'm)	she will (she'll)	we would (we'd)
he had (he'd)	you have (you've)	who is (who's)

Exercises

A. Write the possessive form of each noun.

1. men	**6.** oxen	**11.** rhinoceros
2. family	**7.** singers	**12.** Mr. Hess
3. dog	**8.** Sonia	**13.** horses
4. teachers	**9.** painter	**14.** children
5. girl	**10.** writers	**15.** lawyer

B. In the sentences below write each group of under-lined words as either a contraction or a possessive form with an apostrophe.

EXAMPLE: Ken <u>has not</u> seen <u>the shoes of his sister</u>.
ANSWER: hasn't, his sister's shoes

16. <u>The camera of my friend</u> <u>does not</u> take good pictures without a flash attachment.
17. <u>I am</u> going to the museum to see <u>the paintings of the artists</u>.
18. <u>The contributions of the alumni</u> <u>are not</u> enough to pay for a new addition to the school.
19. <u>Who will</u> go to <u>the picnic of the fire fighters</u> at Mountainview Park?
20. <u>They had</u> given many performances to <u>the delight of their fans</u>.
21. <u>Have not</u> any of the guests arrived as yet at <u>the party of Billy</u>?
22. <u>The house of Mr. Jones</u> <u>could not</u> have been any closer to the river.
23. When she goes to the library, <u>she will</u> return <u>the library books of her sister</u>.
24. <u>The letter of his brother</u> <u>did not</u> arrive until the day before yesterday.
25. <u>Is not</u> the day after tomorrow the day of <u>the recital of the pianist</u>?

Additional Exercises

A. Write each sentence, adding commas where necessary.

1. I ate my lunch rode my bike and went to the store.
2. The plane we took to Texas a 747 was filled.
3. No Andrea I do not agree with you at all.
4. In addition your comments are not logical.
5. Who lives at 301 Roy Street Provo Utah 84601?
6. July 4 1776 was an eventful day.
7. Donna swam a few laps and then she rested before going home.
8. I think Rona that the watch can be fixed.
9. We planted corn peas tomatoes and cucumbers in our garden.
10. Li ate some lunch but she could not finish it.

B. Write each sentence, adding quotation marks where necessary.

11. Imagine is a fine song.
12. Amy, asked Pete, are you going to the game?
13. Ligeia is a short story by Edgar Allan Poe.
14. Phil said, That show was really interesting.
15. My camera, said Carmen, is a good one.
16. Write to Ann, Dad urged. It has been a while.
17. The Narrow Escape is a chapter in this book.
18. Denise said, This quiz is going to be a snap.
19. The record for rain, Hector said, was set this April.
20. Let's leave. It is getting late, Sara said.
21. Are you feeling better? asked Byron.
22. San Francisco is the greatest! Jon exclaimed. I hope I can go back again.
23. They ate all the grapes, Kara said.
24. Stop joking! My sides hurt! wheezed Ed.
25. When, Jay asked, will you call me?

Application

Punctuation is not only important in school. Correct punctuation is important in the world outside school as well. Punctuation is required in many applications and forms. Using punctuation and capitalization correctly helps create a good impression with an employer.

Below is an example of a job application form you might fill out to apply for a job.

CHELSEA PUBLIC LIBRARY
Employment Application
Date _____

Name_____
      Last   First

Address _____
                  Street and Number

City   State   ZIP

Telephone Number (   ) _____ Date of Birth _____
             Area Code

School _____ Grade _____

Why do you want to work in the library? _____

_____

List three books you have read and enjoyed. _____

_____

Your Signature _____

Exercise

Copy the application form above. Complete the application as though you were applying for a job with the library. Use commas with your address and your list of books. Also use a comma with your date of birth and with today's date.

Use a comma to separate your last name from your first name: Robinson, Gail.

Chapter Review

A. Write each sentence, adding correct end marks.

1. We buy the Sunday papers on Saturday night
2. At what time is the Video Club meeting
3. I cannot believe how hot it is today
4. Please don't stay up too late
5. Which way is it to the Egyptian gallery

B. Write each sentence, adding commas where necessary.

6. Well to be honest I cannot go with you Ken.
7. Jingles our cat climbed up the tree.
8. "Be healthy wealthy and wise" said Franklin.
9. Cook dinner now or you will waste time later.
10. Wendy's date of birth is Friday December 6 1973.

C. Write each sentence, adding quotation marks where necessary.

11. That is a foolish thing to say! cried Luis.
12. What on earth, exclaimed Martha, is that?
13. What flower is this? Do you know? asked Gwen.
14. She has just read the poem City Trees.
15. Who was the winner? asked Amber.

D. Write each sentence, adding an apostrophe where necessary.

16. Horses tails swat flies.
17. James wont be able to join us today.
18. The geeses honking was heard for miles.
19. Tias jeans need to be patched.
20. Theyve set up a new show at the museum.

Write Arnie's letter, adding correct punctuation marks.

July 21 1986

Dear Ms. Hayes

I want to thank you the other librarians and all your staff for helping me locate books and articles about the East Coast My family and I appreciated your cooperation before our recent trip and we are sending this letter to tell you We found the following books very useful Atlanta Georgia—A Peach of a City Jeffersons Home Town and The Nations Capital Joan my sister enjoyed bike riding along the Potomac River Yes these cities were as wonderful as you said they were

There was some information of course that books and articles could not give us For example prices change so quickly that no book can ever be current about them and some restaurants are not as good as guidebooks say they are In general however the books were accurate about such small items as the U.S. Mints closing time of 4 45 P M The books were also right about the Air and Space Museums exhibits They were fantastic By the way we have pictures from the following cities Philadelphia Williamsburg Baltimore Richmond and Atlanta

Well I will not mention all the things we saw on the trip there is no space here for that We enjoyed the trip more because of your help

Very truly yours

Arnie S. Craig

Cumulative Review

Capitalization and Punctuation
Capitalization (pp. 224–235)

End Marks (pp. 242–243)   Semicolons (pp. 258–259)

Commas (pp. 244–251)   Colons (pp. 258–259)

Quotations (pp. 252–255)   Apostrophes (pp. 260–261)

A. Write each sentence, adding capitals where necessary.

1. kerry moved to miami, florida, on wednesday.
2. the french instructor was professor parrish.
3. joel went to hunter college in new york city.
4. whose birthday is on september 27?
5. wendy said, "do you know sunday's date?"
6. the american greeting company is in ohio.
7. dr. stein's office closes only on new year's day.
8. new england is famous for its fall foliage.
9. marlon uses ivory soap on his car.
10. few people in the middle ages could read.
11. the koran is the holy book of islam.
12. grandfather fought in world war I.
13. labor day is always the first monday in september.
14. the constitution is in the national archives.
15. e.a. robinson wrote the poem "richard cory."
16. my brother was born at 12:01 a.m.
17. that english tea is delicious!
18. "where," said dr. verner, "is my appointment book?"
19. next year i must take chemistry I.
20. my aunt crossed the atlantic ocean on her way to africa.

B. Write this poem by A. E. Housman, adding capitals where necessary.

21. the night is freezing fast

22. the night is freezing fast,

23. to-morrow comes december;

24. and winterfalls of old

25. are with me from the past;

26. and chiefly i remember

27. how dick would hate the cold.

28. fall, winter, fall; for he

29. prompt hand and headpiece clever,

30. has woven a winter robe,

31. and made of earth and sea

32. his overcoat for ever,

33. and wears the turning globe.

C. Write each sentence, adding capitals where necessary. Change incorrect uses of capital letters.

34. janet washes her face with Soap.

35. dad asked, "will you join us at the Movies?"

36. mom works for the boy scouts Of america.

37. the letter ended this way: "Sincerely Yours."

38. i always shop at the Store on first avenue.

D. Write each sentence, adding the correct end marks.

39. At 10:00 P.M. the fireworks went off

40. George Washington was born in 1732

41. You look unbelievably terrific

42. Please clean up Deena's room

43. What's her favorite rock group

44. Look out

45. Dawn said, "Why are you late "

E. Write each sentence, adding commas where necessary.

46. It rained on Monday Tuesday and Sunday.
47. Yes Dan we would love some yogurt.
48. Kim bought eggs but some of them were broken.
49. Mr. Bell Sally's teacher was out sick today.
50. "Besides" said Anna "he will be out for a week."
51. The package goes to 2 Rye Street Boise Idaho 83702.
52. Spring arrived and the flowers bloomed in the yard.
53. Milk juice and fish were on the shopping list.
54. They are moving on Tuesday August 6 1985.
55. It seems however that there was an error.

F. Write each sentence, adding quotation marks where necessary.

56. I made the track team! cried Yoko.
57. Rory said, You really deserved it.
58. You are the fastest in the school, agreed Jason.
59. Yoko listened to the song Running Wild.
60. She read the chapter called Your Feet and You.
61. This, she said, gives a lot of information.
62. My feet, she declared, are my best friends!
63. She said, From now on, I will take care of them.
64. When is your first race? asked Rory.
65. I think it is on May 15, Yoko replied.

G. Write each sentence, adding semicolons and colons where necessary.

66. The play starts at 8 00 P.M. sharp.
67. Ted broke the glass he did not hurt himself.
68. Remember the following names Ray, Stan, Ronald, and Terry.
69. Take a break now otherwise, you will get tired.
70. Lend me a quarter I will pay you back later.

H. Write each sentence, adding an apostrophe where necessary.

71. Sandys shoelaces just broke.
72. The dancers costumes glittered in the light.
73. Thomass notebook is still in his locker.
74. Giraffes necks are long.
75. The childrens voices carried in the wind.

I. Write the correct contraction in each line.

76.	I'll	Ill'l	Ill'
77.	shouldn'ot	should'nt	shouldn't
78.	theyre'	they're	theyr'e
79.	wasno't	wasn't	was'nt
80.	you've	youv'e	yo'uve

J. Write the dialogue with the correct punctuation marks. Do not write the sentence number.

81. Which was your favorite city Arnie asked
82. Well its hard to say but I think Charleston was replied Joan
83. Do you remember the night of June 6 asked Dad
84. We got there about 9 30 P M
85. Yes I remember we couldnt find a vacant hotel room said Joan
86. Mom asked Did you collect a map from every place we visited Joan
87. No but I have saved maps from the following cities Williamsburg Baltimore Richmond and Atlanta
88. Ill trace our route on each map to remind us where weve been Joan replied
89. Arnie said On this map for example youll see the Rock Creek Hotel in Washington
90. Mom concluded This is a good collection we can take our trip over again without leaving home

WRITING, SPEAKING and

LISTENING, STUDY SKILLS

UNIT FIVE

The Basics of Writing

You are living in the age of information. To live and work successfully, you must learn to acquire and exchange this information.

Unit Five focuses on writing—a skill that allows you to exchange information with others. Unlike speech, writing becomes a permanent record. People you do not even know can be influenced by your writing. Some people may be helped by what you write. Others may be moved to action. People will also form opinions of you based on how you write. For these and other reasons, you will want your writing to be clear, accurate, and effective.

Each of the four chapters in Unit Five concentrates on one skill that will improve your writing ability. In Chapter 12 you will practice writing sentences. You will discover that writing means making word choices. You will generate and expand sentences until they say exactly what you want them to. You will also use sentence combining techniques to improve the clarity and flow of your writing.

To communicate effectively in writing, you must be aware of your purpose and audience. Chapter 13 focuses on these factors. You will learn to identify the purpose for a piece of writing. You will also learn the importance of identifying and analyzing an audience—the people who read what you write. In addition, you will gain an understanding of the many forms writing can take.

Since well-developed paragraphs are essential for clear writing, Chapter 14 presents the basics of paragraph writing. You will practice writing the main idea in a topic sentence, supporting main ideas with details, and concluding a paragraph with a clincher sentence.

All writers should go through the stages of the writing process. Chapter 15 examines this process of how writers write. It begins with a six-page photo essay comparing a writer using the writing process with an artist creating a vase from clay. This book divides the writing process into four stages. The first stage is prewriting. During prewriting, writers generate ideas and clarify their purpose and audience. Writing ideas down in a first draft is the second stage. In revising, the third stage, writers rewrite, edit, and proofread using appropriate editing symbols. During the fourth stage, publishing, writers display their work for public view.

The *Writers at Work* pages are a unique feature of the unit. Each page highlights a person who has made a significant contribution to American life through writing. Laura Ingalls Wilder's writings, for example, made frontier history come alive. Richard Sears showed the importance of writing to a successful business, and Andrew Carnegie described new ways to help the less fortunate. Finally, Rachel Carson's books gave rise to a new interest in the preservation of the environment.

12 Sentence Combining and Revising

"Word-carpentry is like any other
kind of carpentry: you must
join your sentences smoothly."

—*Anatole France*

1 — Combining Sentences with Repeated Ideas

> ● Combine short sentences with repeated ideas.

A sentence is a group of words that expresses a complete thought. As a writer, you must make continuous choices. One of your most important choices will be how to construct sentences. Read the three sentences below. Notice that they repeat the same idea.

> Sandy went to school.
> Brian went to school. **(,)**
> I went to school. **(, and)**

Each of the sentences above expresses a complete thought. However, these short sentences sound too abrupt. Notice how these three sentences with a repeated idea can be combined into one sentence by using commas and the word *and.*

> Sandy, Brian, <u>and</u> I went to school.

Now read the four sentences below.

> I walk to school.   I walk to school,
> I jog around the block. **(,)**   jog around the block,
> I run to the store. **(, and)**   <u>and</u> run to the store.

The three sentences on the left were combined into the one sentence on the right also using commas and the word *and.*

To avoid choppy writing, combine sentences with repeated ideas. In the first set of sentences, the verb was repeated, so the sentences could be combined. In the second set of sentences, the subject was repeated, so the sentences could be combined.

Exercises

A. Combine the following sentences, using the clues in parentheses. Write the new sentence that results.

1. Someday I will fly an airplane.
   Someday I will pilot a steamship. **(,)**
   Someday I will engineer a train. **(, and)**
2. Tim had fun on the subway.
   Henry had fun on the subway. **(,)**
   Kevin had fun on the subway. **(, and)**
3. The student edited the report.
   The student proofread the report. **(and)**
4. Her sister applauded her performance.
   Her brother applauded her performance. **(and)**
5. The doctors praised the emergency room.
   The nurses praised the emergency room. **(,)**
   The patients praised the emergency room. **(, and)**

B. Combine the following sentences. Write the new sentence that results. The sentences do not have clues.

6. Juanita went on vacation to Florida.
   Alexis went on vacation to Florida.
   Miriam went on vacation to Florida.
7. The police officer monitors traffic.
   The police officer issues tickets.
   The police officer helps pedestrians.
8. My family often rides in an automobile.
   My family never rides on a train.
   My family sometimes rides on a bus.
9. I tossed the discus in the first event.
   I ran the broad jump in the second event.
   I threw the javelin in the third event.
10. The seals performed for the audience of children.
    The bears performed for the audience of children.

– 2 – **Combining Compound Sentences**

> ● Combine two sentences that express equally important ideas with *and, but,* or *or.*

Often you will need to combine two sentences that have equally important ideas by using *and, but,* or *or.* These sentences are compound sentences. A compound sentence is one that has two separate but equal ideas joined by a coordinating word. Study these sentences.

> My brother wants to fly an airplane.
> I want to be his copilot. **(, and)**

These sentences can be joined by a comma and the word *and.* Both ideas can be expressed in one sentence.

> My brother wants to fly an airplane, and I want
> to be his copilot.

The word *but* can also create a compound sentence. However, it joins two sentences that express contrasting but equal ideas. These sentences can be joined by a comma and the word *but.* Study the example below.

> My father rides the subway to work.
> Sherri's father drives his own car. **(, but)**
> My father rides the subway to work, but Sherri's
> father drives his own car.

The third word, *or,* indicates a choice between equal ideas. Two sentences with different choices can be joined by a comma and the word *or.* Study the example.

> Will we walk home from the game?
> Will our parents pick us up? **(, or)**
> Will we walk home from the game, or will our parents
> pick us up?

Exercises

A. Combine the following sentences, using the clues in parentheses. Write the new sentence that results.

   1. Mother likes to ride the elevator.
      I prefer the escalator. **(, but)**
   2. We can walk to the party.
      My mother can drive us. **(, or)**
   3. Bill Taylor is a good student.
      He is a safe motorcycle driver. **(, and)**
   4. I ride the bus to the shopping center.
      I take the subway home. **(, but)**
   5. Will the hose put the fire out?
      Will we need to call the fire department? **(, or)**

B. Combine the following sentences with *and, but,* or *or.* Write the new sentence that results. The sentences do not have clues.

   6. In early times individuals carried their belongings.
      They trained animals to bear them.
   7. The invention of the wheel revolutionized early transportation.
      Early roads were very poor.
   8. Smooth roads were not needed in early times.
      The invention of wheeled vehicles made them necessary.
   9. The chariot revolutionized early warfare.
      It aided communication between empires.
  10. Many roads were eventually built.
      Laws regulated the vehicles that used them.
  11. The invention of the wheel aided land travel.
      The invention of the sail aided water travel.
  12. The Phoenicians used boats for trade routes.
      The Romans were the best engineers of the time.

3 — Expanding Sentences

> ● Expand sentences by adding descriptive words to make sentences more specific.

A sentence is a group of words that expresses a complete thought. Although it is very short, the following group of words is a sentence.

The horse galloped.

If you add descriptive words to the sentence above, you can give more information to your readers. Notice how the sentence becomes more specific when descriptive words are added.

The <u>black</u> horse galloped <u>smoothly</u>.

The word *black* is an adjective; it tells *what kind*. The word *smoothly* is an adverb; it tells *how* the horse galloped. This one sentence combines three sentences that could have been written like the ones below.

The horse galloped.
The horse was <u>black</u>.
The horse galloped <u>smoothly</u>.

Sometimes a group of words can be added to a sentence to give more information. Study the group of words, called a prepositional phrase, added to the second sentence below.

The black horse galloped smoothly.
The horse galloped <u>on the bridle path</u>.
The black horse galloped smoothly on the bridle path.

Sometimes more than one group of words can be added.

The black horse galloped smoothly on the bridle path <u>by the lake</u>.

Exercises

A. Combine the following sentences, using the underlined clues. Write the new sentence that results.

1. The horse dragged the wagon.
   The horse was <u>old</u>.
   The horse dragged the wagon <u>slowly</u>.
2. The child rode the pony.
   The pony was a <u>palomino</u>.
   The child rode the pony <u>gracefully</u>.
3. The burro carried the pack.
   The burro was <u>frisky</u>.
   It carried the pack <u>down into the canyon</u>.
4. The stallion appeared.
   The stallion was <u>beautiful</u>.
   The stallion appeared <u>in the clearing</u>.
5. The children petted the animals.
   The children were <u>happy</u>.
   The animals were <u>grateful</u>.
   They petted the animals <u>during the intermission</u>.

B. Use descriptive words and phrases to expand each sentence below. Write each new sentence.

6. The spectators cheered.
7. The runners waited.
8. The gun sounded.
9. The race began.
10. The runners finished.
11. The winner beamed.
12. The coach shouted.
13. The award was given.
14. The winner spoke.
15. The audience left.

Application USING SENTENCE COMBINING

Write ten short sentences about one topic, as in Exercise **B.** Your topic could be a sport such as swimming. Then expand the sentences with descriptive words.

4 — Combining Sentences with Subordinate Ideas

> ● Use the words *who* and *that* to combine sentences that have subordinate ideas.

In a previous lesson you learned to combine sentences with two equal ideas. Often, however, two sentences contain *unequal* ideas. When sentences contain unequal ideas, you must subordinate one idea to another. A subordinate idea is one that is lesser in rank or importance than another. Two connecting words that subordinate information are *who* and *that.* To subordinate information about *people* in a sentence, use *who.* Study the example below.

> The girl won first place in our school's one-mile race.
> She lives next door to me. **(who)**
> The girl <u>who</u> lives next door to me won first place in our school's one-mile race.

When the information you add is necessary to clarify the meaning of a sentence, use *who* to combine ideas. When you only want to add additional information, use *, who.*

> Laurel won first place in our school's one-mile race.
> Laurel lives next door to me. **(, who)**
> Laurel, <u>who</u> lives next door to me, won first place in our school's one-mile race.

To subordinate information about *things* in a sentence, use *that.* Study the example below.

> The bus picks up students in front of my house.
> It is the one I ride to school. **(that)**
> The bus <u>that</u> I ride to school picks up students in front of my house.

Exercises

A Combine the following sentences, using the clues in parentheses. Write the new sentence that results.

1. Terri wants to travel around the world.
   She likes to read about foreign countries. **(, who)**
2. The woman is my cousin.
   She works at the new department store. **(who)**
3. Michael is my cousin.
   He just wrote me a letter from Alaska. **(, who)**
4. The boy collects model trains.
   He is riding in the locomotive. **(who)**

B. Combine the following sentences, using *that.* Write the new sentence. You may need to delete some words.

5. Christopher fixed the small sailboat.
   I found it in the attic. **(that)**
6. Barbara has a collection of miniature racing cars.
   She plans to display it in class. **(that)**
7. This is the book.
   I want you to read it. **(that)**
8. The riverboat still travels on the Mississippi.
   I toured the riverboat. **(that)**

C. Combine the following sentences. Write the new sentence that results. Decide whether to use *who* or , *who.*

9. I wrote a letter to Joanna.
   She is touring Mexico with her parents.
10. The girl is from France.
    The girl is sitting next to Alexander.
11. Manuel enjoys doing aerobic exercises.
    He dislikes jogging.
12. People should register before Wednesday.
    They want to win the bicycle.

5 — Revising Windy Sentences

- Revise windy sentences that ramble on and on.

Young writers often overuse such words as *and, but,* and *so.* They string together several sentences using these words. Study the windy sentence below.

A fire just started on State Street <u>and</u> it looks very bad <u>so</u> I called the Fire Department <u>and</u> told them to go to North State Street in the 1600 block to fight the fire <u>and</u> I also told them the exact location of the burning house <u>but</u> I'm not sure about the house number <u>and</u> I don't know how long the firefighters will take to arrive.

Revising Step 1 The windy sentence above should first be broken down into separate sentences.

A fire just started on State Street. It looks very bad. I called the Fire Department. I told them to go to North State Street in the 1600 block to fight the fire. I also told them the exact location of the burning house. I'm not sure about the house number. I don't know how long the firefighters will take to arrive.

Revising Step 2 The single windy sentence has been broken down into six choppy sentences. Your second step should now be to combine *some* of the choppy sentences using the combining techniques you have just learned. In the revised sentences below, compound verbs and a compound sentence have been used.

A fire just started on State Street and looks very bad. I called the Fire Department and told them to go to North State Street in the 1600 block to fight the fire. I also told them the exact location of the burning house, but I'm not sure about the house number. I don't know how long the firefighters will take to arrive.

Exercise

Combine the windy sentences below. First, break down each sentence into separate sentences. Then combine the sentences, using appropriate techniques.

1. I was away from home and I lost my wallet and I needed money for a telephone call to my parents and I saw a stranger nearby so I asked him for money.
2. My father was painting the house but he was too close to the edge of the roof and the ladder fell and he was clinging to the ledge so I called for help.
3. My best friend and I went camping but she stepped into quicksand and I tried to help her but I had a great deal of difficulty.
4. An automobile accident occurred at the corner of Elm and Washington Streets and a man was injured but no one could identify him.
5. The young woman saw the accident and the young woman reported the accident but she was very upset and the police officer could not calm her.

Application USING SENTENCE COMBINING

Write eight sentences filling in details about the situation in the picture below.

6 — Revising Choppy Sentences

> ● Revise short, choppy sentences by combining them.

Many writers compose short, choppy sentences when writing first drafts. When revising, they should combine choppy sentences into smoother ones. Revising helps the sentences flow better. Read the paragraph below.

> Sentence combining builds skills. Sentence combining builds writing skills. It helps writers improve. Writers can combine short, choppy sentences into smoother-sounding ones. They can write sentences combining equally important ideas. They can combine sentences with subordinate ideas. Writers can avoid choppy writing by using good sentence-combining techniques.

Combining most of the above sentences achieves a smoother flow of ideas. Read the revised paragraph.

> Sentence combining builds writing skills. It helps writers improve because they can combine short, choppy sentences into smoother-sounding ones. They can write sentences combining equally important ideas, and they can combine sentences with subordinate ideas. Writers can avoid choppy writing by using good sentence-combining techniques.

Seven choppy sentences in the first paragraph were combined into four smoother-flowing sentences in the second. Often, as in the second sentence above, choppy sentences can be combined by using such words as *after, although, because, before, if, since, when,* and *while* to show the relationship between ideas. When a noun is the subject of the subordinate sentence, it is often changed to a pronoun when the sentences are combined.

Exercise

Combine the following sentences. Use the words *although*, *because*, *before*, *if*, or *since* to combine some of the sentences below. Sentences using these connecting words have clues. Other sentences do not.

EXAMPLE: You want to ride a bicycle. You must have balance. **(if)**

ANSWER: If you want to ride a bicycle, you must have balance.

1. My little brother wants to keep the training wheels on his bicycle. He is afraid. **(because)**
2. At a circus I once saw an acrobat ride a bicycle. She was brave. The bicycle was on a wire. The wire was high above the arena floor.
3. Bicycles cost much less than cars. They do not pollute the air.
4. Bicycle racers practice many hours a day. They enter contests. **(before)**
5. I could ride in a spaceship. I would travel around the world many times. **(if)**
6. Spaceships do not take off and land easily. I still would enjoy riding in one.
7. Social studies is my favorite school subject. I want to travel around the world to see all the famous places from history. **(since)**
8. I could see all the continents. I could see all the oceans.
9. I would visit the Taj Mahal. I would climb the Sphinx. I would fly over the Grand Canyon. I would explore ancient Roman ruins.
10. I am frightened of the feeling of weightlessness. Traveling on a spaceship has always been a dream of mine. **(although)**

Chapter Review

A. Combine the sentences, using the clues. Write the new sentences that result.

1. Rachel played tennis in the park.
   Dana played tennis in the park. **(,)**
   Ricki played tennis in the park. **(, and)**
2. Rachel hit the ball accurately.
   Dana wasn't able to return it. **(, but)**
3. Ricki hit the ball.
   Ricki hit the ball <u>hard</u>.
   Ricki hit the ball <u>into the net</u>.
4. Sonia won the tennis tournament trophy.
   Sonia is a fast, agile player. **(, who)**
5. Dana may go to tennis camp.
   It is <u>an excellent</u> camp.
   She may go there <u>next summer</u>.

B. Combine the sentences. Write the new sentence that results. The sentences do not have clues.

6. The tennis court is behind the library.
   It is the one I play on.
7. You could play on a clay court today.
   You might want to choose a harder playing surface.
8. Look at Jason's backhand shot. It is smooth.
   Look at his powerful serve.
9. Mr. Abrahamson maintains the tennis courts.
   Mr. Abrahamson gives tennis lessons by appointment.
10. Rod's tennis racket shone in the sun.
    Rod's tennis racket was new.
    Rod's racket was made from aluminum.

On a small mountain farm in Missouri in the late 1920s, sixty-year-old Laura Ingalls Wilder began work on her first book. Before her were the yellowed pages of the journals she had kept since girlhood. Wilder had been a pioneer, and the journals were a vivid record of the hardships and pleasures of frontier life. Now she planned to use that record to help young Americans appreciate their heritage.

Writing is hard work. Even using her journals as a guide, Wilder did not finish *Little House in the Big Woods* until 1932. When the book was published, however, it was an immediate success. By 1943 she had completed eight *Little House* books.

Today, increased by viewers of the long-running television series, Laura Ingalls Wilder's readers number in the millions. To Wilder, reaching her goal as a writer, however, was what was most important: "I wanted the children today to understand more about the beginning of things, to know what is behind the things they see—what it is that made America as they know it."

Application CAREERS

Strong writing skills are required for careers in book publishing. Research in the library how a book is made. Then create a poster explaining the process.

13 *Purpose and Audience in Writing*

"When a man does not know to
what port he is steering,
no wind is favorable to him."

—Seneca

1 — Identifying a Purpose

> • In writing, **purpose** means the writer's intent.

Writers make important decisions in the early stages of writing. They define their purpose. They identify an audience, their readers. They select a form to use—a letter, a poem, an editorial.

Defining a writing purpose is probably the most important decision. To write well, you must have a purpose for communicating clearly in mind.

Purpose is the reason you are writing. It is your intent. For example, do you intend *to entertain* your readers with a poem or a short story? Do you want *to persuade* them to accept your views through an editorial? Perhaps you want *to inform* them with a how-to essay. Sometimes you simply want *to express* your ideas.

Choosing a purpose for your writing is an essential step. If this step is omitted, you may not communicate what you really want to say. To write well, your purpose must be clear in your mind and in your writing.

Below are two writing forms, or products. Decide on the writer's purpose for each.

An English textbook   A mystery novel

Both are books, of course, but the purposes for them are different. The textbook writer's purpose is *to inform*, and the novel writer's purpose is *to entertain*.

A writer's purpose is extremely important because it influences all the other choices a writer will make.

Exercises

A. Write the purpose for each writing form below.

1. science fiction story
2. letter to the editor
3. travel poster
4. editorial
5. report on jobs
6. one-act play
7. poem
8. crossword puzzle
9. advertisement
10. menu

B. Read each paragraph below. Tell the writer's purpose for each.

Dear Grandmother,

Tonight I became a member of the National Junior Honor Society. Both students and parents attended our initiation ceremony, and I wish you could have been here. Mr. Black, our school principal, talked about setting goals in his speech, and what he said made me think about my own goals. I have set some of my own that I wanted to share with you. I am going to make the varsity football team in high school and be the star halfback. Just wait and see!

Love,
Kevin

Better bus safety can be accomplished in several ways. First, every bus needs a seat belt for every student. In case of accident, seat belts can prevent serious injury to passengers. Second, bus drivers need more training in how to drive safely and how to handle discipline problems on the bus. Third, an all-school campaign for bus safety would help students understand the problem. Implementing these suggestions would improve the safety on all school buses.

2 — Identifying an Audience

- Before beginning to write, decide who your readers will be. These readers are your writing **audience.**

The people who read what you write are your audience. To communicate with them, you need to identify your audience clearly before beginning to write. Analyzing them carefully will help you to know them better.

Keeping a specific audience in mind as you write is essential. For example, the information you include and the sentences you compose are influenced by the audience you want to reach. A letter to your best friend about a Saturday night party would be quite different from a letter to your parents about the same party.

Some audiences you know well—yourself, friends, parents, relatives, or teachers. Sometimes, however, you write for general audiences. You may not know any member of such a group. Particularly in this latter situation, you must identify your audience and analyze their general characteristics. Selecting one person from the group as a representative reader is helpful. The Audience Checklist below is useful for establishing a specific audience in your mind before you begin to write.

Audience Checklist

- For whom am I writing?
- How old are they?
- What do I want to tell them?
- How much do they already know about this subject?
- How can I capture their interest?

Exercises

A. For each writing form below, identify one audience.

1. travel brochure
2. news release
3. invitation
4. school song
5. petition
6. recipe
7. want ad
8. exercise booklet
9. sports column
10. movie review

B. For each writing form below, identify two audiences.

11. television review
12. essay question
13. dictionary
14. questionnaire
15. textbook
16. how-to essay on dieting
17. stock market newsletter
18. business letter
19. greeting card
20. traffic rules

C. Identify the writing audience for this excerpt from Madeline L'Engle's novel *A Wrinkle in Time*.

It was a dark and stormy night.

In her attic bedroom Margaret Murry, wrapped in an old patchwork quilt, sat on the foot of her bed and watched the trees tossing in the frenzied lashing of the wind. . . .

The house shook.

Wrapped in her quilt, Meg shook.

She wasn't usually afraid of weather.—It's not just the weather she thought.—It's the weather on top of everything else. On top of me. On top of Meg Murry doing everything wrong. . . .

During lunch she'd rough-housed a little to try to make herself feel better, and one of the girls said scornfully, "After all, Meg, we aren't grammar-school kids any more. Why do you always act like such a baby?"

3 — Writing for Different Audiences

- Writing for different audiences requires you to make changes in what you write.

When you write for different audiences, you need to make important changes. You will use different words and different details. What you decide to emphasize will also change. For example, read the following paragraphs. They are both about the same topic. However, the first is written for a sixth-grade audience, and the second is written for grandparents.

If you like animals, you will love our hometown zoo. It has many different animals. Some special ones are a baby elephant, a baby giraffe, and a panda. The snake house has a twenty-foot python, and you will enjoy the chattering, colorful birds in the trees and beside the many ponds.

A visit to the zoo in my hometown should be on every traveler's schedule. It is one of the largest zoos in the United States. You will see many different animals in natural settings—carved-out hills, large rocks, and pools. New additions include a baby elephant and a baby giraffe. If you like unusual animals, you will love the panda and the twenty-foot python. Our zoo is certainly an interesting place to visit.

When you write for different audiences, select your words carefully. The words you choose for one audience may not communicate well with another audience. The details you decide to include will also change, because the readers' interests will be different. Finally, the overall emphasis, or focus, of what you write will change for each different audience.

Exercises

A. For each writing situation below, identify two different audiences. Write your answers.

1. a description of your school
2. a biographical sketch of your best friend
3. a report on endangered animals
4. an opinion on school electives
5. a summary of a student questionnaire on television viewing

B. Study the writing situations below. Tell how the writing for each one would change if it were written for two different audiences—seventh graders and senior citizens. Include changes in words, details, and emphasis.

6. a menu for a restaurant
7. a school newsletter
8. a news story on an international event
9. a how-to booklet on exercise
10. a guidebook to your school

Application WRITING FOR DIFFERENT AUDIENCES

Select assignment **1** or **2** below. Notice how your writing changes when your audience changes.

1. You are planning to create a travel poster for a city you know well. Think about outstanding sites, landmarks, or other places of special interest that visitors would like to see. Write a travel poster that would be appropriate (**a**) for teens and (**b**) for retired citizens.
2. Imagine you are writing a saying for a greeting card. Create a "Happy Birthday" card (**a**) for a fifteen-year-old friend and (**b**) for a forty-year-old woman.

4 — Choosing a Form for Writing

> • After deciding upon purpose and audience, writers select a **form** that is appropriate.

Writers must select a form that will best convey the ideas they want to express.

In writing, a form provides a frame for your ideas. It gives writing structure and helps organize ideas in ways readers are familiar with. A writer has an almost limitless list of forms from which to choose. Examples include short stories, plays, poems, songs, menus, news stories, editorials, essays, and contest jingles.

Different forms require different organizations. For example, if you choose to write an editorial, you would define the problem, present both sides of the issue, and offer a solution. A letter to a principal, however, may offer a solution and present clear supporting reasons.

Study the photograph below. Look for details.

A school football game may be a familiar scene to you. It could be the stimulus for writing about many ideas.

Below is an idea list that you might make based upon the photograph. Some ideas do not have to be based on something you see in the photograph. They can be ideas you just imagine. You may add others.

1. appearance of the stadium   5. noise level
2. behavior of students   6. cheerleaders
3. behavior of visitors   7. band
4. academics vs. athletics   8. colorful uniforms

A football game provides many ideas for writing. Suppose you want to write about injuries to the players because your best friend was hurt during a game. Your purpose is to inform other teens about advances in football equipment over the past few years, an advance you believe prevented more serious injury to your friend. What form would you choose for this writing situation? All of the forms listed below are possible choices.

- Feature article for teen magazine
- Column for school newspaper
- Research report for a class assignment and oral report
- Short story

The form you choose will determine how you will organize your ideas. The chart on the following page illustrates just some of the choices you have when selecting forms for your ideas.

Forms for Writing

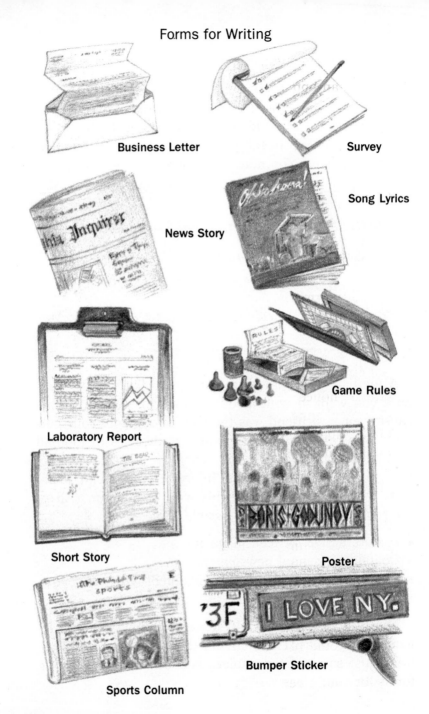

Business Letter

Survey

Song Lyrics

News Story

Game Rules

Laboratory Report

Short Story

Poster

Sports Column

Bumper Sticker

Exercises

A. Identify an appropriate form for each writing situation below. The purpose and audience are provided.

1. To inform parents about Open House
2. To tell a story about friendship
3. To persuade the principal to extend lunch period
4. To explore your own ideas about friendship
5. To inform others about work you can do
6. To report an accident you witnessed
7. To persuade classmates to vote in a school election
8. To entertain others thorugh poetry
9. To inform other teens about nutritional snacks
10. To express ideas on extending the school year

B. For each writing form listed below, provide a purpose and an audience. Write your answers.

11. sale notice	21. television commercial
12. school song	22. research paper
13. job application	23. invitation
14. club minutes	24. inscription
15. poem	25. postcard
16. adventure story	26. almanac
17. accident report	27. cookbook
18. brochure	28. poster
19. sports column	29. record jacket
20. political speech	30. menu

Application CHOOSING A FORM FOR WRITING ——————

List five writing assignments you have completed or ones you would like to complete. For each writing situation, list your purpose and audience and then select a form that would be appropriate.

A. Write the purpose for each writing form below.

1. an election speech
2. a math textbook
3. a diary page
4. a situation comedy
5. a novel
6. a historical marker
7. hospital records
8. a soup advertisement
9. a recipe for soup
10. an editorial

B. For each writing form below, identify one audience.

11. a school dress code
12. a real estate ad
13. a graduation speech
14. instructions for using a computer program
15. a list of common French expressions
16. a plan to redevelop part of a city
17. bicycle safety rules
18. a review of the ten most popular running shoes
19. a thesaurus
20. a record review

C. Identify an appropriate form for each writing situation. The purpose and audience are provided.

21. To persuade your town council to build a public swimming pool in town
22. To inform your friend about jogging
23. To entertain others musically
24. To express feelings of joy on the first spring day
25. To inform friends about your birthday party
26. To entertain others with an adventure you had at summer camp
27. To persuade a television audience to buy a certain brand of soap
28. To record the trees you see on a camping trip
29. To tell about a used bicycle you wish to sell
30. To inform friends how to bake bread

"Now class, it's time for grammar. Take out your Sears and Roebuck catalogs and read the advertisement on page 7."

Using a Sears or Montgomery Ward catalog to teach grammar might sound strange to you, but in rural turn-of-the-century America, it was a common practice. The free catalogs saved the expense of textbooks. Moreover, they were well written with a large vocabulary.

The catalogs were written by the company founder—Richard Sears. He began a mail-order business in 1886 with a few watches bought on credit. In less than ten years, he was president of a multimillion-dollar business. The key to his success was persuasive writing.

Sears's purpose was to provide low-cost, quality goods. His catalogs were jammed with information about the advantages of the pictured products. Sears also knew his audience. He appealed to the needs of the people who were his customers. As more and more Americans read and used the catalogs, Sears, Roebuck & Company became the largest retailer in the entire world.

Application CAREERS

Writing skills are important for careers in advertising. Write an advertisement for an object you own but would like to sell. Be accurate as well as appealing.

14 Organizing Ideas into Paragraphs

"The order of ideas in a sentence
or paragraph should be such
that the reader need not
rearrange them in his mind."

—Robert Graves

1 Paragraph Basics

- A **paragraph** is a group of related sentences about one main idea.

Paragraphs have two special functions. First, paragraphs separate main ideas. When you see a new paragraph, you know the writer has shifted from one main idea to another. Second, paragraphs make reading easier. They help to interrupt the constant flow of black type on the page by creating some white space for relief.

Paragraphs are indented. The first line of a paragraph may begin about five spaces in from the left margin. The rest of the lines in the paragraph begin at the left margin. Indenting signals a new paragraph. Paragraphs vary in length, but they are long enough to develop the main idea. Rarely write one-sentence paragraphs.

A paragraph is a group of related sentences about one main idea. In a paragraph you will usually find a **topic sentence** that states the main idea, **supporting sentences** that provide more detailed information, and when appropriate, a **clincher sentence.** The clincher sentence summarizes or restates the paragraph's main idea. In the paragraph below, the topic sentence is tinted blue, the clincher sentence is tinted red, and the three supporting sentences are without tint.

A paragraph is like a building block. You may have seen children playing with building blocks, carefully placing one on top of another. Although a single paragraph may stand alone, it is usually one small part of a larger whole. You will find two or more paragraphs in almost everything you read. Paragraphs are the building blocks of writing.

Exercises

A. Answer the following questions about paragraphs. Write your answers in complete sentences.

    1. What is a paragraph?
    2. Why do writers use paragraphs?
    3. What signals a new paragraph?
    4. How long does a paragraph have to be?
    5. Can a paragraph stand alone?
    6. Why are paragraphs the building blocks of writing?
    7. Must every paragraph have a clincher sentence?

B. Read the paragraph below. Then answer the questions that follow. Write your answers in complete sentences.

Making good grades is rewarding. I feel wonderful when I know that I did my best, and I like to believe good grades mean I learned something. My parents are pleased with my report card. My teachers are proud and complimentary. Sometimes I receive recognition from the principal. Good grades never bring bad responses.

    8. What is the main idea?
    9. What is the topic sentence of the paragraph?
  10. Does the topic sentence state the main idea?
  11. How many supporting sentences give more information about the main idea?
  12. Is there a clincher sentence?

C. Locate one paragraph from each of the sources below. Then, working with a classmate, tell whether each paragraph has the elements of a good paragraph. Use the five questions in Exercise **B** as a checklist.

Social Studies textbook	Class assignment
Daily newspaper	Short story

2 — Selecting and Narrowing a Topic

> ● Select a topic that interests you and that you know. Then narrow the topic until it is manageable.

Selecting a topic to write about is an important decision. Sometimes your writing topic is determined for you. At other times, however, you will select your own topic. Two suggestions will make your choice easier.

- Write about what interests you.
- Write about what you know.

To select a writing topic, use three sources. First, consider your own interests, hobbies, and activities. Second, think about who and what you see around you every day—people, places, the media, posters, and even billboards. Third, think about what you have read. Textbooks, newspapers, and library books are all good sources for writing ideas.

When you select a topic, focus on the ideas you want to communicate. Think about your purpose for writing and about your readers. If you will be writing a short article, for example, a general topic would be too hard to discuss adequately. You will need to narrow and focus it. In the example below, a general topic is narrowed into ones that are more specific.

General Topic	More Specific Topics
Computers	How I Use My Home Computer Using a Computer for Homework My Favorite Computer Game

Exercises

A. The following writing topics are too broad and unfocused for a single paragraph. For each one, write two topics that are more specific.

1. school	**6.** games
2. cars	**7.** Saturday
3. family vacations	**8.** summer
4. sports	**9.** school subjects
5. shopping malls	**10.** school cafeterias

B. Each sentence below is a writing topic that is too broad. Write each one, narrowing it so that it can be developed in a single paragraph.

EXAMPLE: Computers help students learn.

ANSWER: Computers help students learn to read better.

11. Shells are fun to collect.

12. I know some annoying people.

13. I once had a part-time job.

14. Scientists are making new discoveries daily.

15. My favorite film stars have been in many movies.

16. My family is big.

17. Some students have problems.

18. Everyone was happy with the results.

19. Crime should be punished.

20. Our city needs some changes.

21. Someone needs to do something about pollution.

22. Winter is a good time to enjoy the weather.

23. Arguments are a waste of time.

24. Nothing ever happens here.

25. All students should be required to take certain subjects.

3 — Main Ideas and Topic Sentences

> ● The **main idea** is the central idea in a paragraph.
> ● The **topic sentence** states the main idea.

The main idea is the writer's central message. It is the idea that the writer wants to convey to readers. The topic sentence is the most important sentence in a paragraph because it states the main idea. The topic sentence, therefore, tells the reader what the paragraph is about.

Most paragraphs have a topic sentence. The topic sentence is usually the first sentence in a paragraph, but it may appear anywhere. If it is not the first sentence, then it is most often the last sentence. Until you gain more writing experience, you may want to make the topic sentence the first sentence in every paragraph that you compose.

Each sentence in a paragraph must relate to the topic sentence. The supporting sentences give more information about the main idea by providing specific details, facts, examples, and reasons. Look for the topic sentence in the paragraph below.

> When I chose an elective for next year, I selected journalism. I chose journalism because I wanted to work on the school newspaper. I also wanted to improve my writing skills. Moreover, I thought journalism would help me prepare for a career as a television news reporter. I am looking forward to journalism class.

Notice that the main idea is stated in the first sentence, which is the topic sentence. Three supporting sentences then give reasons why this student selected journalism as an elective. The last sentence is the clincher sentence.

A. In each pair of sentences below is a topic sentence and a supporting sentence. Write the topic sentence.

1. Bicycling is inexpensive fun. Cars need gasoline, but bicycles need only pedal power.
2. Bicycling is fun for people of all ages. Both young children and older adults enjoy it.
3. Exercise bicycles are part of many people's daily fitness programs. Bicycling is good exercise.
4. In city traffic a bicycle can move more rapidly than an automobile. Delivery agencies have long utilized bicycles for fast, short-distance travel.
5. Bicycles can help you earn money. Bicycles have helped news carriers deliver newspapers.

B. Below is a group of five sentences. Write an appropriate topic sentence for them.

6. When riding a bicycle on a street, you must be aware of safety rules.
7. Obey all signs and lights.
8. Give pedestrians the right-of-way.
9. Be especially watchful for parked cars that may pull onto the street.
10. Do not weave in and out of traffic.

Application WRITING A PARAGRAPH ────────────

Write a paragraph about one of the following general topics. First, narrow the topic. Then state the main idea in a topic sentence, underline the sentence, and complete the paragraph.

Bicycles	Skating	Records
Motorcycles	Swimming	Tapes

4 — Developing Paragraphs by Examples

> ● Use examples to explain or prove a point.

A good way to develop a paragraph is to use examples. Examples support a main idea, and they create word pictures that help readers understand your ideas. A paragraph usually has two or three examples if it is fully developed, but one example is enough if it includes complete information. Read the following paragraph. Notice how examples are used to add specific details.

> A bicycle is a good means of transportation. When I need to run an errand for my mother, I ride my bicycle to the store. I get there faster than by walking, and the items I buy easily fit into my basket. On weekends my best friend and I take all-day trips into the country. We see many different sights, and we enjoy riding through the countryside. A bicycle gets me where I want to go.

General statements can be used as topic sentences, but specific examples are needed to add more information. Using examples is an effective way to develop a paragraph that explains or proves a point. In the following paragraph only one example is used, but a great deal of specific information is included.

> A bicycle is a good means of transportation. I ride my bicycle to school every day. Instead of getting up at six o'clock to catch the early bus, I can sleep a little longer. I enjoy being outdoors in different types of weather, and bicycling to school allows me to be outside more often.

Paragraphs that explain or prove a point are called **explanatory paragraphs.** The two paragraphs above *explain* why a bicycle is a good means of transportation.

Exercises

A. Some of the sentences below would be good examples to prove the statement "Teenagers spend too many hours on the telephone." Write those sentences. Write *no* if a sentence would not prove the statement.

1. My older sister talks to her high school friends every night for two or three hours.
2. My mother has established a twenty-minute time limit for calls.
3. I spend at least one hour a day talking to my friends from school on the phone.
4. When people call my home, the line is busy.
5. Although I see my best friend almost every day, I call her every day to talk about "teenage things."

B. Write two examples to develop each topic sentence.

6. Some fast foods can be good for you.
7. Learning to play a sport requires practice.
8. Everyone should develop a daily exercise routine.
9. Playing team sports develops cooperation.
10. America has had many great presidents.
11. A sports coach has many duties.
12. I have established good study habits.

Application · WRITING A PARAGRAPH

Write a paragraph on one of the following topics or on a topic of your own choice. Use examples to develop the main idea.

Team sports create team spirit
Homework is necessary
Pets make good friends
Summer jobs provide work experience

5 — Developing Paragraphs by Facts

> • Use facts to prove that the main idea of a paragraph is true.

A fact is something that can be proven true. Its accuracy can be checked or verified through reference books such as encyclopedias. Many paragraphs you write will be developed by facts. For instance, most reports for science or social studies will require facts to support your research. Facts are always used in news stories. They answer the questions *who, what, when, where, why,* and *how.* In news stories, facts are presented in the order of their importance, with the most important fact first. In a historical report, however, facts would most often be presented in chronological order.

The writer of the paragraph below used facts in chronological order to support the statement made in the topic sentence.

> The bicycle has an interesting history. The first one was made in France in the late 1700s. It had no pedals and could not be steered. About 1816 a German forester, Baron Karl von Drais, built a bicycle whose front wheel could be turned for steering. The first U.S. patent for a pedal-powered bicycle was granted to Pierre Lallement in 1866. Newer versions appeared rapidly, including one with a very large front wheel. By 1900 bicycles had many of the safety features that are on today's bicycles.

If the writer had used only one fact to support the topic sentence, the paragraph would not have presented enough information. One fact would not have proved that the bicycle has an interesting history. The topic sentence must be fully developed.

Exercises

A. Read the paragraph below. Then answer the questions that follow. Write your answers in complete sentences.

Bicycling boomed in the United States in the 1960s. Americans needed exercise, and bicycling was encouraged by many doctors, including heart specialists. With a greater amount of leisure time and more money for recreation, many American adults began to buy and use bicycles. By 1971 more than seventy million Americans were bicycling. Sales of bicycles to adults accounted for more than twenty-five percent of annual totals. Many Americans wanted to return to a simpler life. Bicycling offered opportunities for family activities. The bicycling boom is continuing today.

1. What is the topic sentence?
2. Do all the facts support the topic sentence?
3. How many supporting sentences are there?
4. In what order are the facts presented?
5. Is there a clincher sentence?

B. Read the topic sentences below. Then write three facts you could use to support each one.

6. Art is the most popular elective in our school.
7. The cost of school lunches is too high.
8. Six cheerleaders were selected after the tryouts.
9. John Turner was elected president of our student council on Thursday.
10. May Li won the writing contest.

Application WRITING A PARAGRAPH

Write a paragraph using facts. You may choose one of the topic sentences above or make up one of your own.

6 — Developing Paragraphs by Reasons

> ● Reasons are used to develop paragraphs that persuade, explain, or state an opinion.

Many paragraphs you write will be **persuasive paragraphs.** These paragraphs can persuade readers to take some action, justify a position on a subject, or state an opinion. In a persuasive paragraph that states an opinion, the opinion should be presented in the topic sentence and supported by convincing reasons.

Reasons answer the question *Why?* in clarifying a writer's opinion. They offer proof for the position the writer takes. Most topic sentences need at least three reasons for full development. Study the example below. The topic sentence states an opinion. The other three sentences contain reasons supporting that opinion.

Topic Sentence	Military service provides good experience for young people.
Reason One	Training and exercise programs make them physically fit.
Reason Two	Technical training furnishes young people with job skills useful in civilian life.
Reason Three	The opportunity to serve their country helps young people develop a spirit of patriotism.

Choose reasons that are appropriate for your audience. Reasons that persuade one audience may not necessarily persuade another. Always consider the concerns, interests, and prejudices of your audience.

Exercises

A. Below are ten writing situations. Write the ones you could develop by reasons. Be prepared to explain your choices.

1. A review of your favorite book
2. An editorial on freedom of speech for the school newspaper
3. A description of your room for a blind classmate
4. A paragraph recommending a stricter dress code
5. A summary of the plot of a short story
6. A paragraph persuading teens to do more reading
7. A letter to the editor about raising the voting age
8. A comparison of two animals
9. A description of an accident you witnessed
10. An explanation of the causes of air pollution

B. Below is a topic sentence followed by a number of reasons that support it. Choose three reasons that would be appropriate for each audience below. Some reasons may be appropriate for both audiences.

seventh graders   teachers

Topic Sentence: The school day should be longer.

11. Students need more time in each class.
12. More courses could be offered.
13. Too much time is wasted in changing classes.
14. Teachers need more time with their students.
15. Students would have a longer lunch period.
16. Longer classes would permit more teaching time.
17. Students would have more time to study while in school.
18. School hours would correspond more closely to the working hours of parents.

7 — Paragraph Unity

- In a unified paragraph every sentence contributes to the main idea.

Have you ever woven three colors of yarn into a braid? Although the colors can be identified individually within the braid, they combine to make a unified whole. This is similar to the makeup of a paragraph. The main idea, topic sentence, and supporting sentences should be so interwoven as to create a unified paragraph.

Main Idea

Topic Sentence

Supporting Sentences

No unrelated or unnecessary thoughts should enter the paragraph. Each word and each sentence should contribute to the whole. Notice the unrelated sentence in the paragraph below.

> Two very brave men were trying to catch an alligator with a wire rope and a net. The alligator beat the water with its tail. It was trying to escape into the muddy swamp. The men wanted to capture it in order to put it in a zoo for everyone to see. One man had the rope around the alligator's jaws. The other man held the net over its head. The alligator fought hard but lost.

Just as some braids need the threads tied at the ends to keep them together, some paragraphs need a restatement of the main idea at the end. This summary is the clincher sentence. *The alligator fought hard but lost* is the clincher sentence in the paragraph above.

Exercise

Each paragraph below contains a sentence that does not belong in it. Write the unrelated sentence from each paragraph.

1. Baseball players enjoy arguing with umpires. A player may stand nose to nose with an official and shout as loudly as possible. Sometimes the spectators throw bottles onto the playing field. The umpire never backs down. He always wins. If a player kicks dirt or hits an umpire, he or she may be ejected or suspended. Such confrontations are often looked forward to by baseball fans.

2. Many people do not know how to take care of a city. Without thought they litter the streets. They pollute the air by burning trash. They leave their broken appliances in vacant lots. Litter laws should be enforced. Some citizens even cut the flowers, shrubs, and trees in city parks. How beautiful the city would be if people took care of it!

3. A birthday card is much more than a piece of paper. It represents the time and money a person has spent to send you a greeting. It reveals the taste and personality of the sender and is his or her idea of what you would enjoy reading. Never send a card without signing it. Whether the card is humorous or serious is unimportant. That you received it is what matters. Remember, the card is more than paper. It is a message from a friend.

Application WRITING A PARAGRAPH

Imagine that the school cafeteria manager has asked you to write a paragraph about proper behavior in the lunchroom. Write the paragraph, making sure that it is unified.

8 — Order of Ideas in Paragraphs

> ● How ideas are organized in paragraphs depends upon the purpose for writing.

Paragraphs may be organized in many ways. Generally the organizational pattern you select is determined by your purpose for writing and by the form you choose to use. If you are writing a short story, for example, you would probably use time order, but a news story would require that facts be presented in the order of their importance.

Organizing your ideas clearly and logically creates clear, readable writing. Paragraphs that do not have a clear organization will confuse your readers. Four ways to organize ideas are presented in this lesson: time order, space order, order of importance, and climactic order.

Time Order   In time order, also called chronological order, ideas are arranged according to the order in which they occur. You can use time order to tell a story, describe a series of events, and give directions. Read the paragraph below, written in time order.

> I have a busy day planned. Before school I need to buy some string for my science project. After my first class I am going to meet with my guidance counselor. At lunch I have to practice with friends on our clarinet ensemble. After school I have a baby-sitting job, and tonight I have to study for a test.

Space Order   Space order is usually used to describe persons, places, or things in a variety of logical sequences. For example, a room could be described from left to right or from inner to outer. A writer should choose an order that helps his or her readers understand how one object or thing relates to another. Read the following paragraph, written in space order.

> The school cafeteria was transformed for the homecoming dance. In the center of the room was a large revolving ball that sprinkled silver pieces of light on the floor and walls. Cafeteria benches circled the dance floor, and crepe-paper streamers of blue and white draped the walls.

Order of Importance   In order of importance, ideas are arranged in descending order. In a news story, for example, the most important facts are written first and are followed by ones of lesser importance. Read the news story below, written in order of importance.

> James Long won first place in a national short story contest, sponsored by the National Council of Teachers of English. Over one thousand middle school students submitted stories. James is a seventh grader at Rice Middle School in Dallas, Texas. His short story, entitled "If Bicycles Could Speak," is about a young boy's dream of becoming a famous bicycle racer.

Climactic Order In climactic order, details are arranged to build interest. The most important detail is presented last. Climactic order is most often used in short stories and other fictional forms. Read the following paragraph, written in climactic order.

> Amy walked into the dark garage as her family watched. She heard laughter as light flooded the room. In front of her was a bright red ten-speed bicycle. "Happy birthday," everyone yelled.

Exercises

A. Read each paragraph below. Write the order of ideas used in each.

Monday was bluer than blue. First, my alarm clock did not go off. Then when I finally woke up, I rushed to take a shower. There was no hot water. Next, I could not eat breakfast because the milk was sour. After that, rain soaked me while I walked to school. The day got no better as I sneezed through it. Thank goodness the week has only one Monday.

The valley was beautiful. As I sat on the mountainside, I could see the tall grass and wild flowers waving in the gentle breeze. The sun beamed down on a small mountain stream cutting a jagged path through the middle of the clearing. Tall pines guarded the valley on every side.

B. Write the order of ideas you would use for each writing situation below.

1. A story with a surprise ending
2. A description of your own backyard
3. Directions to your school
4. A story in the newspaper about a disastrous fire

A Paragraph Checklist

1. Have I indented each new paragraph?
2. Have I selected a topic that interests me and that I know about?
3. Have I narrowed my topic so that it can be covered adequately?
4. Have I included only one main idea in each paragraph?
5. Have I stated the main idea in a clearly written topic sentence?
6. Have I used specific details to support my main idea and topic sentence?
7. Have I developed the paragraph fully by using examples, facts, or reasons?
8. Are all the sentences closely related to the topic sentence, or did I include any sentence that does not belong?
9. Do I have a clear organization throughout the paragraph?
10. Is the organizational pattern appropriate for the writing form I have chosen?
11. If necessary, have I used a clincher sentence to sum up the main idea?
12. Have I used transitions to achieve a flow from one sentence to another, or from one paragraph to another?

9 — Using Transitions

> ● Transitional words or phrases show how ideas relate to one another.

A transitional word or phrase is like a bridge that connects two sides of a river. A bridge helps people get from one place to another. In writing, transitional words and phrases do the same thing. They bridge ideas within paragraphs and between paragraphs. Without transitions, your writing would be choppy and your ideas unclear. The chart below lists some frequently used transitions.

Transitional Words and Phrases			
Space	Time	Logical	Comparison/Contrast
above	after	as a result	by contrast
behind	before	because	different from
below	during	consequently	instead of
beyond	earlier	evidently	just as
inside	finally	however	less than
outside	first	so	more than
through	later	therefore	on the other hand
under	meanwhile	thus	similarly

How you have organized the ideas in your writing influences the transitional words or phrases you will use. For example, if you were comparing and contrasting, you would use words such as *similarly* or *by contrast.* If you were using time order, you would use words such as *first, second,* and *third.* You will often use transitions when you need to write more than one paragraph to develop your ideas more fully. A piece of writing that contains several paragraphs is called a **composition.**

Exercises

A. Write the sentences below, adding a transitional word or phrase in place of each blank.

1. Jim plans to run for the Student Council. ____, he plans to be elected.
2. All words are composed of letters. ____, all musical scores are composed of notes.
3. Some people dislike rainy days. ____, some people enjoy the opportunity to read and study.
4. Mario had never sold a painting. ____, he had a great deal of confidence in his own ability.
5. The bike raced out of control. ____, it hit a tree.

B. Write the paragraph below, replacing each blank with a transitional word or phrase.

It is difficult to find time to think. ____, you really have to set time aside during the day for it. In school you move from class to class about six times. ____ you get to one class, it seems you have to change to another. ____, you do have to think when you are listening to the teacher in class. ____, you cannot stare out the window, or the teacher will believe you are daydreaming. You must pay attention in class. ____ trying to do all your thinking in school, reserve some time at home to think. Your room is a good place to think and study.

Application WRITING A PARAGRAPH

Write a paragraph about how and where you do your best thinking. Perhaps you need the quiet seclusion of your room. Use transitional words and phrases from the chart on the opposite page to connect ideas. Underline the transitional words and phrases.

Chapter Review

A. Write a definition for each term below.

1. paragraph
2. main idea
3. topic sentence
4. supporting sentences
5. clincher sentence

B. Each pair of sentences contains a topic and a supporting sentence. Write the topic sentence.

6. Most dreaming takes place during stage 1, or REM sleep. Scientists describe four stages of sleep.
7. Your heartbeat slows and your blood pressure lowers. Many body changes take place during sleep.
8. Everyone dreams. Dream periods usually occur at about ninety-minute intervals.
9. Some experts think we try to solve problems in dreams. There are many explanations for dreams.
10. No one really sleeps "like a log." Most sleepers make more than twenty moves a night.

C. Write the unrelated sentence in the paragraph below.

11. An active person burns up more calories than someone who gets little exercise. Swimming, for example, requires about 350 calories an hour. Watching television, however, requires less than 100 calories an hour. Your age, sex, and size partially determine the number of calories you need.

D. Write the order of ideas for each writing situation.

12. A description of a model railroad layout
13. Directions for cutting a piece of glass
14. A ghost story with a frightening ending
15. A news story about the closing of a school

Writers at Work

Imagine coming to America as a penniless immigrant, acquiring a fortune of half a billion dollars, and then giving most of it away! It sounds fantastic, but that is exactly what Andrew Carnegie did. He also wrote constantly, and his articles and opinions have had considerable impact on everyday life in America.

The nineteenth century was a time of industrialization. Arriving in Pennsylvania in 1848, the Scottish-born Carnegie realized this growth would require steel. Starting with a small investment in an iron mill, he built a vast network of mines, railways, and steel mills.

In an article entitled "Wealth" published in 1889, Carnegie outlined his ideas on how wealthy people should use their fortunes for the common good. In 1901 he put his ideas into practice by selling his empire and giving the proceeds away. His favorite gift was libraries, and he paid for more than 2800 of them. Carnegie's writings and deeds set an example for others. As a result, philanthropy, or help given to the less fortunate, continues to be an important tradition in American life.

Application CAREERS

Lawyers are often asked to give advice about financial matters. Imagine you had been Carnegie's lawyer. What would you have advised him to do with his money?

15 *The Writing Process*

"Write the way an architect builds,
who first drafts his plan
and designs every detail."

—Schopenhauer

1 — A Photo Essay

> • The artist and the writer use similar processes to create their finished products.

Forming clay into a vase is similar to forming ideas into a finished piece of writing.

1. Prewriting and Gathering Ideas

The artist's purpose is to create a work of art that others can enjoy. Her audience is a friend to whom she intends to give a gift.

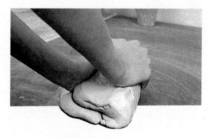

The writer's purpose is to describe something. Students in his English class will read what he writes. They are his audience.

The artist begins to experiment with her clay. She tries different approaches. She thinks about what her friend would like. She chooses a form—a vase.

The writer explores ideas. He experiments by getting thoughts down on paper. At this point, ideas are more important than anything else, and they do not need to be in final shape. The writer also chooses a form. He will write a descriptive paragraph for a poster.

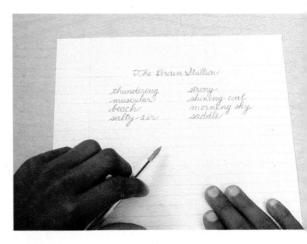

2. Writing and Shaping Ideas

The artist molds her clay into a recognizable shape. The potter's wheel helps her create the form of her vase. She now has a clear vision of the vase she will create.

The writer molds ideas into shape by writing a first draft. His ideas are organized by the form he has chosen—a description for a poster.

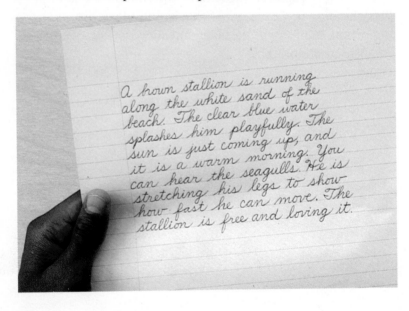

A brown stallion is running along the white sand of the beach. The clear blue water splashes him playfully. The sun is just coming up, and it is a warm morning. You can hear the seagulls. He is stretching his legs to show how fast he can move. The stallion is free and loving it.

3. Revising and Polishing

After the basic structure is shaped, the artist begins
to apply finishing touches. She uses a piece of wood
to smooth out lumps on the surface.

The writer begins to revise his first draft by reading
it. He takes a very critical look. He checks first for

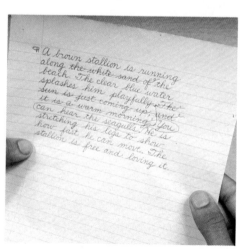

major changes,
such as ideas
that are out of
order or ones
that do not
belong. Secondly,
he edits his work,
using editing
symbols.

The artist adds finishing touches by painting, glazing, and polishing her vase. As a final step, the vase is fired in a kiln. It is now ready for display.

The writer prepares a final copy and proofreads it for errors. He looks for mistakes in spelling, capitalization, and punctuation.

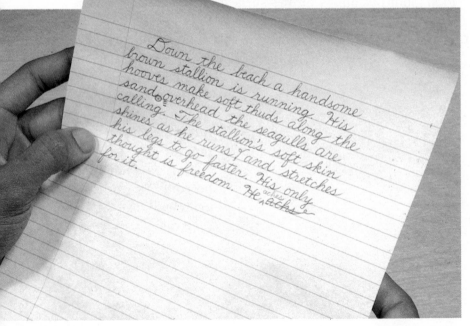

Down the beach a handsome brown stallion is running. His hooves make soft thuds along the sand overhead the seagulls are calling. The stallion's soft skin shines as he runs, and stretches his legs to go faster. His only thought is freedom. He watches for it.

4. Publishing and Sharing

The artist gives the vase to her friend for display.

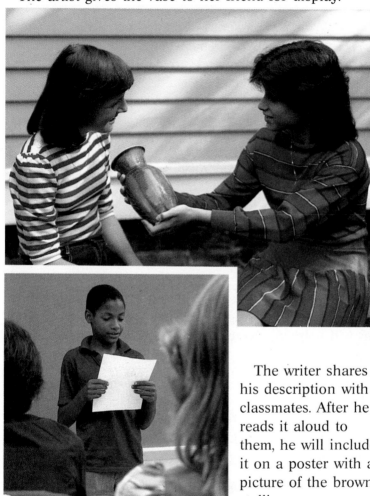

The writer shares his description with classmates. After he reads it aloud to them, he will include it on a poster with a picture of the brown stallion.

—2—The Stages of the Writing Process

> ● Writers use a series of stages called **the writing process.** These stages are prewriting, writing, revising, and publishing.

In the photo essay on the previous pages, you observed the process both artists and writers use. The writing process includes four stages—prewriting, writing, revising, and publishing. All writers go through these stages, although the time they spend on each stage varies. For instance, some writers spend more time prewriting, while others spend more time revising.

1. Prewriting

For most writers, getting started is difficult. A blank page can be frightening. Learning some prewriting strategies will help you overcome this stumbling block.

Writers warm up, or practice, by reading, researching, brainstorming, or just writing to explore or find ideas. They record ideas in journals, they scribble notes on scraps of paper, and they jot down lists on the backs of envelopes and on napkins. Some writers do most of their prewriting while staring into space, deep in thought.

On the following page is a list of prewriting strategies that you can use in the writing lessons in this book. Look them over carefully. These methods are the ones writers frequently rely upon. If you learn to use each one, you will always be able to get started on any writing assignment. You may also discover that some techniques work better for you than others.

Prewriting Methods	
Brainstorming	A group activity. Record all thoughts and ideas about a topic without judging or classifying.
Timed Writing	Write nonstop for a specified amount of time.
Journal Writing	Record ideas, experiences, and re-actions for later use.
Listing	Rapidly list words and phrases that come to mind. Later, examine the list for patterns or classifica-tions.
Dialoguing	Write a conversation between two persons or between two sides of yourself.
Reporter's Formula	Ask the questions *who*, *what*, *when*, *where*, *why*, and *how*.

In later lessons you will practice some of these tech-niques. Which of the techniques do you think will be your favorite?

2. Writing

In the writing stage, concentrate on getting ideas on paper. Stop practicing and start shaping ideas into some form, such as a short story, an article, a report, or a let-ter to the editor. At this point, write without worrying about sentence structure, punctuation, or capitalization. Save the polishing for the third stage of the process—re-vising. Revising is the stage in which you will learn to use editing symbols.

3. Revising

Most writers spend a great deal of time revising what they write. Some spend more time on this stage than on any other. Revising includes at least three parts.

Revision *Revision* literally means "to see again." Revision is like being in a parade and then seeing the parade on the nightly television news. Your first piece of writing is called a first draft. When you look at your first draft critically, you will see places that need filling in or thoughts that need clarifying. A good technique is to read your writing aloud, either to a partner or to yourself. Your hearing will tell you which parts need improvement.

Editing In editing, you look for small parts, or units, that need improvement. You prune excess words, cut overused phrases, substitute specific words for general ones, or correct usage errors. Editors use some standard symbols to make corrections. Study the editing symbols below. Then study the corrections made with them and the rewritten copy on the facing page.

SYMBOL	MEANING	EXAMPLE
ℓ	delete	I won't ~~never~~ go.
∧	add	He *has* been there.
◯↰	move	We him saw.
¶	indent	...to us. We also
≡	capital letter	New mexico
/	small letter	Give me the Ball.
∧	put in comma	May 12ˏ 1985
⊙	put in period	I like you⊙

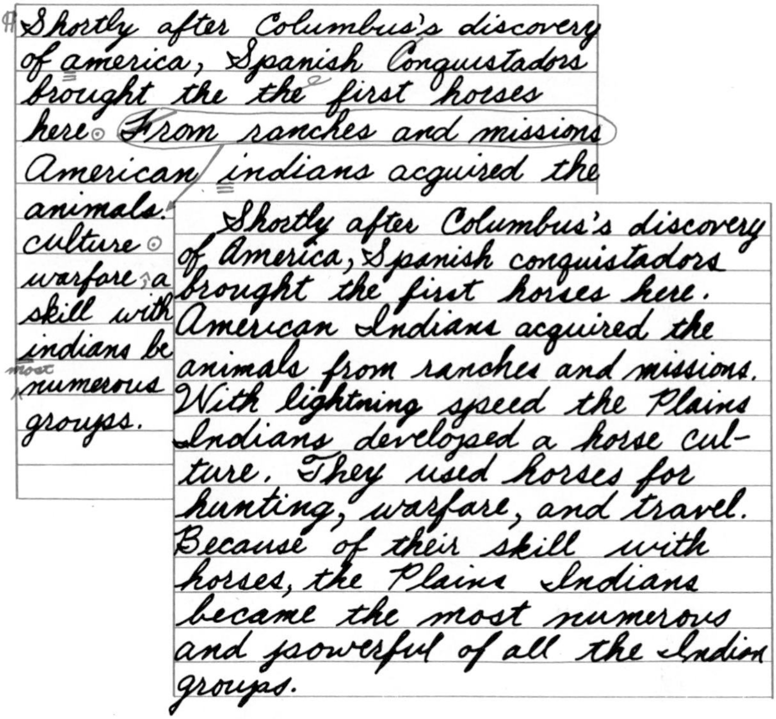

[Handwritten draft, first version with proofreading marks:]

Shortly after Columbus's discovery of america, Spanish Conquistadors brought the the first horses here. From ranches and missions American indians acquired the animals. culture warfore a skill with indians be numerous groups.

[Handwritten draft, revised version:]

Shortly after Columbus's discovery of America, Spanish conquistadors brought the first horses here. American Indians acquired the animals from ranches and missions. With lightning speed the Plains Indians developed a horse culture. They used horses for hunting, warfare, and travel. Because of their skill with horses, the Plains Indians became the most numerous and powerful of all the Indian groups.

Proofreading The final part of the revising stage is proofreading. When you proofread, you look for surface errors, such as spelling, punctuation, and capitalization. You look for careless errors. If you want your audience to read and understand what you write, proofread carefully.

4. Publishing

Publishing is the final stage of the writing process. You may think that printing is the only way to publish your writing. It is, of course, an excellent and effective way, but it is not the only one. There are many ways to publish your writing. You can post it on the class bulletin board, for example, or read it orally to another person or to an entire group or class.

Writer's Checklist

1. Is my purpose for writing clear?
2. Have I identified and analyzed my audience?
3. Is the writing appropriate for my audience?
4. Have I chosen a form that communicates my ideas to my audience?
5. Have I spent enough time prewriting—listing ideas, exploring the topic, brainstorming, jotting notes, collecting information?
6. Have I made my main idea clear to my readers?
7. Have I supported my main idea with specific details, examples, or facts?
8. Does my introduction capture the interest of my readers?
9. Do I have a conclusion, or did I simply stop writing?
10. Do my ideas flow smoothly?
11. Have I used effective transitions, both words and phrases?
12. Do I have only one main idea in a paragraph?
13. Did I include any unnecessary details?
14. Did I stay on the topic, or did I digress to something else?
15. Have I edited my writing carefully for such items as sentence structure, usage errors, and order of ideas?
16. Have I used sentence combining techniques wherever possible?
17. Have I proofread carefully for surface errors such as spelling, capitalization, and punctuation?
18. Have I read my writing *aloud* to hear how it sounds?
19. Have I made a final copy that is as correct and neat as possible?
20. Have I shared my writing with my audience?

Exercises

A. Now that you are familiar with the writing process, answer these questions about it. Write complete sentences for your answers. Some answers may require more than one sentence.

1. What are the four stages of the writing process?
2. Which stage usually causes most writers the greatest difficulty? Why?
3. What is brainstorming? What is listing?
4. What should you concentrate on in the writing stage?
5. What are the three parts of the revising stage?
6. What kind of changes should you make when you edit?
7. What kind of changes should you make when you proofread?
8. In addition to printed materials, how else can writers publish their work?
9. What stage do you think will give you the most difficulty when you write? Why?
10. For what purpose do you write most often? Who is your usual audience?

B. Review the photo essay on the writing process. Tell in your own words how the process used by the artist and the writer is similar.

Application THE WRITING PROCESS

Think about how you write. Jot down some notes and/ or use one of the prewriting strategies you have just learned. Then write a paragraph telling how you write. Keep your purpose and audience in mind. When you finish your paragraph, read it to a classmate.

A. Rewrite the paragraph below. Make all changes indicated by the editing symbols.

Trees are the oldest living things on earth. Live oaks for example can live for 1,000 years some California Redwoods are 3,200 years old! There is a bristlecone pine in the white mountains of California that has been growing for 4,800 years. The tree that grows the longest is the bristlecone pine. Many animals have long life-spans, too. A lake sturgeon a type of fish once lived for 152 years and a 116-year-old turtoise. Who would have thought tortoises could live so long? Although it is rare humens can live to be 110 or older. Seventy years was the longest lifespan ever recorded for an elephant a whale once lived to be eighty-seven.

B. Write the paragraph as it appears below. Then use editing symbols to correct errors in the paragraph. One sentence should be deleted completely, and one sentence should be moved to another location. After you edit the paragraph, rewrite it correctly.

If you think trains are old-fashuned, You should visit japan. Engineers for the japan national railways are testing trains that do not need no rails instead they floats on air. Maglev trains can travel at speeds over 300 miles per hour. These trains are called maglev trains because they are propelled by magnetic forces, And because they float above a guideway. Ordinary Trains are slowed down by friction between there wheels and rails. The Maglev trains they eliminate this friction and travel much more faster. But most Americans prefer planes to trains these days.

Every once in a while, a book appears that changes the way people live. One such book was *Silent Spring,* the first and one of the most powerful protests against destroying the environment ever written.

Its author Rachel Carson had dreamed of being a writer since the age of six. In college, however, marine biology had fascinated her, and she became a dedicated scientist. She worked at fisheries, visited wildlife refuges, and lived aboard research ships. Her knowledge and love of the sea grew and grew. To share what she loved, she began to write.

Her books introduced readers to the wonders of the ocean. Her writing not only provided information about the sea but also revealed its beauty and mystery.

In her studies Carson became aware of the deadly effects of pesticides on the environment. Pesticides were poisoning food and animals. To make others aware of the danger, she wrote her now famous *Silent Spring.* Her book drew public attention to the problem.

Application CAREERS

Environmental scientists keep records on the pollution sites they inspect. Write a paragraph describing an air, water, or land pollution problem with which you are familiar. Include the problem's cause and how to solve it.

UNIT SIX

Writing

Have you ever thought about why you write what you write? The number of reasons for writing is actually rather small. By being aware of the exact reason you are writing something, you can improve the quality of your work.

Unit Six examines eight major reasons for writing: informing, describing, narrating, creating, researching, persuading, classifying, and reasoning. Each chapter in the unit concentrates on two reasons, emphasizing the skills needed when writing for each. The chapters also provide opportunities to practice forms of writing that apply these skills.

Chapter 16 discusses informing in the context of the newspaper. You will become more familiar with the parts of a newspaper, distinguish facts from opinions, and develop interviewing techniques. To practice informative writing, you will write a **news story**.

This chapter also focuses on describing. Lessons on using the senses, writing comparisons, and noting details stress the importance of description. To put your descriptive skills to work, you will write a **character sketch.**

Narrating and creating are also reasons for writing. In Chapter 17 you will learn to write dialogue, identify the elements of a story, and narrate from different points of view. To further develop these skills, you will write a **personal experience narrative** and create a **mystery story.**

Chapter 18 concentrates on researching and persuading. You will explore researching by developing survey questions and writing a **survey summary.** By writing letters, especially a **letter of opinion,** you will become more familiar with persuasive writing.

Two final reasons for writing are classifying and reasoning. In Chapter 19 you will develop your ability to classify and then practice this skill by writing a **media review.** The reasoning portion of the chapter stresses cause and effect, drawing conclusions, and comparison and contrast. To apply these important reasoning skills, you will write a **consumer report** about a service or product.

The final chapter in the unit, Chapter 20, deals with literary forms, such as plays, poems, and myths. By the time you finish Unit Six, you should realize that writing is not just something you do in English class. The writing skills you practice in this unit will be useful in almost every other subject you study. The special-feature pages called *Building Bridges* highlight this by showing how writing is important in mathematics, social studies, science, and computer studies. Even after you finish school, however, your writing skills will help you. Writing well can lead to success in business, in community affairs, and in your personal life.

16 *Informing and Describing*

"While knowledge of facts does not guarantee intelligent decisions, intelligent decisions are difficult to make without knowledge of facts."

—Bayless Manning

1 — Learning About Newspapers

> ● A newspaper contains information in many different forms, such as news stories, feature articles, and editorials.

Although news is communicated by television and radio, newspapers and news magazines are the main sources of printed news. Printed news provides in-depth information and a written record of events.

A newspaper includes several types of information in its different sections. For instance, opinions in the form of editorials, cartoons, and letters to the editor are located in the editorial section. Sports stories are printed in their own section. Feature articles and news stories are usually located in the front part of the newspaper. Feature articles provide stories about people, places, things, and events of particular interest. The greatest amount of information, however, is communicated through the news story, a factual account of an event.

Read the news story below. Notice that the story originated in New York. The letters (*AP*) mean that the story came from the Associated Press, a national news service.

Lewis Carroll materials given to New York University library

NEW YORK (AP)—Those looking for Alice need not go so far as Wonderland. The Alfred Berol collection of Lewis Carroll materials including original editions of *Alice in Wonderland*, *Through the Looking Glass* and other writings by Carroll (real name, Charles Dodgson) has been donated to New York University's Bobst Library.

This is one of the most extensive collections of Carroll material in the world and contains many of his photographs as well. Carroll was considered to be one of the great pioneers of early photography.

He wrote his first book at the age of 14 and went to teach math at Christ Church College, Oxford, where he met the real "Alice," Alice Liddell, daughter of one of the deans. The collection contains letters to Alice Liddell from Carroll and photographs he took of her.

Exercises

A. Write where each form of writing below would be found in a newspaper. Use *front page, editorial section,* and *sports section* for your answers.

1. a letter to the editor
2. an account of a major accident
3. a column about football by a sports writer
4. a story about an international crisis
5. an editorial about raising taxes

B. Newspapers in large cities and Sunday newspapers have many sections. For each section named below, write a form of writing you could find within it.

6. business
7. travel
8. living or at home

9. classified
10. entertainment
11. magazine

C. Clip examples of the following forms of writing from your school newspaper or from your local town or city newspaper.

12. a news story
13. an editorial
14. a sports column
15. a movie review

16. an advertisement
17. a feature article
18. a letter to the editor
20. a help wanted ad

2 — Fact and Opinion

> ● A **fact** can be proven or checked. An **opinion** is a person's own thoughts or beliefs.

It is important to know the difference between fact and opinion. When you read, you need to distinguish between fact and the writer's opinion. When you watch a television commercial, you may be misled if you cannot tell what is fact and what is opinion.

A fact is something that can be proven true. It can be checked or verified. An opinion, however, is what someone thinks or believes. It is a statement of a person's viewpoint. Study the two examples below.

Fact: Eight hundred students are enrolled in the seventh grade at my school.
Opinion: All students at my school are outstanding.

The first statement is a fact. It can be proven by enrollment cards or other school records. The second statement is an opinion because it *cannot* be verified. You may either agree or disagree with it.

Facts can be checked in different ways. You can verify facts through your own observation. For example, you can check the following by looking out the window: *A dark rain cloud is looming in the east.* You can also verify facts in printed reference books such as an encyclopedia.

Some paragraphs you write will contain facts, and others will contain opinions. To develop paragraphs in a news story or research report, you would use facts. In an editorial, however, you would use your own opinion supported with appropriate, logical reasons.

Exercises ————————————————————————

A. Write *fact* or *opinion* for each sentence below.

   1. The Junior Honor Society initiated new members on April 21 of this year.

   2. Thirty seventh graders were initiated.

   3. All seventh graders were looking forward to the important event.

   4. The initiation was held in the school auditorium at 7:30 in the evening.

   5. Dr. Richard Santos was the featured speaker.

   6. Kurt Smith, Honor Society president, conducted the initiation ceremony.

   7. Everyone who attended had a great time.

   8. Kurt Smith has been a good president.

   9. Kurt is the president of the Junior Honor Society.

  10. Other officers are Kathy Baldwin, vice president, and Laura Knight, secretary.

B. Choose one of the opinion sentences below. Then write three reasons that could logically support it.

  11. My friends work hard after school.

  12. Television can be educational.

  13. Football is America's favorite sport.

  14. Country music is popular at my school.

  15. Science is hard but interesting.

Application USING THE NEWSPAPER ————————————

Using a daily newspaper, locate three statements of fact and three statements of opinion. Then try to verify the three facts by checking a reference book or by observation, if possible. Write one reason to support each opinion statement.

3 — Conducting an Interview

> ● An interview is a planned meeting to obtain information.

Conducting an interview is an effective way to collect information. It is one method that reporters use to gather news, and you can use the technique in your own writing. Because an interview has a specific purpose, it must be more structured than a conversation. Successful interviews are carefully planned. To conduct an interview, follow the steps outlined in the chart below.

Steps to Successful Interviewing	
Before the Interview	Select an appropriate person. Schedule an appointment. Research the subject or person. Write specific questions.
During the Interview	State your purpose. Listen attentively. Take accurate notes. Keep on the topic. Close with thanks.
After the Interview	Check notes and fill in details. Verify facts. Write the story immediately.

Good questions are the key to successful interviewing. Questions require careful preparation. After determining exactly what information you want to know, write down the questions you want to ask. They should be simple and direct. They should contain specific information that requires specific answers. However, avoid questions that encourage only *yes* and *no* responses.

Exercises

A. Imagine your teacher has invited the manager of the school's cafeteria to your class for an interview. Students in your class developed the following list of questions, but later they noticed that they only required *yes* and *no* responses. Rewrite the questions so that they encourage more specific information.

1. Do you like your job?
2. Do you have many responsibilities?
3. Are the menus nutritionally balanced?
4. Is much food wasted?
5. Are hamburgers your best-selling item?
6. Do many students buy lunch at the snack bar?
7. Do you ever ask students what they think about food in the cafeteria?
8. Do you think the food service could be improved?

B. Select two persons from the list below. For each person write six questions you might ask in an interview.

9. the President of the United States
10. a famous musician
11. a college football coach
12. the first female to go on a space mission
13. a teacher who has written an English textbook
14. the owner of a computer store
15. a seventh grader from China

Application INTERVIEWING

Think about three people you know whom you would like to interview. Using the checklist on the opposite page, follow all the steps for successful interviewing. Write five questions before you conduct each interview.

4 — Informing–A News Story

> ● A **news story** presents facts about people or events.

News stories compose a large portion of daily newspapers. A news story does not include the writer's opinion. It contains facts that can be proven or checked. News stories are written to inform quickly and efficiently. Facts in a news story, therefore, are presented in the order of their importance. The most important facts are included first, and the less important facts are included in descending order. This arrangement allows news editors to shorten stories quickly without leaving out vital facts.

A news story usually has a **headline** and **lead**. The headline, in large type, states the main idea of the story and captures the reader's interest. The lead is usually the first paragraph in a news story. The lead includes the most important facts. The remainder of the story includes facts that are important but not as essential.

In this lesson you will write a news story on a subject of your choice. You will use each stage of the writing process: prewriting, writing, revising, and publishing. Your *purpose* for writing will be to inform. Your *audience* will be students in your school.

1. Prewriting

Reporters use specific questions to gather information called the **Reporter's Formula.** Five questions begin with a *W* and one begins with *H*. They provide a guide for gathering facts for any story. The questions are summarized in the chart on the following page.

The Reporter's Formula	
Who?	Who did it?
What?	What happened?
When?	When did it happen?
Where?	Where did it happen?
Why?	Why did it happen?
How?	How did it happen?

▶ To begin writing your news story, select one of the events below or choose one of your own . Use the Reporter's Formula to gather information. You may want to write the questions on a piece of paper, leaving plenty of room to fill in the answers. If you need to interview a person for some facts, use the techniques you learned in Lesson 3 on interviewing.

A school play	A science fair
An essay contest	A spelling bee

2. Writing

After you gather the information, you are ready to write your news story. Facts in a news story are written in order of importance. This organizational pattern is like an **inverted pyramid**. The most important facts are written first. Other facts are presented in descending order of importance. Study the inverted pyramid below.

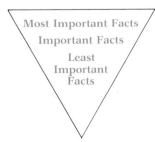

Most Important Facts

Important Facts

Least Important Facts

▶ Use the inverted pyramid pattern to write a first draft of your story. For your lead, select the most important facts from your Reporter's Formula questions. The lead can include most of the answers to the Reporter's Formula questions or only one or two. Your news story will probably contain more than one paragraph.

3. Revising

▶ Use the following Revision Checklist to revise your first draft. Every piece of writing needs revision. Revision checklists focus your thoughts on ways to improve your writing. The checklist below lists the essential elements for a good news story.

Revision Checklist—The News Story

1. Is my purpose for writing clear?
2. Is my story appropriate for my audience?
3. Have I answered all the questions in the Reporter's Formula?
4. Is my story written in the inverted pyramid pattern?
5. Does the lead contain the most important facts?
6. Does the lead contain the main idea of the story?
7. Have I omitted my own opinions?
8. Are all my facts accurate?
9. Have I placed any direct quotations within quotation marks?
10. Have I used vivid action verbs?

Editing for Verbs Action verbs are the muscle behind forceful writing. If you use too many *to be* verbs, such as *is, are, was,* and *were,* the overall impact of your story will lessen. Study how the verbs are edited in the following example news story.

Teen Rescues Drowning Child

Dana Graye [of Bayton] became a ~~H~~ero today. Last night the brave, quick-thinking teenager ~~got~~ [rescued] a Montville child from the swirling waters of the Mucatee ~~r~~iver. Using lifesaving skills learned at ~~C~~amp, Dana saved two-year-old Brian Cole of River's Landing.

The Cole child ~~was on~~ [wandered onto] the pier by the river at about 8:00 P.M. Dana, fifteen years old, ~~was also~~ [arrived] on the pier at the same time and saw the boy ~~go~~ [tumble] into the deep water.

With no other help in sight, Dana ~~went~~ [leaped] in after the youngster. Finding him in the muddy water took about ninety seconds. After carrying the unconscious tot back to the pier, the Hill School sophomore ~~helped~~ [revived] the boy with mouth-to-mouth resuscitation. Dana will be awarded the mayor's Medal of Valor.

Use the editing symbols on the *inside back cover* to insert stronger verbs and to make any other necessary corrections. Then make a final copy.

Proofreading To proofread, check for errors in spelling, capitalization, and punctuation. Refer to the Index to Rules beginning on page 575 if you have a question about one of these three items.

4. Publishing

▶ Choose one of the following ways to share your news story.

1. Submit your story to your school newspaper.
2. Display your story on the class bulletin board.

5 — Writing Sensory Details

> ● Choose details that appeal to a reader's senses.
> **Sensory details** make writing more concrete.

Think how many roads lead to your school. Each morning students come from many directions. If you are accustomed to taking the same route each day, you probably do not know all the roads others take. There are probably many roads to your school. Similarly, there are many roads to understanding.

One of these roads is sensory. By learning to use your senses fully—seeing, hearing, smelling, tasting, and feeling—you will understand the world better. When you use any of these senses to communicate an idea, you are using **sensory impressions.** In writing, details that appeal to the five senses are called sensory details. These details convey particular sensations to the reader. Study the examples below.

Sensory Impressions and Details	
Seeing	At camp the cabins are nestled among tall, protective pines.
Hearing	At night crickets serenade us to sleep.
Smelling	The heavy summer air captures the smell of the campfire's pine logs.
Tasting	I can almost taste the mellow smoke from roasting marshmallows.
Touching	The marshmallows are too hot to eat until they cool for a minute or two.

Sensory details are specific, colorful words and phrases that engage a reader's sensory impressions. Using these details will make your writing more concrete.

Exercise

To practice using all of your senses, follow each of the directions below.

1. For each of the following items, write a sentence describing how the item *looks*. Include words that describe colors, sizes, and shapes.

   your classroom   your room
   your best friend   your pet

2. For each item below, write one sentence that describes the *sound* of the item.

   a beach   an electric saw
   a motorcycle   a thunderstorm

3. For each of the following items, write one sentence describing how the item *feels*.

   a kitten   a plastic bag
   a peach   a pencil point

4. For each item below, write one sentence describing the *taste* of the item.

   a lemon drop   a baked potato
   a watermelon   a pickle

5. For each item below, write a sentence describing the *smell* of the item.

   a perfume bottle   a haystack
   a campfire   a clothes closet

6 — Writing Comparisons

> ● **Similes** and **metaphors** compare one object or thing to another to create vivid images.

Writers paint word pictures with good sensory details, but they can go one step further. They can also point out resemblances, or similarities, between objects. By comparing one object to another, writers give readers a more vivid image of what an object looks like. Good description, then, relies on specific details, sensory impressions, and certain expressions called **figures of speech** that create word pictures.

Two figures of speech, similes and metaphors, can help you describe objects or things more vividly. Both similes and metaphors are comparisons. A simile directly compares two unlike things with the word *like* or *as*. A metaphor compares two unlike things by implying a similarity between them. The words *like* and *as* are not used.

Simile: The puffy white clouds marching across the sky look like white cotton candy.
Metaphor: The clouds were giant balls of cotton candy.

When you use comparisons in your own writing, create ones from your own experience that are fresh and original. Some similes and metaphors have lost effectiveness from overuse. Overused similes and metaphors are called **clichés.** Phrases such as *quiet as a mouse* and *busy as a bee* are clichés. They should be avoided.

Metaphors and similes are especially useful in descriptive writing. When you need to describe a person, for example, they can make characteristics more colorful and precise.

Exercises ————————————————————

A. Each sentence below contains either a simile or a metaphor. Write *simile* or *metaphor* for each sentence.

1. The rain sounded like a raven pecking on a windowpane.
2. The small boat sliced the water like a sharp knife.
3. Her skin was velvet.
4. The magician was a flash of lightning.
5. Ted smiled like a child with an ice-cream cone.
6. Jack thought the party was as dull as a Sunday afternoon piano recital.
7. The final examination loomed like rapids on a Colorado river.
8. Carrie was a sunrise.
9. Her hair was a field of wild strawberries.
10. James's report card was as welcome as a notice about an overdue library book.

B. Write each sentence below, using an original simile or metaphor for the blank.

EXAMPLE: Morning is ———.
ANSWER: Morning is starlight.

11. The boy was as quiet as ———.
12. The basketball is ———.
13. The class was as interesting as ———.
14. The dress was as beautiful as ———.
15. The steep cliffs of the mountains were ———.
16. The battered automobile looked like ———.
17. The new movie theater is ———.
18. The autumn leaves mingled among one another like ———.
19. When I write, I always feel like ———.
20. The young woman's face was ———.

7 — Writing a Descriptive Paragraph

- To write a **descriptive paragraph,** observe carefully and choose specific details.

As you know, description paints pictures with words. To describe a person or scene, several procedures are involved. The first is observing carefully. The second is noting and recording details, and the third is selecting what details to write.

When describing a person, include both physical characteristics, such as size, shape, and clothing, and personality traits, such as helpfulness, lovableness, and intelligence. Use of both physical characteristics and personality traits creates a general impression of the person. In *I Know Why the Caged Bird Sings,* Maya Angelou uses details to describe the character Mrs. Flowers. Read the paragraph below. Notice how Maya Angelou uses specific details.

Mrs. Bertha Flowers was the aristocrat of Black Stamps. She had the grace of control to appear warm in the coldest weather, and on the Arkansas summer days it seemed she had a private breeze which swirled around, cooling her. She was thin without the taut look of wiry people, and her printed voile* dresses and flowered hats were as right for her as denim overalls for a farmer.

*fine soft fabric used especially for women's summer clothing

Exercises

A. Reread the paragraph about Mrs. Flowers. Write three physical characteristics used to describe Mrs. Flowers. Then write three personality traits used.

B. Rewrite the following sentences to include more descriptive details.

1. The new girl entered our classroom.
2. The man walked down the street.
3. The gas station was closed.
4. The light was bright.
5. The hamburger tempted the dog.

Application WRITING A DESCRIPTIVE PARAGRAPH

Look at the picture below. First, consider the general impression this person makes on you. What are his physical characteristics? What personality traits can you determine? Second, list five descriptive details you could use to support your general impression. Third, organize your descriptive details into a good paragraph.

8 —Describing–A Character Sketch

> ● A **character sketch** is a piece of writing in which a person is described.

In a character sketch a writer creates a strong impression of a person in a reader's mind by using carefully selected descriptive details. Descriptive details in a character sketch describe a person's physical characteristics as well as his or her personality traits. Physical characteristics show how a person looks—height, bone structure, color of hair and eyes. Personality traits include qualities such as kindness, courage, and sincerity.

In this lesson you will describe a person who is important to you. You may want to write about a teacher, a parent, or a friend. Select a person who has made a strong impression on you. Your *purpose* for writing is to describe. Your *audience* is your classmates.

1. Prewriting

Listing is a useful prewriting strategy. A list forces you to look at specific details and to record them for later use. When making a list, write whatever comes to mind. Read the model list below about a jogger.

Prewriting List–Description of a Jogger	
Physical Characteristics	**Personality Traits**
strong legs	determined
healthy	optimistic
blue gym suit	dedicated runner
brown hair	enjoys keeping
green eyes	fit

▶ After choosing a person to describe, list as many details as you can. Include both physical characteristics and personality traits. Reread your list and circle the ideas you want to include.

2. Writing

If you have many details from your prewriting list, you are probably wondering how you will include all of them. Obviously you should choose the ones that are most significant. In your character sketch you will include only those details that help create the impression you want your audience to receive.

Descriptive paragraphs must be organized in a logical way. As you know, most descriptive paragraphs are organized in space order. In space order you can describe a person from top to bottom or from head to foot.

▶ The chart below outlines the structure for a descriptive paragraph. Use it as a guide. The topic sentence should present the overall or main impression of the person. It could be followed by supporting sentences and a clincher sentence. If your sketch is more than one paragraph, you would introduce the overall or main impression in the first paragraph, write one or more supporting paragraphs, and end with a concluding paragraph.

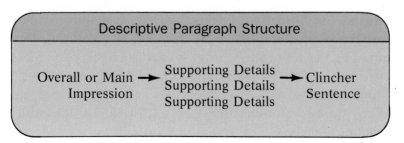

Descriptive Paragraph Structure

Overall or Main Impression → Supporting Details Supporting Details Supporting Details → Clincher Sentence

3. Revising

▶ Use the following checklist as a guide for revising your character sketch.

> ### Revision Checklist—The Character Sketch
>
> 1. What information should I include for an audience that is unfamiliar with this person?
> 2. Is what I have written appropriate for my audience?
> 3. How do I want the reader to feel about this person? Do my words or phrases convey this main impression?
> 4. Is a single main impression clearly presented in my topic sentence?
> 5. Does every detail support the main impression I want to create?
> 6. Are my details arranged in logical order?
> 7. What details can I use to involve the reader's sense of sight, sound, smell, touch, or taste?
> 8. Have I used at least three details to support my main impression?
> 9. Will the details create word pictures in the reader's mind?
> 10. Have I used colorful, vivid adjectives?

Editing for Adjectives Adjectives are descriptive words that make your writing more specific and colorful. For example, the following words vividly describe eyes: shimmering, glossy, blazing, emerald, hollow, or velvety. Hands can be animated, immense, jeweled, slender, or grimy. Study how adjectives are added in the following example sketch.

The jogger was a dedicated ~~regular~~ runner. Every day, for over a year, he ran the five ~~rough~~ *grueling* miles from town out to our farm and back again.

The man's ~~young~~ *boyish* face shone with determination. His bright *intense, green* eyes seemed to flash the message "Keep at it." His nose was open *long, straight* wide to let in the oxygen. His lips formed *finely curved* a smile that seemed to say "I am going faster. I am getting better."

Day after day the jogger wore an ~~old dark~~ *ancient blue* gym suit and running *dirty* shoes. His head, always ~~straight~~ *erect*, faced his *distant* goal. His thin *lean* arms pumped up and down like pistons. His legs, ~~thin~~ *wiry* bundles of muscles, stretched forward powerfully. Last Spring a few days passed with no sign of the runner. I was worried until I heard he had gone to france and won a marathon!

Use the editing symbols on the *inside back cover* to insert more specific adjectives and to make any other necessary corrections. Then, using your best handwriting, make a final copy.

Proofreading To proofread, check for errors in spelling, capitalization, and punctuation. Refer to the Index to Rules beginning on page 575 if you have a question about one of these three items.

4. Publishing

▶ Select one of the following ways to share your character sketch with your audience.

1. Combine your character sketch with those of other students to create a book called *Important People.*
2. Draw a picture of the person you have described and display it on a poster with your sketch.

Building Bridges to Computers

Janet Singh is an architect who designs houses by computer. At the push of a button, she can change the dimensions of a room, add a closet, or take away a window. The computer also calculates building costs in seconds. When a design is completed, the computer prints copies of the final floor plan.

The computer screen below shows the first level of a house that the architect designed.

Janet Singh plans to send the floor plan to a client who wants to build a house. She also plans to send him a written description of the house, indicating its many positive features. Because she is describing a particular place, the architect will organize her description according to space order.

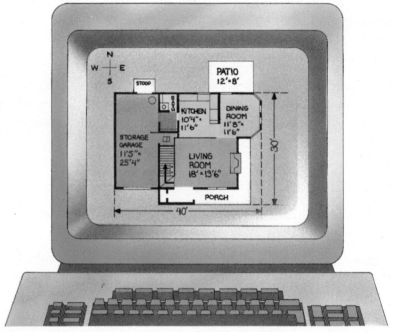

Exercises

A. Read the beginning of the description of the house below. Then, referring to the floor plan on the computer screen on the facing page, complete the description. Organize your description according to space order. You will write more than one paragraph.

Upon entering the spacious living room from the front porch, you will notice the stairs to the upstairs on your left. This provides both convenience and privacy. The focus of the living room is the large fireplace on the east wall. A large picture window looks out onto the porch and beyond.

B. The floor plan below shows the second level of the same house. Using space order again, write a detailed description of this level.

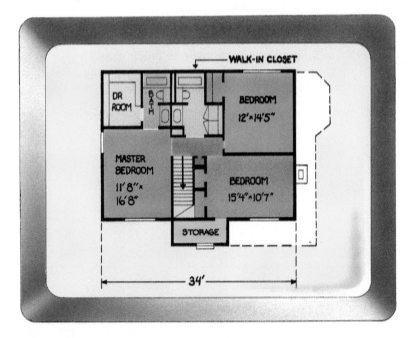

17 Narrating and Creating

"Plots come to me at such odd moments;
when I am walking along a street, or exam-
ining a hat shop with particular interest,
suddenly a splendid idea comes into my
head, and I think, 'Now that would be a
neat way of covering up the crime so that
nobody would see the point.' Of course, all
the practical details are still to be worked
out, and the people have to creep slowly
into my consciousness, but I jot down my
splendid idea in an exercise book."

—*Agatha Christie*

1 — First Person in a Narrative Paragraph

> ● Use first-person **point of view** to write about yourself.

Your point of view is how you look at your world. It is your vantage point. When writing, you must choose a point of view from which to tell a narrative, or story. If you were writing a narrative based on your personal experience, you would use first-person point of view. You would use personal pronouns such as *I, me,* and *mine.*

If you were writing fiction, or a story about something that did not really happen, you could use either first-person or third-person point of view. In third person you would use personal pronouns such as *, he, she,* and *they.* If you used first person to tell a fictional story, the "I" would not be yourself but rather an imaginary character.

In *I Know Why the Caged Bird Sings,* Maya Angelou uses first-person point of view to tell about her childhood in Stamps, Arkansas. Read the personal experience narrative below about her memory of her favorite place.

> Until I was thirteen and left Arkansas for good, the Store was my favorite place to be. Alone and empty in the mornings, it looked like an unopened present from a stranger. Opening the front doors was pulling the ribbon off the unexpected gift. The light would come in softly (we faced north), easing itself over the shelves of mackerel, salmon, tobacco, thread. It fell flat on the big vat of lard and by noontime during the summer the grease had softened to a thick soup. Whenever I walked into the Store in the afternoon, I sensed that it was tired. I alone could hear the slow pulse of its job half done.

Exercises

A. Each sentence below is written in either first-person or third-person point of view. For each sentence, write *first person* or *third person.*

1. His family plans a camping trip this summer.
2. My family also plans a camping trip this summer.
3. I am looking forward to the vacation.
4. It provides an opportunity to observe nature.
5. They enjoy camping because they like the outdoors.
6. I like the outdoors also.
7. Next summer her family plans to camp in the Rocky Mountains.
8. Mine is going to camp in the Sierra Nevada.
9. My favorite activity is white-water rafting.
10. More families should try camping vacations.

B. The paragraph below is written in the third person. Rewrite the paragraph in the first-person point of view.

Brian dreamed about his family's camping vacation. A trip to the Rocky Mountains offered a wide variety of fun. Activities included white-water rafting, horseback riding, and all-day hiking trips to ranger stations high on mountain peaks. Brian liked being close to nature. He enjoyed sitting in pine forests and watching deer and chipmunks. He could even observe mountain trout lurking in crystal streams. Brian could hardly wait until June when his family's vacation would begin.

Application WRITING A PARAGRAPH

Using the topic sentence below, write a narrative paragraph in the first-person point of view.

I love Saturdays because _____.

–2—Writing Dialogue

> • Dialogue is written conversation.

Dialogue in a story is conversation between characters. In writing, dialogue serves special functions. First, dialogue reveals a character's personality. Second, dialogue advances the story. It helps create action and reveals what characters plan to do. Third, dialogue creates a sense of immediacy. The audience feels as if it were in the middle of the action. Fourth, dialogue makes a story more like real life. Below is an example showing how dialogue is written. The dialogue was written by a student.

"Jane," called my sister. "Jane, where are you?"

"Oh, no!" groaned my friend Kim. "Do you have to leave now, Jane? We're in the middle of this computer program."

"I'll ask if I can stay longer," I answered, "but I'm not sure my sister will agree."

My sister walked into the computer room. She smiled and said, "Would you like to work some more on the computer?"

"Yes!" I said, grinning shyly.

Dialogue is written in a special way. To be understandable, it must be indented and punctuated correctly. Begin a new paragraph each time a different person speaks. Additionally, be sure to establish the name of the speaker the first time he or she speaks. If you do this, you do not need to repeat the speaker's name each time, or *he said* and *she said* over and over again.

Writing dialogue requires a good knowledge of punctuation. The box below reviews some of the rules about quotation marks. You may wish to refer to pages 252–255 for more information on writing quotations correctly.

How to Write Dialogue

1. Indent each time another person speaks.
2. Enclose a speaker's exact words in quotation marks.
3. Begin each direct quotation with a capital letter.
4. Put a comma after *he said* or *she said* in the second part of a divided quotation if it is not a separate sentence.
5. Do not put quotation marks around every sentence spoken by the same person. Put them around the entire uninterrupted speech.

Exercise

Select one of the situations below. Then write a dialogue between the two persons.

1. A twelve-year-old girl talking to a sales clerk about buying a bicycle
2. A student explaining to a librarian why a library book was lost
3. A twelve-year-old boy talking to an employer about a summer job
4. A student asking a parent for help with homework
5. Two friends making plans for Saturday

3 — Narrating— A Personal Experience Narrative

> ● A **personal experience** narrative tells a story about yourself.

A narrative is a story. The story may be real, as in personal experience narratives and autobiographies, or the story may be imagined, as in short stories and novels. In a personal experience narrative, the writer tells about his or her own life. The writer uses first-person point of view and first-person pronouns such as *I, me, my, mine, we, us,* and *ours*. You must be consistent and maintain the first-person point of view. You are limited to events that you know from your own experience.

In this lesson you will develop your narrative skills by writing a story about yourself. Later you will share it, with your classmates as your *audience*. Your writing *purpose* is to tell a story to entertain.

1. Prewriting

You have had many interesting experiences to write about. Think about the most memorable. Perhaps you received an honor, won a contest, or learned something important to you. You may want to write about a special holiday or birthday. When you decide upon an experience, think of just *one word* that represents that experience such as *vacation, award,* or *birthday*. This one word will form the center, or nucleus, of your narrative.

A good way to generate ideas for writing is to develop a word cluster. Clustering is a form of word association. To create a cluster, choose a word or phrase and write it in the center of a clean piece of paper. Then write words that associate with the word or phrase. The words will spread out like ripples on a pond. A cluster takes about ten minutes. Write rapidly. Study the example below.

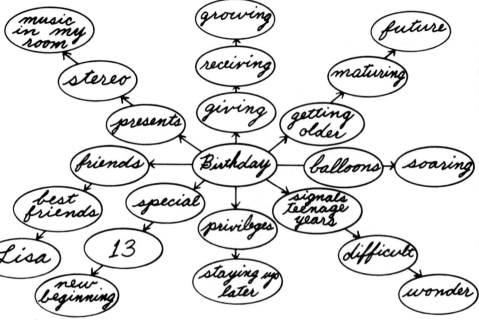

▶ Now select your own topic. Choose a central word or phrase, and write a word cluster. When you finish clustering, select the ideas you like best.

2. Writing

Use the cluster you developed to organize your ideas for your narrative. In personal experience narratives, details are usually organized in the order they happen, or in time order. As you write, you may want to use some of the connecting words in the box on the following page. They can help connect your ideas and make your writing read more smoothly and clearly.

after	later	then
before	meanwhile	next
finally	at the same time	soon

▶Now write a first draft of your story. Be sure to include dialogue and a title.

3. Revising

▶Read your first draft aloud to yourself or to someone else. How does it sound? How can it be improved? Use this checklist to help you revise.

Revision Checklist—The Personal Experience Narrative

1. Will my story appeal to my audience?
2. Have I used first-person point of view?
3. Have I used first-person pronouns consistently?
4. Have I used specific details?
5. Have I included only those events or details that I have seen or heard personally?
6. Have I used time order to organize my ideas?
7. Have I used connecting words and phrases to help organize my time order?
8. Have I used dialogue?

Editing Use the editing symbols on the *inside back cover* to edit your story. You may have to move some sentences around if they are not in logical order.

Proofreading for Dialogue When you are writing a personal narrative, dialogue can help you tell your story. Study how the dialogue is proofread in the following example story.

Caught in the Whirlwind

Tornado! The word makes my hair stand on end and my shoulders shake. Why is my reaction so strong? Three months ago I was caught in the path of one of those violent clouds of destruction.

I was visiting my cousin Biff at the time. It had been a humid morning, and a thunderstorm began at noon. A little later, I heard a strange roar like a freight train.

"what was that?" I asked Biff. I was confused. He screamed, "twister!" Then my Aunt Lena commanded "Everyone, get to the cellar!"

Through the dusty cellar window, I caught a glimpse of the giant black funnel. It seemed half a mile wide, rising and falling as it crossed the landscape.

"Look!" I gasped "it's heading toward us!"

"Get away from that window!" barked Biff. Finally, the noise grew so loud I hid my head and saw nothing.

Minutes later it was over. We were safe, but Aunt Lena's house had lost part of its roof. The screams of sirens filled the air, and I stood shivering, thinking about the fury that had passed so near.

4. Publishing

▶ Choose one of the following ways to share your personal experience narrative with your audience.

1. Read it aloud before the class.
2. Post it on the class bulletin board.

4 — Third Person in a Narrative Paragraph

- Use third-person point of view to write about people you know or characters you create.

Writers often use third-person point of view to write about real people besides themselves or fictional characters they create. Using third person allows writers to write from someone else's point of view. They can become other people. They use personal pronouns such as *he, she, it,* and *they* and not *I, me, my,* and *mine*. With this point of view, the thoughts and feelings of many characters can be shown.

The paragraph below is from *The Red House Mystery*. Writer A. A. Milne uses third-person point of view to describe the feelings and thoughts of one character, Antony Gillingham. Notice the use of the pronoun *he*.

To Antony, who was older and who realized into what deep waters they were getting, it did not seem fun. But it was amazingly interesting. He saw so much, and yet somehow it was all out of focus. It was like looking at an opal, and discovering with every movement of it some new color, some new gleam of light reflected, and yet never really seeing the opal as a whole. He was too near it, or too far away; he strained his eyes and he relaxed his eyes; it was no good. His brain could not get hold of it.

Exercises

A. The sentences below are written in either first-person or third-person point of view. For each sentence write *first person* or *third person.*

1. I like to read mystery stories.
2. The search had yielded nothing. They were completely lost and defeated.
3. Charles said that many stolen items ended up with the police. Perhaps he should check with them.
4. I saw Nancy take the jacket and hang it in the closet. However, that is all I saw.
5. Exhilarated by their searches, they had entered into the spirit of the mystery.
6. The criminal in a mystery story never succeeds in entirely covering up his or her tracks.
7. A detective usually finds clues that lead to the individual who committed the crime.
8. When I write a mystery story, I become completely involved. I like to work out all the details.
9. Clues can be objects that belong to the criminal or that in some way are associated with him or her.
10. In a mystery a chase is usually physical, but it may also be a contest of wits.

B. Select one of the topic sentences below. Then write a paragraph using third-person point of view.

11. Maria was determined to win first place.
12. Evan had always wanted to be a singer.
13. When Jeff awoke, the water was already two inches deep on his bedroom floor.
14. When Alice noticed that the purse was missing, she alerted her classmates.
15. The teacher had just finished the writing lesson.

5 Elements of the Short Story

> • The basic elements of a short story are **setting, plot,** and **character**.

People love stories. Storytelling was a popular form of entertainment long before stories were copied by hand or printed. Storytelling is still a popular form of entertainment, and many books of short stories are published and read each year.

Unlike novels, short stories are short pieces of fiction. They can be written about different subjects—science fiction, adventure, mystery. A short story always has three basic elements; they are setting, plot, and characters.

The setting is the time and place in which the story occurs. For example, a story could be set in New Jersey in 1962. The plot is the story plan. It is the action, or sequence of events, and contains the **conflict,** or problem to be solved. The characters are the people (or animals) in a story. How the characters behave or act in the story creates the plot. Without plot and action, there is no story.

Every story has a beginning, a middle, and an end. In the beginning the writer often establishes the setting, provides the conflict, and introduces the characters. The middle is often a series of action-packed episodes, or scenes, that advance the plot and build toward a **climax**. In the climax something happens to conclude the conflict. In the end the writer resolves the problem and ties up loose ends. To summarize, a short story essentially relates a main character's attempt to attain a goal.

Read the following short story, which is a mystery. Be prepared to answer questions about the basic elements of the story.

The Pet Shop Rip-off

"Let's see if there are any puppies in the pet shop window," Sara said to Bill Tawson. "Poor Mr. Gray hasn't been doing so well, but there might be some. This isn't a very good location."

They crossed the quiet street, but there was no quiet inside the little shop. Through the shop window they could see two teenaged boys struggling fiercely with each other, and Mr. Gray slumped unconscious over the counter.

Like a shot, Bill surged through the door and the boys fell apart.

As Sara called an ambulance, one boy cried, "It was he! He was trying to rob the cash register and I jumped him!"

"You lie!" yelled the other boy. "I caught you!"

"I know both these boys," Sara said after completing her call. "George Simmons and Hal Ferrell. They both worked for Mr. Gray up until about three months ago, when his business began to get so bad. I can't believe either one of them would do this. How did you both happen to be here today?"

"I've been coming in to teach the myna birds to talk," George answered. "You can check. One of them says 'Hi, George.' People like them to be able to say something when they buy them. Of course, they just pick some things up—"

"I came to see if the baby rabbits had been born yet," Hal said, glaring at George. "Some were expected when I left, and Mr. Gray said I could have one."

"Oh, now, come on," George began, making a move toward Hal. Bill stiffened, and Sara shook her head.

"No more trouble please," she said. "I know who the thief is, and which one is the hero, and I think both these boys know that I do."

Which one was it?

The answer appears upside down below.

Hal The gestation, or pregnancy, period of rabbits is thirty-one days. Both boys knew that if they'd been expected three months before, they'd hardly be "babies" now.

This mystery story has its setting in a pet shop, a plot that involves a theft, and five characters. In addition to these basic elements common to all stories, mystery stories also include some special elements. They are summarized in the chart below.

Elements of a Mystery Story

A Crime

A criminal

A detective

Suspects

Police

Clues

Exercises

A. Write complete sentences to answer the questions below about the short story.

1. What is the setting?
2. What is the basic plot?
3. What is the plot's central problem?
4. How does Sara solve the problem?
5. Is the ending believable and logical? Why?

B. Write a plan for a story based on the pictures below. You will have to create a main character who must solve a problem to reach a goal. The maze represents some obstacles, or complications, that the main character must overcome to find a missing jewelry box. You will also have to create a setting and some clues to help find the missing jewels. Your plan should include how the character solves the problem, or overcomes the complications. You do not need to write a complete story. Just write a paragraph telling your story plan.

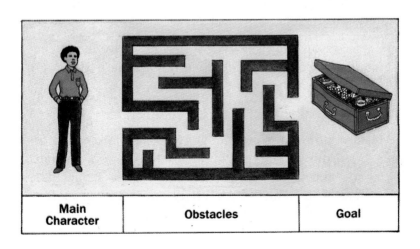

| Main Character | Obstacles | Goal |

6 – Creating–A Mystery Story

> • A **mystery story** creates suspense and directly involves the reader in the plot.

You are probably familiar with the adventures of the most famous detective in literature—Sherlock Holmes. You may have read about the cases of other famous detectives, or you may have seen movies based upon Agatha Christie novels. These popular stories are mysteries, stories about "who-did-it?"

Mystery stories are popular with all age groups. Everyone loves a secret, and as a mystery story unravels, one person, often a detective, uncovers a secret, usually the criminal's. A mystery story is about "who-did-it" and why. Plot, therefore, is the most important element in a mystery story.

In this lesson, you will write a mystery story for a teenage *audience.* Your *purpose* for writing will be to entertain.

1. Prewriting

Mystery stories are fun to write. To explore ideas for your story, draw a chart similar to the one on the next page. The chart includes six headings. They name most of the basic elements of a mystery story. To get started, some examples are already included. Add three examples of your own under each category.

Prewriting List

Crime	Criminal	Motive	Crime Solvers	Setting	Clues
arson (setting a fire to cause harm)	tenant in apartment building	anger at landlord's negligence	police officer	city apartment building	discarded matches
theft	servant in wealthy household	money in safe	detective	country estate	finger-prints

▶ Circle one entry from each category. Write at least three sentences to describe the crime, the criminal, the motive, the crime solver, the setting, and the clues.

2. Writing

Most mystery stories follow a formula readers expect. To organize your story, use the formula below.

Mystery Story Formula

- A crime is committed. (What crime? Where?)
- The crime is discovered. (How? By whom?)
- Someone decides to solve the mystery. (Who? Why?)
- Suspects are named. (What are their motives?)
- The crime solver looks for clues. (These may be objects or statements from witnesses.)
- While pursuing suspects, the crime solver usually gets into a dangerous position.
- The mystery is solved, and the criminal confesses.

Remember that every story has a beginning, a middle, and an end. The beginning of your mystery story should hold the reader's interest and set the stage for the rest of the action. The middle should detail the action. Remember that your story will seem more believable if you use dialogue. Toward the end of the story, in the climax, let the reader know the mystery is solved, but do not tell them *how* it is solved. Reveal the solution in the ending.

▶ Now use the formula to write a draft of your own mystery story. First, reread the example mystery story on page 383.

3. Revising

▶ Read your first draft aloud to yourself or to someone else. How does it sound? Can you improve it? Use the checklist below to revise your story.

Revision Checklist—The Mystery Story

1. Does my story have a beginning, a middle, and an ending?
2. Does my story follow the Mystery Story Formula?
3. Have I written an interesting beginning?
4. Do I have a suspenseful, action-packed plot?
5. Is each character, especially the criminal and the crime solver, motivated by believable reasons?
6. Have I provided at least three legitimate clues to the criminal's identity?
7. Have I used dialogue to advance the action and to make the characters more real?
8. Is my climax suspenseful?
9. Is my solution logical?
10. Have I used verbs tenses consistently?

Editing for Verb Tense   Tense indicates time, and time is critical in a mystery story. Also critical in a good mystery is action. The words that convey both time and action are verbs. Unnecessary shifts from one verb tense to another hurt the telling of the story. You should use one verb tense consistently unless the time changes. For example, do not use present tense, past tense, and then future tense in the same sentence or passage. Study how the verbs are edited in the following example.

> I talked with my teacher after class. She ~~says~~ *said* that I ~~write~~ *wrote* a good mystery story. I thanked her. I told her I ~~will~~ *enjoyed* enjoy the writing assignment.

All the verbs in the above passage should be in the past tense. Use the editing symbols on the *inside back cover* to correct verb tenses and to make other corrections in your mystery story. Then make a final copy.

Proofreading   To proofread, check for errors in spelling, capitalization, and punctuation. Refer to the Index to Rules beginning on page 575 if you have a question about one of these three items.

4. Publishing

▶ Select one way to share your mystery story.

1. Prepare copies for classmates.
2. Record your story. Create a "Mystery Hour" radio program, using your story and those of classmates.

Building Bridges to Social Studies

As part of a social studies project, Travis had to write a two-paragraph report about the first fifteen years of Virginia's colonial history. He decided to use time order to organize his report because it is a clear and logical way to describe a series of events.

While doing research for the report, Travis constructed a time line. A time line shows both when important events occurred and the order in which they occurred. A time line also shows which events or conditions were occurring simultaneously within a particular period. In a way, the time line acts like an outline. It helps Travis to include important events in their correct order.

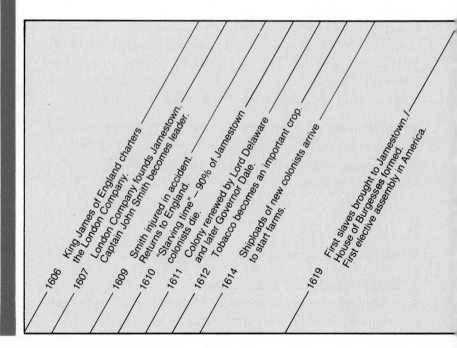

King James of England charters the London Company. 1606

London Company founds Jamestown. Captain John Smith becomes leader. 1607

Smith injured in accident. Returns to England. 1609

"Starving time" – 90% of Jamestown colonists die. 1610

Colony renewed by Lord Delaware and later Governor Dale. 1611

Tobacco becomes an important crop. 1612

Shiploads of new colonists arrive to start farms. 1614

First slaves brought to Jamestown. House of Burgesses formed. First elective assembly in America. 1619

Exercises

A. Read the first paragraph of Travis's report below. Then use the time line on the facing page to write the second paragraph.

In 1607, only one year after it received its charter from King James of England, the London Company established the colony of Jamestown in Virginia. The first colonists depended heavily on their resourceful leader, Captain John Smith. After Smith returned to England in 1609 because of an accident, conditions in Jamestown became very bad. Approximately ninety percent of the settlers died of starvation and sickness in 1610.

B. The following time line shows key events in the history of New Netherland. Use the time line below to write a two-paragraph report about its history.

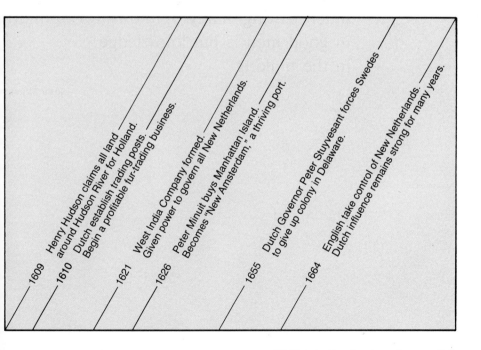

1609 — Henry Hudson claims all land around Hudson River for Holland.

1610 — Dutch establish trading posts. Begin a profitable fur-trading business.

1621 — West India Company formed. Given power to govern all New Netherlands.

1626 — Peter Minuit buys Manhattan Island. Becomes "New Amsterdam," a thriving port.

1655 — Dutch Governor Peter Stuyvesant forces Swedes to give up colony in Delaware.

1664 — English take control of New Netherlands. Dutch influence remains strong for many years.

18 *Researching and Persuading*

"Where there is much desire to learn, there of necessity will be much arguing, much writing, many opinions; for opinion in good men is but knowledge in the making."

—John Milton

1 — Taking a Survey

> ● A **survey**, or poll, gathers information from people about specific subjects.

Polls and surveys influence lives every day. Your favorite television program may be canceled because of a survey. A new traffic light near your house may result from a survey of traffic patterns.

Surveying is a big industry in the United States. Many people make surveying a career. Advertising agencies often study survey results before planning advertising campaigns or before introducing new products on the market. Politicians consult opinion polls before voting on controversial issues or before deciding whether or not to seek a political office. Presidents consult poll results to learn the views of people on important topics. Hollywood movie producers have paid pollsters to survey Americans to learn what kinds of films they enjoy most.

Polling is a good way to get information. The first surveys were simple head counts. The word *poll* comes from an old English word for *head.* During the Middle Ages, the English held elections by counting heads, or *pols.* The sophisticated polling known today began in the 1930s with the work of such famous pollsters as George Gallop, Elmo Roper, and Archibald Crossley.

You can use polling and survey techniques to gather information and then summarize the results in writing. You can also use survey results as factual support for writing editorials, letters to the editor, and news stories for your school newspaper.

To conduct your own survey, use the following checklist as a guide.

How to Conduct a Survey

1. Think about the information you need. Then write a sentence stating what you need to know.
2. Define your audience. Who are the people you want to survey?
3. Decide how the survey will be conducted—by mail, telephone, or personal interview.
4. Choose a sample of people to be surveyed.
5. Develop a survey questionnaire. Make it simple so that the results will be easy to figure out.
6. Try out, or pretest, the questionnaire to see if questions receive the responses you want.
7. Conduct the survey and check the responses.
8. Record the results. Summarize the information in written form.

Exercise

Write answers in complete sentences to the following questions about surveys.

1. Why do people take surveys?
2. Do you think a survey is a good way to gather information? Why or why not?
3. List three industries that use surveys to gather information.
4. Which type of survey do you think would get the most responses—mail or personal interview? Why?
5. Do you think polling and surveying will become even more important in the future? Explain your answer.
6. Why is it important for you to know about polls and how they are conducted?
7. How can you use surveys in your writing?

2 — Writing Survey Questions

> ● Word survey questions carefully.

Every survey begins with a general question. This general question summarizes the main information you want to know. The next step is then to write specific questions to gather detailed, supporting information. To receive valid information, word your questions carefully.

When developing a survey, keep it simple. Generally, ask questions that can be answered either by *yes* or *no*. If questions are open-ended, or ask for opinions, answers may stray off the topic. Next, use a quick method, such as simple addition, to figure out the results. Finally, decide how you will summarize the information in writing when you complete the survey. Study the sample survey questionnaire below.

		SURVEY QUESTIONNAIRE
		General Question: Should the school library be called the Learning Resource Center?
Yes	**No**	
☐	☐	**1.** Do you prefer the title *Library Services?*
☐	☐	**2.** Do you prefer the title *Learning Resource Center?*
☐	☐	**3.** Are you satisfied with present library services?
☐	☐	**4.** Would you like to see library services expanded?
☐	☐	**5.** Do you think the library is mainly a place for books?
☐	☐	**6.** Do you think the library should have more films, records, and tapes?
☐	☐	**7.** Do you think more students would use the library if more services were available?

After a questionnaire has been developed, it should be distributed to a large number of people. For the library questionnaire, it should reach as many students and teachers as possible. Selected individuals should also be interviewed to support survey findings.

SURVEY FINDINGS—215 people surveyed		
Prefer title Library Services	65	
Prefer title Learning Resource Center	150	
Satisfied with present services	102 yes	113 no
Like to see services expanded	180 yes	35 no
Library is mainly for books	55 yes	160 no
Should have more films, etc.	165 yes	50 no
More students would use the library	130 yes	85 no

Survey findings should be summarized in paragraph form.

About three fourths of the students and teachers in our school who were questioned would prefer the library to be called a Learning Resource Center. Although almost half of those surveyed were satisfied with present services, they would still like to see them expanded. Most do not think the library is only a place for books. Films, records, and tapes are also important library services that students and teachers want and need. In addition, the survey revealed that approximately two thirds of those questioned thought more students would use the library if services were increased. Follow-up interviews also supported these findings.

Exercise

Using the general topic "Commercials in Children's Television Shows," develop a survey questionnaire of your own.

3 — Researching–A Survey Summary

> • A **survey summary** records in writing the results of information gathering.

Conducting a survey gives you experience with *primary* research. Often you acquire information from reading what someone else has written about a subject. When you read, you are getting information from a *secondary* source. Although reading secondary sources is a good way to acquire information and verify facts, thorough research also involves primary research—research conducted from an original source such as a survey.

In previous lessons you learned about polling and surveying. In this lesson you will conduct your own survey on a topic of your choice and summarize the results. Your *purpose* will be to inform through your research. Your *audience* will include everyone in your school community—students, teachers, administrators, and other workers. You will share results with your classmates.

1. Prewriting

To select a subject for your survey, work with a few classmates to brainstorm appropriate topics. Brainstorming is a group activity that helps generate ideas. It can be used in many situations, but it is especially good for prewriting. Some in the group may want to survey the television preferences or career choices of students. Others may want to survey some topic of special interest in your school, such as gymnasium facilities, social gatherings, or field trips.

There are general guidelines you will need to follow to brainstorm effectively. First, everyone in the group needs to contribute. Second, the purpose of brainstorming is to write as many ideas as possible. One idea will generate another and another. Third, brainstorming sessions are usually brief. They should last only five or ten minutes. Some brainstorming tips are listed in the chart below.

Brainstorming Tips

1. Spill out ideas as quickly as possible.
2. Choose one student to record *all* ideas.
3. Do not criticize or judge. Record all ideas, including what may seem to be "silly" ones.
4. Consider quantity to be more important than quality.
5. Keep trying even if you run out of ideas before time is up. Do not give up.

Brainstorming will help you generate ideas for your survey. Keep thinking of different questions about your school. For example, you may want to know how teachers or students spent the summer, or you could conduct a survey on the school newspaper. Your brainstorming session should result in numerous possible topics.

▶ Working in groups of three to five, brainstorm topics for a survey. The topics should be collected and then combined into a class list. From the class list, choose a topic for individual research. After selecting a topic, plan and conduct your survey, using the guidelines presented in the previous lessons.

2. Writing

When your survey has been completed, total the responses. Study your totals and try to draw some conclusions from them. Take notes of ideas that occur to you. For example, you may note that "most students went on a two-week vacation with their families during the summer."

▶ Now you are ready to write your survey summary. Remember that your purpose for writing is to inform. Like a news story, your summary should report the facts. You should not include personal opinions. First, reread the example survey summary on page 397.

Begin with a clear statement, or topic sentence, that draws a conclusion about the results of your survey. Use order of importance to organize your summary. Begin with the most important fact or finding and then include those of lesser importance. You may need to write more than one paragraph if you want to add details about your findings.

3. Revising

▶ Use the following checklist as a guide for revising your survey summary.

Revision Checklist—The Survey Summary

1. Have I followed the guidelines for conducting a survey?
2. Have I used good interviewing techniques?
3. Have I asked *yes* or *no* questions?
4. Have I counted the results accurately?
5. Have I chosen an appropriate topic?
6. Have I kept my audience in mind?
7. Have I written a clear statement of the survey results as my opening sentence?
8. Have I written a factual summary, or have I included personal opinions?
9. Have I used order of importance?
10. Do subjects agree with verbs in all the sentences I have written?

Editing for Subject/Verb Agreement Every subject must agree with its verb. In writing, however, it is easy to use a wrong verb, especially when a prepositional phrase comes between the subject and the verb. Sometimes beginning writers choose verbs that agree with the *closest* noun instead of the subject of the sentence. Study how the verb is edited in the following example.

> The results of my survey ~~shows~~ show that most students in my school went on vacation during the summer. Slightly more than one half of the students surveyed went on two-week vacations.

Use the editing symbols on the *inside back cover* to correct subject-verb agreement and to make any other necessary changes. Then recopy your summary in final form. Use your best handwriting.

Proofreading To proofread, check for errors in spelling, capitalization, and punctuation. Refer to the Index to Rules beginning on page 575 if you have a question about one of these three items.

4. Publishing

▶ Select one of the following ways to share your survey summary with your audience.

1. Post it on a bulletin board the school will see.
2. Submit it to the school newspaper.

4 – Friendly Letters

> • Friendly letters are personal letters. Write them to friends or family members.

In a friendly letter you write more informally than you do in business letters. Write as if you were talking to a friend. In a friendly letter write about your own interests or experiences, but choose them according to the audience—the person—to whom you are writing. Include specific details so that your letter will be more interesting and appealing. If you are replying to a letter, you should always answer any questions the person may have asked.

Study the example below. Notice the five parts of a friendly letter.

Heading

403 Meadows Road
Grand Lake, CO 80447
March 17, 1986

Salutation

Dear Jody,

Body

It was great to hear from you. I'm excited that you will be able to visit for three whole weeks this summer. I'm looking forward to seeing you.

I am planning some wonderful adventures. I think you will enjoy a horseback ride one evening, complete with a campfire, a barbecue and real cowhands. On another day we can go on a white-water rafting trip. There will be plenty of time to talk.

Write soon and let me know what you think about my plans.

Closing

Your friend,

Signature

Jill

The following example shows the arrangement of the five parts in outline form.

Friendly Letter Format

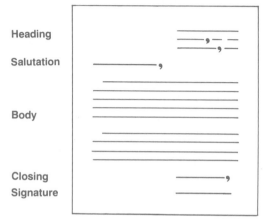

Heading

Salutation

Body

Closing

Signature

Letters should be written as neatly as possible. You may use tinted paper, but white paper of good quality is always suitable. If the letter is handwritten, blue or black ink should be used. Center the letter on the page. Keep equal margins on the sides and on the top and bottom.

Exercises

A. Write answers in complete sentences to the questions below.

1. What are the five parts of a friendly letter?
2. What punctuation mark is used in the heading, salutation, and closing?
3. What is the salutation of the letter on the opposite page?

B. Imagine that you are Jody. Write an answer to Jill's letter. Use the correct form for a friendly letter.

5 — Social Notes

- A social note is a short letter, such as a **thank-you note** or an **invitation.**

A social note is usually written to thank someone for something or to invite someone to a special occasion. A bread-and-butter note is a special thank-you note written when you have stayed overnight at the home of a friend or relative. Write a thank-you note promptly. A social note is also written to accept or decline an invitation.

Social notes are similar in form to friendly letters and have a heading, salutation, body, closing, and signature. Sometimes a social note includes only the date in the heading. Study the thank-you note below.

May 29, 1986

Dear Uncle Glen,

Thank you so much for the subscription to _Photography_ magazine. It was the perfect gift. Can you believe the first issue arrived on my birthday?

Before I had a chance to read it, John was already sitting at the table reading an article. I am sure the magazine will be a help when I start my photography class.

Once again thanks for the gift.

Love,
Katrina

An invitation often has the abbreviation R.S.V.P. written at the bottom. R.S.V.P. is a French abbreviation meaning "please respond." The person sending the invitation needs to know as soon as possible how many people plan to attend. You should reply to such an invitation by sending a note of acceptance or regret. If you send a note of regret, you should state a reason for not attending. Study the invitation below.

203 Palm Street
Hartford, CT 06112
August 1, 1986

Dear Dale,

You are cordially invited to attend a back-to-school barbecue on Saturday, August 13, at 1:00 P.M. The barbecue will be held at my house. I hope you can attend.

Sincerely,
Melissa

R.S.V.P.

Exercises

A. Write a reply to Melissa's invitation above. Imagine that you are Dale, and that you *cannot* attend.

B. Write a social note for the following situations.

   1. Your grandfather has sent you and your friends three tickets for a baseball game.
   2. You have just returned home from a weekend visit with a friend who lives on a ranch.

6 – Business Letters

> ● Business letters should be clear and concise.

Business letters may request information, clarify problems, place orders, or state opinions. A business letter has six parts instead of the five in a friendly letter. A business letter also has an inside address. Study the persuasive letter below. Notice that a colon is used after the salutation in a business letter.

<table>
<tr>
<td>Heading</td>
<td></td>
<td align="right">20 Whitaker Way
Modesto, CA 94611
April 9, 1986</td>
</tr>
<tr>
<td>Inside
Address</td>
<td colspan="2">Mr. R. D. Thomas
Los Amigos School District
201 Westfield Road
Modesto, CA 94611</td>
</tr>
<tr>
<td>Salutation</td>
<td colspan="2">Dear Mr. Thomas:</td>
</tr>
<tr>
<td rowspan="3">Body</td>
<td colspan="2">   A recent survey I conducted for a writing project at Carter Middle School revealed a need for additional personal computers. Eighty-three percent of the students said they would like to have more access to computers. Although there are five computers in the library, many students never get to work with them, even for brief periods.</td>
</tr>
<tr>
<td colspan="2">   More computers will give students extra opportunities for hands-on experience. More students could practice skills or do supplemental work in basic subjects, such as math and reading. More students could become computer literate, a modern necessity instead of a privilege. In addition, teachers could be freed of routine drill to work individually with students.</td>
</tr>
<tr>
<td colspan="2">   As superintendent of schools, I am sure you are aware of the growing interest in and need for computers in schools. By the time my class graduates from high school, computers will be linked to more than eighty percent of jobs. I would appreciate hearing from you on this subject.</td>
</tr>
<tr>
<td>Closing</td>
<td colspan="2" align="right">Sincerely,</td>
</tr>
<tr>
<td>Signature</td>
<td colspan="2" align="right">Bill Mannus
Bill Mannus</td>
</tr>
</table>

The following example shows the arrangement of the six parts in outline form.

Business Letter Format

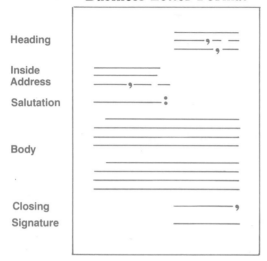

Heading

Inside Address

Salutation

Body

Closing

Signature

White paper is appropriate stationery for business letters. If you type well, write your letter on a typewriter. If you do not, write using blue or black ink. Be concerned about the physical appearance of your business letter. Neatness counts and creates a good impression. Center the letter properly on the page and keep equal margins.

Exercises

A. Write answers to the questions below.
1. What are the six parts of a business letter?
2. What are four reasons for writing a business letter?

B. In Exercise A you listed four reasons for writing a business letter. Select one of the reasons and write a business letter, using correct form. Use your own address for the heading. Make up the inside address.

7 — Preparing Letters for Mailing

> ● An envelope must contain a mailing address and a return address.

When you finish writing any type of letter, you must prepare it for mailing. First, you must fold your letter so that it is easy for the reader to open. Second, you must address the envelope.

Folding a letter neatly is important. Readers prefer letters that are smooth, unwrinkled, and folded so that they open easily. A business letter is usually folded in thirds by folding the bottom third up and the top third over it.

Addressing an envelope is extremely important. If you make even a slight mistake, your letter may never reach its destination. Every letter must contain a mailing address and a return address. The return address includes your name, street address, city, state, and ZIP code. The mailing address includes the name and complete address of the person to whom you are mailing the letter. Study the example below.

Mr. Bill Mannus
20 Whitaker Way
Modesto, CA 94611

Mr. R. D. Thomas
Los Amigos School District
201 Westfield Road
Modesto, CA 94611

The following is a list of mailing abbreviations for the fifty states, the District of Columbia, Puerto Rico, and the Virgin Islands.

Alabama	AL	Nebraska	NE
Alaska	AK	Nevada	NV
Arizona	AZ	New Hampshire	NH
Arkansas	AR	New Jersey	NJ
California	CA	New Mexico	NM
Colorado	CO	New York	NY
Connecticut	CT	North Carolina	NC
Delaware	DE	North Dakota	ND
District of Columbia	DC	Ohio	OH
Florida	FL	Oklahoma	OK
Georgia	GA	Oregon	OR
Hawaii	HI	Pennsylvania	PA
Idaho	ID	Puerto Rico	PR
Illinois	IL	Rhode Island	RI
Indiana	IN	South Carolina	SC
Iowa	IA	South Dakota	SD
Kansas	KS	Tennessee	TN
Kentucky	KY	Texas	TX
Louisiana	LA	Utah	UT
Maine	ME	Vermont	VT
Maryland	MD	Virginia	VA
Massachusetts	MA	Virgin Islands	VI
Michigan	MI	Washington	WA
Minnesota	MN	West Virginia	WV
Mississippi	MS	Wisconsin	WI
Missouri	MO	Wyoming	WY
Montana	MT		

Exercises

A. Write each address below as it should be written on an envelope. Use correct punctuation.

1. Ms. Dorothy Jenkins 425 Lansing Avenue Evanston Illinois 60201
2. The Poster Company 4021 Peachtree Street Atlanta Georgia 30359

B. Bring an envelope to class. Address it correctly to a person whom you know.

8 —Persuading–A Letter of Opinion

> • A **letter of opinion** attempts to persuade others to your point of view.

Persuasion is a skill you use almost every day. For example, you may convince your parents to let you stay up later on school nights, or you may persuade a friend to take the same course as you. In persuasive writing your main objective is to sway readers to change their minds about something or to urge them to take action.

In this lesson you will use the writing process to write a letter of opinion. You will choose and write about an issue that concerns you, using the business letter form. Your *purpose* for writing is to persuade. Your *audience* will be a real one of your own selection, such as a public official.

1. Prewriting

▶ Choose one of the topics below or select one of your own. Then write a one-sentence statement telling how you feel about the subject. Include the words *should* or *should not*.

- Automobile drivers should/should not be required to wear seat belts.
- Schools should/should not be in session twelve months a year.
- Women should/should not be required to register for the draft.

After you have chosen a topic, explore your ideas about it. A good prewriting strategy for discovering ideas is timed writing. In timed writing you write for a few minutes, perhaps five, without stopping. Even if you "can't think of anything to say," do not lift pen from paper. Simply write whatever comes to mind.

Write your one-sentence statement on the top of a clean piece of paper. Then write nonstop for five minutes. When time is up, review what you have written. Underline the best ideas, and evaluate them to see which reasons should be included in your letter.

You might spend some time in the library to gather background knowledge. Look in recent newspapers and magazines for articles or editorials on your topic. Furthermore, you may need to include some background information in your letter if you believe your audience has little knowledge of the subject. You may also need to use the library to find out the address of your audience, if he or she is a public official.

2. Writing

To organize a persuasive piece of writing, state your opinion in either the topic sentence or the introduction. Use carefully selected, convincing reasons to support your opinion. It is best to include at least three reasons. Study the organization below.

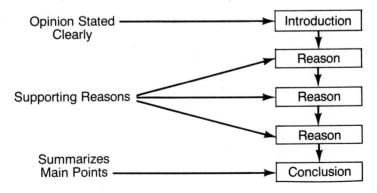

This organizational pattern is the same for a paragraph or a longer composition of two or more paragraphs. If you decide to write just one paragraph, it should contain all five parts of the organization—introduction, three reasons, conclusion. For a longer composition, you might write three paragraphs—one for the introduction, one containing the three reasons, and one for the conclusion.

▶ Be certain your reasons are supported by details or examples. Seldom are they effective if they simply stand alone without any supporting evidence. You can provide more support for your reasons by using actual events from your own experience, by including facts, and by using statements from authorities. Be sure to review the example letter of opinion on page 406.

3. Revising

▶ Use the following checklist as a guide for revising your letter of opinion.

Revision Checklist—The Letter of Opinion

1. Have I stated my opinion clearly?
2. Have I chosen the correct audience?
3. Have I supported my opinion with at least three convincing reasons?
4. Have I included supporting evidence?
5. Have I selected the appropriate number of paragraphs to organize my letter?
6. Have I tried to answer any questions my audience may have?
7. If discussing a problem, have I proposed a reasonable solution?
8. Have I used the correct business letter form?
9. Have I used the correct inside address?
10. Have I written any run-on sentences?

Editing for Run-On Sentences A sentence that should be broken into two or more sentences is a run-on sentence. One way to correct a run-on sentence is to make the second sentence a separate sentence. Another way is to use a conjunction such as *and, but,* or *or* to join the two sentences if they are of equal importance. Study how the sentences are edited in the example below.

Letters are important means of communication. they bring together people who live far away. I often write letters; but my best friend does not.

Use the editing symbols on the *inside back cover* to correct run-on sentences and make other necessary changes. Then make a final copy.

Proofreading To proofread, check for errors in spelling, capitalization, and punctuation. Refer to the Index to Rules on page 575 if you have a question about one of these three items.

4. Publishing

▶ Select a way to publish your letter.

1. Mail it to the person to whom it is addressed.
2. Send the letter to the local newspaper.

Building Bridges to Mathematics

The information you collect in a survey will often be numerical. In order to use such information efficiently, you may organize it in tables or graphs.

Todd conducted a survey to find out if the recycling of resources was on the rise in Davis County. He organized the results of his survey in a table. A **table** is an orderly arrangement of facts and figures.

Resource	1983	1984	1985
Paper	23%	41%	68%
Glass	11%	16%	26%
Metal	3%	7%	8%

Information from surveys can also be presented in graph form. A **graph** is a diagram that pictures the relationships between different facts. A circle graph, for example, shows percentages both as numbers and as parts of the whole area.

One of Todd's survey questions asked what communities should do with funds earned from recycling. The results are shown on this circle graph.

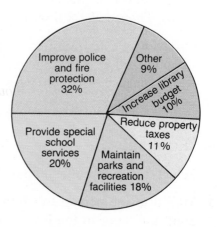

Bar graphs can also organize information. In a survey sent to managers of recycling centers in the county, Todd asked about earnings of the centers. The bar graph below shows the results.

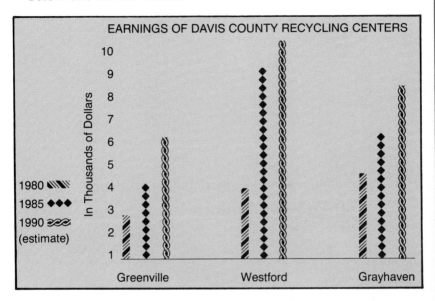

EARNINGS OF DAVIS COUNTY RECYCLING CENTERS

Exercises

A. Write a paragraph summarizing the information in the table. You may use the following topic sentence: *Over the last three years, Davis County residents have significantly increased their recycling efforts.*

B. Write a business letter to Mayor Kucik of Bridgeton, a town in Davis County. The purpose of your letter is to persuade him to start a recycling center in Bridgeton. To persuade the mayor, summarize the information contained in the circle and bar graphs.

19 *Classifying and Reasoning*

"Good order is the foundation of all good things."

—Edmund Burke

1 — The Media

> • The **mass media**—such as television, radio, newspapers, and films—provide information to large numbers of people.

People communicate in many different ways. When they converse with others, they exchange ideas. This communication is two-way communication. Most people also acquire much of their information through the mass media, which are methods of one-way communication. People receive information and news from the mass media, but there is no opportunity to talk back. The media are called *mass* media because they reach so many people. The mass media include television, radio, books, newspapers, magazines, film, records, and tapes. Many opinions are shaped by the mass media.

To summarize, the mass media are means of one-way communication that reach large numbers of people. Printed information is transmitted through books, magazines, and newspapers. Television presents news, information, and entertainment. Film is a major business in the United States. Records, tapes, comic books, and cartoons also communicate with large numbers of people. Technological advances are constantly improving the mass media. In recent years a revolution has occurred in video cassette recorders, videodiscs, and cable television.

Since the mass media are produced for audiences, you must remember that the audiences—including yourself— have the final control. For example, if no one watched television, it would disappear. The audiences ultimately control the mass media.

Exercise

To determine what role the mass media play in your own life, take a personal inventory. Write answers in complete sentences to the questions below. After completing your inventory, decide how many hours you spend with the mass media each week and each year.

1. How many library books do you read in a year?
2. How much money do you spend each year on books?
3. What kinds of books do you prefer?
4. How many hours each week do you spend reading, either for pleasure or for school assignments?
5. What magazines or comic books do you buy? How much time do you spend each week reading them?
6. What are your favorite television shows?
7. How much time each week do you spend watching television?
8. How much time each week do you spend listening to records, tapes, or the radio?
9. How much money each year do you spend on records or tapes?
10. What types of mass media equipment (television, stereo equipment, radio, record player, video cassette recorder) are available in your home?
11. How many movies do you pay to see each year? How much time do you spend seeing movies?
12. Does your family own a personal computer? If so, how much time do you work with it each week?

Application WRITING A PARAGRAPH

What is your reaction to the information you discovered about yourself in the personal inventory above? Write a paragraph telling about your reaction, and whether or not you were surprised.

2 – Classifying Information

> ● To classify information, sort items that belong together into categories.

Classifying is a way of organizing information. It is a way of sorting items that belong together into categories. To classify is to categorize information.

Categories can be created by either *dividing* or *grouping*. If you begin with a general topic that is too broad, you can *divide* it into categories. For example, the general topic *dogs* can be divided into kinds of dogs—such as Doberman pinscher, bulldog, poodle, collie, German shepherd, and cocker spaniel.

Sometimes you need to *group* items in order to organize them. Group items by their common features. How could you group the following list of animals?

robin	spider	cricket	pelican
donkey	crow	cat	ant
turtle	giraffe	dolphin	cow
horse	tarantula	shark	whale
snake	frog	crab	peacock

You could group them according to size, number of legs, intelligence, type of animal, or many other ways.

Both dividing and grouping are useful ways to classify information for writing. Sometimes you may need to break down a general topic into specific categories. Other times you may want to group specific items that share a common feature. Sometimes you may want to do both. Whatever you decide to do, classifying will help you organize your ideas for writing.

Exercises ————————————————————

A. Write each specific example of a fruit or vegetable under its appropriate category: *Fruits* or *Vegetables*.

1. strawberry
2. carrot
3. string beans
4. pineapple
5. spinach
6. plum
7. peach
8. asparagus
9. cauliflower
10. blackberry

B. Write each specific example of a state under its appropriate category: *Eastern States, Southern States, Western States*.

11. Georgia
12. California
13. Oregon
14. Mississippi
15. Massachusetts
16. Alabama
17. Connecticut
18. New York
19. New Jersey
20. Washington

C. Write four specific examples for each general category below.

21. trees
22. sports
23. countries
24. planets
25. circus attractions

Classifying

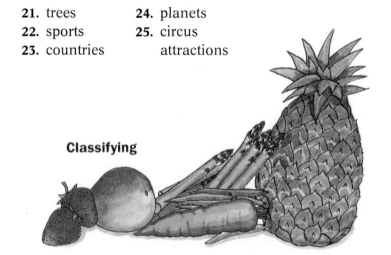

3 — Classifying–A Media Review

> ● A **review** provides an opinion and recommendation on some segment of the media.

Many people read reviews. A review helps people understand better what they see, read, or hear by presenting another person's viewpoint. Many critics are professional reviewers who write for newspapers and magazines. They review movies, television shows, records, books, and plays.

Perhaps you have read a review that made you want to see a certain movie, or you may have disagreed with a review of your favorite television show. A review usually contains a short summary, the reviewer's opinion with supporting reasons, and advice on whether or not others would enjoy it. A review should be brief. Reviews are not usually given much space, so when writing a review it is important to be concise.

In this lesson you will write a review on some segment of the media. For example, you may review a book, a movie, or a television program. Your *purpose* is to inform. Your *audience* is your classmates.

1. Prewriting

A useful prewriting strategy is notetaking. You record your thoughts and feelings on what you see, hear, or read. Begin by choosing something that you would like to review. Read a book, view a film, watch a television program, listen to a record album, or see a performance of a play. Take notes.

A review is a judgment. Before you can make a judgment on anything, you must know what standards you will be using. *Criteria* are standards for judgment. (One standard is called a *criterion*.) Before writing a review, you must develop standards to use in evaluating what you have seen, heard, or read.

Suppose, for example, you plan to review a film. A good way to start is by rating the film according to other films in the same category. To develop a standard, compare what you are reviewing with other films you have seen. Classify the film into a category. Is it intended to entertain, or does it have a more serious purpose? Is it a comedy, drama, science fiction film, or suspense film? Make a list of films and then classify them into categories. What characteristics do the films in each category have in common? Where does the film you have selected belong?

▶ After you have finished your classification, develop criteria to judge the film. Below are general criteria.

General Criteria for Films

- Was the film informative or entertaining?
- Was the plot believable and well developed?
- Were the characters realistic?
- Was the acting good and the dialogue convincing?
- Was casting of the lead roles appropriate?
- How does it compare with films in the same category?
- Was originality displayed in the film?

---

2. Writing

To write your review, use the general guidelines below. Notice that a review should have four parts. You may want to write a paragraph for each part. While writing, refer frequently to the notes you have taken.

Guidelines for Writing a Review

1. **Introduce**   Get the reader's attention.
                    Identify the work clearly and specifically.
                    State a general opinion.

2. **Summarize**   Summarize the work.
                    Be brief but informative.

3. **Evaluate**   Apply the standards you have established.
                    Discuss strengths and weaknesses.
                    Use evidence, or specific examples, to
                    support your opinion.
                    Make a judgment, good or bad.

4. **Respond**   Conclude with your own reaction.
                    Include a recommendation for others.

▶ Write a first draft of your review.

3. Revising

▶ Use the following checklist as a guide for revising your media review.

Revision Checklist—The Media Review

1. Does the introduction identify what I am reviewing and state a general opinion?
2. Did I summarize the work briefly?
3. Does the review make clear the criteria I used?
4. Did I support my opinion with clear examples?
5. Does the review include my personal reaction and recommendation?
6. Have I used indefinite pronouns correctly?

Editing for Indefinite Pronouns Pronouns such as *each, anyone, somebody,* and *everybody* are singular. *Few, several,* and *both* are plural. Study how the indefinite pronouns are edited in the following review.

Almost everyone ~~love~~ *loves* suspense and adventure movies. That is why almost everybody ~~enjoy~~ *enjoys* *Wait Until Spring*, a new film from Crocker Studios. In the first thirty minutes, the hero fights off a Wolf Pack, becomes buried in an avalanche, and shares a cave with a hungry bear. Then his adventures get even more exciting!

The hero is Ben Moore, fourteen years old and the only survivor of an ill-fated wagon train. Alone in the Rockies, he faces a long and harrowing winter. Not only must he overcome the elements but his own fears and weaknesses as well.

Directed by Lily Davoe, *Wait Until Spring* is both an informative and entertaining film. The story is well developed, the photography is majestic, and the setting is realistic. Harry Childs, who plays Ben Moore, is very effective. Each of his actions in the story *is* ~~are~~ believable. *Wait Until Spring* is one of the best movies of its kind I have ever seen. Don't wait until spring to see it!

Use the editing symbols on the *inside back cover* to make your corrections. Copy your review in final form. Use your best handwriting.

Proofreading To proofread, check for errors in spelling, capitalization, and punctuation. Refer to the Index to Rules beginning on page 575 if you have a question about one of these three items.

4. Publishing

▶ Select one of the following ways to share your media review with your audience.

1. Present it orally to your classmates.
2. Post it on a bulletin board entitled Critic's Corner.

4 — Identifying Cause and Effect

> - A cause is *why* something happened. An effect is *what* happened. Writers often explain events in terms of causes and effects.

Much of what you read and write is based on cause-and-effect relationships. When writers talk about why an event happened, they are discussing causes. A cause is the reason why something happens. An effect is the result produced by the cause. It can be a single event or a series of events. You see causes and effects in life every day. Rain causes people to carry umbrellas, injuries cause athletes to retire, and tests cause students to study.

Writing can be organized by cause and effect. In some paragraphs the topic sentence can state the cause. Then several supporting sentences can list effects resulting from the cause. This organization can also be reversed. You might want to start with an effect, and then the remainder of the paragraph could list the causes, or reasons, for its happening.

Certain words usually signal cause-and-effect relationships. Some of these words are listed below.

so	since	therefore
because	as a result	consequently

Because and *since* are used most frequently.

Cause-and-effect organization is often used in both scientific and historical writing. Understanding cause-and-effect relationships, however, will help you in *all* your school subjects.

Exercises

A. Determine whether the statement contains a cause-and-effect relationship. Then write *yes* or *no*.

1. In 1962, Rachel Carson published a very important book called *Silent Spring*.
2. She described the dangers of synthetic pesticides.
3. Since pesticides can remain in or on the soil for years, Carson was concerned about their long-range effects.
4. She presented facts showing that birds might die because they ate bugs killed by pesticides.
5. Rachel Carson's book caused much controversy.

B. Write one possible cause for each effect below.

6. The meeting was rescheduled.
7. The cat climbed the tree.
8. Unemployment is declining.
9. Farmers are leaving agriculture.
10. An elderly woman fell on the sidewalk.
11. The principal instituted a dress code.
12. Absenteeism at my school has decreased.
13. Fast-food restaurants are increasing rapidly.
14. The whale is an endangered species.
15. All grades on the report card were excellent.

C. Each sentence below is a cause. Using the word in parentheses, connect the cause with an effect. Add to the sentence or write a second sentence.

16. The game was canceled. (so)
17. I caught a bad cold. (therefore)
18. Kay bumped into the door. (as a result)
19. Rusty woke up very late. (consequently)
20. Steven was awarded the scholarship. (therefore)

5 — Interpreting Data

> ● To interpret data, such as graphs and charts, draw conclusions from the facts or figures presented.

Data is information used as a basis for reasoning and drawing conclusions. Data usually consists of facts or figures that need to be interpreted.

Data is often presented in charts or graphs. Sometimes it is summarized in paragraphs or longer reports. Look at the bar graph below. The figures on the left represent the number of students. The items on the bottom indicate different extracurricular activities that teens prefer. What conclusions can you draw from this data?

EXTRA CURRICULAR ACTIVITIES THAT TEENS PREFER

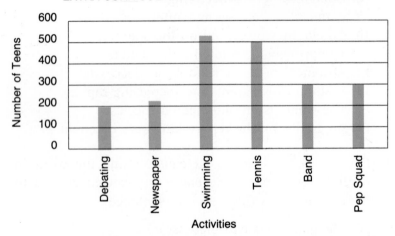

You may conclude that more teens in this school prefer sports as extracurricular activities, for example. You could also point out that equal numbers of students like band and pep squad.

Exercises

A. Look at the circle graph below entitled "How Teens Spend Money." The amount of each dollar spent for various items is shown. Write answers to the questions below the graph.

HOW TEENS SPEND MONEY

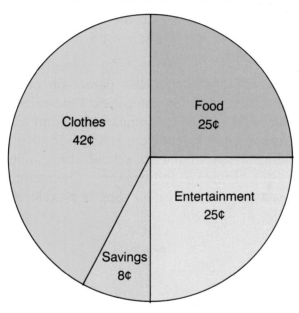

1. According to this circle graph, on what item do teens spend the least money?
2. Out of every dollar, how much money goes for food and entertainment?
3. What conclusion can you draw after analyzing this data? Draw at least one conclusion.

B. Mr. Nakai's English class took a writing skills test. Six of the students received *A*'s. Fifteen students received *B*'s and ten students received *C*'s. Only five students received *D*'s. Create a bar graph to display this data.

6 — Comparison/Contrast Paragraphs

> ● When comparing or contrasting two things, look for similarities or differences.

The words *comparison* and *contrast* are often used together. *Comparison* shows the <u>similarities</u> between two things. *Contrast* points out the <u>differences</u>. The word *comparison*, however, is often used to mean <u>both</u> similarities and differences.

Before writing a comparison paragraph or a contrast paragraph, first look for categories. Categories will provide you with points to compare or contrast. For example, if you want to compare riding a bicycle to school with riding a school bus to school, think of categories such as time, freedom, and economy. Then, under the appropriate category, list how riding a bicycle and a bus are similar or different.

Time	Freedom	Economy
different	different	same

The clearest way to organize comparison/contrast paragraphs is by the point-by-point method. In point-by-point organization, you move back and forth between two things, comparing or contrasting each point. If you compare riding a bicycle to school with riding a bus to school, the bicycle would represent the letter *A*, and the bus, the letter *B*, in the following organization: ABABAB.

Some connecting words that can be used in comparison/contrast paragraphs are *similarly, instead, in like manner, in the same way, on the other hand, in contrast, however, both,* and *on the contrary.*

Select topics that can be compared and contrasted in the same kinds of ways. For example, you could compare gerbils and guinea pigs because both are small rodents. But it would be hard to compare gerbils with guitars.

The following paragraph compares similarities between football and basketball. Notice that each sport is discussed in the same order in which it is presented in the topic sentence.

> Football and basketball are similar sports. Football and basketball are played between two opposing teams. Both games are played with a ball. Points are gained by kicking a football through a goalpost and by throwing a basketball through a hoop. As for football players, speed, strategy, timing, and team work are necessary skills for basketball players.

The paragraph below contrasts the differences between football and basketball.

> Football and basketball are two different kinds of sports. Football is played with eleven team members. Basketball, however, is played with only five team members. Football is a contact sport. The players are allowed to touch each other during the game. On the other hand, basketball is not a contact sport. Players are penalized for touching other players.

Application WRITING A CONTRAST PARAGRAPH

Select a topic such as Saturdays and Mondays, cats and dogs, trains and planes, or pencils and pens. Then write a paragraph contrasting the differences between the two. Use the point-by-point method of organization. Use the following as a model for a topic sentence: *Although cats and dogs have much in common, they have many differences between them.*

7 — Reasoning–A Consumer Report

> ● A **consumer report** informs readers about services or products.

When you buy a record, clothes, or school supplies, you are a consumer. Any time you exchange money for services or a product, you are consuming. Similarly you are also a consumer of information from the media.

It is important that consumers spend their money wisely. Consumers need to know how one product compares with another, or how a product has been tested and used by other consumers. Many people write information for consumers in the form of newspaper stories, magazine articles, booklets, and reports.

In this lesson you will write a consumer report. Your writing *purpose* will be to inform. Your *audience* will be teenagers in general.

1. Prewriting

To write a consumer report, you need to analyze the product or service. To *analyze* is to examine something according to a careful plan. You will use reasoning skills such as comparing, contrasting, and drawing conclusions.

▶ Choose some consumer product or series of products to analyze. You may select one from the choices below or one of your own.

a video game	designer jeans
a new toy	sports equipment

You will need to make a list of similarities and differences between your product and other *products of the same kind.* Below is a general list of similarities and differences, organized into categories.

Categories of Similarities/Differences

- Is the *appearance* of the product (color, size, shape) like others of the same kind, or is it different?

- Is the *quality* of the product (how well it is made) like others of the same kind, or is it different?

- Is the *cost* the same or different?

- After *use,* does it still wear as well or work as well as others of the same kind, or is it different?

- If *safety* is a factor, is it safe or is it not safe compared with others of the same kind?

- Does it have some *special feature* that makes it different from others of the same kind, or is it similar?

▶ Use the clock face below to analyze your product, paying special attention to your list of similarities and differences. Follow the four steps on the clock face carefully. Complete each of the four in order, spending only 3 to 5 minutes on each. When time is up, review your notes. Be sure you have carefully identified how your product is *similar* to and how it is *different* from other products of the same kind.

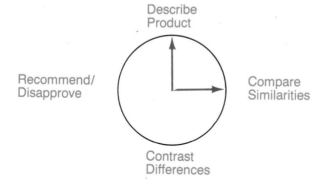

Describe Product

Recommend/ Disapprove

Compare Similarities

Contrast Differences

2. Writing

▶ You must now decide how to organize your ideas for a first draft. Your consumer report will have the standard organization of most reports—an introduction, a body, and a conclusion. The introduction, the beginning paragraph, should describe the product. The body may be any length, but two paragraphs are recommended. The first paragraph in the body should *compare similarities* point by point between your product and other products of the same kind. The second paragraph in the body should *contrast differences,* telling how your product is better or worse than competing brands. Your concluding paragraph should either recommend or disapprove the product and provide a sense of closing.

3. Revising

▶ After you have written your first draft, use the check-list below to revise it.

Revision Checklist—The Consumer Report

1. Does my introduction describe the product?
2. Does the first paragraph in the body compare similarities?
3. Does the second paragraph in the body contrast differences?
4. Did I always move back and forth between my product and others of the same kind?
5. Have I varied my sentences?

Editing for Sentence Variety Sentence variety is important for good writing. Study how the sentences are edited in the following example report.

Strawberry yogurt is both America's and my favorite flavored yogurt. It is made from milk and strawberries. It is a tasty snack. Three brands—Brite Glow, Jansen Farms, and Country Fair—are available in area markets.

The yogurts have much in common. All three come in eight-ounce containers. All three contain twelve grams of protein and four grams of fat. The price of the three is also similar. It ranges from fifty-five cents to sixty-five cents. The yogurts differ in several ways. Jansen Farms contains 220 calories. Brite Glow contains 190 calories. Country Fair has 150 calories. Country fair uses artificial flavors and sweeteners. The others are all natural. Brite Glow tastes freshest, in my opinion. Country Fair has a slightly sour taste. The berries in Jansen Farms yogurt are gooey and jamlike. For these reasons, I would recommend Brite Glow yogurt to the taste-conscious and calorie-conscious consumer.

Use the editing symbols on the *inside back cover* to make your corrections. Copy your report in final form. Use your best handwriting.

Proofreading In proofreading, you check for errors in spelling, capitalization, and punctuation. Refer to the Index to Rules, beginning on page 575, if you have a question about one of these three items.

4. Publishing

▶ Select one of the following ways to share your report with your audience.

1. Display your report on the class bulletin board.
2. Combine your report with those of other students into a *Consumer Reports* magazine for teens.

Building Bridges to Science

Sarah plans to be an ornithologist, a scientist who studies birds. On a field trip she spotted these geese.

In order to classify these geese exactly, Sarah must divide them into categories called species. Each species is different. For example, a barnacle goose has white sides, a black chest to the waterline, and a white face encircling its eyes. Since goose **1** matches this description, Sarah classifies it as a barnacle goose.

Exercises

A. Match each description below with a picture above.

Canada Goose—black head and neck, pale chest, and a white patch or "chinstrap" at each side of head

White-Fronted Goose—gray goose with white patch on front of face and irregular black bars on belly

Brant Goose—black head and neck except for a small fleck of white, black chest, and white sides

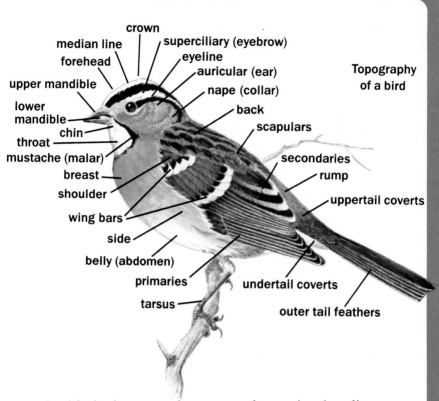

Topography of a bird

crown
median line
forehead
upper mandible
lower mandible
chin
throat
mustache (malar)
breast
shoulder
wing bars
side
belly (abdomen)
primaries
tarsus

superciliary (eyebrow)
eyeline
auricular (ear)
nape (collar)
back
scapulars
secondaries
rump
uppertail coverts
undertail coverts
outer tail feathers

B. Ornithologists use the terms shown in the diagram above to describe the features of a bird. Use the terms to write a description of a "Baltimore" oriole below.

20 *Literature*

I Am Looking For a Book

I am looking for a book
I do not know its title
or what it is about

but if I find it
and turn to the right page

it will read me

it will put a pen into my hands
that will sprout iridescent feathers
and fly.

—*Eve Merriam*

A SILVER CLASSIC

The Call
of the Wild
and Other Stories

JACK LONDON

1 — Plays

> ● A play uses dramatic **scenes** and **dialogue** to tell a story.

As in a story, the major elements of a play are plot, character, and setting. The plot and characters are revealed through dialogue (the words the characters speak) and through actions. Unlike stories, plays are written to be performed on a stage. When you read a play, imagine a performance of it in your mind. Picture the play's setting. Imagine the characters speaking to one another as you read their dialogue. Picture the actions they perform as described in the **stage directions.** (Stage directions often appear in parentheses.)

Many plays, especially longer ones, consist of a number of scenes. The scenes advance the plot of the play as a whole. However, each scene has its own dramatic point and its own beginning and ending.

The following scene is from Sidney Kingsley's play *The Patriots*. The play is about the early days of the United States. Thomas Jefferson has just returned from France, where he was the American ambassador. George Washington, the young nation's first president, wants Jefferson to be his secretary of state. As you read the scene, imagine it being performed on a stage.

Characters	George Washington
	Thomas Jefferson
	Colonel Humphreys, Washington's aide
Scene	New York, spring 1790. The presidential residence. Washington and Jefferson are sitting in chairs facing one another.

Washington (*rises, fetches a dish of biscuits*). I've had two attacks of illness this year. I doubt if I'd survive a third. Oh well, tomorrow or twenty years from now, we are all in the hands of a Good Providence. Try one of these biscuits.

Jefferson. Thank you. (*He takes a biscuit.*)

Washington (*goes to his desk, sits down*). I'm organizing the ministers of the various departments into a cabinet to advise me. As our Secretary of State, you're …

Jefferson. General Washington.

Washington. Mm?

Jefferson. In your letter, you did give me the option of refusal.

Washington. You can't mean to refuse?

Jefferson. I must.

Washington. Why?

Jefferson. I've been away so long. I know none of the duties of this office. I may bungle it. I have forebodings.

Washington. We're all groping. This will be a government of accommodation.

Jefferson (*shakes his head*). I'm sorry. I want you to understand. Whatever spice of political ambition I may have had as a young man has long since evaporated. (*He rises, places the half-nibbled biscuit on a dish.*) I believe every man should serve his turn. I think I've done my share. Now I want to go home. I must complete my house. Twenty years it's waited. Patsy and her husband have come to stay with me at Monticello. The truth of the matter is, I've lived with my children so long, I've come to depend on their affection and comfort.

Washington. Tom, have you ever thought of marrying again?

Jefferson. No.

Washington. She was a wonderful woman, your Martha.

Jefferson. Yes. (*He pauses.*) When I came home—she

was in every room. (*He pauses.*) I've learned one thing. For me there's no place anywhere else in the world but Monticello. You understand why I must refuse your offer? (*Humphreys enters.*)

Humphreys. Excuse me, Sire.

Washington. Yes, Humphreys?

Humphreys. The theater box and guard of honor are arranged.

Washington (*dryly*). Good.

Humphreys. And I've discovered the Ambassador of the Sultan of Turkey is going to be present.

Washington (*with a notable lack of enthusiasm*). Mm, mm.

Humphreys. A suggestion, Excellency?

Washington. Yes?

Humphreys. Wouldn't it be advisable to return to six horses on the coach?

Washington. I thought we compromised on four.

Humphreys. When I was at the court of Louis ...

Washington (*making a great effort to contain his impatience*). Colonel Humphreys, I recognize the importance of these forms to the dignity of a state, particularly one so young as ours. Understand, I know nothing of these matters. I've never been to the courts of Europe. I'm just an old soldier. I leave the ceremonies in your hands. (*The impatience wears thin, and he growls.*) But it seems to me four horses and that canary coach with the pink and gilt angels will be enough to impress even the Ambassador of the Sultan of Turkey.

Humphreys. But, Sire ...

Washington. Four will do—that's final (*He ruffles some papers, frowns.*) On second thought, I won't be free to go to the theater tonight. Cancel it!

Humphreys. Sire, if I may ...

Washington (*rises, thundering*). Don't "Sire" me! How many times must I tell you? By the Eternal! I am not a king! I am the elected head of our people. This is a republic. Can you get that through your skull? (*He controls himself.*) All right! (*wearily*) Go!

Humphreys. Very well, Mr. President. (*He goes. Washington sighs heavily.*)

Washington. I was offered the crown.

Jefferson. The crown!

Washington. Twice. (*He pauses.*) I don't want to be a king, Tom. (*He crosses to the cabinet, takes up a lamp, fills it with oil from a jug.*)

Jefferson. I know you don't, Mr. President.

Washington. You've no idea. (*He touches a taper to a burning candle.*) Every eye is on this office. A number of our people suspect me. As God is my judge, I would rather live and die on my farm than be emperor of the world. (*He lights the lamp, frowning angrily.*)

Jefferson (*after a pause*). I know. And yet—since I've been back—particularly here in New York—I find alarming yearnings. Our fashionable folk appear to be looking wishfully for a king and a court of our own.

Washington. Yes. I suppose so. (*He sighs, puts the lamp by the window, extinguishes the taper.*) On the other hand, there is equal danger of anarchy. We came close to it while you were away! (*He nervously adjusts the lamp.*) We walk between these two pitfalls. Our people don't take to discipline. But, without it—we shall be lost. We've yet to see how large a dose of freedom men can be trusted with. Tom, from the earliest days in Virginia, you were close to them, you seemed always to understand them. In this office, I find myself removed from direct contact with them. I need your agency. I need their faith in you. This is the last great experiment for promoting human happiness. I need the hand that wrote, "All men are created equal." I can't let you go home yet! I need you here.

(*A long pause. Jefferson turns to Washington.*)

Jefferson. It's for you to marshall us as you see fit.

Washington (*goes to him, grips his shoulder*). Good!

Jefferson. It's a great honor. I hope I can be worthy of it.

About the Play

1. The dramatic point of the scene from *The Patriots* concerns a decision Thomas Jefferson must make. What is the decision about? What does he finally decide? What reason does he give for his reluctance?

2. President Washington points out two dangers to the young nation. (He calls them "pitfalls.") One is anarchy. What is the other? Point out the dialogue in which he discusses them. In what way is Colonel Humphreys an example of one of the dangers?

3. Point out the dialogue that helps you understand what kind of people Washington and Jefferson are. What dialogue part reveals Washington's attitude toward Humphreys?

4. Point out stage directions that help you imagine a performance of the scene. What actions, described in the stage directions, reveal Washington's feelings?

5. Some stage directions do not describe feelings. They indicate how certain lines of dialogue should be spoken. Point out two examples.

Writing About Literature

Write a brief character sketch of George Washington. (A character sketch describes the personality traits of an individual.) Base your sketch on what you have learned about Washington from the scene from *The Patriots*. Include specific references to dialogue and actions in the scene.

2 – Myths

> ● A **myth** is a story that attempts to explain a natural phenomenon and that usually involves supernatural beings.

When the world was much younger, people wondered about natural phenomena and tried to find explanations for them. They wondered about the creation of the world, the change of the seasons, and the moon and the stars they observed in the sky. In ancient Greece and Rome, in Africa and Scandinavia, in the South Pacific and the American continents, people made up myths to explain such phenomena. They invented stories about gods and goddesses who created mountains and rivers, hurled thunderbolts, and changed people into flowers, rivers, animals, and stars.

Myths were also created to show what qualities people valued or disliked in others. There were myths about lovers whose love for each other was so strong it survived horrible catastrophes and continued even after death. There were myths about great warriors, great liars, and great fools.

As you read the following Greek myth, notice what attitude toward people it shows. Notice also what natural phenomenon it explains.

Midas

Midas, whose name has become a synonym for a rich man, had very little profit from his riches. The experience of possessing them lasted less than a day, and it threatened him with speedy death. He was an example of folly being as fatal as sin, for he meant no harm; he merely did not use his intelligence. His story suggests that he had none to use.

He was king of Phrygia, the land of roses, and he had great rose gardens near his palace. Into them once strayed old Silenus, who, intoxicated as always, had wandered off from Bacchus's train [group of followers] where he belonged and lost his way. The fat old drunkard was found asleep in a bower of roses by some of the servants of the palace. They bound him with rosy garlands, set a flowering wreath on his head, woke him up, and bore him in this ridiculous guise to Midas as a great joke. Midas welcomed him and entertained him for ten days. Then he led him back to Bacchus, who, delighted to get him back, told Midas that whatever wish he made would come true. Without giving a thought to the inevitable result, Midas wished that whatever he touched would turn into gold. Of course, Bacchus, in granting the favor, foresaw what would happen at the next meal, but Midas saw nothing until the food he lifted to his lips became a lump of metal. Dismayed and very hungry and thirsty, he was forced to hurry off to the god and implore him to take his favor back. Bacchus told him to go wash in the source of the river Pactolus and he would lose the fatal gift. He did so, and that was said to be the reason why gold was found in the sands of the river.

Later on, Apollo changed Midas's ears into those of an ass; but again the punishment was for stupidity, not for any wrongdoing. He was chosen one of the umpires in a musical contest between Apollo and Pan. The rustic god could play very pleasing tunes on his pipes of reed, but when Apollo struck his silver lyre, there was no sound on earth or in heaven that could equal the melody, except only the choir of the Muses. Nevertheless, although one umpire, the mountain-god Tmolus, gave the palm to Apollo, Midas, no more intelligent musically than in any other way, honestly preferred Pan. Of course this was double stupidity on his part. Ordinary prudence would have reminded him that it was dangerous to side against Apollo with Pan, infinitely the less powerful. And so he got his ass's ears. Apollo said that he was merely giving to ears so dull and dense the proper shape. Midas hid them under a cap especially made for that purpose, but the servant who cut his hair was obliged to see them. He swore a solemn oath never to tell, but the secrecy so weighed upon the man that he finally went and dug a hole in a field and spoke softly into it, "King Midas has ass's ears." Then he felt relieved and filled the hole up. But in the spring reeds grew up there, and when stirred by the wind, they whispered those buried words—and revealed to men not only the truth of what had happened to the poor, stupid king, but also that when gods are contestants the only safe course is to side with the strongest.

—from Mythology
by Edith Hamilton

About the Myth

1. Is the myth of King Midas mainly concerned with natural phenomena or human qualities? Explain.
2. Two sentences in the myth explain natural phenomena. Identify them.
3. The author who retells the myth of King Midas says, "He was an example of folly [stupidity] being as fatal as sin...." The myth tells of two mishaps in Midas's life. How is the first an example of "folly being as fatal as sin"? How is the second?
4. The author says that Midas's name is a synonym (another name) for a rich man. Do you think this myth reveals the ancient Greeks' attitude toward the very rich? Why or why not?
5. A number of Greek myths concern quarrels between gods. The myth of King Midas suggests a rule of conduct for humans who are caught up in such a quarrel. Find a sentence that states this rule of conduct.

Writing About Literature

1. Three myths that explain a natural phenomenon are those of Narcissus and Echo, of Daphne, and of Arachne. Read and then retell one of these myths in your own words.
2. Write your own myth to explain a modern phenomenon, such as a power blackout, smog, or a traffic jam. You may also want to invent a mythical god or goddess as part of your explanation.

3 — Poetry—Sound and Form

> ● The sound of a poem depends on such elements as **rhythm** and **rhyme.** The form depends on the pattern of lines and the pattern of rhymes.

Sound All language has rhythm, but most poems have a regular rhythm consisting of a pattern of stressed syllables, or beats, and unstressed syllables. In the following lines from "The Oak," a poem by Alfred, Lord Tennyson, the beats have been marked.

> Líve thy Lífe,
> Yoúng and óld,
> Líke yon oák,
> Bríght in spríng,
> Líving góld.

Notice that each line has two beats and one unstressed syllable between them, thus creating a regular rhythm.

Notice also that two lines—the second and fifth—rhyme. Rhyme is the repetition of similar sounds at the ends of words, such as *old* and *gold.* In the following group of words, all but one rhyme: *cat, sat, hat, tan, bat.* Which word does not rhyme?

Two other elements of sound are alliteration and onomatopoeia. **Alliteration** is the repetition of beginning consonant sounds of words. It occurs not only in poems but in common phrases, such as *might and main.* Point out the alliteration in the first line of "The Oak."

Onomatopoeia is the use of words that sound like what they mean. *Crack* imitates the sound of something cracking. *Whisper* suggests the sound of whispering.

Read the poem below. Notice the use of rhythm, rhyme, alliteration, and onomatopoeia.

The Wolf Cry

The Arctic moon hangs overhead;
The wide white silence lies below.
A starveling[1] pine stands lone and gaunt,
Black-penciled on the snow.

Weird as the moan of sobbing winds,
A lone long call floats up from the trail;
And the naked soul of the frozen North
Trembles in that wail.

—*Lew Sarett*

Form   The form of a poem results from several patterns: the pattern of stressed and unstressed syllables, the pattern of the number of beats per line, and the pattern of rhymes. Many poems are made up of groups of lines called **stanzas.** In some poems all the stanzas have the same—or nearly the same—pattern.

Two common forms of poetry are the couplet and the ballad. A **couplet** is a pair of lines that rhyme. Some poems are made up of several couplets. A **ballad** is a poem that tells a story and is made up of many stanzas. Read the poems that follow and notice their forms.

The Centipede

I objurgate[2] the centipede,
A bug we do not really need.
At sleepy-time he beats a path
Straight to the bedroom or the bath.
You always wallop where he's not,
Or, if he is, he makes a spot.

—*Ogden Nash*

1. Thin as if from starvation.
2. Denounce or rebuke.

The North Ship

I saw three ships go sailing by,
Over the sea, the lifting sea,
And the wind rose in the morning sky,
And one was rigged for a long journey.

The first ship turned towards the west,
Over the sea, the running sea,
And by the wind was all possessed
And carried to a rich country.

The second turned towards the east,
Over the sea, the quaking sea,
And the wind hunted it like a beast
To anchor in captivity.

The third ship drove towards the north,
Over the sea, the darkening sea,
But no breath of wind came forth,
And the decks shone frostily.

The northern sky rose high and black
Over the proud unfruitful sea,
East and west the ships came back
Happily or unhappily:

But the third went wide and far
Into an unforgiving sea
Under a fire-spilling star,
And it was rigged for a long journey.

—*Philip Larkin*

About the Poems

1. In "The Wolf Cry" what words rhyme in lines 1–4? In lines 5–8?
2. Point out two examples of alliteration.
3. Point out an example of onomatopoeia in line 5.
4. Which poem is made up of couplets? Identify the words that rhyme.
5. Reread the first stanza of the ballad "The North Ship." Where do the rhyming words occur? Do the other stanzas follow the same pattern of rhyming words?
6. Like many ballads this one suggests a story instead of telling it directly. What story does it suggest? Explain what happened to each of the ships.

Writing About Literature

1. A poem is meant to be spoken and heard as well as read silently. Read "The Wolf Cry" aloud several times so that you can appreciate its sounds. Then write which words have sounds that are especially effective in suggesting the "soul of the frozen North." List other words the poet might have used. Explain why you chose the words on your list.
2. Write a paragraph explaining why you think either "The Centipede" is a funny poem or "The North Ship" is a sad poem. Defend your opinion with specific references to words or phrases in the poem.

UNIT SEVEN

Speaking and Listening

At first glance you might wonder why an entire unit of this book is needed to teach speaking and listening. After all, speaking seems easy enough. Most people learn to speak by age three. Listening, or at least hearing, also seems easy. People do not even have to learn how to hear.

Actually, many everyday speaking and listening situations are quite simple. You talk about weekend plans with a friend. You listen to a ball game on the radio. You telephone a classmate for a homework assignment. You have been in these situations so often that you do not even have to think about them.

Other speaking and listening activities, however, are not so automatic. Do you ever have trouble starting and continuing conversations with adults? Does listening to complicated directions give you difficulty? Does the thought of giving a talk to a roomful of people make your palms sweat? In this unit you will practice speaking and listening in situations that are often difficult for students of your age.

As you grow older, you experience more situations in which good speaking and listening skills are necessary. Already you know how important listening is for success in school. The ability to listen well can help you to

- determine the main idea of what you hear.
- remember important details.
- take better notes.
- follow directions correctly.
- evaluate, or judge, the information you hear.

Speaking skills, too, can lead to success in school. Speaking well allows you to

- participate actively in class discussions.
- ask questions concisely.
- make announcements clearly.
- present a short talk confidently.

At parties and other social occasions, your speaking and listening skills will also be useful. Among other things, they will help you to

- practice good telephone manners.
- introduce strangers to one another correctly.
- start and continue conversations with people you do not know well.
- give directions and instructions clearly.
- speak comfortably to a group of people.

In the years ahead you will use speaking and listening skills in many life situations. Whether you are being interviewed for a job or making a new friend, questioning a salesperson about a product you wish to buy or running for President, good speaking and listening skills are important. Indeed, the ability to communicate well will greatly increase your chances for success.

21 *Speaking*

"It usually takes me more than three weeks to prepare a good impromptu speech."

—Mark Twain

1 — Introductions

> • Introductions allow people to meet one another and feel at ease.

Have you ever gone to a party and found yourself in a room filled with strangers? Most people are uneasy in this type of situation. Introductions can help overcome this uneasiness.

Whenever you are in a social situation in which you know two people who do not know each other, it is important to introduce them. The following guidelines will help you make and respond to introductions.

Making Introductions

• Give the full name of each person you introduce. If you are introducing an adult to a younger person, say the adult's name first.

> Mr. McGee, I'd like you to meet my cousin, Charlene Karr. Charlene, this is my music teacher, Mr. McGee.

• Tell each person a little bit about the other. This will help put the people at ease and serve as a "conversation starter" between the two.

> Grandma, this is David Grippo. David is our school's top tennis player. David, my grandmother, Mrs. Pickett, is visiting us from her ranch in Nebraska.

• Sometimes it is necessary to introduce yourself. Simply tell your name and give a little information about what you do.

> Hello, I'm Aaron Stone. My family and I just moved here from West Virginia. I'll be going to Riverview High next September.

- When you introduce someone to a group, say the name of the group first.

> Team, this is Beth Santos. Beth played softball in Mayfield. She moved here last week and wants to join our team.

Responding to an Introduction

- When someone is introduced to you, listen carefully for the person's name. You might want to repeat the name in order to remember it.

- Respond with a smile and a friendly greeting. To people your own age you may say "Hi." "How do you do?" is a more formal response.

- It is polite to rise from your seat and shake hands during an introduction. Usually the older person takes the lead in handshaking.

- Begin a conversation with your new acquaintance in order to get to know him or her better.

Exercise

Form groups of three students to make the following introductions before the class. Two members of each group take the parts of the persons being introduced. The third member makes the introduction. Be sure that each member of the group takes a turn making an introduction. Your classmates will evaluate how you make and respond to introductions.

1. Introduce your grandfather to your best friend.
2. Introduce your sister to your science teacher.
3. Introduce yourself to two students you do not know.
4. Introduce a beginning rock collector to the other members of your geology club.

2 — Conversations

> ● Knowing how to start and continue a conversation is an important life skill.

Starting a Conversation   After you have been in-troduced, do your part to get the conversation going.

- Give your partner your full attention.
- Focus on your partner's interests.
- Ask questions that will "draw out" a partner.
- Answer questions in a way that will lead to further conversation.

Dana and Ellen have just been introduced. Which girl is not following the tips given above?

Dana: Jack says you have just moved to Cedar Valley. Do you like our town?
Ellen (Waving to her friend Bill): Yes, I do.
Dana: You live out by the lake, don't you?
Ellen: Sort of.
Dana: My brother and I sail at the lake in the summer.
Ellen (Rocking in time to the music): That's nice.

Notice that Ellen did not give Dana her full attention. Her answers to Dana's questions tended to block conversation. To build conversation Ellen could have told Dana what she liked or disliked about Cedar Valley and exactly where she lived. Ellen also failed to focus on Dana's interests. She could have asked Dana about sailing and other activities at the lake.

Exercise

Rewrite the conversation between Dana and Ellen. Have both girls follow the tips for starting a conversation.

Continuing a Conversation   A conversation is a good opportunity to express yourself and to learn more about others. Once a conversation has started, do your best to keep it moving. The following tips will help you.

- Take part in the conversation. State your own ideas briefly and clearly. Do not shout or mumble.
- Give others an opportunity to speak. If necessary, ask questions or ask for another's opinion on a topic.
- Listen when others speak. Do not interrupt or start a side conversation with someone else.
- Watch your conversational manners. Avoid bragging or making comments that will embarrass or offend. Be pleasant, even when you disagree with someone.

Exercises

A. Discuss what is wrong with this conversation.

Ann: Last Sunday, Nancy and I rode to Columbus and—
Dan: I study every Sunday in order to get all A's.
Ann: We saw the new movie *Space Patrol.*
Jill: You're crazy to be friends with Nancy, Ann.
Ann: I like Nan—
Jill: She's very strange, and you know it!

B. Hold a conversation with a partner before the class, based on one of the situations listed below. Your classmates will evaluate your conversational skills.

1. You meet an old friend of your mother's at a store.
2. In the lunchroom you find yourself sitting next to a student who has recently moved to your town.
3. An uncle you have not seen in five years has come to visit.

3 — Class Discussions

- A discussion is an opportunity to share ideas and solve problems.
- Answering questions in class develops speaking skills and self-confidence.

Discussions   In a good group discussion, people share ideas and try to solve common problems. Follow these guidelines when taking part in a group discussion.

- Listen to the discussion, and contribute ideas.
- Give everyone a chance to speak. Do not talk too long at one time. Do not interrupt other speakers.
- Keep to the original topic of discussion.
- If you disagree with a speaker, explain why pleasantly.

Exercises

A. Read the group discussion. Which speaker does not keep to the subject? Which speaker makes statements that block discussion? Who does not contribute?

Jack: The seventh grade fair earned $300. We agreed to buy a gift for the school. What should we get?

Ray: How about a new water fountain for the gym?

Al: I like that idea! We sure need one!

Dana: I'd like to get a new curtain for the auditorium stage. The curtain we have is old and torn.

Al: That's ridiculous! What a waste of money!

Jane: I saw the senior class's performance of *Help!*

Jack: So far we have two suggestions—a gym fountain and a stage curtain. Do you have any ideas, Ike?

Ike: Huh? Oh, that sounds good to me, too.

B. Hold a discussion with four or five of your class-mates. Discuss one of the topics listed below, or choose your own topic. Other classmates will evaluate your discussion.

1. How to Get Along with Brothers and Sisters
2. Five Ways We Could Improve Our School
3. What We Can Do Now to Get Ready for the Future
4. How Does Television Affect Our Lives
5. The Importance of Sports

Answering Questions in Class   Frequently your teacher will expect you to discuss or answer questions about homework or class assignments. Taking part in such discussions will improve your speaking and listening skills and build your self-confidence. If you have trouble speaking in class, these tips may help.

- Keep up with reading assignments so that you will be prepared to discuss them.
- Pay attention to the discussion, and ask questions when you are confused.
- Do not let the fear of giving a wrong answer prevent you from entering a discussion.
- Try to make at least one contribution to every discussion in class.

Exercise

Keep a record of your participation in class discussions. Note the date, the topic of the discussion, and the number of times you contributed ideas or answers. Also note how your contributions made you feel. Keep the record for at least a month, and check your progress week to week.

4 — Telephoning

> ● Using the telephone is an important life skill.

You know that good speaking skills are important when taking part in conversations and discussions. Speaking skills are also important when talking on the telephone. You will often speak to people on the phone who do not know you. They will form their first impression of you on the basis of your telephone skills. These rules will help you make a good impression.

Making a Telephone Call

- Avoid making calls early in the morning, at meal times, or late at night.
- Make sure you know the correct number. If you dial a wrong number, apologize and hang up.
- When someone answers, say hello, give your name, and tell the name of the person you are calling.
- If the person you are calling is not available to speak, leave a message. The message should include your name, your number, and the reason for your call.
- If you reach the person you are calling, keep the conversation brief. Speak clearly, and use good conversational manners. The person who makes the call usually says good-bye first.

Receiving a Telephone Call

- Answer promptly, and tell the caller your name.
- Listen carefully to the caller and, if necessary, take notes on important information.
- If the call is for someone who is not present or available, take a message. Write the message and repeat it to the caller to make sure it is correct.

Exercise

Working with a partner, conduct a telephone conversation based on one of the situations below. Your classmates will listen and evaluate your telephone technique.

1. You call the fire department to report a small fire in a wooded area near your home. The fire department operator wants specific information.
2. You call a friend to confirm a date to go to the movies on Friday night. The friend is out. The friend's uncle, whom you've never met, answers the phone.
3. After dialing a wrong number, you call Al's Jewelry Shop to see if your watch has been fixed. The clerk can find no record of it and takes a message for the shop owner.
4. The town librarian calls you about two overdue records. You think you may have already returned the records.
5. You call the dentist's office to say you can't keep Thursday's appointment and to make another one.

Application LIFE SKILLS

During emergencies the telephone can be a lifesaver. Knowing the numbers of those who can help will save precious seconds in a crisis. Copy the form below. Fill in the emergency numbers and keep it near your telephone.

EMERGENCY TELEPHONE NUMBERS	
Police _____	Fire Department _____
Ambulance _____	Doctor _____
Poison Control Information_____	Business Number(s) of Parent(s)_____
	_____

5 — Giving Information

- Announcements must be clear and must be attention-getting.
- Directions must be clear and complete.

Making Announcements Announcements have two purposes. They provide information about an event or activity, and they create interest in it. An announcement should clearly answer the following questions.

What is happening?	Who is involved in it?
Where is it happening?	Why should the event
When is it happening?	interest the listener?

Unnecessary information should be left out of an announcement, but key words can be repeated. Notice that this announcement gives all the necessary information.

Would you like to have fun after the class party on Saturday? Then stay and sweep out the gym with us! Don't laugh. Volunteer! To sign up, see Jean Mills in the cafeteria at noon today. That's the clean-up committee sign-up (pause), Jean Mills (pause), in the cafeteria at noon. Be part of the party after the party!

To create interest, an announcement must get the listener's attention. Speak loudly and clearly. A humorous or dramatic announcement is often effective, too.

Exercise

First write and then read aloud an announcement for an event that will take place in your school or community. Use an attention-getting opener. Give and repeat all important details.

Giving Directions Have you ever gotten lost because someone gave you unclear or incomplete directions? If so, you know that good directions are important. These guidelines will help you give clear directions.

- Think of the route that is easiest to follow.
- Organize the directions in logical steps.
- Present the steps in the order they should be followed.
- Give specific details. Mention street names and landmarks that may be helpful.
- Be exact. Say "two blocks," not "a little way."

Exercise

Use the map below to give the following directions. Write the directions, numbering each step.

1. Your uncle is arriving in town by bus and wants to visit you at the Park Avenue School.
2. Your cousin who is visiting from another town wants to drive to the bus station from Tulip Street.

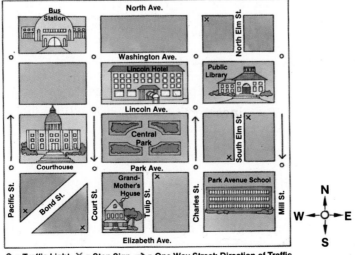

O = Traffic Light X = Stop Sign → = One Way Street; Direction of Traffic

6 — Voice and Speech Techniques

- Use your voice to help express meaning and feeling.

As you practice speaking, you will find there are ways your voice can help you express meaning and feeling. The following techniques can make you a better speaker.

Stress Stress is the emphasis, or force, that you place on a spoken word. Stressing certain words can change the meaning of spoken sentences. Read these sentences.

You ran to town.   (A simple statement—no stress)
You ran to town?   (A question—Was it really you who ran?)
You *ran* to town?   (A question—You didn't get a ride?)
You ran to *town*?   (A question—You ran that far?)

Pitch Pitch, or the rise and fall of a voice, adds variety to speech and also expresses feeling. A rise in voice indicates a question: *Is this the end?* It can also show excitement: *That was great!* The voice falls to show finality or disappointment: *This is the end.* You can vary the pitch of your voice to achieve many effects.

Exercises

A. Say each sentence below several times, stressing a different word each time. What special meaning does the stress give the sentence each time?

1. Jack fell in the swamp.   2. His mom is a dentist.

B. Use pitch to make each sentence a question. Next use pitch to make the sentence show disappointment. Then use pitch to show excitement.

1. They are soldiers.   2. Sue won the race.

Pausing Pausing is another speaking technique that will help you express your meaning. Pause briefly where a comma would be used and longer for end punctuation. Notice how pauses change the meaning of the sentence.

> Lisa, Marie, and Sue buy turkey, soup, and bread.
> Lisa Marie and Sue buy turkey soup and bread.
> Lisa Marie and Sue, buy turkey soup and bread.

Pausing also lets you call attention to an important word or phrase.

> We have nothing to fear (pause) but *fear* itself!

Rate Your rate of speech is the speed at which you say words. You can speed up or slow down your rate according to what you say. A slow rate suggests sadness or thoughtfulness. A fast rate suggests happiness or excitement. At what rate would you describe a horse race?

Volume Changing the volume, or loudness, of your voice adds variety to your speech. You should always speak loudly enough to be heard. Increasing the volume of your voice is also a way to emphasize points you feel strongly about.

Exercises

A. Use pauses to say the sentence below in different ways.

Mr. Douglas James bought the fruit juice and ice.

B. Practice reading aloud a passage from a book. Find out how many words you say per minute. Try speeding up and slowing down. Which sounds better?

C. Practice changing the volume of your voice. Begin speaking in a whisper. Slowly increase your volume to a shout. Then decrease the volume to a whisper.

7—Giving a Talk

- Choose a topic for a talk that is appropriate for your purpose and audience.
- Gather information and organize it into an introduction, a body, and a conclusion.
- Practice presenting your talk.

Why are some talks so interesting and others so boring? The presentation of the talk is important. A speaker must speak clearly and must appear comfortable. More important, though, a good talk requires careful preparation. Learn the steps for preparing a short talk.

Choosing a Topic Often you will have to choose your own topic for a talk. These guidelines will help you.

- Choose a topic in which you are interested. Your interest will help make your talk interesting.
- Choose a topic about which you have some knowledge. Your knowledge will make the process of gathering and organizing information easier. Telling personal experiences will add "life" to the talk.
- Narrow your topic so that you can cover it in a short time. If your topic is too broad, there will be no time for anything but general statements. "Airplanes," for example, is too broad a topic. "My Ride in a Biplane," however, is a suitable topic for a short talk.

Exercise

List three topics for a talk that interest you and about which you have knowledge. Be sure to narrow the topics so that they are not too broad for a short talk.

Knowing Your Purpose and Audience As you choose a topic, you should consider the purpose of the talk. Most talks inform, persuade, or entertain the audience.

An informative talk helps an audience understand or appreciate a topic. Such a talk usually includes many facts. "How to Print Your Own Photographs" is an example of an informative talk topic.

A persuasive talk tries to win the audience over to the opinion of the speaker. The topics of such talks have at least two sides to them. "The Best Candidate for Mayor" and "Why Summer Vacations Should Be Shorter" are examples of persuasive talk topics.

Any talk you give should be enjoyable. Certain talks, however, have entertainment as their main purpose. "The Skunk Who Moved Into Our Basement," for example, might be the topic of an entertaining talk.

A good speaker also considers his or her audience, the people who will listen to the talk. For most of the talks you give, the audience will be your classmates. Since they are your age and share many of your interests, it should be easy to pick appropriate topics for them.

You may also have the opportunity to speak to groups outside your class or school. If so, you should ask these questions about the group.

1. **What is the purpose of the group?** Is the group meeting to learn something? Is it meeting to have fun? Your talk should be on a topic that will help the group achieve its purpose.
2. **Who is in the group?** Your talk should contain information appropriate for the age, interests, and educational level of the audience.

Exercises

A. Tell the purpose of a talk on each topic below.

  1. Maintaining a Ten-Speed Bicycle
  2. Living with Twenty-seven Cats and a Canary
  3. Soccer Is Better Than Football!

B. List three audiences you might speak to. Then write an appropriate talk topic for each audience.

Gathering Information   Once you have chosen your topic, it is time to begin gathering information. The gathering of information is like the prewriting stage of the writing process. List the many ideas and facts you might include in your talk. Do not worry now about organizing them. Most material will come from the following sources.

- **Personal Experiences** Topics you have firsthand knowledge of or experience about make lively short talks. Jot down everything you know or can remember.
- **Experiences of Others**   Other people with experience or knowledge related to a topic are good sources of information. Interview these people, taking good notes. Ask them to suggest other sources, too.
- **Library Research**   The library offers a wide variety of resources. Refer to Chapter 23 on the library for specific suggestions. Again, be sure to take careful notes.

Exercise

Choose one of the topics that you listed in the exercise on page 470. Find four different sources of information for this topic. List each source on a note card along with the information the source provides. (You may wish to refer to the lesson on taking notes, pages 500–501.)

Organizing Your Talk   Your talk should have a logical organization so that it will be easy to follow. Divide your talk into an introduction, a body, and a conclusion.

The introduction should attract the attention of the listeners. A humorous statement or unusual fact helps to get the audience's interest. The introduction should also state the purpose of the talk.

> My talk today is about a lot of garbage. No, my talk isn't garbage. Rather, it's about the 640 tons of trash that Midvale produces each day. Specifically, I will explain why this trash must be disposed of ecologically.

The body is the main part of your talk. It includes the main ideas and details that explain and support your topic. Outline the information on note cards. (Refer to the lesson on outlining, pages 504–505.) Write one card for each main idea. Remember, you are giving a talk, not reading a report. Do not write down everything you will say. Instead, write phrases that will remind you of important points. Also note where to use visual aids.

III. Advantages of a recycling program
(Show photographs of Elmtown
Recycling Center.)
A. Inexpensive — provides funds
sources

II. Options suggested by sanitation
Chief Lee
A. Build large-scale incinerator
dollars
worsen

I. Problems with present dumping
system
A. Cost of using present site —
$800,000 a year
(Hold up graph showing how much
of total city budget goes for dumping.)
B. Declining space
1. Dump will be full in 5 years
2. No alternate site available nearby

The conclusion is a brief summary of the main points you have made. If your purpose was to persuade, your conclusion for you talk should reemphasize your point of view.

> Because of high costs and dwindling available land, Midvale must change its garbage disposal practices. Chief Lee suggests two options—a garbage incinerator or recycling. An incinerator will be expensive to build. Recycling will save resources and provide funds for the town.

Exercise

Use the topic you researched on page 472. Write a short introduction for a talk on this topic. Next organize your information logically in outline form. (To complete the outline, you may need to gather more information.) Then write a brief conclusion for the talk.

Practicing Your Talk   After you have organized your talk, you will need to practice it. Follow these guidelines.

- Read through your note cards, making sure the information is in correct order. See that visual aids are in order, too.
- Underline or star the material you will emphasize. Experiment with voice techniques such as stress, pitch, and volume to place emphasis on certain points.
- Practice in front of a mirror to make sure your gestures and facial expressions appear natural.
- Memorize portions of the talk so that you can look at the audience frequently, not always at your note cards. (Do keep your cards handy, however.)
- Practice giving your talk to several family members or friends. Ask them to make specific suggestions about how you can improve your talk.

Exercise

Following the steps listed in this section, practice presenting the talk you have been working on. If you feel you should make changes in or additions to your talk, now is the time to do it.

Presenting Your Talk By now you should be familiar enough with the content of your talk to feel comfortable as you deliver it. However, just standing up in front of a group makes many people nervous. The following suggestions should help you overcome any nervousness you may be feeling.

- *Do* relax before your talk. Breathe deeply and try to relax all your muscles.
- *Do* look at the audience as you speak. Move your eyes slowly from face to face. Their faces may tell you whether they can hear and understand you.
- *Do not* stare at the floor or out the window. *Do not* check the clock or a watch frequently.
- *Do* stand in a natural position with your weight evenly balanced on both feet.
- *Do not* shift your weight from leg to leg or pace back and forth nervously.
- *Do not* scratch your head, yawn, or make other distracting movements.

Exercise

Deliver your talk to the class. Listen carefully as other members of the class present their talks. As you listen, evaluate the content and presentation of each talk. When each talk is over, discuss it, telling what you liked about it and what you feel needs improvement.

22 *Listening*

"Instead of listening to what
is being said to them,
many people are already listening to what
they are going to say."

—Anonymous

1 – Listening

> ● Listening is paying careful attention to what you hear.

Speaking is an important communication skill. When you give a speech, however, you must have an audience to listen. Listening is the "other side" of speaking. You need both skills for communication to take place.

Learning how to be a good audience is just as important as learning how to be a good speaker. Listening manners will help you pay attention to someone giving a speech.

Listening Manners The way you listen will determine how much you will learn from a speaker. To be a good listener, you should practice listening manners.

1. Look at the speaker. Focusing on the speaker shows your interest. It helps you concentrate, too.
2. Sit comfortably and quietly. Fidgeting, whispering, or doodling will distract you and others.
3. Do not interrupt the speaker. Interruptions make it harder to follow a speaker. If you have questions, wait until the end of the speech to ask them.

Exercises

A. Think of the last time you listened to a speech. Tell in what ways you showed good listening manners.

B. The next time you are a member of an audience, observe the listening manners of those around you. Share your findings with the class.

Listening Techniques In addition to practicing listening manners, you will also need to practice certain techniques to become a good listener. The EARS technique, which follows, will help you become a more skillful listener.

E. Examine the speaker's purpose. Keep that purpose in mind as you listen.

A. Anticipate the points the speaker will make. Questions such as "What point will be made next?" will keep you listening actively.

R. Remind yourself of the purpose of the talk if your mind begins to wander. This will help you return your attention to the speaker.

S. Summarize the speaker's points from time to time. Take notes if possible. Jot down in brief the speaker's main ideas. They will help you recall the information.

Exercises

A. Write a short paragraph. Then read your paragraph to the class. All listeners should use the EARS techniques. See if the listeners can tell the main idea of the paragraph.

B. Bring a short newspaper or magazine article to class, and read it aloud. When you have finished, see if your listeners can state the purpose of the article and summarize its main points.

C. Write a description of a person or place that most of your classmates are familiar with. Do not identify the person or place in your description. Read the description aloud, and have your listeners guess who or what you are describing.

2 – Listening to Learn

> • Listening to learn is paying attention to what you hear and remembering what you hear.

Learning by listening can be much harder than learning by reading. When you are reading, you can always reread a page again to check important information. When you are listening, however, you often have only one chance to remember what you hear. Memory techniques can be a big help when listening to learn.

Memory Techniques A memory technique is any method that helps you remember information. One memory technique is **cumulative repeating.** Each time a speaker makes a point, mentally repeat it and all the preceding points. For example, suppose a new friend is giving you directions to his or her home in another part of town. Your friend's directions and your use of cumulative repeating could go something like this.

> Friend: Turn left on Van Buren Avenue.
> You (mentally): Left on Van Buren.
> Friend: Ride six blocks until you get to Kent Place.
> You (mentally): Left on Van Buren, six blocks to Kent.
> Friend: Then turn right on Kent Place.
> You (mentally): Left on Van Buren, six blocks to Kent, turn right.
> Friend: My house is number 348 Kent Place.
> You: Left on Van Buren, six blocks to Kent, turn right, number 348.

Another memory technique is **mental mapping.** To use this technique, mentally place the information you want to remember at various points in a room you know well, such as the classroom. Read the following example.

Teacher: Columbus sailed in 1492.
You (mentally): Write *1492* on the classroom door.
Teacher: He had three ships named the *Niña*, the *Pinta*, and the *Santa Maria*.
You (mentally): Place the three ships along the top of the chalkboard.
Teacher: Queen Isabella was Columbus's sponsor.
You (mentally): Place Queen Isabella in the teacher's chair.

Reviewing the mental map from time to time will help you remember it.

Exercise

This exercise will let you practice the two memory techniques you have studied. Form groups of six to eight students. The first student begins the activity by naming an important event and date in history. A second student repeats this information and adds a second event and date. Read the following example.

First student: Columbus discovered America in 1492.
Second student: Columbus discovered America in 1492, and the English settled Jamestown in 1607.
Third student: Columbus discovered America in 1492. The English settled Jamestown in 1607, and the Pilgrims landed at Cape Cod in 1620.

Each student in the group repeats the sequence and adds an event and date. See how many events and dates you can remember.

Listening for the Main Idea   The most important listening skill is understanding a speaker's main idea. If you grasp the main idea, the details will be easier to remember. If you try to remember details without understanding the main idea, you may become confused.

Exercise

Close your book and listen as your teacher reads the paragraph below. After listening to the entire paragraph, write what you think is the main idea.

> Many tourists come to this seaside resort in the summer, making the shops and restaurants very busy. The construction and fishing industries also employ many local people during the summer. In the winter, though, everything stops. The tourists have left, and there is little winter fishing. It is even too cold for construction work. Because it is hard to make a living here during the winter, some year-round industries are needed.

Listening for Details It is important to remember the details that support a speaker's main idea. Details may be facts, examples, or descriptions. As you listen to details, think about how they help explain the main idea.

Think back to the paragraph about the seaside resort. Suppose someone were to ask you, "Why does that town need year-round industry?" What details from the paragraph can you remember that would answer the question? Do not reread the paragraph. Use your memory.

Exercise

Close your book and listen as your teacher reads the speech below. Then answer the question that follows.

> Hector Santos has been a city councilman for eight years. Before that he was active in community groups. He founded the Parks for Parkville Committee and raised money for three new parks. He has worked tirelessly for the redevelopment of downtown Parkville. Hector Santos understands city government. His opponent, however, has never held public office and has no record of community service. Elect Hector Santos mayor this November!

Why might some citizens vote for Hector Santos?

Taking Notes Taking notes will help you remember the information you hear. You should take your notes in outline form to keep up with the speaker.

To write notes in outline form, write each main idea the speaker presents. Identifying the main ideas may take some detective work, since it is not always easy to know the direction a speaker may take. Still, this detective game will keep you alert and involved. The main ideas will be the main headings of your outline. After you write a main idea, identify the speaker's supporting details that give information about the idea. Write these supporting details under the appropriate heading of your outline.

Do not get so involved in writing that you forget to listen, though. If necessary, write incomplete words or initials. Later, you can write your notes in paragraph form.

Exercise

Close your book and listen as your teacher reads the science selection below. Take notes in outline form.

> Your body grows and replaces parts by the addition of cells. Cells are the basic units of structure and function of all living things. The bodies of all plants and animals are made up of cells.
> A cell membrane surrounds the cell. The membrane helps control the flow of materials into and out of the cell.

Listening for Context Clues As you listen to someone speak, you will sometimes hear an unfamiliar word. Often you can get clues to the meaning of a new word from the surrounding words, or context. For example, read the sentence on the following page and tell what the word *mendacious* means.

Since she tends to be a <u>mendacious</u> person, we
rarely believe her stories.

The words *rarely believe* are clues indicating that *mendacious* means "not truthful."

Exercise

Write the words *obdurate, incensed, chastise, winsome,*
and *enamored.* Then close your book and listen as your
teacher reads the paragraph below. Using context clues,
tell what each word means.

Young Helen can be quite obdurate at times. She continues to behave as she wishes, despite the con-
sequences. This behavior causes her parents to become
incensed, and sometimes they chastise her by sending
her to her room. At other times, Helen is so winsome
that everyone loves her. Still, no matter what her behavior, her adoring parents are completely enamored of
their darling daughter.

Listening to Directions   Have you ever written a correct answer on a test only to have it marked wrong because you did not follow directions? Listening to directions is an important listening skill. Think of these
situations, and consider what might happen if you failed
to follow directions.

1. The coach is explaining a new play for use in a
   championship game.
2. The band leader is telling you how to play your
   trumpet solo.
3. You are filling out a job application.
4. You are conducting an important experiment in
   your science class.

The following steps will help you learn to listen and to follow directions.

1. Mentally repeat each step of the directions as you listen to the speaker.
2. When the speaker has finished, summarize the directions in your mind.
3. Ask questions about steps you do not understand.

Exercises

A. Close your book and follow the directions your teacher will read to you. Each direction will be read only once. How well can you listen?

1. Write *yes* if your first name begins with *W, P, T,* or *R.* Otherwise, write *no.*
2. Of the words *school, paper,* and *book,* write the longest.
3. Even if cows are larger than dogs, write *no.*
4. If fourteen plus nine equals twenty-two, draw a circle; if it does not, draw a square.
5. Are you in Europe? Give the wrong answer.
6. If your birthday is in the first half of the year, draw a star in a circle. Otherwise, do the opposite.
7. If you are left-handed, write your first name. Otherwise, write your last name.

B. Carefully draw a design consisting of geometric shapes, such as straight lines, circles, and squares. Then choose a partner and give him or her directions for drawing your design. Do not show your design to your partner. Compare the two designs afterward, and discuss whether your directions were clear and whether your partner followed them. Then trade roles.

3 — Critical Listening

> ● Critical listening means evaluating the statements that you hear.

Good listeners do not accept everything they hear. Instead, they evaluate, or judge, the merits and faults of a speaker's statement. One way to do this is to evaluate the reasoning behind a statement.

Evaluating Reasoning To evaluate a speaker's reasoning, ask yourself the following questions.

1. Does the speaker use sound logic?
2. Does the speaker support his or her statements and opinions with examples or facts?

At a school board meeting, these statements were made.

A. Park High is a fine school. I went there thirty years ago, so I should know!
B. Park High is not any good. The students are lazy, and the teachers give too much homework.
C. Park High has serious problems. Only ten percent of its graduates go to college. Its absentee rate is the third highest in the state!

Statement **A** is not logical; it does not make sense. What was true thirty years ago may not be true today.

Statement **B** contains only opinions. An opinion is a judgment or belief formed in the mind.

Statement **C** begins with an opinion but contains facts that support it. Critical listeners use the facts and examples in a statement to decide whether it is logical and acceptable.

Exercise

Evaluate the reasoning behind these statements.

A. My doctor went to Park High, so it must have good science teachers.
B. We would all be proud of Park High if it had better teams. The football team is terrible, and not enough students go out for baseball.
C. Park High's new library is impressive. There are fifty thousand books, a media center, and two full-time librarians on the staff.

Viewing Television Critically   Television provides much information and entertainment. Many people, however, view television uncritically. Some accept everything they see and hear without evaluating it. Others remember nothing about shows they watch. These steps will help you view television critically.

1. Decide in advance what show to watch.
2. Determine whether the show is based on fact or fiction. If fact, try to identify any opinions you hear.
3. Decide whether the commercials are logical. Do they contain facts to support their claims?
4. Summarize your impressions of the show. Do you think you will watch it again?

Exercises

A. Make tape recordings of television commercials for your class. What facts and opinions can you hear?

B. Bring last week's television listings into class. Discuss the shows that you and other class members watched. List your reasons for watching these shows. Summarize your impressions of them.

UNIT EIGHT

Study Skills

> ## UNIT PREVIEW
> ### What Are Study Skills?

Now that you are in the upper grades, your schoolwork is becoming more challenging. You must learn to study on your own and to set up a daily study schedule. You must learn to do research and to prepare oral and written reports. To meet these challenges, you must develop study skills.

The unit begins with library skills. You will learn to find your way around the library by using the card catalog and the book classification system. The next lesson covers reference works and how to use them to find information. Doing research for a written or an oral report may now seem difficult to you. However, the lessons on taking notes, paraphrasing (putting ideas into your own words), outlining, and the parts of a report provide step-by-step guides that will help you learn how to compile a report.

To develop your study skills, you must use reading skills. The skills of skimming and scanning will help you find information quickly. Use skimming to get a general idea of what the material is about. Use scanning to find a specific piece of information. Vocabulary skills are also necessary for effective study. In this unit you will learn how to study vocabulary, how to use the dictionary, and how to understand context clues in learning new words.

Another study skill to master is how to study for tests. You will learn how to take notes as you listen in class, how to use the reading aids in your textbooks, and how to organize information in your notebook to make studying easier. You will learn how to review for a test and how to answer objective and essay questions on a test. You will also get practice in one special type of test question—the analogy. Analogies are comparisons that help you sharpen your thinking skills.

This unit will teach you the skills you need to become a good student. You must put them into practice yourself, however, if you want to do well in school. Good study habits must become part of your daily life. Set aside the same time each day for study. During this time, complete your homework, review your class notes, and work on reports.

Suppose you decide you need two hours a day to accomplish your study goals. Choose an afternoon hour and an evening hour for study. Leave yourself free time in between for other activities. Alternating study time and relaxation time will keep you motivated. Find a good place to study, with good lighting and enough space for your books and supplies. Do not let radio, television, or anything else distract you when you study.

As the year goes by, your good study habits will bring improvement. You will become a better student and will be able to accomplish more in less time because of effective study skills and study habits.

23 *Library and Reporting Skills*

Public Library

Up three
worn
steps,

Through a heavy door,

Into
the midst
of books.

From them, anything.

From here, anywhere.

—*Robert Froman*

1 **Using the Library**

> ● The **card catalog** is your guide to books.

To find the information you need in the library, learn to use the card catalog—a file cabinet that contains information cards for every book in the library. Some libraries have a computer listing in addition to the card catalog. Also learn how books are arranged on the library shelves.

The Card Catalog The cards in the catalog are arranged in alphabetical order in drawers. On the outside of each drawer is a guide label that shows the beginning letters on the first and last cards inside. For example, a drawer labeled *La–Me* would contain cards for books on Lapland and meteorology, among other topics. Inside the drawer are guide cards to help you locate topics.

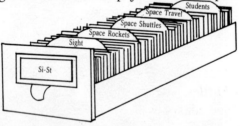

Each nonfiction book usually has three kinds of cards filed in the card catalog: a **title card**, an **author card**, and a **subject card**. Each card gives the same information.

If you know the title of the book you want, look up the title card. Title cards are filed by the first important word of a title. For example, the book *Flying to the Moon* would be found under *Flying*; however, *The Survivors* would be listed under *Survivors*. If you know only the author's name, look up the last name on an author card. If you are doing research on a particular subject, such as space travel, look for a subject card on *space travel.*

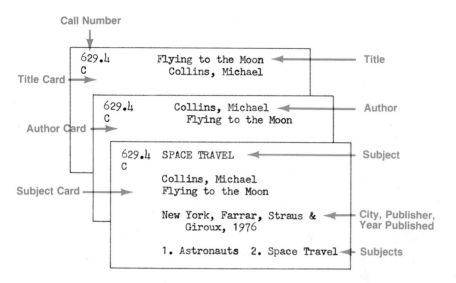

You may also find cross-reference cards in the card catalog. A cross-reference card will direct you to another subject heading that lists books you can use. If you look up *space shuttles*, you may find a cross-reference card that says, "See reusable space vehicles."

The Arrangement of Books Books in the library are shelved systematically. Fictional books are found in their own section. They are arranged alphabetically by the author's last name. Biographies are also often in a special section. These books are arranged alphabetically by the last name of the person being written about.

To find any nonfiction book in the library, you need to know its **call number**. The call number of a book appears on the side or spine of the book. It also appears in the upper lefthand corner of its corresponding card in the card catalog. Nonfiction books are shelved numerically, according to their call numbers. One of two numerical systems is used. Most libraries use the **Dewey decimal system**, which places all nonfiction books within ten categories, or subject areas. The following chart shows the number ranges of the Dewey decimal system and their corresponding subject areas.

Numbers	Subjects
000–099	**General Works** (reference works such as the encyclopedia, atlas, almanac)
100–199	**Philosophy** (includes psychology)
200–299	**Religion** (includes myths)
300–399	**Social Sciences** (includes education, government, folktales, fairy tales)
400–499	**Language** (includes the thesaurus, foreign language versions of the dictionary)
500–599	**Science** (includes mathematics, biology, chemistry, physics)
600–699	**Technology** (includes medicine, engineering, aviation, farming)
700–799	**The Arts** (includes painting, music, sports)
800–899	**Literature** (includes plays, poetry, essays, television scripts, but not fiction)
900–999	**History and Geography** (includes travel)

Each subject is divided further into more specific topics. For example, *the arts* (700's) is divided into categories such as *architecture* (720's), *painting* (750's), and *music* (780's). Each book within a category has a call number that includes the initial of the author's last name. The **Library of Congress system** uses a different combination of numbers and letters in its call numbers.

Exercises

A. Write which card you would look for—title, author, or subject—to find each of the following. Then write the word the card would be alphabetized under.

    1. A book by Pura Belpré
    2. A book called *A Treasury of Poems*
    3. A Mexican-American cookbook
    4. *Who's Who of American Women*
    5. Books by Myra Cohn Livingston

B. For each book title, write the number range under which it would appear in the Dewey decimal system.

EXAMPLE: *Travels in Africa*
ANSWER: 900–999

    6. *Whales and Porpoises*
    7. *The World Book Encyclopedia*
    8. *Poetry in Our Time*
    9. *Vietnamese Folktales*
    10. *Psychological Testing*
    11. *Square Dancing*
    12. *Spanish-English Dictionary*
    13. The Bible
    14. *The Government of the U.S.A.*
    15. *Spacecraft*

C. Go to the card catalog and write a title, author, and call number for each of the following.

    16. A book about ancient Rome
    17. A book about skiing
    18. A collection of poems
    19. A thesaurus
    20. A book about computers

2 — Using Reference Books

> ● Reference books supply specific information.

The library contains a variety of reference books that you can use for researching a report. Learn which reference book will provide the information you need.

Encyclopedia An encyclopedia contains thousands of articles on a wide variety of topics. An encyclopedia article is a good place to begin research for a report. It will give you an overview of the topic.

Encyclopedia articles are arranged in alphabetical order within books, or volumes. Each volume lists on its spine the number of the volume and the beginning letters of its first and last entries. At the top of each page of the volume are guide words showing the first and last entries on the page. At the end of many entries are cross-references to other related entries. For example, the entry "Space Flight" might be followed by this cross-reference: "*See also* Astronaut; Satellite; Space Shuttle."

To discover all the information an encyclopedia contains on your topic, use the index, which is usually in the last volume. The index lists each entry in alphabetical order, followed by its volume number (or the letter with

Photograph of *The World Book Encyclopedia* by permission of World Book, Inc.

which that volume begins) and its page number. There are cross-references to help you find more information.

Atlas An atlas contains maps that show countries, cities, mountains, rivers, and other geographic features. Other maps and tables illustrate facts such as population distribution. Keys, or legends, help you read the maps. Maps in an atlas are usually more detailed than those in an encyclopedia.

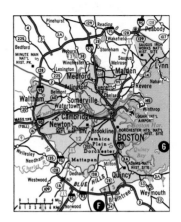

Almanac Almanacs are published yearly and contain facts and figures mostly in chart, table, or list form. If you need the answer to a specific question on current events, sports, weather, natural phenomena, population figures, and many other subjects, the almanac is a good place to look. The almanac index is the quickest guide to the location of a subject. A chart from the *Information Please Almanac* is shown below.

Highest Waterfalls of the World

Waterfall	Location	River	Height (feet)	Height (meters)
Angel	Venezuela	Tributary of Caroní	3,281	1,000
Tugela	Natal, South Africa	Tugela	3,000	914
Cuquenán	Venezuela	Cuquenán	2,000	610
Sutnerland	South Island, N.Z.	Arthur	1,904	580
Takkakaw	British Columbia	Tributary of Yoho	1,650	503
Ribbon (Yosemite)	California	Creek flowing into Yosemite	1,612	491
Upper Yosemite	California	Yosemite Creek, tributary of Merced	1,430	436
Gavarnie	Southwest France	Gave de Pau	1,384	422
Vettisfoss	Norway	Mörkedola	1,200	366
Widows' Tears (Yosemite)	California	Tributary of Merced	1,170	357
Staubbach	Switzerland	Staubbach (Lauterbrunnen Valley)	984	300

Readers' Guide to Periodical Literature Your library probably has a room or section for periodicals. **Periodicals** are newspapers and magazines that are published at regular periods, such as daily, weekly, or monthly.

If you need magazine articles to complete research for a report, use the *Readers' Guide to Periodical Literature* to find them. This reference book indexes articles from magazines. A paperback *Readers' Guide* is published periodically during the year. At the end of the year, all the information is put in a hardbound edition.

Magazine articles are listed in the *Readers' Guide* by subject and author. Here is a subject entry.

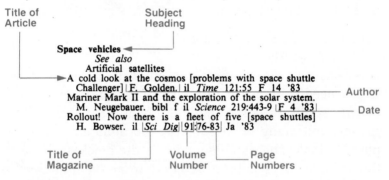

Several abbreviations are used in this entry. The abbreviation *il* stands for illustrated, *bibl* stands for bibliography, and *Ja* for January. At the front of the *Readers' Guide* is the Key to Abbreviations. Cross-references within the entries list related articles.

When you know exactly what periodical you want, fill in its name, date, and volume number on a periodical request form. The librarian will take the request form and give you either the periodical itself or a reproduction of it on microfilm. A device called a *reader* is needed to read microfilm. Ask your librarian how to use it.

Exercises

A. Use the section of an encyclopedia index to write the volume letter and page number of each item.

Space travel So:560 *with pictures and maps*
See also the Reading and Study Guide on this topic
Altitude **A:372b**
Astronomy (Space Exploration) **A:813**
Computer (In Engineering) **Ci:742** *with picture*
Cosmic Rays (Effects of Cosmic Rays) **Ci:857**
Guided Missile (Postwar Developments) **G:413-414**
Life (The Search for Life on Other Planets) **L:245**
Mercury (Flights to Mercury) **M:340**
Moon (Future Exploration on the Moon) **M:651**

1. Flights to Mercury
2. Effects of cosmic rays
3. Astronomy
4. Future exploration of the moon
5. An article with maps and a cross-reference

B. Write whether each of the following questions can be answered by an atlas, an almanac, or both.

6. Which team won the World Series last year?
7. How far is it from Seattle to San Francisco?
8. Who is the governor of Illinois?
9. What is the population of Japan?
10. What states contain part of the Rocky Mountains?

C. Use this excerpt on football from the *Readers' Guide to Periodical Literature* to answer the questions below.

Super Bowl
The great Super Bowl debate: why I hate it. G. Waggoner. il *Sport Mag* 74:32+ F '83
The great Super Bowl debate: why I love it. K. Lamb. il *Sport Mag* 74:33-4 F '83
Hail to the Redskins! P. Zimmerman. il *Sports Illus* 58:16-26+ F 7 '83
Our chance to be great [views of Washington Redskins quarterback]; ed. by John Papanek. J. Theismann. il *Sports Illus* 58:44-6+ F 14 '83

11. Who is the author of "Hail to the Redskins!"?
12. Which magazine has "The Great Super Bowl Debate"?
13. Which magazine has two issues listed?
14. Write the volume number of each: 74:32; 58:44.
15. What do the other numbers stand for?

3 — Taking Notes

> ● Take notes on index cards for a report.

The first step in learning to do research is learning to use the sources of information in the library. The second step is learning to take useful notes from these sources. You need to take notes to record important information. If you are taking notes for a written or an oral report, your notes should contain the main ideas you will cover in your report, along with the facts and details that support these ideas. You should also include definitions of important terms and a few quotations from experts.

As you do research for your report, you will be gathering information from many different sources—nonfiction books, reference works, and magazine articles. A good way to take notes from any source is to write them on 3" × 5" index cards. Each index card should contain notes on one main idea and from one source only. Because the information is on index cards, you can easily rearrange the cards to fit the order you want to use.

At the top of each note card, write the main idea. Then write the title of the source, the author, the publication date, and the pages covered. Next write your notes, which will include important details that support or explain the main idea. Be sure to express what you write down in your own words. Keep each note as brief and as simple as possible.

If you use quotations in your notes, copy the exact words, put quotation marks around them, and list the name of each person quoted. Do not use too many quotations. Study the chart and note card on the next page.

How to Take Notes

1. Write your notes on index cards, using one card for each main idea.
2. Write the main idea at the top of each card.
3. List the source of your information.
4. Write brief notes in your own words.
5. If you use quotations, copy the exact words, add quotation marks, and name each person quoted.

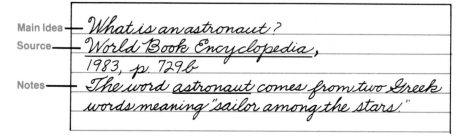

Main Idea — *What is an astronaut?*
Source — *World Book Encyclopedia,*
1983, p. 729b
Notes — *The word astronaut comes from two Greek words meaning "sailor among the stars."*

Exercise

Write the answers to the following questions.

1. What information about the source goes on each note card?
2. What rules must you follow when writing a quotation on a note card?
3. What are three reasons for taking notes on index cards?

Application TAKING NOTES FOR A REPORT

Choose a topic for a report that you will write later. First refer to the lesson "Selecting and Narrowing a Topic" on pp. 308–309. Then use two reference books to find information about your topic. Write four note cards for each source. Keep your cards for your report.

4 — Paraphrasing

> ● **Paraphrasing** is expressing in your own words ideas you have read or heard.

Some students find it difficult to write notes in their own words. If this is your problem, the skill you need to learn is paraphrasing, or putting information you have read into your own words.

First, identify the information you want to record in your notes. In the following example paragraph, the information is underlined.

> Since the year 1883 when it was built, the <u>Brooklyn Bridge</u> has been a symbol of human achievement. It represented the highest technological achievement of its time. It was <u>an engineering marvel, as daring as this century's space shots</u>.

The underlined material should not be copied word for word unless you enclose the words in quotation marks. Copying word for word, without using quotation marks or giving credit to the source of the material, is a form of stealing ideas known as **plagiarism**. Instead of copying, use the basic ideas and state them in your own words. For example, "an engineering marvel" can become "a feat of engineering." *Marvel* and *feat* are synonyms. The second underlined words could be restated: "Brooklyn Bridge—achievement as great in its time as space flights today." If you were to use these notes in your report, you might write the following.

> The Brooklyn Bridge was a great engineering feat. It was as impressive an achievement in its day as space flights are in our time.

Another way to express ideas in your own words is by **summarizing**. Unlike paraphrasing, when you summarize you write the most important ideas in as few words as possible. A summary should begin with a statement of the main idea. The supporting sentences should tell only the most important facts and details. To summarize a longer piece of writing, paraphrase the main idea of each paragraph into a single sentence. Then combine the sentences to form a summary paragraph.

Exercises

A. Write this passage. Underline the most important information. Then write notes, using paraphrasing.

Talk of a bridge over the East River in New York began as early as 1800. In those days Brooklyn was a separate city. People crossed the river in ferries. In winter, they were often stranded in storms or when ice choked the river. Legend has it that John Roebling thought of the bridge in 1853 when he and his son, Washington Roebling, were stranded on a ferry in the East River ice. In 1867, state legislators approved his design.

Tragedy haunted the construction. John Roebling died after a freak accident before ground was broken. Between twenty and forty workers died before the bridge was completed. Soon after Washington Roebling took over the construction, he was stricken by caisson disease—the bends. He spent most of the fourteen years of construction in a sickbed. His wife, Emily, carried his dictated instructions to the bridge builders.

B. Write a summary paragraph of four or five sentences about the Brooklyn Bridge. Use the information from the notes you took in Exercise **A**.

5 — Outlining

> ● An **outline** organizes material into main ideas, supporting ideas, and supporting details.

Always make a plan before you start to write a composition or a report. Your plan should follow outline form. By the time you write an outline, you will have decided on the subject you will cover. If you did research, you will have main ideas or topics on your note cards.

The first step is to arrange your ideas in outline form. In an outline all main topics are preceded by Roman numerals. Subtopics, or supporting ideas related to the main topics, are preceded by capital letters. Supporting details are set off by Arabic numerals.

There are two kinds of outlines. One has full sentences and is called a **sentence outline**. The other has topics and is called a **topic outline**.

An outline follows a logical and rigid structure. Study the chart below and the sample outline on the following page to learn how to write a topic outline.

How to Write an Outline

1. Center the title at the top of the outline.
2. You must write at least two items at each level of the outline. For example, there must be at least two main ideas, labeled I and II.
3. Place a period after each numeral or letter.
4. You should indent each new level of an outline.
5. Each Roman numeral, capital letter, and Arabic numeral should be in line with others of its kind.
6. Capitalize the first word of each item.

What Makes a Successful Astronaut?

I. How astronauts are chosen
  A. Physical qualities needed
  B. Personality traits needed
  C. Education needed
  D. Career training needed
II. How astronauts are trained
  A. Physical training
    1. Fitness training
    2. Survival skills training
  B. Psychological training
    1. Teamwork
    2. Space flight stress
    3. Emergency procedures
  C. Flight training
    1. Military aircraft
    2. Spacecraft
  D. Scientific training

Exercise

Refer to the sample topic outline above to write the answers to the following questions.

1. What is the title of the report outlined above?
2. What are the two main topics?
3. How many subtopics does topic II have?
4. How many details are included under "flight training"?
5. Which subtopic has no details listed?

Application OUTLINING A REPORT

Decide on a title for your report. Review your note cards. The main ideas on the note cards can become main topics in your outline. Write a topic outline for your report, showing main topics, subtopics, and details.

6 — Structure of a Report

> • A **report** presents information that you have gathered arranged in a well-organized form.

After you have completed your research and have written an outline, you can use your note cards again in writing the report. Your report will have three main parts: the introduction, the body, and the conclusion.

The **introduction** tells the purpose of the report and how the purpose will be accomplished. Here is a sample introduction: *A home computer has many different uses. Each member of the family can find ways to use one.* This introduction tells that the purpose of the report is to give information about home computers. The purpose is going to be accomplished by telling how each member of the family can use the home computer. An introduction to a report should fill a paragraph.

The **body** of the report contains all the information necessary to cover your subject thoroughly. It should follow the structure of your outline. For a short report, you should have a full paragraph for each main topic in your outline. Write a topic sentence for each paragraph in the body. The supporting sentences should furnish details that are based on your notes and topic outline.

The **conclusion** is the last paragraph of your report. The conclusion restates your main points.

At the end of the report, list all the sources of information you used in preparing your report. This list is called the **bibliography**. As you do your research, make up a bibliography card for each source. On an index card write the author's name, the title of the article, and the name of the magazine, book, or reference book. Other information must also be included, depending upon the type of source used. Below are sample bibliographical entries and a sample short report.

Reference: Cromie, William. "Astronaut." The World Book Encyclopedia, 1983.

Book: Collins, Michael. Carrying the Fire: An Astronaut's Journeys. New York: Farrar, Straus & Giroux, 1974.

Magazine: Abramson, Pamela, and Jerry Adler. "Sally Ride: Ready for Liftoff." Newsweek, June 13, 1983, pp. 36–51.

Catching the Wind

introduction — Wind power could be an important source of clean and cheap electricity someday. Scientists are now looking for better ways to use this valuable resource.

body —
Years ago, all farms had windmills. When cheap electricity became available, they fell into disuse. Power is no longer cheap. Windmills may make a comeback.

Large windmills, or wind machines, are more efficient than small ones. Doubling the size of a windmill blade produces four times as much power. One design for a future windmill has blades taller than a fifteen-story building.

The seas are the windiest parts of the world. Windmills on floating platforms could harness ocean breezes. Coastal areas could get much electricity in this way.

Application WRITING A REPORT

Use your outline and note cards to write a first draft of your report. Read over your first draft. Then rewrite the report, using the Writer's Checklist on page 340.

7 — Writing a Book Report

> ● A **book report** contains a description of a book and your judgment about it.

A book report is a way of sharing your thoughts about a book with others. It is a way to recommend or not to recommend a book to your classmates. Writing a book report helps you form your reasons for liking or not liking a book. By expressing your reasons you will find out what your standards or guidelines are for judging a book.

There are three parts to a book report: the introduction, the body, and the conclusion. In the **introduction** tell the title, author, and kind of book. Is your book fiction or nonfiction? Next, tell about the author. Is he or she a popular writer? If the book is nonfiction, why is the author an expert on the subject?

The **body** of the report has two parts. The first is a summary of the book. Describe briefly the setting (where the story takes place), the main characters, and the plot (story line). The plot usually centers around a problem or conflict that is solved toward the end of the book. Be careful not to give the ending away. Also take care not to give too many details of the plot. Your summary should be about two paragraphs long.

In the second part of the body, give your reasons for liking or not liking the book. Answering one or more of the following questions can help you explain your opinion. What made you select the book? Was the plot interesting, or was it dull and confusing? Did the characters seem real? Why? What did you get out of reading the book? After reading it, did you understand life better than you did before? Did you enjoy an imaginary world of fantasy?

The final paragraph of your book report is the **conclusion.** In it you should recommend or not recommend the book. Give a summary of the reasons for your judgment.

Read the sample book report below. The first paragraph is the introduction. The next three paragraphs make up the body. The final paragraph is the conclusion.

The Adventures of Tom Sawyer is a novel by Mark Twain, one of America's greatest authors. Twain grew up in Hannibal, Missouri, on the Mississippi River. In *Tom Sawyer*, Twain tells what life on the river was like.

The story takes place during the nineteenth century in St. Petersburg, a small town along the Mississippi River. The main character of the book is, of course, Tom Sawyer. The book also has many other interesting characters, especially Becky Thatcher, a girl whom Tom really likes.

Although this book was written over one hundred years ago, its story is still exciting today. Tom has many suspenseful adventures; a creepy cemetery, a mysterious cave, and a buried treasure all play important roles in the plot. It truly is difficult to put the book down once you are caught up in Tom's story.

Even more than for the suspense, however, I liked the book because of its characters and the author's understanding of human nature. Tom seemed as real to me as one of my own friends. As the story progresses, you can see Tom's character change from that of a mischievous boy to a person who cares about other people.

I highly recommend *The Adventures of Tom Sawyer.* If you enjoy lots of action and stories about the feelings and problems of other young people, you will like this book.

Application WRITING A BOOK REPORT

Write a report about a book of fiction you have read. Include an introduction, a body, and a conclusion.

24 Vocabulary and Word Study

"Perhaps of all the creations of man
language is the most astonishing."

—Giles Lytton Strachey

— 1 — How to Study Vocabulary ——————

> ● A person's **vocabulary** is the stock of words he or she understands or can use.

Building a good vocabulary is one of the most important things you can do for yourself as a student. To build vocabulary, you should develop ways to learn new words. You can do this best by reading more. If you learn new words in your reading rather than from lists, you will develop a better sense of how they are used.

To improve your chances of remembering the new words you meet, you should develop the habit of looking them up in a dictionary and writing them down. Keep a dictionary handy whenever you read, and use it.

Vocabulary Notebooks and Flash Cards To record new words, you can use a special vocabulary notebook, a section in your school notebook, or flash cards (index cards). Write each new word, along with its meaning and an example of how it is used in a sentence.

You will find it a great help to group your new words in some logical way, such as by subject. Make a division for each subject you are studying in school and one for general subjects (that is, words you find in books you read for pleasure as well as in textbooks). You may also want separate divisions for special interests.

Making New Words Your Own To help you remember the words you record, you will want to review them regularly. Review one group at a time. Especially helpful times to go over the words from a school subject are before beginning a reading assignment and before a test. Go through your list or flash cards and see how many meanings you can remember without looking at your written definition. Try to think of tricks for remembering the most difficult words. The hint on the flash card is a good memory aid.

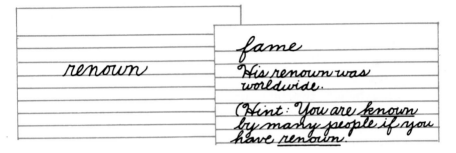

renown

fame

His renown was worldwide.

(Hint: You are *known* by many people if you have *renown*.)

To be able to use a word correctly as well as to recognize it when you see it, you must practice using it. Try to choose a different word from your notebook or card box each day and use it at least twice.

Exercises

A. Choose ten words from the list below that you would like to know better. Write a definition and an example sentence for each. Use your dictionary.

antonym	immigrant	cumulus	denominator
concerto	tenacious	irate	legislature
igneous	equation	colony	replenish
tedium	infinitive	lyrics	conjunction
rhombus	membrane	radius	overture
treaty	crescendo	simile	protozoa

B. Write these topics for a vocabulary notebook or card box. Then write the four words from Exercise **A** that belong under each topic. Use your dictionary.

Science Social Studies English Math Music General

2 — The History of English

> ● Learning the origins of words can help you understand and remember words.

Languages, like people, belong to families. And languages, like families and nations, have histories. Learning about people's cultural roots can help you to understand people better. Learning the origins of words can also help you to understand and remember words better.

The family of languages that English belongs to is called the Indo-European family. All the languages in this family have as a common ancestor an ancient language that scholars call Indo-European. Within this large family there are several subgroups of languages that are more closely related.

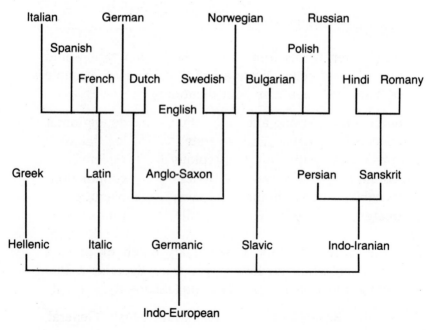

Old English As the chart shows, English belongs to the Germanic branch of the Indo-European family. The origins of English are in the languages of Germanic tribes—the Angles, Saxons, and Jutes—that invaded Britain in the fifth century. The language spoken by these tribes from about 450 to 1100 is known as Anglo-Saxon, or Old English. Many of the most common English words have come from this time with little change.

Middle English In 1066, England was invaded by French armies from Normandy. Following this invasion, known as the Norman Conquest, French became the language of England's ruling class. As a result, hundreds of French words entered the English vocabulary. The language that evolved from this combination of Anglo-Saxon and Norman French is known as Middle English. It was used from about 1100 to 1500.

Modern English During the Renaissance, roughly from the fourteenth through the sixteenth centuries, interest in classical learning was revived. During this period hundreds of words from Latin and Greek entered English. Writers turned to these ancient languages to express ideas for which they felt English words were not adequate. Some common words that entered English in this way are *education, medium, modern, urban, imitate.*

By the year 1500, English looked and sounded much like the language spoken today. Modern English is said to date from about this time.

English Keeps Growing Since 1500, thousands of new words have entered the language in a variety of ways. Many of the new words have been borrowed from other languages. As English-speaking people began to explore and trade with other lands, they absorbed words from the many new languages they came in contact with.

Words from Other Languages

Spanish: canyon **Hebrew:** amen
Italian: cartoon **Turkish:** tulip
German: nickel **Hindi:** jungle
Dutch: skate **Native American:** pecan
Arabic: mattress **African languages:** banjo

Other new words have come from names of persons and places. A new product or idea is often named for its inventor or place of origin. Notice the words illustrated below named for the following people and places: Jodhpur, India; Levi Strauss; Amelia Bloomer; Paisley, Scotland; Madame de Pompadour; and the seventh Earl of Cardigan.

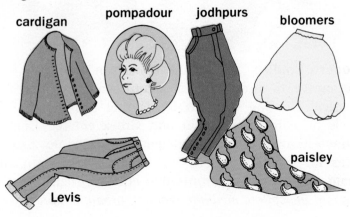

cardigan pompadour jodhpurs bloomers Levis paisley

Still other new words have been formed from existing words. A great many English words have been made by putting together two or more shorter words in a process known as **compounding.** Some examples of compound words are *foolproof, setback,* and *loudspeaker.* Others have been formed by joining parts of two words. Words formed in this way, such as *brunch* (*breakfast* + *lunch*) and *moped* (*motor* + *pedal*), are known as **blends.** New shorter words have been made by dropping syllables from longer words in a process known as **clipping.** Many common words are clipped forms: *bus* (from *omnibus*), *pants* (from *pantaloons*), *flu* (from *influenza*).

Etymologies   To learn how a word was formed or what language it came from, you can look up its history, or etymology, in a dictionary. Abbreviations, such as *L* for *Latin,* are used to show sources for words. The abbreviations are explained at the front of a dictionary.

Exercises

A. Write the language from which we get each food name below. Use the etymologies in a dictionary.

1. apricot	**5.** jambalaya	**9.** coleslaw
2. sauerkraut	**6.** taco	**10.** catsup
3. chop suey	**7.** broccoli	
4. smorgasbord	**8.** hominy	

B. Write *clip, blend, compound,* or *proper name* to show how each word originated. Use a dictionary.

11. motel	**15.** sunshine	**19.** smog
12. homesick	**16.** diesel	**20.** chauvinism
13. zoo	**17.** telecast	
14. tuxedo	**18.** wig	

3 — Using a Dictionary

- A dictionary gives aids to finding, pronouncing, and understanding words.

Study the sample dictionary entries below and the explanations of the numbered features that follow.

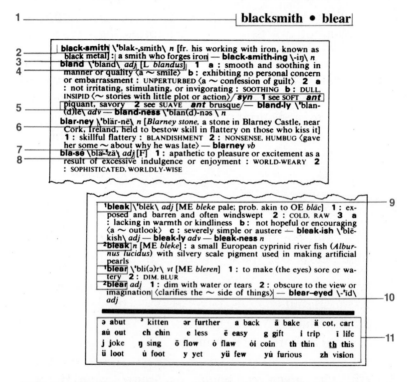

Aids to Finding Words Words in a dictionary are arranged alphabetically. The **guide words (1)** tell you the first and last words on the page. Each **entry word (2)** appears in dark type. **Homographs (9)**—words that are spelled alike but have different meanings—have separate entries preceded by superscripts, such as ¹ and ².

Aids to Pronouncing Words The **phonetic respelling (6)** is made up of symbols and special marks that show how a word is pronounced. The symbols are explained in the **pronunciation key (11)**. Spaces, dots, or hyphens in the respelling show syllable divisions. A **stress mark (7)** indicates a syllable that is spoken with more force.

Aids to Understanding Words A **part-of-speech label (8)** shows a word's part or parts of speech. A word's meanings, or **definitions (3)**, are grouped by part of speech and are usually numbered. **Example sentences and phrases (10)** show how a word is used. A word's history, or **etymology (4)**, can deepen your understanding of the meaning. **Synonyms** and **antonyms (5)** for a word are often given. Abbreviations in entries are explained at the front of the dictionary.

Exercises

A. Use the sample dictionary entries on page 518 to answer the questions below.

   1. Where does the word *blarney* come from?
   2. Which definition of *blarney* means "nonsense"?
   3. What part of speech is *blacksmith*?
   4. What is a synonym for *bland*?
   5. Which entry words are homographs?

B. Write each word below that could be found on a dictionary page with the guide words *desert* and *detail.*

6. desertion	**11.** design	**16.** dessert
7. derrick	**12.** desolate	**17.** destiny
8. deserve	**13.** desk	**18.** depress
9. desiccate	**14.** detach	**19.** destination
10. deride	**15.** deposit	**20.** destroy

4 — A Dictionary as a Writing Aid

> ● A dictionary answers questions about the correct spellings and forms of words.

Questions about the correct spellings and forms of words often arise when you are writing the final draft of a paper. Answers to such questions can be found in a dictionary. Learn to use it to avoid unnecessary errors.

Checking Spellings The basic procedure for checking a spelling is simple. Think of the possible spellings for a word's beginning sounds and look under each of these.

For other questions about spellings and forms, you will need more detailed knowledge of a dictionary's features. Study the sample entries. The following sections explain the numbered features.

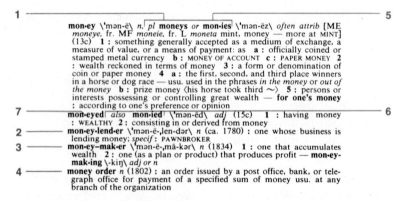

1 ——————————————————— 5

mon·ey \'mən-ē\ *n,* *pl* **moneys** *or* **mon·ies** \'mən-ēz\ *often attrib* [ME *moneye,* fr. MF *moneie,* fr. L *moneta* mint, money — more at MINT] (13c) **1** : something generally accepted as a medium of exchange, a measure of value, or a means of payment: as **a** : officially coined or stamped metal currency **b** : MONEY OF ACCOUNT **c** : PAPER MONEY **2** : wealth reckoned in terms of money **3** : a form or denomination of coin or paper money **4 a** : the first, second, and third place winners in a horse or dog race — usu. used in the phrases *in the money* or *out of the money* **b** : prize money ⟨his horse took third ∼⟩ **5** : persons or interests possessing or controlling great wealth — **for one's money** : according to one's preference or opinion

7 ——————————————————— 6
mon·eyed *also* **mon·ied** \'mən-ēd\ *adj* (15c) **1** : having money : WEALTHY **2** : consisting in or derived from money

2 —— **mon·ey·lend·er** \'mən-ē-,len-dər\ *n* (ca. 1780) : one whose business is lending money; *specif* : PAWNBROKER

3 —— **mon·ey–mak·er** \'mən-ē-,mā-kər\ *n* (1834) **1** : one that accumulates wealth **2** : one (as a plan or product) that produces profit — **mon·ey-mak·ing** \-kiŋ\ *adj or n*

4 —— **money order** *n* (1802) : an order issued by a post office, bank, or telegraph office for payment of a specified sum of money usu. at any branch of the organization

Related Forms (1) The related forms of words—the plurals of nouns, the principal parts of verbs, the comparatives and superlatives of adjectives and adverbs—are included in entries whenever the forms are irregular or hard to spell.

Compounds **(2, 3, 4)** Compounds can be written in three ways: as one word, as a hyphenated word, or as two separate words. The acceptable style for writing compounds changes frequently. Check a dictionary to find the accepted form for any compound.

Alternate Spellings **(5, 6)** Sometimes a dictionary lists two spellings for a word. Both are correct. Although the first is preferred, you may safely use either spelling.

End-of-Line Division **(7)** A dictionary shows where words may be divided at the end of a writing line by the use of dots or spaces in entry words. Check the entry word when you are in doubt. Remember these rules:

- One-syllable words cannot be divided.

- A single letter cannot be left alone on a line.

Exercises

A. Write each word with hyphens where it can be broken at the end of a line. Use a dictionary.

1. apostrophe	**3.** throughout	**5.** ordinary
2. traveling	**4.** equitable	**6.** equivalent

B. Make compounds by combining *soft* with each word below. Use a dictionary to write them correctly.

7. boiled	**9.** drink	**11.** cover	**13.** spoken
8. ware	**10.** spot	**12.** touch	**14.** hearted

C. Write the entry words you would look up to check the spelling of each related form.

15. picnicked	**17.** choosing	**19.** volcanoes
16. scarves	**18.** livelier	**20.** rallies

5 — Prefixes and Suffixes

- A **prefix** is a letter or letters added to the beginning of a word.
- A **suffix** is a letter or letters added to the end of a word.

Notice the underlined word in the sentence below.

The voters' underline{disenchantment} with the mayor became clear on election day when he was soundly defeated.

It is made up of three parts: *dis-enchant-ment.* Do you know what *disenchantment* means? If not, you might be able to figure it out if you recognize the three parts that make up the word and know what each means.

At the center is a **base,** or root, word *enchant,* meaning "to charm" or "to attract." The letters added to the beginning of a base word form a prefix. A prefix has meaning of its own and changes the meaning of the base it is added to. The prefix *dis-* means "away from" or "opposite of." The letters added to the end of a base word form a suffix. A suffix changes a word's meaning or part of speech. The suffix *-ment* means "state of" and is used to make nouns.

Put these three parts and their meanings together and you get "away from—or no longer in—a state of being charmed." This is very close to the dictionary meaning of *disenchantment.*

Familiarity with common prefixes and suffixes in the following chart can help you learn the meanings of new words. Watch for spelling changes that may occur when adding a suffix. Check a dictionary when in doubt.

Common Prefixes and Suffixes

Prefix	Meaning	Example
de-	from, down	detoxify
mis-	wrong, badly	misprint
pre-	before	preshrunk
re-	again, back	refinish
un-	not, opposite of	uncertain

Suffix	Meaning and Part of Speech	Example
-able	worthy of, able to (*adj.*)	manageable
-ion	act of, state of (*noun*)	invention
-ize	cause to be, become (*verb*)	visualize
-or	one who (*noun*)	editor
-ous	full of, having (*adj.*)	courageous

Exercises

A. Eight of the words below contain prefixes. Write those words and underline the prefixes. Write *none* for the words without prefixes.

1. replace	**5.** precaution	**9.** unreliable
2. dishonor	**6.** mission	**10.** defame
3. district	**7.** misspell	**11.** deep
4. misinterpret	**8.** uncle	**12.** untied

B. Add a suffix to each word below that will change its part of speech. Write the word and its part of speech. Check a dictionary for correct spelling if necessary.

EXAMPLE: desire
ANSWER: desirable, adjective

13. place	**15.** zeal	**17.** enjoy	**19.** legal
14. honor	**16.** apology	**18.** critic	**20.** prosper

6 — Denotation and Connotation

> - **Denotation** is the exact meaning of a word.
> - **Connotation** is the positive or negative meaning associated with a word.

Read these two impressions of a place in New York City at rush hour.

> Times Square at rush hour—what an experience! You are carried <u>along</u> by the <u>bustling crowds</u>, <u>energized</u> by their <u>lively</u> pace. The <u>exotic</u>, <u>tempting aromas</u> of street foods <u>envelop</u> you. A <u>dazzling display</u> of neon <u>lights</u> your way down the street.

> Times Square at rush hour—what an experience! You are <u>jostled along</u> by <u>swarming masses</u>, <u>rattled</u> by their <u>frenzied</u> pace. The <u>strange smells</u> of street foods <u>bombard</u> you. A <u>dizzying array</u> of neon <u>blinds</u> you as you go down the street.

Both passages describe the same experience. They even use words with similar meanings. However, the two descriptions convey very different feelings about Times Square. This difference in feeling is created by the connotations of the underlined words.

There are two aspects to the meaning of a word. The first is its denotation, or exact meaning, which is found in the dictionary. The second is its connotation—the feelings or reactions, positive or negative, that it suggests.

Words with the same denotation can have very different connotations. For example, *bustling crowds* and *swarming masses* both mean "large, moving groups of people." But the first expression suggests a positive reaction to the people, and the second, a negative one.

To write or speak well, you must be aware of the connotations of words. It is not enough just to use words with the correct denotation.

For help in thinking of a variety of words with similar denotations, use a thesaurus. For help in sorting out the connotations of similar words, use a dictionary.

Exercises

A. Write each numbered word below. Beside it write the word from the list with a similar denotation. Circle the word in each pair with the more positive connotation.

demand	magnificent	antique	hoard	take
skinny	hasty	shack	plump	artful

1. pompous
2. out-of-date
3. grab
4. cabin
5. slim

6. request
7. save
8. fat
9. slapdash
10. subtle

B. Write each sentence. Choose the word in parentheses with the more negative connotation.

11. Jack's remarks are often (sarcastic, witty).
12. Mrs. Ramos wears (quaint, odd) hats.
13. Are you a (finicky, dainty) eater?
14. The portions they serve are too (skimpy, modest).
15. Your ideas are (innovative, newfangled).
16. My boss has a (brusque, direct) manner.
17. A person with all A's is a (bookworm, scholar).
18. Our neighbors are (nosey, concerned).
19. She often (relaxes, goofs off) with friends.
20. Our (jalopy, automobile) needs to be painted.

7 — Using Context Clues

> ● A **context clue** helps you understand the meaning of an unfamiliar word.

English contains so many thousands of words that few people can hope to learn them all. If you stop to look up in a dictionary each new word you meet, reading will be very tedious. Fortunately you do not always need to look up a new word to understand its meaning.

Often you can figure out what a new word means by using clues from its context. The context of a word is formed by the surrounding words and sentences. For example, look at the underlined word in the sentence below.

> I can't believe such a shy man had the temerity to make that bold accusation.

You can probably figure out from the way *temerity* is used in the sentence that it means "reckless courage."

There are several kinds of context clues. Some are used more effectively in a specific subject area. You should become familiar with the kinds of clues found in the various types of reading you do.

Using Context Clues in Science Books and articles on scientific topics contain many little-known words with very specialized meanings. Science writers know that their readers are likely to be unfamiliar with many of the special terms they use. Therefore they provide an especially helpful kind of context clue—a full *definition*. Read the paragraph on the next page. Notice that each term in dark type is fully defined shortly after it is first used.

The **ecosystem,** or specific situation in which a group of living organisms interact with their environment, is the basic unit of ecology. A pond, a forest, and a marsh are all examples of ecosystems. The conditions that define an ecosystem can be divided into **biotic** and **abiotic** factors. The biotic factors are all the living things found in the ecosystem. The abiotic factors are all the nonliving forces, such as temperature and light, that affect the ecosystem.

Using Context Clues in Social Studies Social studies materials and other kinds of nonfiction writing also contain special terms that readers may not know. The authors of these books and articles, like science writers, try to help readers by providing context clues for unfamiliar words. A lengthy definition is not always necessary or possible. Two other kinds of context clues are common in social studies writing.

An everyday vocabulary often contains a simpler word that means nearly the same thing as a specialized term. Authors frequently add these *synonyms* as context clues. In other instances authors give *further information* about words as clues to their meanings. Read the passage below. Notice how synonyms are provided for three of the terms in dark type. See if you can figure out what the other words in dark type mean from the additional information about them.

After flax had been harvested, it had to be **swingled** to knock bits of stalk out of the fibers. A swingle was used to beat the flax as it lay over the end of a plank. Wool had to be cleaned and untangled by **carding,** or dragging bits of it between two flat pieces of wood studded with short wire teeth. After being swingled and carded, the fibers were spun into yarn, then tied into **hanks,** or coils, and set aside to be woven. Most cloth woven on the frontier was **"linsey-woolsey"**—so-called because it was made by using linen for the **warp**, or lengthwise threads, and wool for the **weft**, or crosswise threads.

Using Context Clues in Literature Many times when you meet a word you do not know, you will find that no obvious clues to its meaning have been provided. This is especially true when you read literature. Gifted authors use less familiar words to make their writing fresh and precise. To explain each of these would make their sentences or verses clumsy. Also, you frequently read novels, poems, and plays by writers who lived a long time ago. Many words familiar to readers then are no longer in common use.

Still you can often figure out from the context what an unfamiliar word means. Read the opening paragraph of Edgar Allan Poe's short story "The Tell-Tale Heart." Look for clues that help you understand the meaning of the word *acute* in the fourth line.

> True!—nervous—very, very dreadfully nervous I had been and am; but *why* will you say that I am mad? The disease had sharpened my senses—not destroyed—not dulled them. Above all was the sense of hearing **acute**. I heard all things in the heaven and in the earth. I heard many things in hell. How, then, am I mad? Hearken! and observe how healthily—how calmly I can tell you the whole story.

Notice that Poe tells you that the disease *sharpened* the speaker's senses. Right after the word *acute* he writes, "I heard all things in the heaven and in the earth." From these clues you know that *acute* means "keen" or "especially responsive to impressions."

In addition, look for examples that will help you guess the meaning of an unfamiliar word.

Exercises

A. Write the word below that is closest in meaning to each underlined word.

> party   leaf-shedding   loyalty   mild   inactive

1. Most plants thrive in temperate climates.
2. Oaks, maples, and birches are deciduous trees.
3. After a wedding came the festivity of a shivaree.
4. Reptiles in a dormant state need very little food.
5. A vassal took an oath of fealty to his lord.

B. Write the word below that is closest in meaning to each numbered word. Look for context clues.

> occur   mood   endless   remarkable   springy
> sleeps   leave   continuous   sleepiness   beginning

The morning, which is the most **(6)** memorable season of the day, is the awakening hour. Then there is least **(7)** somnolence in us. Some part of us awakes which **(8)** slumbers all the rest of the day and night. All memorable events **(9)** transpire in morning time and in a morning **(10)** atmosphere. To him whose **(11)** elastic and vigorous thought keeps pace with the sun, the day is a **(12)** perpetual morning. Morning is when I am awake and there is a **(13)** dawn in me. We must learn to keep ourselves awake by an **(14)** infinite expectation of the dawn, which does not **(15)** forsake us in our soundest sleep.—Adapted from *Walden*, by Henry David Thoreau

Application WRITING A PARAGRAPH

Write a paragraph about types of ancient Greek literature. Include these words: *epic, bard, lyric poetry, drama.* Provide a context clue for each. Use an encyclopedia.

25 Reviewing and Taking Tests

If you would have your learning stay,
   Be patient,—don't learn too fast:
The man who travels a mile each day,
   May get round the world at last.

—from McGuffey's Reader

STUDY SCHEDULE

4:30-5:00-history
5:00-5:30-English
5:30-6:00-science
6:00-6:45-dinner
6:45-7:15-free time
7:15-7:45-math
7:45-8:30-Study for
English test

1 — Taking Notes in Class

> ● Keep a notebook of well-organized study notes.

A notebook can be a valuable study aid if it is well organized. If your study notes are complete and neatly written, they will make studying for a test easier. A properly kept notebook eliminates the need to reread every word of a textbook when studying.

Include in your notebook the most important ideas that the teacher presents each day. Listen carefully in class and make sure you understand what you write. Ask questions if you do not understand something. Copy all rules, charts, and definitions that the teacher puts on the board. Also use your notebook to take notes as you do your homework assignments.

You will not make your notebook a valuable study aid, however, simply by writing important facts. You must organize your notebook. The chart below will help you to do so effectively.

How to Organize Your Notebook

1. Divide your notebook into sections, by subject.
2. Keep all class and textbook notes for the same subject in the same section.
3. Write a heading for each page of notes, listing subject, date, and class or textbook.
4. Keep homework and quiz papers that will help when you study for a test.
5. Rewrite notes to make them better organized.

Step 5 in the chart should not be overlooked. You may take notes in class too quickly to write important facts clearly. You may repeat them or include too many unimportant ideas. Make it a practice to rewrite your notes at the end of each week.

> **Rewriting your notes will help you to**
> 1. organize them and make them easier to understand.
> 2. eliminate repetition and unimportant ideas.
> 3. restate important ideas more clearly.
> 4. memorize material for tests. The process of rewriting is a study technique.

Keep an accurate record of all your homework assignments in a pocket-size notebook. One way to organize an assignment book is to divide each page into five columns. (See illustration below.) Write a complete description of the assignment, including any special instructions. Also mark all upcoming tests in your assignment book.

Date	Subject	Assignment	Due	Completed
11/16	English	Read ch. 3, pp. 24-30. Answer all questions.	11/17	✓
11/16	Math	Study pp. 21-32 for test Fri.	11/20	

Exercises

A. Team up with a classmate for one week. Each day after class compare both sets of notes. Help each other identify the most important information. Then underline it. At the end of the week, rewrite your notes to include only the most important information.

B. Follow the five rules in the chart, "How to Organize Your Notebook," to improve your notes. See if organizing your notebook makes studying easier.

2 How to Review for a Test

- Reviewing is going back over material you have read to make sure you understand it.

To do your best on a test, you must know how to review. The first step is to have good study notes. As you read each chapter, turn the **titles, headings,** and **subheadings** into questions. Then read to find the answers. Write a summary sentence for each answer.

You might find it helpful to write the following question words, one on a line, beneath each question you have written: *Who? What? When? Where? How? Why?* Each section under a heading or subheading will give you the answers to at least some of these questions. Put the information next to the question word. This exercise will give you a list of important ideas and facts to study.

As you read, look up unfamiliar words in a dictionary (or in the book's glossary if there is one). Reread difficult parts of the chapter, and make a list of questions to ask in class about parts you do not understand.

When it is time to study for a test, review your class notes, textbook notes, and your homework assignments. Also use reading aids that your textbook may have. Reading aids include textbook features such as chapter introductions and summaries. Reread them to review the main ideas of the chapter. The headings and subheadings in a chapter are reading aids that organize the information into main topics and subtopics just as an outline does. Go through the chapter again, mentally turning these headings and subheadings into questions. See if you can give the answers from memory.

Use the questions and exercises at the end of each chapter to test how well you remember the material. Finally, make up some possible questions the teacher might ask, and write the answers for practice.

How to Review for Tests

1. Study in a quiet, comfortable place with good light and as far away from distractions as possible.
2. Gather all the books, study notes, and supplies you will need. Keep a dictionary nearby.
3. Take a short break every half hour to relax.
4. Use the reading aids in your textbooks.
5. Look over previous tests to see what kinds of questions the teacher might ask. Make up some possible questions and answers.

Exercises

A. Look over two of your textbooks to find the reading aids they contain. Then answer these questions.

1. Does each chapter have a preview or introduction, a summary of main ideas, and review questions?
2. Copy the main headings in one chapter. Under each main heading, list the subheadings. Does this give you a good outline of the information in the chapter?

B. Go back to a chapter that you have already read in one of your textbooks. Then do the following.

3. Practice turning each heading and subheading into a question. Write the answer in a sentence or two.
4. Write the question words *Who? What? When? Where? How? Why?* Read the section under one heading, and write the answers you find.

3 — How to Take a Test

- Learning to take tests successfully is a skill you can master.

Robin and Dave studied hard for a test, but Dave's score was much higher. Robin asked him why. Dave replied that it was partly because he was "test wise." Dave knew how to follow the test directions and answer questions to achieve the highest possible score. Anyone can become "test wise." It just takes knowledge and practice.

Most of your tests will be either objective tests or essay tests. An **objective test** asks specific questions for which you provide short answers. There are many kinds of objective test questions. You may be asked to choose an answer from *multiple choices,* to tell if a statement is *true or false,* to *complete a sentence,* or to *fill in the blank* with a fact, name, date, or definition. If your teacher tells you that the test will be objective, you should stress facts, names, dates, and important definitions in your studying.

How to Take an Objective Test

1. Study the sample test question and answer to understand how to write or mark a correct answer.
2. For each question, read all the answer choices.
3. If you are not sure of an answer, eliminate all of the obviously wrong choices.
4. If your test score will be based only on correct answers, you might guess at an answer. If wrong answers will count against you, do not guess.
5. In test questions look for words such as *never* and *always* so that you are not trapped into writing wrong answers.

An **essay test** consists of questions that must be answered with short compositions, usually several paragraphs long.

How to Take an Essay Test

1. Read each test question carefully so that you understand exactly what you are being asked.
2. In the questions look for words that tell you how to answer. Examples are *list, describe, explain, discuss, compare,* and *contrast.* Write your answers accordingly.
3. Write a brief outline of your answer, listing the main points in proper order.
4. Use the test question to compose the topic sentence for your answer. If the question is "What causes earthquakes?" you can begin with the topic sentence "Earthquakes are caused by the following factors."

Exercise

Be sure to follow each direction carefully.

1. Write *true* or *false.*
   You should never guess on an objective test.
2. Write the correct answer from the choices you are given. Which of the following is not a kind of objective test?
   a. multiple choice   **c.** true or false
   b. essay question   **d.** fill in the blank
3. Write the letter of the correct ending.
   An essay test may ask you to
   a. complete a sentence.   **b.** describe or explain.
4. Complete the definition begun below.
   Reviewing is going back ____.
5. Write your answer in essay form.
   Choose one of the four rules in the chart on how to take an essay test. Explain why that rule is important.

4 — Verbal Analogies

> ● An **analogy** compares two things and shows the relationship between them.

Some standardized tests measure how sharp your thinking skills are. They contain a kind of puzzle involving relationships that is called an analogy. The more you practice solving analogies, the easier they will become for you. Here is an example of an analogy.

<u>flower</u> is to <u>garden</u> as <u>tree</u> is to _____
(Choose one.) **a.** bark **b.** branch **c.** forest **d.** leaf

How is a flower related to a garden? A flower is part of a garden. What is a tree part of? The answer is **c.,** <u>forest</u>.

An analogy always begins with a pair of items (such as *flower, garden*) that are related in some way. In this case the relationship is part to whole. Then a second pair of items (such as *tree, forest*) completes the analogy. A tree is part of a forest. To solve an analogy you must figure out the relationship between its first two items. The relationship could be part to whole, cause to effect, or some other relationship. Then you must select the word in the second pair of items that has the same relationship.

Here is a second analogy, written in the form you will probably see on tests. (The symbol : is read "is to." The symbol :: is read "as.")

glass : smooth :: sandpaper : _____
a. beach **b.** rough **c.** wood **d.** rock

Smooth tells what *glass* feels like. The word <u>rough,</u> **b,** tells what *sandpaper* feels like. The relationship between each pair of words in the analogy is similar.

Exercise

Write the following analogies, completing them with the correct word choices.

1. elephant : herd :: fish : _____
    a. fins   **b.** school   **c.** lake   **d.** swim
2. telephone : talk :: stove : _____
    a. dish   **b.** bake   **c.** hot   **d.** cook
3. meter : kilometer :: liter : _____
    a. kilogram   **b.** millimeter   **c.** kiloliter   **d.** hectogram
4. dog : puppy :: flower : _____
    a. bud   **b.** leaf   **c.** stem   **d.** tree
5. door : house :: zipper : _____
    a. jacket   **b.** open   **c.** close   **d.** metal
6. leaf : tree :: hair : _____
    a. branch   **b.** head   **c.** feather   **d.** brown
7. street : city :: room : _____
    a. wall   **b.** furniture   **c.** window   **d.** house
8. wind : howl :: baby : _____
    a. teeth   **b.** mouth   **c.** cry   **d.** grow
9. apple : seed :: chicken : _____
    a. egg   **b.** rooster   **c.** feather   **d.** peck
10. glove : hand :: scarf : _____
    a. silk   **b.** neck   **c.** shirt   **d.** suit
11. wheel : car :: wing : _____
    a. feet   **b.** fly   **c.** bird   **d.** leg
12. kite : string :: dog : _____
    a. cat   **b.** leash   **c.** collar   **d.** tag
13. water : flood :: snow : _____
    a. flake   **b.** avalanche   **c.** skiing   **d.** sled
14. belt : buckle :: suitcase : _____
    a. leather   **b.** trunk   **c.** lock   **d.** clothes
15. Spanish : Mexico :: English: _____
    a. Spain   **b.** language   **c.** American   **d.** U.S.A.

Improving Your Spelling

As you probably know, in English the same sound may be spelled in more than one way. For example, *suite, meat,* and *fleet* spell the same vowel sound in three different ways. Other words, such as *tough, bough, cough,* and *dough,* have similar spellings, but different sounds. As a result, learning to spell English words can be a challenge. However, the following guidelines will help you master the task if you use them patiently and consistently.

- Use a dictionary as a bridge to better spelling. Whenever possible, look up the spellings of words you are unsure of. A dictionary will take the guesswork out of your spelling. It will also provide you with a better understanding of a word's meanings and pronunciation.

- Pronounce words carefully when you speak. Many people misspell common words because they pronounce them incorrectly. For example, if you misspell *February* as *Febuary,* you are probably mispronouncing it, too. For new and unfamiliar words, the dictionary's phonetic respelling and pronunciation key should always be checked.

- Look at words carefully when you read them. If you see each and every letter in a word, you are more likely to remember the word's spelling. This is especially important for the new words you encounter. Maintain a list of your personal spelling "demons." If you are like most people, there are certain words that you misspell over and over again. By listing these words in your notebook and reviewing them frequently, you can master them.

- Make up a spelling memory device if you think it will be helpful. Many people remember troublesome spellings with devices such as the following:
  capitol (*o*) The capitol building has a d*o*me.
  capital (*a*) Every st*a*te has a capital.
  The familiar rhyme, "*i* before *e* except after *c*, or when sounded like *ā* as in *neighbor* and *weigh*," has helped countless people.

- Mentally divide a difficult word into syllables as you spell it. Since most syllables have only a few letters, it is relatively easy to master them. Then you can put all the pieces together and spell the entire word.

- Proofread your writing to correct spelling errors. Many students are so anxious to express an idea in writing that they make careless spelling errors. Proofreading your work means checking the spelling of every word. Train your eyes not to skip over misspellings when you proofread.

- Learn the eight rules for spelling listed on page 542. Most words in the English language are spelled according to certain rules. Learning the rules will let you spell these words easily.

Use this summary of the rules to help you **SPELL**!

S ee all the letters in each word you read and write.
P ronounce words carefully, syllable by syllable.
E xamine the dictionary entry for each unfamiliar word.
L ist and review your personal spelling demons.
L earn the eight most common spelling rules and use them!

The 8 Most Useful Spelling Rules

1. If a word ends in *e*, usually drop the *e* when you add a suffix that begins with a vowel. Keep the *e* when you add a suffix that begins with a consonant.

    hope + ing = hoping   hope + ful = hopeful

2. If a word ends in a vowel and *y*, keep the *y* when you add a suffix.   play + ing = playing

3. If a word ends in a consonant and *y*, change the *y* to *i* when you add a suffix unless the suffix begins with *i*.

    try + es = tries   try + ing = trying

4. If a word ends in one vowel and one consonant and has one syllable or is stressed on the last syllable, double the last consonant when you add a suffix that begins with a vowel.

    sad + er = sadder   confer + ing = conferring

5. When you choose between *ie* and *ei*, use *ie* except after *c* or for a long *a* sound. (Exceptions: *leisure, neither, seize, weird*)

    conceit   shriek   view   reign   weight

6. The suffix *-s* can be added to most nouns and verbs. If the word ends in *s, ss, sh, ch, x,* or *zz,* add *-es.*

glass	glasses	dish	dishes
birch	birches	box	boxes

7. If a word ends in a single *f* or *fe,* usually change the *f* to *v* when you add *-s* or *-es.*

    calf   calves   wife   wives

8. The letter *q* is always followed by the letter *u* in English words.   quarter   require   inquest

99 Spelling Demons

1. ache
2. again
3. aisle
4. all right
5. always
6. among
7. answer
8. anything
9. assignment
10. been
11. beginning
12. believe
13. break
14. business
15. busy
16. calendar
17. children
18. color
19. coming
20. committee
21. cough
22. could
23. country
24. different
25. doctor
26. done
27. early
28. easy
29. especially
30. every
31. exaggerate
32. experience
33. February
34. foreign
35. forty
36. friend
37. governor
38. grammar
39. guess
40. handkerchief
41. hear
42. heard
43. height
44. here
45. imagine
46. interested
47. it's
48. knew
49. know
50. knowledge
51. laid
52. library
53. loose
54. lose
55. many
56. meant
57. minute
58. much
59. necessary
60. neighbor
61. often
62. once
63. opposite
64. piece
65. pretty
66. raise
67. receive
68. said
69. separate
70. shoes
71. since
72. some
73. sometime
74. stationary
75. sugar
76. sure
77. surprise
78. their
79. there
80. therefore
81. they
82. though
83. threw
84. through
85. tired
86. together
87. too
88. truly
89. Tuesday
90. two
91. unusual
92. very
93. Wednesday
94. where
95. whether
96. woman
97. women
98. would
99. you're

Exercises

A. Write the word in parentheses that is spelled correctly.

1. We should (exercize, exercise) more often.
2. The apples had a (pecular, peculiar) taste.
3. (Parallel, Paralell) lines never intersect.
4. On (ocassion, occasion) we order a pizza.
5. We visited a (quaint, qaint) village.
6. Does the car get good (milage, mileage)?
7. After (desert, dessert) we will go outside.
8. (You're, Your'e) not talking loud enough.
9. Asa has no (knowledge, knowlege) of mechanics.
10. Don't feel (embarrassed, embarassed) about that.

B. If a word in a sentence below is spelled incorrectly, write it correctly. If all words in a sentence are spelled correctly, write *All Correct.*

11. A curious calender hung on the captain's wall.
12. The police analized the clothes in the laboratory.
13. Did lightning strike the superintendant?
14. The secretary said the neighbor was a nuisance.
15. Did he criticise the physician's appearance?
16. A vacuum cleaner is a necessary possession.
17. Go to the library tomorrow or Teusday.
18. By Independance Day the situation was desperate.
19. Keep your mathamatics homework separate.
20. He liked the rhythm of the restaraunt work.

C. Check each of your answers above in a dictionary. Write any word you misspelled in your list of spelling demons. Then look through any of your writing that your teachers have checked. If the writing contains any misspelled words, add them to the list. Spelling errors will hurt the impact of your written work.

D. Add *-s* or *-es* to each noun.

21. gas	**26.** box	**31.** berry
22. branch	**27.** bush	**32.** shelf
23. top	**28.** wife	**33.** buzz
24. knife	**29.** caress	**34.** bushel
25. monkey	**30.** waltz	**35.** trench

E. Add the suffix in parentheses to the word beside it.

36. value (-able)	**41.** complete (-ness)
37. imagine (-ary)	**42.** endorse (-ing)
38. love (-ing)	**43.** manage (-ed)
39. encourage (-ment)	**44.** agree (-ment)
40. nerve (-ous)	**45.** fate (-ful)

F. Add the suffix in parentheses to the word beside it.

46. try (-ing)	**51.** amplify (-er)
47. atrophy (-es)	**52.** grin (-ing)
48. lazy (-ness)	**53.** pretend (-er)
49. employ (-ment)	**54.** prefer (-able)
50. commit (-ed)	**55.** shop (-er)

G. Write the incomplete word in each sentence. Fill in the *ie* or *ei*.

56. We visited several for--gn lands.

57. Whose footprints are on the c--ling?

58. My n--ce and nephew sent the flowers.

59. The fr--ght train had one hundred cars.

60. N--ther Peter nor Toya came to the play.

61. She had no sales rec--pt for the book.

62. What a w--rd dream I had last night.

63. They may try to dec--ve us again.

64. Please save me a p--ce of this velvet ribbon.

65. Seeing you was a great rel--f.

Sentence Parts

A **diagram** is a line drawing that explains something. Just as an architect uses a diagram to show the structure of a building, you can use a diagram to show the structure of a sentence.

A sentence diagram is made up of horizontal, vertical, and slanting lines. Each word is placed at a certain location on the diagram to show its use in the sentence. Diagraming sentences will strengthen your ability to identify parts of speech and sentence structure.

Subjects and Verbs The simplest sentence diagram shows a subject and a verb. Both the subject and the verb are placed on a horizontal line. They are separated by a crossing vertical line. If a sentence has a verb phrase, the entire phrase appears on the horizontal line.

subject | verb

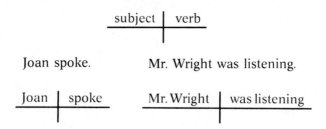

Joan spoke.   Mr. Wright was listening.

Joan | spoke   Mr. Wright | was listening

To diagram an interrogative sentence, put the subject before the verb. To show the subject of an imperative sentence, put *you* in parentheses in the subject place.

May I go?   Leave!

I | May go   (you) | Leave

Notice that a sentence diagram shows the capital letters of a sentence but not the punctuation.

Compound subjects and compound verbs are diagramed on separate horizontal lines. The conjunction that joins the subjects or verbs is written on a vertical broken line linking the horizontal lines.

You and I should go.   It blinks, beeps, or hums.

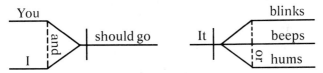

Adjectives and Adverbs All sentences have a subject and a verb. Most sentences also have adjectives and adverbs. These parts of speech can be shown in a sentence diagram.

In a sentence diagram an adjective is written on a slanting line connected to the noun or pronoun the adjective modifies. When more than one adjective modifies a word, each is written on a separate slanting line. The articles *a, an,* and *the* are also diagramed in this way.

Three cars passed.   A tall blond man waved.

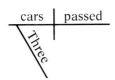
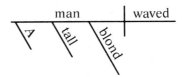

Adverbs, like adjectives, are diagramed on slanting lines. If an adverb modifies a verb, it appears directly below the verb.

We ran quickly.   The child stood there quietly.

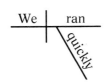
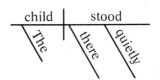

Diagram an adverb modifying an adjective or an adverb on a slanting line attached to the word modified.

A really strange thing happened.   Kate laughs very loudly.

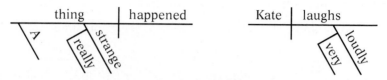

As you have seen, conjunctions are placed on broken lines between the words they connect.

The young but lame pony limped slowly and painfully.

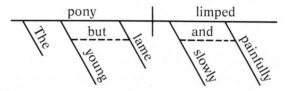

Prepositional Phrases A prepositional phrase is diagramed below the word it modifies. The preposition is placed on a slanting line connected to the word modified. Its object is placed on a horizontal line connected to the slanting line.

The boys in the red balloon soon returned.
They traveled over two tall mountains.

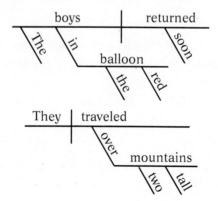

Other Sentence Parts A direct object appears on the horizontal line after the verb. It is separated from the verb by a short vertical line that does not cross the horizontal line.

The trainer finally found the lost tiger.

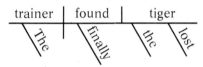

An indirect object is placed on a horizontal line below the verb. A slanting line connects the indirect object to the verb.

That doctor gave the school a computer.

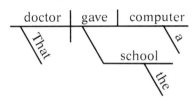

Predicate nouns, predicate pronouns, and predicate adjectives are placed on the horizontal line after the verb, just like direct objects. However, they are separated from the verb by a line that slants backward toward the subject and that does not cross the horizontal line.

James is the pitcher.   The girl in the picture is she.
The stew tasted delicious.

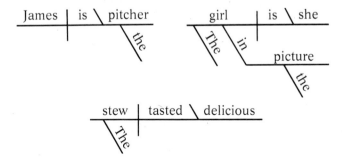

Exercises

A. Diagram each sentence.

1. Birds were singing.
2. Grass grows.
3. Go!
4. Do hurry.
5. Did they run?

6. Will Emma sing?
7. We have finished.
8. Have they been eating?
9. Jay listens.
10. He might have heard.

B. Diagram each sentence. Remember to write each conjunction on a broken line.

11. Biff barked and growled.
12. Dad will write or call.
13. You and they must agree.

14. He and I argued.
15. Mona or Myra dances.

C. Diagram each sentence. Place each adjective and adverb below the word it modifies.

16. The hot air shimmered steadily.
17. The nervous young puppy was behaving poorly.
18. Did the class sing clearly?
19. Only one child could speak persuasively.
20. The small girl skates so gracefully.
21. We worked hard but barely finished.
22. Listen carefully and quietly.
23. Two very fine artists were painting quite busily.
24. Did young Madge ski very slowly?
25. Tom should arrive rather early.

D. Diagram each sentence. Be sure each prepositional phrase is placed below the word it modifies.

26. The purple mountains towered in the distance.
27. Shrubs with big yellow berries grew nearby.
28. A large flag hung from the window.

29. The ring with nine diamonds should be in a safe.
30. The costumes for the green monsters are stored inside the small gymnasium.

E. Diagram each sentence. Be sure your diagrams indicate which words are direct objects; indirect objects; and predicate nouns, pronouns, and adjectives.

31. Is Ms. Gray the new teacher?
32. Rod sent Cliff a secret message.
33. Ella and Clay seem undecided.
34. Bruce could not finish the puzzle.
35. Show me the hidden staircase.
36. The actors definitely were we.
37. The clever coach gave the runner a signal.
38. The players and the fans are happy.
39. Our third President is the author.
40. Has Mr. Warner already given Alice the trophy?

F. Diagram each sentence. The sentences contain various sentence parts and parts of speech that you have studied in this section.

41. A thing of beauty is a joy forever.
42. Tom and Fred worked quickly and efficiently.
43. The terrible flood destroyed thousands of homes.
44. Its chief feature was a long, clear, high note.
45. Anyone can catch a firefly in his or her hand.
46. Mrs. Pringle and her lawyer showed the mayor a copy of the petition.
47. The weary campers gave the brave ranger a loud cheer of thanks.
48. The writer of the almost illegible message was unfortunately I.
49. Two angry cats clawed and yowled.
50. In the morning give her your old but unused hat.

Compound and Complex Sentences

The sentences you have diagramed so far have been simple sentences. A simple sentence, as you remember, has only one subject and one verb, although each may be compound. You can use the same diagraming techniques that you have learned to diagram more complicated sentences. In this section you will study how to diagram compound and complex sentences.

Compound Sentences A compound sentence is made up of two or more independent clauses joined by a conjunction or a semicolon. (For a review of compound sentences, see pages 110–111.) Each independent clause in a compound sentence is diagramed like a simple sentence. The first clause is diagramed above the second. The clauses are joined by the conjunction as shown below.

> We thoroughly enjoyed the band, but the singer could barely carry a tune.

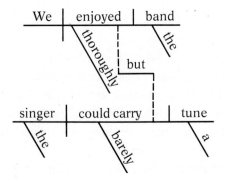

Notice that the line that connects the two independent clauses is drawn from verb to verb. If the clauses are joined by a semicolon, a broken line connects the two verbs.

Complex Sentences A complex sentence contains two or more clauses. However, only one clause is independent. The other clause or clauses are subordinate. (To review subordinate clauses and complex sentences, see pages 112–115.)

When diagraming a complex sentence, diagram the independent clause first. Then diagram the subordinate clause below the independent clause. You should be able to identify the subordinate clause by the subordinating conjunction—such as *after, because, before, if, since, while,* or *where*—that begins the clause.

Connect the verbs of the two clauses with a slanting broken line. Write the subordinating conjunction on the slanting line. Study the diagrams of the complex sentences that follow.

> He kept his pet outside, since it was an elephant of some size.
> If you like elephants, visit him.

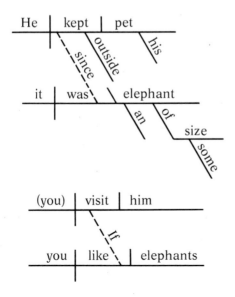

553

Exercises

A. Diagram each compound sentence.

1. The journey was long, and the wind was cold.
2. They won the game, but we will win the match.
3. Should I send Jill the mango, or may I eat it?
4. Jane was ill, but the other actors rehearsed.
5. Each actor must learn his or her part, or the play will be a complete failure.
6. In the early morning we fished, and later we explored the lighthouse.
7. You must hurry, or you will miss the bus.
8. Everyone agrees with your conclusions, but can anything be done in three days?
9. I took my camera to the picnic, but I forgot the film.
10. The solution is simple, or I would not have discovered it so quickly.

B. Diagram each complex sentence.

11. If you need any help, call me.
12. I must study now because my test is tomorrow.
13. If wishes were horses, beggars would ride.
14. She left before anyone could ask her any more questions.
15. While she worked, the dentist hummed softly.
16. They will repair your shoes while you wait.
17. When all danger of frost had passed, we planted the tomatoes in a sunny spot.
18. After I told my teacher the plot, I began work on the story.
19. This season was a complete success for our team because we won the state championship.
20. Before the phone rang twice, Sophie answered it.

Thesaurus

What Is a Thesaurus?

In a thesaurus, entry words are listed in alphabetical order. Under each entry word, synonyms and sometimes antonyms are shown. Below is part of a thesaurus entry from this book.

Entry word → **important** (adj)— marked by significant worth or value. The important news bulletin was broadcast last night.

Synonym → *noteworthy*— worthy of attention because of special excellence. Her fine performance in the competition was noteworthy.

Antonym → ANTONYM: insignificant

The entry word is in bold type, synonyms are in italic type, and antonyms are in blue type.

Using the Thesaurus Index

The Index lists every word in the Thesaurus. To find a word that appears only as a synonym or antonym, you first have to look up its entry word.

Below are examples from the Index. They show that to find *noteworthy* or insignificant you must look under **important**. The entry for **important** begins on page 567.

>   **important** (adj) 567
>   *noteworthy* **important** (adj) 567
>   insignificant **important** (adj) 567

A cross-reference (marked "See also") lists an entry that gives additional synonyms, related words, and antonyms.

>   **important** (adj) 567
>   See also **urgent** (adj) 573

See also the lesson "Using a Thesaurus" on page 4.

THESAURUS INDEX
A list of all the words in this thesaurus

A

accept **believe** (v) 561
accomplish **win** (v) 574
achieve **win** (v) 574
acquire **buy** (v) 562
acquire **give** (v) 565
acute **urgent** (adj) 573
address **talk** (v) 573
adjacent **far** (adj) 564
adjacent **near** (adj) 570
adjoining **near** (adj) 570
affluent (adj) **poor** (adj) 571
affluent **rich** (adj) 571
afraid **brave** (adj) 561
answer (v) **ask** (v) 561
anxiety **fear** (n) 564
appear **disappear** (v) 563
apprehend **know** (v) 568
article **object** (n) 570
articulate **say** (v) 572
artifact **object** (n) 570
ask (v) 561
association **group** (n) 565
auction (v) **buy** (v) 562
author **write** (v) 574

B

band **crowd** (n) 563
bankrupt (adj) **rich** (adj) 571
be in stitches **laugh** (v) 568
believe (v) 561
benevolent **kind** (adj) 567
big-league **important** (adj) 567
bleach **clean** (v) 563
blistering **hot** (adj) 566
blunder **mistake** (n) 569
bold **brave** (adj) 561
boldness **fear** (n) 564
bordering **near** (adj) 570
brave (adj) 561
bravery **fear** (n) 564
break (v) 562
break (v) **fix** (v) 562
bring home the bacon **win** (v) 574
broke **poor** (adj) 571
bunch **crowd** (n) 563

burning **hot** (adj) 566
burst (v) **fix** (v) 565
buy (v) 562
buy **believe** (v) 561

C

cabin **house** (n) 567
call (v) 562
call **say** (v) 572
careful (adj) 562
careless **careful** (adj) 562
castle **house** (n) 567
cautious **careful** (adj) 562
chancellor **leader** (n) 568
chat **talk** (v) 573
cheer **call** (v) 562
chief **important** (adj) 567
chuckle **laugh** (v) 568
clean (v) 563
close (adj) **far** (adj) 564
close **near** (adj) 570
cold **hot** (adj) 566
collapse (v) **fix** (v) 565
comfortable **easy** (adj) 564
comfortable **rich** (adj) 571
commander **leader** (n) 568
compassionate **kind** (adj) 567
compelling **urgent** (adj) 573
complicated **easy** (adj) 564
comprehend **know** (v) 568
confidence **fear** (n) 564
conscientious **careful** (adj) 562
contaminate **clean** (v) 563
contribute **give** (v) 565
corral **win** (v) 574
correspond **write** (v) 574
cottage **house** (n) 567
courage **fear** (n) 564
courageous **brave** (adj) 561
cowardly (adj) **brave** (adj) 561
crack (v) **fix** (v) 565
crawl **move** (v) 570
crew **group** (n) 565
crisp **hot** (adj) 566
critical **urgent** (adj) 573
crowd (n) 563
   See also **group** (n) 565

crucial **urgent** (adj) 573
cruel **kind** (adj) 567
crush **crowd** (n) 563
cry (v) **laugh** (v) 568

D

dash **move** (v) 570
debate **talk** (v) 573
debilitated (adj) **strong** (adj) 572
decimate **break** (v) 562
deliberate **careful** (adj) 562
deliver **give** (v) 565
depart **disappear** (v) 563
despot **leader** (n) 568
destitute **poor** (adj) 571
destitute **rich** (adj) 571
destroy **break** (v) 562
device **object** (n) 570
difficult **easy** (adj) 564
difficult **hard** (adj) 566
dirty (v) **clean** (v) 563
disappear (v) 563
disbelieve **believe** (v) 561
discontinue **move** (v) 570
discreet **careful** (adj) 562
dispute (v) **believe** (v) 561
distant **near** (adj) 570
doctor **fix** (v) 565
doohickey **object** (n) 570
double-barreled **important** (adj) 567
doubt (v) **believe** (v) 561
dread **fear** (n) 564
drop **lose** (v) 569
dry-clean **clean** (v) 563
dwelling **house** (n) 567

E

easy (adj) 564
easy **hard** (adj) 566
effortless **easy** (adj) 564
emerge **disappear** (v) 563
endow **give** (v) 565
energetic **strong** (adj) 572
energetic **weak** (adj) 574
error **mistake** (n) 569
evaporate **disappear** (v) 563
expire **disappear** (v) 563

F

facile **hard** (adj) 566
fade out **disappear** (v) 563

fail **lose** (v) 569
fail (v) **win** (v) 574
faint **weak** (adj) 574
fainthearted **brave** (adj) 561
fall **lose** (v) 569
fall (v) **win** (v) 574
far (adj) 564
far **near** (adj) 570
faraway **far** (adj) 564
faraway **near** (adj) 570
far-off **far** (adj) 564
fathom **know** (v) 568
fear (n) 564
fearful **brave** (adj) 561
fearlessness **fear** (n) 564
feeble **strong** (adj) 572
filter **clean** (v) 563
find (v) **lose** (v) 569
fix (v) 565
fix (v) **break** (v) 562
flock **group** (n) 565
flop **lose** (v) 569
flop (v) **win** (v) 574
flow **move** (v) 570
follower **leader** (v) 568
forceful **strong** (adj) 572
foreboding **fear** (n) 564
forfeit (v) **win** (v) 574
formidable **easy** (adj) 564
fragile **weak** (adj) 574
frail **strong** (adj) 572
frail **weak** (adj) 574
fright **fear** (n) 564
frigid **hot** (adj) 566
frosty **hot** (adj) 566
frown **(v) laugh** (v) 568
frozen **hot** (adj) 566
funk **fear** (n) 564
furnish **give** (v) 565

G

gab **talk** (v) 573
gadget **object** (n) 570
gain (v) **give** (v) 565
gain (v) **lose** (v) 569
get **buy** (v) 562
get **know** (v) 568
giggle **laugh** (v) 568
give (v) 565
glower (v) **laugh** (v) 568
grasp **know** (v) 568
great **kind** (adj) 567
grill **ask** (v) 561

group (n) 565
 See also **crowd** (n) 563
guffaw **laugh** (v) 568
gutsy **brave** (adj) 561

H

halt (v) **move** (v) 570
hard (adj) 566
hardy **strong** (adj) 572
hardy **weak** (adj) 574
harsh **kind** (adj) 567
hasty **careful** (adj) 562
have down pat **know** (v) 568
have no doubt about **believe** (v) 561
hefty **hard** (adj) 566
heroic **brave** (adj) 561
high rise **house** (n) 567
hike **walk** (v) 573
hold (v) **lose** (v) 569
holler **call** (v) 562
horde **crowd** (n) 563
hot (adj) 566
hot as a furnace **hot** (adj) 566
house (n) 567
howl **call** (v) 562
humane **kind** (adj) 567

I

immediate **far** (adj) 564
immediate **near** (adj) 570
implement **object** (n) 570
important (adj) 567
 See also **urgent** (adj) 573
impoverished **poor** (adj) 571
impoverished (adj) **rich** (adj) 571
imprudent **careful** (adj) 562
inconsequential **important** (adj) 567
inconsiderate **kind** (adj) 567
indiscreet **careful** (adj) 562
individual (n) **group** (n) 565
inferior **poor** (adj) 571
inherit **give** (v) 565
inhumane **kind** (adj) 567
inquire **ask** (v) 561
inscribe **write** (v) 574
insignificant **important** (adj) 567
instrument **object** (n) 570
interrogate **ask** (v) 561

J

judicious **careful** (adj) 562

K

keep (v) **lose** (v) 569
kind (adj) 567
kingpin **leader** (n) 568
KO **break** (v) 562
know (v) 568

L

laborious **easy** (adj) 564
laugh (v) 568
laugh it up **laugh** (v) 568
launder **clean** (v) 563
leader (n) 568
leery **careful** (adj) 562
listless **strong** (adj) 572
listless **weak** (adj) 574
loaded **rich** (adj) 571
long-distance **far** (adj) 564
lose (v) 569
lose **win** (v) 574
lumber **walk** (v) 573
luscious **rich** (adj) 571

M

magnanimous **kind** (adj) 567
malevolent **kind** (adj) 567
manageable **easy** (adj) 564
mansion **house** (n) 567
market (v) **buy** (v) 562
materialize **disappear** (v) 563
melt **disappear** (v) 563
mend (v) **break** (v) 562
mend **fix** (v) 565
merciless **kind** (adj) 567
migrate **move** (v) 570
miscalculation **mistake** (n) 569
misjudgment **mistake** (n) 569
misplace **lose** (v) 569
misprint **mistake** (n) 569
mistake (n) 569
mistrust (v) **believe** (v) 561
misunderstand **know** (v) 568
mob **crowd** (n) 563
momentous **important** (adj) 567
monarch **leader** (n) 568
moneyed **poor** (adj) 571
move (v) 570
 See also **walk** (v) 573
multitude **crowd** (n) 563
muscular **strong** (adj) 572
mutter **say** (v) 572

N

near (adj) 570
near **far** (adj) 564
nearby **far** (adj) 564
nearby **near** (adj) 570
needy **poor** (adj) 571
needy (adj) **rich** (adj) 571
negligent **careful** (adj) 562
neighboring (adj) **far** (adj) 564
neighboring **near** (adj) 570
not to be sneezed at **important** (adj) 567
noteworthy **important** (adj) 567

O

object (n) 570
obtain **buy** (v) 562
obtain **give** (v) 565
opulent **poor** (adj) 571
opulent **rich** (adj) 571
orchestra **group** (n) 565
outlying **far** (adj) 564
outlying **near** (adj) 570
overhaul **fix** (v) 565
overheated **hot** (adj) 566
oversight **mistake** (n) 569

P

pace **walk** (v) 573
pack **group** (n) 565
painless **easy** (adj) 564
paramount **important** (adj) 567
pause (v) **move** (v) 570
penniless **poor** (adj) 571
petty **important** (adj) 567
philanthropic **kind** (adj) 567
phobia **fear** (n) 564
plain (adj) **rich** (adj) 571
pollute **clean** (v) 563
poor (adj) 571
poor (adj) **rich** (adj) 571
powerful **weak** (adj) 574
powerless **strong** (adj) 572
powerless **weak** (adj) 574
premier **leader** (n) 568
present **give** (v) 565
president **leader** (n) 568
pressing **urgent** (adj) 573
presume **believe** (v) 561
prevail **win** (v) 574
procure **buy** (v) 562
procure **give** (v) 565
progress **move** (v) 570

propel **move** (v) 570
prosperous **poor** (adj) 571
prosperous **rich** (adj) 571
provide **give** (v) 565
prudent **careful** (adj) 562
purchase **buy** (v) 562
purify **clean** (v) 563
put into words **say** (v) 572
put through the third degree **ask** (v) 561

Q

question **ask** (v) 561
question (v) **believe** (v) 561
quiz **ask** (v) 561

R

ramble **walk** (v) 573
rap **talk** (v) 573
ravage **break** (v) 562
receive **give** (v) 565
reckless **careful** (adj) 562
recognize **know** (v) 568
recondition **fix** (v) 565
reconstruct **fix** (v) 565
record **write** (v) 574
recover **lose** (v) 569
relinquish **lose** (v) 569
remote **far** (adj) 564
remote **near** (adj) 570
removed **near** (adj) 570
repair (v) **break** (v) 562
repair **fix** (v) 565
report **talk** (v) 573
request **ask** (v) 561
residence **house** (n) 567
respond **ask** (v) 561
restore **fix** (v) 565
retain **lose** (v) 569
rich (adj) 571
rich (adj) **poor** (adj) 571
rigorous **easy** (adj) 564
rolling in money **rich** (adj) 571
rugged **hard** (adj) 566
ruin **break** (v) 562

S

say (v) 572
   See also **talk** (v) 573
scalding **hot** (adj) 566
scowl (v) **laugh** (v) 568
scream **call** (v) 562
scribble **write** (v) 574

sell (v) **buy** (v) 562
service **fix** (v) 565
shout **call** (v) 562
shriek **call** (v) 562
shriek **laugh** (v) 568
simple **easy** (adj) 564
simple **hard** (adj) 566
slipup **mistake** (n) 569
smudge (v) **clean** (v) 563
snap (v) **fix** (v) 565
snicker **laugh** (v) 568
soft **easy** (adj) 564
soft (adj) **hard** (adj) 566
soft (adj) **strong** (adj) 572
soil (v) **clean** (v) 563
solid **hard** (adj) 566
split (v) **fix** (v) 565
spunky **brave** (adj) 561
stain (v) **clean** (v) 563
sterilize **clean** (v) 563
stern **hard** (adj) 566
sticky **hot** (adj) 566
stop (v) **move** (v) 570
strenuous **easy** (adj) 564
strict **hard** (adj) 566
stride **walk** (v) 573
strong (adj) 572
strong (adj) **weak** (adj) 574
strong as a bull **strong** (adj) 572
sturdy **strong** (adj) 572
sturdy **weak** (adj) 574
subordinate (n) **leader** (n) 568
subsidize **give** (v) 565
succumb **lose** (v) 569
superficial **important** (adj) 567
superior (adj) **poor** (adj) 571
suppose **believe** (v) 561
surmise **believe** (v) 561
sweltering **hot** (adj) 566
sympathetic **kind** (adj) 567

T

take (v) **give** (v) 565
take down **write** (v) 574
talk (v) 573
    See also **say** (v) 572
team **group** (n) 565
telephone **call** (v) 562
terror **fear** (n) 564
think **believe** (v) 561
thoughtless **careful** (adj) 562
throng **crowd** (n) 563
timid **brave** (adj) 561

timorous **brave** (adj) 561
titter **laugh** (v) 568
torrid **hot** (adj) 566
tough **strong** (adj) 572
traipse **walk** (v) 573
travel **move** (v) 570
triumph **win** (v) 574
trivial **important** (adj) 567
troupe **group** (n) 565
trudge **walk** (v) 573
trust **believe** (v) 561

U

unable to make ends meet **poor** (adj) 571
unafraid **brave** (adj) 561
undauntedness **fear** (n) 564
underprivileged **poor** (adj) 571
understand **know** (v) 568
unimportant **important** (adj) 567
unimportant **urgent** (adj) 573
unkind **kind** (adj) 567
unmanageable **easy** (adj) 564
urgent (adj) 573
    See also **important** (adj) 567
utter **say** (v) 572

V

valiant **brave** (adj) 561
vanish **disappear** (v) 563
vend **buy** (v) 562
vigorous **strong** (adj) 572
vigorous **weak** (adj) 574

W

walk (v) 573
    See also **move** (v) 570
wanting (adj) **rich** (adj) 571
wash **clean** (v) 563
weak (adj) 574
weak **strong** (adj) 572
wealthy **poor** (adj) 571
wealthy **rich** (adj) 571
whisper **say** (v) 572
win (v) 574
win (v) **lose** (v) 569
worthless **important** (adj) 567
wreck **break** (v) 562
write (v) 574

Y

yap **say** (v) 572

A

ask (v)—**1** to question; to call on to answer. Our teacher will <u>ask</u> us questions about the homework assignment. **2** to request something of someone. <u>Ask</u> the librarian to help you find the book.

interrogate—to question systematically. The detective will <u>interrogate</u> the witness.

inquire—to ask about someone or something. I will <u>inquire</u> about the price of tickets.

question—to ask of or about. Did the doctor <u>question</u> the nurse about the test results?

quiz—to question carefully. Our history teacher will <u>quiz</u> us on ancient Greece.

request—to ask for. The pilot of the private plane has <u>requested</u> permission to land.

grill [informal]—to question with intensity. The police officer will <u>grill</u> the suspect.

put through the third degree [idiom]—to question unmercifully. After coming home very late from school, Mark was <u>put through the third degree</u>.

ANTONYMS: answer (v), respond

B

believe (v)—to accept with trust and faith; to have a firm conviction of the reality of something. I <u>believe</u> that the climate of our area is changing.

accept—to receive as true or satisfactory. I <u>accept</u> his explanation for the delay.

presume—to suppose to be true without any proof. We <u>presume</u> that all the arrangements for the trip have been made.

suppose—to have as an opinion; to believe. I <u>suppose</u> that what she said about the earthquake is true.

surmise—to imagine on slight proof to be true; to guess. I <u>surmise</u> that the storm has delayed the arrival of the flight.

think—to have an opinion. I <u>think</u> that we must protect the wilderness areas of the world.

trust—to rely on the honesty or truthfulness of. Do you <u>trust</u> his judgment on the subject?

buy [slang]—to accept as true. Do you <u>buy</u> the ridiculous explanation that he just gave you?

have no doubts about [idiom]—to believe totally. I <u>have no doubts about</u> the safety of this automobile.

ANTONYMS: disbelieve, dispute (v), doubt (v), mistrust (v), question (v)

brave (adj)—having or displaying courage. The <u>brave</u> fire fighters entered the burning building.

bold—fearless when facing danger. The <u>bold</u> rider urged her horse over the difficult jump.

courageous—possessing or characterized by bravery. The <u>courageous</u> individual dove into the icy water to save a child who had fallen from the bridge.

heroic—marked by courage and daring. The mountain climber made a <u>heroic</u> effort to reach the summit.

unafraid—without fear. The seriously ill patient faced the operation <u>unafraid</u>.

valiant—having or exhibiting valor; courageous. Although in extreme pain, the <u>valiant</u> marathon runner stayed in the race.

spunky [informal]—spirited; brave. The <u>spunky</u> individual refused to let anything get her down.

gutsy [slang]—courageous. Trying to steal home is a <u>gutsy</u> play in baseball.

ANTONYMS: afraid, cowardly (adj),

brave *(continued)*

Thesaurus

fainthearted, fearful, timid, timorous

break (v)—to reduce to pieces with sudden or violent force. Please do not <u>break</u> that valuable vase.

decimate—to destroy a large portion of. Spraying the area with a pesticide will <u>decimate</u> the insect population.

destroy—to break into pieces; to ruin. Lack of sufficient rainfall can <u>destroy</u> farm crops.

ravage—to damage greatly; to destroy. The fire <u>ravaged</u> an entire city block.

ruin—to destroy; to devastate. Certain stains can <u>ruin</u> a shirt.

wreck—to destroy or ruin. Improper maintenance procedures can <u>wreck</u> a power lawn mower.

KO [slang]—to knock out or destroy. Nothing can <u>KO</u> me faster than the flu.

ANTONYMS: fix (v), mend (v), repair (v)

buy (v)—to acquire ownership of something by the payment of money. My sister will <u>buy</u> a new coat tomorrow.

acquire—to gain possession of. A motion picture studio <u>acquired</u> the movie rights to that popular novel.

get—to obtain possession of. I will <u>get</u> a loaf of bread and a quart of milk at the store.

obtain—to attain usually through planned action. Judy will <u>obtain</u> two tickets to the basketball game.

procure—to obtain or acquire. The stockbroker will <u>procure</u> one-hundred shares of the stock of that company.

purchase—to obtain through the payment of money. Where did you <u>purchase</u> those tennis shoes?

ANTONYMS: auction (v), market (v), sell (v), vend

C

call (v)—to say; to cry out or shout. The team captain <u>called</u> the plays.

cheer—to shout support or praise. The fans at the basketball game <u>cheer</u> every time the home team scores a basket.

howl—to give a long mournful cry. The crowd <u>howled</u> when the football team fumbled the ball.

scream—to make a loud, piercing cry. Some of the passengers <u>screamed</u> when the plane jolted because of severe turbulence.

shout—to cry out suddenly and loudly. Almost everyone applauded and <u>shouted</u> after the pianist had finished playing.

shriek—to make a shrill sound. The parrot <u>shrieked</u> when I came near.

telephone—to communicate with someone by telephone. I will <u>telephone</u> my best friend tonight.

holler [informal]—to shout loudly. When angry, the coach can really <u>holler</u>.

careful (adj)—having caution; showing concern over what one says or does. A pedestrian should always be <u>careful</u> when crossing a street.

cautious—extremely careful; not taking any chances. A <u>cautious</u> driver never tailgates.

conscientious—careful to do whatever is right; scrupulous. A <u>conscientious</u> student hands in homework assignments on time.

deliberate—done on purpose; thought over ahead of time. He made a <u>deliberate</u> effort to improve his grades.

discreet—careful in action or speech; prudent. Being <u>discreet</u>, she did not tell anyone about the confidential information.

judicious—having good judgment;

sensible. A judicious physician tries not to alarm a patient.

prudent—showing wisdom; thoroughly planing ahead of time. A prudent individual saves some money for the future.

leery [slang]—wary, suspicious. The police were leery of the suspect's story.

ANTONYMS: careless, hasty, imprudent, indiscreet, negligent, reckless, thoughtless

clean (v)—to free from dirt or impurities. When will you go upstairs and clean your room?

bleach—to remove stains or make lighter in color. Can you bleach those towels?

dry-clean—to clean clothes with naphtha, or the like, and little or no water. You must dry-clean that stained suit jacket.

filter—to pass a liquid or gas through a porous mass in order to separate out matter or impurities. My cousin's fish tank has a device that filters all of the water.

launder—to wash clothes with water. I will launder all of my shirts today.

purify—to clear from material imperfection. A huge plant purifies the city water supply.

sterilize—to free from living germs or microorganisms, as by heating. Hospital personnel will sterilize all the surgical instruments that will be used in the operation.

wash—to clean by using a liquid such as water. When should I wash this dirty floor?

ANTONYMS: contaminate, dirty (v), pollute, smudge (v), soil (v), stain (v)

crowd (n)—a large number of people collected together. A crowd gathered near the stadium entrance.

band—a number of persons or animals acting together. A band of scientists worked ceaselessly to find a cure for the disease.

crush—a group of people crowded together. The crush jammed the subway train during rush hour.

horde—a loosely organized crowd. A horde of students left the school building at the end of the day.

multitude—a large group of people. A somber multitude gathered near the site of the mine cave-in.

throng—a great number of people. A loud cheer arose from the throng at the stadium.

bunch [informal]—a group of people. That bunch always sticks together.

mob [slang]—a lawless crowd of people. The angry mob started to move toward city hall.

See also *group* (n).

D

disappear (v)—to pass from sight; to cease existing. The freight train disappeared as it rounded the curve.

depart—to leave or go away. The plane will depart for Honolulu in about an hour.

evaporate—to change from liquid or solid into vapor; to disappear. Soon after the heavy rain, all the water evaporated from the street.

expire—to terminate; to come to an end. The time left in the first half of the game expired.

melt—to change from solid to liquid; to dissolve. These mild March temperatures are melting the ice on the pond.

vanish—to disappear quickly; to cease existing. The brilliant golden sunset vanished into darkness.

fade out [slang]—to disappear gradually. The singer's popularity began to fade out about a year ago.

disappear *(continued)*

Thesaurus

Thesaurus

ANTONYMS: appear, emerge, materialize

E

easy (adj)—**1** not difficult to do or obtain. Learning to speak French was
easy for me. **2** free from pain or
worry. Vacationing at this tropical
island is certainly the easy life.
comfortable—having ease. I certainly
feel comfortable in this soft reclin-
ing chair.
effortless—needing or showing little
exertion; easy. The runner in the
lead has an effortless stride.
manageable—capable of being han-
dled or controlled. That simple task
is certainly manageable.
painless—without physical or emo-
tional distress or suffering. The
tooth extraction was painless.
simple—free of complications; easy to
do or understand. Fortunately, the
directions for assembling the
model airplane were simple.
soft—requiring little effort. Stacking
these boxes is a soft task.
cushy [slang]—requiring little difficulty; comfortable. I wish I had a
cushy job like yours.
easy as pie [idiom]—not difficult. For
me, riding a bicycle is easy as pie.
ANTONYMS: complicated, difficult,
formidable, laborious, rigorous,
strenuous, unmanageable

F

far (adj)—not near; remote in time or
space; distant. They moved to a far
country.
distant—not near; far away in time or
space. I wonder if everyone will be
able to travel to other planets in
the distant future.
faraway—remote; located at a great
distance. I would like to travel to
faraway places.

far-off—located far away, distant. He
gazed across the wheat fields toward the far-off mountains.
long-distance—over or for a long distance. My uncle made a long-distance telephone call to Fairbanks,
Alaska.
outlying—distant or far from the center. The meteorologist said the outlying suburbs would receive more
snow than the city.
remote—far away; far removed in
space or time. There are no paved
roads in that remote wilderness
area.
ANTONYMS: adjacent, bordering (adj),
close (adj), immediate, near (adj),
nearby (adj), neighboring (adj)

fear (n)—an unpleasant emotion
caused by belief that danger is
present or near. As he glanced
down from the steep mountain
path, my friend was studdenly overcome by fear.
anxiety—uneasy or painful thoughts
about what might happen. My anxiety over the upcoming history test
continues to grow.
dread—to look forward to with great
fear. I dread our class trip to the
snake farm.
foreboding—a warning or prediction
of coming evil; an omen. She
boarded the plane even though she
had a foreboding that something
bad would happen during the
flight.
fright—sudden fear; terror. The sound
of the door slamming shut behind
him gave him a fright.
phobia—a persistent abnormal fear of
a certain thing. She has a phobia
about elevators.
terror—a state of great fear. We felt
terror as we watched the tornado
approach.

funk [informal]—a state of fear; a depressed state of mind. The gloomy weather left me in a blue funk.
ANTONYMS: boldness, bravery, confidence, courage, fearlessness, undauntedness

fix (v)—to repair or mend. Can you fix my broken guitar?
mend—to repair; to put into good shape again. I will mend these torn socks.
overhaul—to examine and make any necessary repairs. Even though the automobile mechanic overhauled the engine last month, the automobile still is not running right.
recondition—to restore to a good condition; renovate. The mechanic will recondition the automobile in order to make it perform as if it were brand new again.
reconstruct—to build or construct again; to restore. The carpenters will reconstruct that dilapidated old house.
repair—to fix by putting together what is broken or by replacing a part. Someone must repair the broken refrigerator quickly before all of the food spoils and we have absolutely nothing to eat.
restore—to bring back to an original condition; to renew. I will restore the finish on this old table.
service—to repair or perform maintenance on. Airlines periodically service the engines on each of their airplanes.
doctor [informal]—**1** to repair. We doctored the leaning wooden fence. **2** to alter or tamper with. The dishonest executive doctored the company records.
ANTONYMS: break (v), burst (v), collapse (v), crack (v), snap (v), split (v)

G

give (v)—to hand over as a gift; to grant by formal action. I will give my brother a new camera for his birthday.
contribute—to give in common with others. I will certainly contribute to the fund for the new children's hospital.
deliver—to hand over; to carry and give out. We must deliver this package to Los Angeles.
endow—to give money or property in order to provide an income. The wealthy person generously endowed the hospital.
furnish—to provide with something necessary. The sponsor will furnish uniforms for the baseball team.
present—to give to; to offer formally. The principal will present the awards during the assembly.
provide—to supply what is needed or wanted. The volunteers will provide transportation to anyone who wants to attend the football game Saturday afternoon.
subsidize—to assist with a grant of money. Does the government subsidize commuter bus lines that do not make a profit?
ANTONYMS: acquire, gain (v), inherit, obtain, procure, receive, take (v)

group (n)—a usually comparatively small number of persons, animals, or things together. A group of children played in the sandbox.
association—a group of people with a common purpose. The recreation association of our town has done much for everyone.
crew—the people needed to work a ship. The crew of a cruise ship includes chefs and doctors.
flock—a group of animals of one kind keeping or herded together. A flock

group *(continued)*

Thesaurus

of geese just flew over the horizon.

orchestra—a group of musicians, including string players, organized to perform together. The symphony orchestra played Beethoven's Fifth Symphony at our high school auditorium.

team—a group of persons joined together in a certain activity. A team of mountain climbers is on its way up Mt. Everest.

troupe—a band, especially of actors, dancers, or other entertainers. The city ballet troupe will perform *Swan Lake* next month.

pack [informal]—a set or number of persons or things together. Do you think that everything you just heard was a pack of lies? See also *crowd* (n).

ANTONYM: individual (n)

H

hard (adj)—**1** not easy to penetrate. The thick ice on the lake is frozen hard. **2** difficult to do. Painting that lattice fence is hard. **3** unyielding to influence. He is a hard person when it comes to accepting excuses.

difficult—not easy to do or understand. It is very difficult for me to read that handwriting.

formidable—difficult to overcome or to deal with. Inclement weather can be a formidable challenge for airplane pilots.

rugged—having a rough and uneven surface; covered with rough edges. This rugged gravel road is filled with dangerous ruts.

solid—neither gaseous nor liquid; put together strongly; hard, firm. The solid form of water, ice, is lower in density than the liquid form of water.

stern—strict, harsh, severe. A stern person does not smile very often.

strict—careful in following a rule or in making other people follow it. My English teacher is strict when it comes to handing in homework assignments on time.

hefty [informal]—considerable; having bigness or bulk. Reshelving all of the books in our school library is a hefty job.

ANTONYMS: easy, facile, simple, soft

hot (adj)—**1** having a temperature that is relatively high. It is really hot outside. **2** having the sensation of high bodily heat. The fever from the illness made him feel extremely hot and uncomfortable.

blistering—capable of causing blisters; extremely hot. After playing baseball all morning, the blistering heat was too much to endure.

burning—hot; being on fire; affecting with heat. Immediately after running the race, Sue was overcome by a burning sensation.

overheated—warmed beyond a safe or desired point. The overheated car was parked on the shoulder of the highway.

scalding—hot enough to burn with hot liquid or steam. Don't drink that scalding coffee.

sweltering—oppressively hot. On that sweltering summer day, thousands of people headed for several of the local beaches.

torrid—parched with heat; scorching. The torrid heat caused some people to become dizzy.

sticky [informal]—hot and humid. In sticky weather like this, I cannot stop perspiring.

hot as a furnace [idiom]—having unbearable heat. The tennis court is hot as a furnace today.

ANTONYMS: cold, crisp, frigid, frosty, frozen

house (n)—a building in which one or more families live. Jessica lives in the blue house on the corner just one block from my house.

cabin—a roughly built small house. There are many cabins in the wooded area that surrounds the lake.

castle—a large building or set of buildings with thick walls and battlements for defense. Many medieval castles can be found in Europe.

cottage—a small house, especially in the country or suburbs. We stayed at a cottage near a picturesque lighthouse.

dwelling—the place in which a person lives; a house. We live in a modest dwelling on Maple Avenue.

high rise—a building having many stories. We live in an apartment in the new high rise on Brinker Street.

mansion—a large, imposing house. Some movie stars live in impressive mansions in Beverly Hills.

residence—the place where a person lives; a home. Did your sister take up residence in Colorado yet?

I

important (adj)—marked by significant worth or value. The important news bulletin was broadcast last night.

chief—of greatest importance or significance. The chief member of the crew on a plane is the pilot.

momentous—very important; consequential. The anniversary celebration was a momentous occasion.

noteworthy—worthy of attention because of special excellence. Her fine performance in the competition was noteworthy.

paramount—superior to all else. The final exams are of paramount significance.

big-league [informal]—something outstanding of its kind. Linda gave a big-league performance in the play last Wednesday evening.

double-barreled [slang]—important; having a dual purpose. The lawyer asked the witness a double-barreled question.

not to be sneezed at [idiom]—of considerable importance. His chances in the race are not to be sneezed at.

See also *urgent* (adj).

ANTONYMS: inconsequential, insignificant, petty, superficial, trivial, unimportant, worthless

K

kind (adj)—having a gentle and considerate nature; tending to be helpful. A kind person usually manages to find time to help others.

benevolent—wanting to promote the happiness of others; disposed to doing good. The benevolent king was kind to all of his subjects.

compassionate—sympathetic; desiring to help those that suffer. The compassionate nurse comforted the severely injured accident victim by reassuring him.

humane—merciful; compassionate; not cruel. A humane person treats animals, as well as people, with kindness.

magnanimous—noble of mind; free from mean acts; generous in forgiving. In a magnanimous gesture, the senator who had just lost the election asked everyone to support his victorious opponent.

philanthropic—kind and helpful toward people in general; charitable. The philanthropic organization in

Thesaurus

kind (continued)

our town raised enough money to build a new senior citizen center.

sympathetic—showing kind feelings toward other people. My sympathetic friend always lifts my spirits when I feel sad.

great [slang]—noble; kind and generous. Your brother is a great guy to pay for our hot dogs.

ANTONYMS: cruel, harsh, inconsiderate, inhumane, malevolent, merciless, unkind

know (v)—**1** to have understanding of the facts of. I know the geography of North America quite well. **2** to be acquainted with. I know that person very well.

apprehend—to become aware of; to perceive. He clearly apprehended the risks involved in skydiving.

comprehend—to understand the nature or meaning of something. I cannot comprehend her complex report about lasers.

fathom—to fully understand. I cannot fathom the vastness of outer space.

grasp—to lay hold of with the mind; to understand. Can you grasp the meaning of what I am saying?

recognize—to be aware of someone or something as previously known. Do you recognize that television personality?

understand—to grasp the meaning of. I understand why we must conserve all natural resources.

get [slang]—to understand. I get what you mean.

have down pat [idiom]—to understand something quite well. I have the entire plan down pat.

ANTONYM: misunderstand

L

laugh (v)—to show happiness or scorn with a smile and a chuckle

or a very loud sound. I laughed uncontrollably at the joke that she told me.

chuckle—to laugh quietly or inwardly. I happily watched and chuckled when my dog danced excitedly with my slipper between its teeth.

giggle—to laugh in a silly manner. The two children giggled almost every time they glanced at each other.

guffaw—to laugh coarsely and loudly. When I dropped the ice-cream cone into my lap, all of my companions guffawed.

shriek—to utter a sharp, shrill, loud sound. When her parents first showed the young girl her new bicycle, she shrieked with delight.

snicker—to laugh in a partly suppressed and often disrespectful manner. The two political opponents frequently snickered at each other's remarks during the televised campaign debate.

titter—to laugh in a partly suppressed manner because of nervousness. The two children tittered when the famous actor approached them.

laugh it up [slang]—to act happy by use of laughter. I hope you guys will laugh it up when I tell my funny story.

be in stitches [idiom]—to laugh uncontrollably. You will be in stitches when you hear that comedian do his monologue.

ANTONYMS: cry (v), frown (v), glower (v), scowl (v)

leader (n)—someone who has commanding authority or influence. The leader of a symphony orchestra is called a conductor.

chancellor—the prime minister or other high official in some European countries. Who is the chancellor of West Germany?

commander—someone in an official position of control. The naval commander has just issued new orders.

despot—**1** a ruler having unlimited power and authority. A despot can put laws into effect without anyone else's approval. **2** one who exercises power abusively or oppressively. The despot proclaimed that nearly all private property would now belong to the government.

monarch—someone, such as a queen or king, who rules over a kingdom or empire; usually a hereditary leader. In some countries a monarch exercises only limited authority.

premier—the prime minister or other chief officer. I saw the premier of the Soviet Union on the television newscast last night.

president—the chief officer of a governmental body; the chief officer of an organization such as a corporation or an institution. The president of the company announced that profits were up ten percent from the previous year.

kingpin [informal]—the most important person. Without doubt their all-star center fielder is the kingpin of the team.

ANTONYMS: follower, subordinate (n)

lose (v)—**1** to fail to win or obtain. Do you think that the football team will lose more than four games this season? **2** to be unable to find; to fail to keep. It seems as if I always lose pens and pencils.

fail—to be unable to do or become what is attempted, expected, or desired. I have never failed to get a good grade in all of my school subjects.

fall—to come down from a higher place. Our team will fall from first place if it loses the game.

misplace—to put in a wrong place. I must have misplaced my wristwatch; I can't find it.

relinquish—to release; to give up; to stop holding physically. The governor relinquished his authority to his newly elected successor.

succumb—to give way or yield to superior strength or overpowering appeal. The dieter succumbed to temptation and devoured some extra rolls and butter with dinner.

flop [informal]—to utterly fail. The new musical play flopped after just one performance.

drop [slang]—to lose. The New York Yankees dropped last night's game to the California Angels.

ANTONYMS: find (v), gain (v), hold (v), keep, recover, retain, win (v)

M

mistake (n)—**1** a misunderstanding of the meaning of something. My mistake was in not realizing the impact that lack of sufficient rainfall can have upon a harvest. **2** a wrong action, judgment, or thought. While driving to the airport, my father made a mistake by turning off of the highway at the wrong exit.

blunder—a careless or stupid mistake. How could I commit the blunder of not putting my name on my test paper?

error—something done that is incorrect or wrong; something that is not the way it should be. I made an error by putting too much fertilizer on the lawn.

miscalculation—a mathematical error such as in addition or subtraction. When I added the column of numerals, I made a miscalculation.

misjudgment— a wrong or unjust opinion or estimate. Thinking that this class would be easy was a terrible misjudgment on my part.

misprint—an error in printing. The misspelled word on the very first page of that book is a misprint.

oversight—a failure to notice or to think of something; an error. Not checking the weather forecast before planning the picnic was an oversight on my part.

slipup [informal]—a mistake; an error. Do you think you can do what I ask without any slipups?

move (v)—**1** to change or cause to change the position or place of; to put in motion; to keep in motion. A bulldozer will move that large pile of rocks. **2** to advance or proceed; to make progress. The construction project is moving on schedule.

crawl—to move slowly by pulling the body across the ground. I saw the snake crawl behind the rock.

dash—to move with a sudden speed. The runner dashed across the finish line.

flow—to move in a current or a stream. The molten lava flowed slowly down the mountainside.

migrate—to move from one place or locality to another. Some animals migrate from mountain slopes to valleys for winter protection and food.

progress—to move forward; to go ahead; to advance. We must progress by working very hard and avoiding any unnecessary conversation.

propel—to push or drive forward or onward by means of a force. Powerful engines propel the space shuttle into orbit.

travel—to journey; to move from one place to another. We will travel to Florida during our vacation this year.

See also *walk* (v).

ANTONYMS: discontinue, halt (v), pause (v), stop (v)

N

near (adj)—not distant in time, place, or degree; close. Please remember that I will wait for you at the near entrance to the theater.

adjacent—lying close or near; neighboring; having a common border. The supermarket is adjacent to the pharmacy.

adjoining—being next to or in contact with; touching. There is a door between the two adjoining rooms in this apartment.

bordering—touching at the boundary; nearby. The bordering property is for sale.

close—having little space between; near. When in a movie theater, you should be aware of a close exit in case of fire.

immediate—close or near; near at hand. Many exotic birds can be found right in the immediate vicinity.

nearby—close by; near. The nearby mountains are about ten-thousand feet high.

neighboring—being near; bordering; adjacent. Although the neighboring town is larger in area than ours it does not have as many people.

ANTONYMS: distant, far, faraway, outlying, remote, removed

O

object (n)—**1** something that can be seen, touched, or otherwise sensed. That metal object must weigh about five pounds. **2** a person or thing toward which action, feeling, or thought is directed. The object of the geological study is the Grand Canyon.

article—a particular item or thing. This article of clothing is quite expensive.

artifact—a usually simple object made by human skill. Those pieces of pottery are artifacts of an ancient civilization.

device—something made for a particular use or special purpose; a mechanism. What is the name of the device that a plumber uses to clean out clogged pipes?

gadget—a small mechanical or electronic device. An electric pencil sharpener is a handy gadget to have around.

implement—a useful piece of equipment; a tool or utensil. A plow is, of course, an extremely important farm implement.

instrument—1 something used to do something; a tool. Surgical instruments of various kinds are utilized during an operation. 2 a device that produces musical sounds. I think that the instrument we are now listening to is an oboe.

doohickey [informal]—a gadget or thing whose name is unknown or forgotten. Hand me the doohickey that goes on this faucet.

inferior—lower in quality; below average; of little value or merit. Purchasing an inferior automobile may lead to costly repairs.

needy—poverty-stricken; not having enough necessities to live on. Some charitable organizations give food and clothing to needy people.

penniless—not having any money; extremely poor. Having lost my wallet at the airport, I found myself penniless.

underprivileged—not having many of the advantages that most people have, especially because of poor social or economic status. The underprivileged people of some nations have horrible living conditions.

broke [slang]—penniless; without money. I can't buy tickets for the game because I'm broke.

unable to make ends meet [idiom]—not having enough money. With so many bills to pay this month, I'm unable to make ends meet.

ANTONYMS: affluent (adj), moneyed, opulent, prosperous, rich (adj), superior (adj), wealthy

P

poor (adj)—1 lacking money or property; having few things or nothing at all; needy. Many poor people have very little to eat. 2 not good in quality or value; lacking something necessary. This soil is too poor for agriculture.

destitute—lacking things that are necessary such as food, clothing, and shelter. Destitute people cannot afford new clothes.

impoverished—extremely poor. The impoverished family worried from day to day about food and other necessities that many people take for granted.

R

rich (adj)—1 having an abundance of money, land, goods, or other material possessions. The rich fashion designer lives in a penthouse in New York. 2 having great value or quality; sumptuous. The rich decor increased her enjoyment in the meal she was served.

affluent—having a generous supply of material possessions; wealthy. The affluent attorney owns condominiums in Florida.

comfortable—having enough money to be content or secure. Maybe we are not wealthy, but at least we are comfortable financially.

rich *(continued)*

Thesaurus

luscious—very delicious to taste or smell; richly sweet. I savored every bite of that luscious peach dessert.

opulent—displaying wealth often to the point of showing off; luxurious. The opulent home of the millionaire impresses every visitor.

prosperous—having economic well-being; successful; thriving. The computer industry is certainly prosperous in this country.

wealthy—extremely affluent; rich. The wealthy investor just purchased bonds worth $1,000,000.

loaded [informal]—having a large amount of money. She must be loaded to have been able to buy that diamond-studded necklace.

rolling in money [idiom]—extremely well-off financially. Some professional tennis players are so rich they are rolling in money.

ANTONYMS: bankrupt (adj), destitute, impoverished (adj), needy (adj), plain (adj), poor (adj), wanting (adj)

S

say (v)—to speak, state, or express in words; to communicate. I often say things without thinking.

articulate—to speak distinctly; to express in clear and effective words. When speaking before a large group of people, a person must articulate every word so that everyone can hear what is said.

call—to say, especially with a loud voice; to shout. The coach called the players to the bench.

declare—to make known publicly or formally; to state strongly. The senator declared at the press conference that she would run for reelection.

mutter—to speak words indistinctly or with a low voice and with the lips partly closed; to murmur angrily. The child muttered something when told to stop climbing the very high fence.

utter—to give forth as a sound; to express in words; to speak. He finally uttered what was on his mind.

whisper—to speak very softly or low, especially to avoid being overheard. Kristen whispered that she knew who the culprit was.

yap [slang]—to talk or chatter idly and insistently. Some people always yap about what they do.

put into words [idiom]—to speak; to express verbally. Sometimes I cannot put into words how I feel.

See also *talk* (v).

strong (adj)—having much power or force; healthy; vigorous; able to last or endure. Only a very strong person can move that heavy piece of furniture.

energetic—full of the power to do work; eager to do work. The energetic youngster did household chores and homework immediately after school.

forceful—having much strength; powerful or vigorous. Lisa's composition made a forceful statement about the great amount of food wasted in the cafeteria.

hardy—able to withstand the cold weather of winter, or able to bear other adverse conditions. I was told that these hardy chrysanthemums can survive extremely cold winter temperatures.

muscular—of, relating to, or influencing the muscles; having well-developed muscles. Occasional muscular strains are common occurrences in athletics.

sturdy—firmly built; strong and stout. That rickety wooden bridge is not very sturdy.

tough—firm but flexible and not brittle; difficult to cut, tear, or chew. Some animals have <u>tough</u> protective hides.

vigorous—strong and active both physically and mentally; having much strength or active force. That <u>vigorous</u> couple plays three sets of tennis almost every day even though they both work.

strong as a bull [idiom]—possessing great strength or toughness. That professional football player is <u>strong as a bull</u>.

ANTONYMS: debilitated (adj), feeble, frail, listless, powerless, soft (adj), weak

T

talk (v)—to speak; to use words; to exchange words or engage in conversation. Do you think that I <u>talk</u> too much?

address—to deliver a formal speech to; to speak directly to. At the assembly our principal <u>addressed</u> all of the students.

chat—to talk in an informal and familiar way. During dinner my sister and I <u>chatted</u> about homework among other things.

debate—to discuss the reasons for and against something; to argue a topic in a public meeting. The two candidates for mayor <u>debated</u> various issues during a one-hour telecast.

report—to give an account of something seen, heard, read, done, or considered; to relate or tell. I <u>reported</u> the traffic accident I had seen to the police.

gab [informal]—to talk in a rapid and thoughtless manner; to talk too much. That person <u>gabs</u> all the time about almost anything and everything.

rap [slang]—to talk openly and frankly. My dad and I <u>rapped</u> about school all evening. See also *say* (v).

U

urgent (adj)—calling for immediate action or attention; pressing; important. The governor made an <u>urgent</u> request for financial aid for the flood victims.

acute—seriously in need of urgent attention; threatening. The <u>acute</u> housing shortage in this area must be addressed immediately.

compelling—that drives or urges with force. The <u>compelling</u> reason I have for staying home is to finish my book report on time.

critical—important or indispensable for the weathering of a time of difficulty or danger. There is a <u>critical</u> need at this time to reach all of the motorists stranded in the snow.

crucial—very important; essential for resolving a crisis. It is <u>crucial</u> that the supplies reach them no later than tonight.

pressing—requiring immediate attention; critical. There are several <u>pressing</u> deadlines I must deal with today.

See also *important* (adj).

ANTONYM: unimportant

W

walk (v)—to go on foot; to advance by steps. Tom <u>walked</u> to the house.

hike—to take a long walk, especially for pleasure or exercise. Maryann and I <u>hiked</u> in Yellowstone National Park.

lumber—to move along heavily or clumsily. The defeated team <u>lumbered</u> off the field.

walk *(continued)*

Thesaurus

pace—to walk with slow or measured steps. The worried captain <u>paced</u> the deck.

ramble—to wander about aimlessly. People <u>rambled</u> through the shopping mall all day.

stride—to walk with long steps. The guest speaker <u>strode</u> into the auditorium.

trudge—to walk wearily or with effort, but steadily and persistently. The exhausted troops <u>trudged</u> through the deep mud.

traipse [informal]—to walk about aimlessly or needlessly. That guy <u>traipses</u> all over the countryside.

See also *move* (v).

weak (adj)—not having strength; deficient in some way; lacking intensity. I was too <u>weak</u> to budge that heavy table.

faint—not clear; hardly perceptible; lacking in amount, loudness, or intensity. I barely heard a <u>faint</u> voice somewhere off in the distance.

fragile—easily broken or damaged. Be careful with those <u>fragile</u> crystal glasses.

frail—not very strong; weak; delicate. The <u>frail</u> individual had to be helped up the steps.

listless—seeming too tired to care about anything; lacking the inclination to be active. I was so <u>listless</u> from that virus that I could hardly move.

powerless—without strength or force; unable to produce an effect. The king was <u>powerless</u> in the face of so many foes.

ANTONYMS: energetic, hardy, powerful, strong (adj), sturdy, vigorous

win (v)—to gain a victory in a contest; to succeed; to get possession of by work or fortune. You cannot <u>win</u> unless you try.

accomplish—to succeed in completing; to carry to conclusion. The task was <u>accomplished</u> in two days.

achieve—to carry out successfully; to accomplish. Wendy <u>achieved</u> a school record at the track meet.

prevail—to win the victory; to gain supremacy through strength or superiority. In the end our strong defense <u>prevailed</u>.

triumph—to be victorious; to prevail. Many people are working so that medical research will <u>triumph</u> against disease.

corral [informal]—to capture or secure. Our football team <u>corralled</u> the state championship.

bring home the bacon [idiom]—to win. Let's get out on that field and <u>bring home the bacon</u>!

ANTONYMS: fail (v), fall (v), flop (v), forfeit (v), lose

write (v)—to make letters, words, or symbols on a surface with an instrument such as a pen; to be the author of. <u>Write</u> your name.

author—to write or compose. She <u>authored</u> many excellent novels.

correspond—to write letters to each other. Although my friend lives hundreds of miles away, we <u>correspond</u> often.

inscribe—to write or engrave on stone, metal, or other material. The names of the class officers were <u>inscribed</u> on the plaque.

record—to set down in writing so as to retain for future use; to register permanently. The secretary <u>recorded</u> what was said during the meeting.

scribble—to write or draw carelessly; to write illegibly. I <u>scribbled</u> these notes so quickly that I can hardly read them.

take down [idiom]—to write out what is spoken. <u>Take down</u> everything I say to you.

Index to Rules

THE PARTS OF SPEECH

1. Nouns, Pronouns, and Adjectives

1. noun, 8
2. common and proper noun, 10
3. pronoun, 14
4. antecedent of pronoun, 16
5. demonstrative and reflexive pronoun, 18
6. interrogative and indefinite pronoun, 20
7. adjective, 24
8. proper and demonstrative adjective, 26
9. words used as different parts of speech, 28

2. Verbs and Adverbs

1. verb, 36
2. verb phrase, 38
3. adverb, 42
4. facts about adverbs, 44

3. Conjunctions, Prepositions, and Interjections

1. conjunction, 52
2. preposition, 54
3. prepositional phrase as adjective, 58
4. prepositional phrase as adverb, 60
5. interjection, 64

SENTENCE STRUCTURE

4. The Sentence

1. sentence, 76
2. declarative, interrogative, imperative, and exclamatory sentences, 78
3. complete and simple subject, 80
4. complete and simple predicate, 82
5. subject and verb identification, 84
6. compound subject and verb, 86
7. direct object, 90
8. predicate nominative and predicate adjective, 92
9. indirect object, 96
10. verbal and participle, 98
    gerund, 100
    infinitive, 102

5. Simple, Compound, and Complex Sentences

1. simple sentence and compound sentence, 110
2. clause, 112
3. complex sentence, 114
4. run-on sentence and sentence fragment, 116

USAGE

6. Noun and Pronoun Usage

1. singular and plural noun, 136

2. nouns with special plural forms, 138
3. possessive noun, 140
4. pronoun case, 144
5. pronoun errors, 146
6. pronoun errors, 148
7. using interrogative, indefinite, and reflexive pronouns, 150

7. Adjective and Adverb Usage

1. degrees of adjectives, 158
2. using the comparative and superlative degree, 160
3. degrees of adverbs, 162
4. double negative, 164
5. using adjectives and adverbs correctly, 166
6. using *good, well, real, really, sure, surely, most,* and *almost,* 168

8. Verb Usage

1. principal parts of verbs, 176
2. tenses of verbs, 178
3. forms of *be, have,* and *do,* 182
4. irregular verbs, 186
5. using *leave, let, sit,* and *set,* 192
6. using *rise, raise, lie,* and *lay,* 194

9. Subject-Verb Agreement

1. spelling singular verbs, 200
2. using *be, have,* and *do,* 202
3. prepositional phrase between subject and verb, 204
4. agreement with compound subjects, 206
5. subject following verb, 208
6. indefinite pronoun as subject, 210

MECHANICS

10. Capitalization

1. names and titles, 224
2. geographical names, 226
3. other names, 228
4. first words and certain parts of speech, 230
5. titles of works, 232
6. writing numbers, 234

11. Punctuation

1. end marks, 242
2. commas to separate items in a series and to separate independent clauses in a compound sentence, 244
3. commas with appositives and nouns of direct address, 246
4. commas after introductory

words and to set off interrupters, 248
5. commas with dates and
addresses, 250
6. quotation marks, 252
7. divided quotations, 254
8. italics and underlining, 256
9. semicolons and colons, 258
10. apostrophes, 260

THE BASICS OF WRITING

12. Sentence Combining and
Revising

1. combining compound subjects and verbs, 276
2. combining compound sentences, 278
3. expanding sentences, 280
4. combining complex sen-
tences, 282
5. revising windy sentences,
284
6. revising choppy sentences,
286

13. Purpose and Audience in
Writing

1. identifying purpose, 292
2. identifying an audience,
294
3. writing for different
audiences, 296
4. choosing a form, 298

14. Organizing Ideas into
Paragraphs

1. paragraph basics, 306
2. selecting and narrowing a
topic, 308
3. main idea and topic sentence, 310
4. development by examples,
312
5. development by facts, 314
6. development by reasons,
316
7. paragraph unity, 318
8. order of ideas, 320
9. using transitions, 324

15. The Writing Process

1. comparing the processes of
artists and writers, 330
2. the writing process, 336

WRITING

16. Informing and Describing

1. parts of a newspaper, 348
2. fact and opinion, 350
3. interviewing, 352
4. a news story, 354
5. sensory details, 358
6. similes and metaphors, 360
7. descriptive paragraphs, 362
8. a character sketch, 364

Index to Rules

17. Narrating and Creating

1. first-person point of view, 372
2. dialogue, 374
3. a personal experience narrative, 376
4. third-person point of view, 380
5. short story elements, 382
6. a mystery story, 386

18. Researching and Persuading

1. surveys, 394
2. survey questions, 396
3. a survey summary, 398
4. friendly letters, 402
5. social notes, 404
6. business letters, 406
7. preparing letters for mailing, 408
8. a letter of opinion, 410

19. Classifying and Reasoning

1. mass media, 418
2. classifying information, 420
3. a media review, 422
4. cause and effect, 426
5. interpreting data, 428
6. comparison/contrast paragraphs, 430
7. a consumer report, 432

20. Literature

1. plays, 440
2. myths, 446
3. poetry, 450

SPEAKING AND LISTENING

21. Speaking

1. introductions, 458
2. conversations, 460
3. class discussions, 462
4. telephoning, 464
5. giving information, 466
6. voice and speech techniques, 468
7. giving a talk, 470

22. Listening

1. how to listen, 478
2. listening to learn, 480
3. critical listening, 486

STUDY SKILLS

23. Library and Reporting Skills

1. the library, 492
2. reference books, 496
3. taking notes, 500
4. paraphrasing, 502
5. outlining, 504
6. report structure, 506
7. book reports, 508

Index to Rules

24. Vocabulary and Word Study

1. vocabulary study, 512
2. history of English, 514
3. using a dictionary, 518
4. using a dictionary as a writing aid, 520
5. prefixes and suffixes, 522
6. denotation and con-
   notation, 524
7. context clues, 526

25. Reviewing and Taking Tests

1. taking class notes, 532
2. reviewing for tests, 534
3. taking tests, 536
4. verbal analogies, 538

Contributors to the Teacher's Edition: James J. Alvino, gifted notes; Nancy S. Bley, learning disabled notes; Claudia Campbell, translation of Parent Letters into Spanish; Contemporary Perspectives, Inc., marginal notes, Reinforcement Masters, and Practice Masters; Rita M. Deyoe-Chiullán, English as a Second Language notes; National Evaluation Systems, Inc.,tests; Arthur Roth, Reinforcement and Practice marginal activities; Rita Steinglass, language games.

SCHOOL ADVISORY PANEL

CLASSROOM TEACHERS

Levels 7 and 8
Peggy Allen, Mundy's Mill Junior High, Jonesboro, Georgia; Nancy Collins, St. Thomas More School, Baton Rouge, Louisiana; Grace Crispinelli, Alexander Hamilton High School, Elmsford, New York; Joan Devine, Blessed Sacrament School, Washington, D.C.; Marilyn Lewis, San Juan School District, Carmichael, California; Brenda Nuara, Swift Creek Middle School, Midlothian, Virginia; Judith Nuechterlein, Rittmuller Middle School, Frankenmuth, Michigan; Julie Snyder, East Hills Junior High School, Bloomfield Hills, Michigan

SPECIAL CONSULTANTS

Betty Gould, Patchogue, New York; Barbara Todd, Los Angeles, California
Teacher Focus Group, New Jersey Public and Parochial Schools: Marie Antieri, Phyllis Mordente Farese, Constance B. Fenner, Maureen Fulop, Carole Guild, Linda Larner, Eileen C. Molloy, Annette Rauscher, Eileen St. André, Barbara M. Silvernale, Barbara Verian
Thesaurus Lessons Consultant: Rosemary Cooke, Southern Boulevard School, Chatham Township, New Jersey

Index

Abbreviations
  capitalization of, 224–225
  period after, 242–243
Action verbs, 36–37, 40–41, 48, 49, 70
Addresses
  in business letters, 406–407
  commas in, 250–251, 262, 265
  on envelopes, 408–409
  in friendly letters, 402–403
Adjective phrases, 58–59, 67, 70, 71
Adjectives
  articles, 24–25, 33, 70
  comparative, 158–159, 160–161, 170–171,
    172, 173, 217
  definition of, 3, 24
  degrees of comparison, 158
  demonstrative, 26–27, 30, 33
  infinitives as, 102–103
  nouns used as, 28–29, 33
  participles as, 98–99
  predicate, 92–93, 94–95, 107, 123, 125
  prepositional phrases as, 58–59, 67,
    70, 71
  pronouns used as, 28–29, 33
  proper, 26–27, 30, 33, 71
    capitalization of, 230–231
  review of, 32–33, 172–173
  superlative, 158–159, 160–161, 170, 171,
    172, 173, 217
  usage, 158–169, 173, 217, 218, 219
  writing with, 31
Adverb phrases, 60–61, 67, 70, 71
Adverbs, 42–43, 44–45, 46–47, 48, 49, 62
  comparative, 162–163, 170, 171, 172
  definition of, 3, 42
  degrees of comparison, 162
  infinitives as, 102–103
  with -ly, 44
  prepositional phrases as, 60–61, 67,
    70, 71
  review of, 48-49
  superlative, 162–163, 170, 171, 172,
    173, 217
  usage, 158–169, 170–173, 217–219
  writing with, 47

Agreement
  with compound subjects, 206–207
  with indefinite pronouns, 210–211
  in inverted sentences, 208–209
  subject-verb, 200–201, 202–203,
    204–205, 206–207, 208–209, 210–211,
    212, 214, 215, 218
  editing for, 401
Alliteration, 450–453
Almanac, 497
Almost, most, 168–169, 170, 171, 172
Among, between, 132–133
Analogies, 538–539
Announcements, 466–467
Antecedents, of pronouns, 16–17, 23,
  32, 70
Apostrophes
  in contractions, 128, 260–261, 264
  to form plurals of letters or
    numerals used as nouns, 138–139
  in possessive nouns, 140–141, 260–261,
    264, 265
Appositives, 246–247
**Armour, Richard, "Good
  Sportsmanship,"** 108
Article, definite, 24–25, 33, 70
Articles, indefinite, 24–25, 33, 70
At, to, 132–133
Atlas, 497
Audience, writing for an
  changing tone and voice for, 296–297
  choosing appropriate form for, 298–299,
    300, 301, 302
  identifying and analyzing, 294–295, 301,
    302

**Baruch, Dorothy W., "A Horse Is a
  Horse,"** 34
Be
  agreement with subject, 202–203
  conjugation of, 183
  as helping verb, 182–183
  as linking verb, 92–93, 196
  as main verb, 182–185

Beside, besides, 132–133
Between, among, 132–133
Bibliography, 506–507
Book reports, 508–509
Books ˆ
  parts of, xv-xvi
  reference, 496–499
  titles of
    capitalization, 232–233, 236
    underlining, 256–257
Brainstorming, 337, 399
Building Bridges
  to computers, 368
  to mathematics, 414
  to science, 436
  to social studies, 390
Business letters, 406–407

Capitalization
  abbreviations, 224–225
  in direct quotations, 230–231, 236
  first word of sentence, 76, 78, 118,
    230–231
  geographical names, 226–227, 236
  names, 224–225, 236
  in poetry, 230–231, 236
  proper adjectives, 230–231
  proper nouns, 224–225, 226–227,
    228–229, 236, 238–239
  religious terms, 232–233
  review of, 238–239, 266–267
  in salutations and closings, 230–231
  titles for people, 224–225, 236
  titles of written works, movies, works of
    art, 232–233, 236
Card catalog, 492–495
Cause and effect, 426–427
Character, in story, 382–385
Character sketch, 364–367
Charts and graphs, 428–429
Checklists
  A Paragraph Checklist, 323
  Writer's Checklist, 340
Classifying, 420–421
Clauses
  definition of, 112
  distinguishing from phrases, 112–113,
    120
  independent, 112–113, 121, 124, 125
  subordinate, 112–113, 121, 124, 125
Clichés, 360
Clincher sentence, of paragraph, 306–307

Collective nouns, 10-11, 33, 71
Colons, 258–259
Commas
  in addresses, 250–251, 262, 265
  in compound sentences, 110–111,
    244–245, 262, 264, 265
  in dates, 250–251, 262, 264, 265
  after interjections, 64–65
  after introductory words, 248–249, 262,
    264, 265
  with letter parts, 250–251, 265
  in quotations, 252–253
  in series, 244–245, 262, 264, 265
  to set off appositives, 246–247, 262,
    264, 265
  to set off interrupters, 248–249, 262,
    264, 265
  to set off nouns of direct address,
    246–247, 262, 264
Common nouns, 10–11, 12, 32, 70
Comparison
  of adjectives, 158-159, 160–161, 170–171,
    172, 173, 217
  of adverbs, 162–163, 170–171, 172, 173,
    217
Comparison and contrast, 430–431
Comparisons
  metaphors, 360–361
  similes, 360–361
Complex sentences, 114–115, 119,
    120, 121, 125
  combining, 282–283
  using in writing, 119
Composition. *See* Writing.
Compound predicate. *See* Compound
  verb.
Compound sentences, 110–111, 120,
    121, 125
  combining, 278–279
Compound verbs, 86–87, 107, 121, 125
Compounds, 138–139
Conjugation, 179
Conjunctions
  in compound sentences, 110–111
  coordinating, 52–53, 62, 66, 67, 70
  correlative, 52–53, 66, 67, 70
  definition of, 3, 52
  review of, 66–67, 70
  subordinating, 114–115, 121
  using in writing, 63
Connotation, 524–525
Consumer report, 432–435
Content areas, language in. *See* Building
  Bridges.

Context clues
listening for, 483–484
using, 526, 529
Contractions, 130–131, 260–261
definition of, 128
Contrast. *See* Comparison and contrast.
Conversations, 460–461
Coordinating conjunctions, 52–53, 62, 67, 70
Copyright page, of a book, xv-xvi
Correlative conjunctions, 52–53, 66, 67, 70

Dates, commas in, 250–251, 262, 264, 265
Declarative sentences, 78–79
Definite article, 24–25, 33, 70
Demonstrative adjectives, 26–27, 30, 33
Demonstrative pronouns, 18–19, 22
Denotation, 524–525
Descriptive paragraph, 362–363
Details
in descriptive paragraphs, 362–363
listening for, 482–483
sensory, 358–359
specific nouns, 13
supporting sentences, 306–307, 310–311
Dewey decimal system 494–495
Diagraming, 546–554
Dialogue
in plays, 440–445
punctuation of, 254–255
writing, 374–375
Dictionary
parts of, 518–519
as writing aid, 520–521
Different from, 132–133
Direct object, 90–91, 106, 107, 123, 125
Directions
giving, 466–467
listening to, 484–485
Discussions, 462–463
Do, 182–185
agreement with subject, 202–203
conjugation of, 183
Double negatives, 164–165, 173
Drawing conclusions, 428–429

Editing. *See* Writing process.
Encyclopedias, 496–497
End marks, 78–79, 106, 118, 242–243, 264, 265

Entry words, 518–519
Envelope, addressing, 408–409
Exclamation marks
as end marks, 78–79, 242–243
after interjections, 64–65
Exclamatory sentences, 78–79

Fact and opinion, 350–351
Figures of speech, 360–361
Fisher, Aileen, "Comma in the Sky," 240
Fisher, Aileen, "Winter Circus," 50
Form for writing, 298–302
Francis, Robert, "Skier," 198
Friendly letters, 402–403
Future perfect tense. *See* Verbs.
Future tense. *See* Verbs.

Gerunds, 100–101, 104, 106, 107, 124, 125
Good, well, 168–169, 170, 171, 172
Graphs and tables, 414, 428–429
Guide words, 518–519

Handwriting, 403
Have, 182–185
agreement with subject, 202–203
conjugation of, 183
Helping verbs, 38–39, 40, 49, 70
Homographs, 518
Homophones, 127, 128–129

Imperative sentences, 78–79
subject of, 84–85
In, into, 132–133
Indefinite articles, 24–25, 33, 70
Indefinite pronouns, 20–21, 22, 33, 70, 150–151
agreement with verb, 210–211
Indenting, 306–307
Independent clauses, 112–113, 121, 124, 125
Index, of a book, xv-xvi
Indirect objects, 96–97, 107, 123, 125
Infinitives, 102–103, 104, 106, 107, 124, 125
Interjections, 64–65, 66, 71
definition of, 3, 64
Interrogative pronouns, 20–21, 22, 33, 70, 150–151
Interrogative sentences, 78–79

Interviewing, 352–353
Intransitive verbs, 93, 95
Introductions, making and responding to, 458–459
Inverted sentences, 208–209
Invitations, 404–405
Italics, uses of, 256–257
Its, it's, 130–131

Jackson, Kathryn and Byron, "Open Range," 6

Kingsley, Sidney, *scene from* "The Patriots," 440–445

Larkin, Philip, "The North Ship," 452
Lay, lie, 194–195, 196, 218
Leave, let, 192–193, 196
Letters
  addressing envelopes, 408–409
  business, 406–407
  friendly, 402–403
  of opinion, 410–413
  social notes, 404–405
Library, 492–495
Lie, lay, 194–195, 196, 218
Life skills
  job application, 263
  telephone communication, 464–465
  writing a check, 237
Linking verbs, 92–93, 95, 107
Listening
  class discussion, 462–463
  for context clues, 483–484
  critical, 486–487
  for details, 482
  to directions, 484–485
  interviewing, 352–353
  for main idea, 481–482
  manners and techniques, 478–479
  memory techniques, 480–481
  preview of, 454–455
  responding to introductions, 459
  taking notes, 483
  telephone, 464–465
Literature. *See* Myths; Plays; Poems.

Main idea
  listening for, 481–482
  of paragraph, 307–308, 310–311
Main verbs, 38–39, 40, 49, 70

Mass media
  reviewing, 422–425
  viewing television critically, 487
Mechanics
  preview of, 220–221
  See also Capitalization; Punctuation.
Media review, 422–425
Memory techniques, 480–481
Merriam, Eve, "Exploring," 222
Merriam, Eve, "I Am Looking for a Book," 438
Most, almost, 168–169, 170, 171, 172
Mystery story, 386–389
Myths, 446–449

Narrative paragraph, 372–373, 380–381
Nash, Ogden, "The Centipede," 451, "The Guppy," 134
Negative words, 164–165, 173
News story, 354–357
Newspaper, parts of, 348–349
Nominative case, 144–145, 152, 154, 155
Notebook, organizing a, 532–533
Note-taking
  as an aid to listening, 483
  in class, 532–533
  for a report, 500–501
Nouns
  collective, 10–11, 33, 71
  common, 10–11, 12, 32, 70
  compound, 138–139
  definition of, 3, 8
  of direct address, 246–247
  gerunds, 100–101, 104, 106, 107, 124, 125
  infinitives as, 102–103, 104, 106, 107, 124, 125
  letters and numerals as, 138–139
  plural, 8–9, 136–137, 138–139, 142, 154, 155, 216
  possessive, 140–141, 142, 154, 155, 216
    apostrophes in, 140–141, 260–261, 264, 265
  proper, 10–11, 12, 33, 70, 71, 224–225, 226–227, 228–229
    capitalization of, 224–225, 226–227, 228–229, 236, 238–239
  review of, 32–33, 154–155
  singular, 8–9, 136–137, 138, 139, 155, 216
  spelling of, 136–137, 216
  usage, 136–141, 216, 219
  using as adjectives, 28–29, 33
  using in writing, 13, 143

Numbers, writing, 234–235

Object
  direct, 90–91, 106, 107, 123, 125
  indirect, 96–97, 107, 123, 125
  of preposition, 54–55, 67, 70, 71, 123
Object pronouns, 144–145
Objective case, 144–145, 152, 154, 155
Onomatopoeia, 450–453
Opinion. See Fact and opinion.
Oral language. See Speaking.
Organizational patterns for paragraphs
  climactic order, 322
  order of importance, 320–321
  space order, 320–321
  time order, 320–321
Outlining, 504–505

Paragraphs
  checklist, 323
  clincher sentence, 306–307
  comparison/contrast, 430–431
  definition of, 306
  descriptive, 362–363
  developing
    by examples, 312–313
    by facts, 314–315
    by reasons, 316–317
  explanatory, 312–313
  indenting, 306–307
  main idea, 306–307, 310–311
  narrative, 372–373, 380–381
  order of ideas, 320–322
  persuasive, 316–317
  review of, 326
  selecting and narrowing a topic
    for, 308–309
  summary, 503
  supporting sentences, 306–307
  topic sentence, 306–307, 310–311
  transitions, 324–325
  unity, 318–319
Paraphrasing 502–503
Parenthetical expressions, 248–249
Participles, 98–99, 104, 105, 106, 107, 124, 125
Parts of a book, xv-xvi
Parts of speech, 2–3, 68–69
  review of, 68–69
  same words as different parts, 28–29, 69
Past participle, 98–99, 104, 106

Past perfect tense. See Verbs.
Past tense. See Verbs.
Periodicals, 498–499
Periods
  after abbreviations and initials, 242-243
  ending sentences, 78–79, 242–243
Personal experience narrative, 376–379
Personal pronouns, 14–15, 22, 32, 33, 71
Persuasive paragraph, 316–317
Photo essay, "The Writing Process," 330–335
Phrases
  adjective, 58–59, 67, 70, 71
  adverb, 60–61, 67, 70, 71
  definition of, 112
  distinguishing from clauses, 112–113, 120
  prepositional, 54–55, 56–57, 58–59, 60–61, 66, 67, 70, 71, 121
  transitional, 324–325
  verb, 38–39, 40–41, 48, 49
Play, scene from "The Patriots," by Sidney Kingsley, 440–445
Plays, elements of, 440–445
Plot, 382–385
Poems
  "A Horse is a Horse" by Dorothy W. Baruch, 34
  "Comma in the Sky" by Aileen Fisher, 240
  "Exploring" by Eve Merriam, 222
  from "The Oak" by Alfred, Lord Tennyson, 450
  "Good Sportsmanship" by Richard Armour, 108
  "Hard Questions" by Margaret Tsuda, 74
  "I Am Looking for a Book" by Eve Merriam, 438
  "Measure Me, Sky" by Leonora Speyer, 174
  "Open Range" by Kathryn and Byron Jackson, 6
  "Public Library" by Robert Froman, 490
  "Skier" by Robert Francis, 198
  "The Centipede" by Ogden Nash, 451
  "The Guppy" by Ogden Nash, 134
  "The North Ship" by Philip Larkin, 452
  "The Wolf Cry" by Lew Sarett, 451
  "Velvet Shoes" by Elinor Wylie, 156
  "Winter Circus" by Aileen Fisher, 50
Poetry
  elements of, 450–453
  form, 451–453
Point of view, in narrative, 372–373, 380–381

Poll. *See* Survey.
Possessive nouns, 140–141, 142, 154, 155, 216
  apostrophes in, 140–141, 260–261, 264, 265
Possessive pronouns, 14–15, 33, 70, 130–131
Predicate
  complete, 82–83
  compound, 86–87, 107, 121, 125
  simple, 82–83, 88, 95, 106, 123
Predicate adjectives, 92–93, 94–95, 107, 123, 125
Predicate nominatives, 92–93, 94–95, 106, 107, 123
Prefixes
  de-, 522–523
  mis-, 522–523
  pre-, 522–523
  re-, 522–523
  un-, 522–523
Prepositional phrases
  adjective phrases, 58–59, 67, 70, 71
  adverb phrases, 60–61, 67, 70, 71
  definition of, 54
  example of, 55
  identifying, 54–55, 56–57, 66, 121
Prepositions
  definition of, 3, 54
  identifying, 54–55, 56, 62, 66, 121
  object of, 54–55, 67, 70, 71, 123
  in prepositional phrases, 54–55, 56–57, 58–59, 60–61, 66–67, 70, 71, 121
  review of, 66–67
  usage, 132–133
  using in writing, 63
Present participle, 98–99, 104, 106, 125
Present perfect tense. *See* Verbs.
Present tense. *See* Verbs.
Prewriting. *See* Writing process.
Pronouns
  antecedents of, 16–17, 23, 32, 70
  definition of, 3, 14
  demonstrative, 18–19, 22
  indefinite, 20–21, 22, 33, 70, 150–151, 210–211
  interrogative, 20–21, 22, 33, 70, 150–151
  nominative case, 144–145, 152, 154, 155
  object, 144–145
  objective case, 144–145, 152, 154, 155
  personal, 14–15, 22, 32, 33, 71
  possessive, 14–15, 33, 70, 130–131
  reflexive, 18–19, 22, 70, 150–151
  subject, 144–145

  usage, 144–145, 146–147, 148–149, 150–151, 152
  used as adjectives, 28–29, 33
  using in writing, 23, 153
Proofreading. *See* Writing process.
Proper adjectives, 26–27, 30, 33, 71
  capitalization of, 230–231
Proper nouns, 10–11, 12, 33, 70, 71
  capitalization of, 224–225, 226–227, 228–229, 236, 238–239
  geographical names, 226–227
  names, 224–225
  religious terms, 232–233
  titles for people, 224–225, 236
  titles of written works, movies, works of art, 232–233, 236
Publishing. *See* Writing process.
Punctuation
  apostrophes, 128, 138–139, 140–141, 260–261, 264–265
  in business letters, 406–407
  colons, 258–259
  commas, 64–65, 110–111, 244–245, 246–247, 248–249, 250–251, 252–253, 262, 264, 265
  end marks, 78–79, 106, 118, 242–243, 264, 265
  exclamation marks, 64–65, 78–79, 242–243
  in friendly letters, 402–403
  italics, 256–257
  question marks, 78–79, 242–243
  quotation marks, 252–253, 254–255, 262, 264, 265
  review of, 264–265, 267, 268–269
  semicolons, 110, 258–259
  underlining, 256–257
Purpose for writing
  choosing appropriate form for, 298–300, 301, 302
  identifying, 292–293, 301, 302

Question marks, 78–79, 242–243
Questions. *See* Interrogative sentences.
Quotation marks
  direct quotation, 252–253, 254–255, 262, 264
  with titles, 252–253, 262, 264, 265
Quotations
  dialogue, 254–255
  direct, 252–253

divided, 254–255
punctuation of, 252–253, 254–255, 262, 264

Raise, rise, 194–195, 196, 218
Readers' Guide to Periodical Literature, 498–499
Real, really, 168–169, 170, 171, 172
Reasoning. *See* Thinking skills.
Reference books, 496–499
Reflexive pronouns, 18–19, 22, 70, 150–151
Reports
book, 508–509
consumer, 432–435
structure of, 506–507
Reviewing for tests, 534–535
Revising
compositions. *See* Writing Process.
sentences. *See* Sentences.
Revising Checklists. *See* Checklists.
Rhyme, 450–453
Rhythm, 450–453
Rise, raise, 194–195, 196, 218
Run-on sentences, 116–117, 120, 124

Sarett, Lew, "The Wolf Cry," 451
Semicolons, 110, 258–259
Sensory details, 358–359
Sentence
agreement of subject and verb, 200–201, 202–203, 204–205, 206–207, 208–209, 210–211, 212, 214, 215, 218
capitalization of, 76, 78, 118, 230–231
clincher, 306–307
combining, 276–277, 278–279, 282–283, 288
complex, 114–115, 119, 120, 121, 125, 282–283
compound, 110–111, 120, 121, 125, 278–279
declarative, 78–79
definition of, 76
end punctuation, 78–79, 106, 118, 242–243, 264, 265
exclamatory, 78–79
expanding with modifiers and prepositional phrases, 280–281
fragments, 116–117, 118, 120, 124
identifying, 76–77
imperative, 78–79
subject of, 84–85
interrogative, 78–79
inverted, 208–209

kinds of, 78–79, 89, 106, 122, 124, 125
parts of, 72–73
predicate, 76–77
complete, 82–83
compound, 86–87, 107, 121, 125
simple, 82–83, 88, 95, 106, 123
revising, 284–285, 286–287
run-on, 116–117, 120, 124
simple, 110–111, 120, 121
structure, 72–73
subject
agreement with verb, 206–207
complete, 80–81
compound, 86–87, 107, 121, 125
simple, 80–81, 88, 95, 106, 123
supporting, 306–307
topic, 306–307, 310–311
word order in, 84–85, 124
writing with four kinds of, 89
Sentence fragments, 116–117, 118, 120, 124
Set, sit, 192–193, 196, 218
Setting, 382–385
Short story, elements of, 382–385
Similes, 360–361
Simple sentences, 110–111, 120, 121
Sit, set, 192–193, 196, 218
Social notes
invitations, 404–405
thank-you notes, 404–405
Space order in paragraphs, 320–321
Speaking
class discussions, 462–463
conversations, 460–461
giving a talk, 470–475
giving directions, 466–467
interviewing, 352–353
making announcements, 466–467
making introductions, 458–459
preview of, 454–455
telephone, 464–465
voice and speech techniques, 468–469
Spelling, 540–545
homographs, 518
plural nouns, 136–137, 216
verbs, 176–177, 200–201
Speyer, Leonora, "Measure Me, Sky," 174
State-of-being verbs, 36–37, 40, 48, 49, 70
Story
mystery, 386–389
short, 382–385

587

Study skills
book reports, 508–509
outlining, 504–505
paraphrasing, 502–503
parts of a book, xv–xvi
parts of a newspaper, 348–349
preview of, 488–489
reference books, 496–499
report structure, 506–507
reviewing for tests, 534–535
selecting and narrowing topics, 308–309
taking notes
for a report, 500–501
in class, 532–533
taking tests, 536–537
using a dictionary, 518–521
using the library, 492–495
using a thesaurus, 4–5
vocabulary, 514–517, 522–523, 524–525, 526–529
Subject pronouns, 144–145
Subjects
agreement with verbs, 200–201, 202–203, 204–205, 206–207, 208–209, 210–211, 212, 214, 215, 218, 401
complete, 80–81
compound, 86–87, 107, 121, 125, 206–207
of imperative sentences, 84–85
simple, 80–81, 88, 95, 106, 123
using in writing, 213
Subject-verb agreement, 200–201, 202–203, 204–205, 206–207, 208–209, 210–211, 212, 214, 215, 218
with compound subjects, 206–207
editing for, 401
with indefinite pronouns, 210–211
in inverted sentences, 208–209
Subordinate clauses, 112–113, 121, 124, 125
Subordinating conjunctions, 114–115, 121
Suffixes
-*able,* 522–523
-*ion,* 522–523
-*ize,* 522–523
-*ly,* 44–45
-*or,* 522–523
-*ous,* 522–523
Summarizing, 398–401, 415, 502–503

Supporting sentences, 306–307
Sure, surely, 168–169, 170, 172
Survey
taking a, 394–395
writing questions for, 396–397
writing summary of, 398–401, 415

Table of contents, of a book, xv–xvi
Tables and graphs, 414, 428–429
Taking notes
as aid to listening, 483
in class, 532–533
for a report, 500–501
Telephoning, 464–465
Television, critical viewing, 487
Tennyson, Alfred, Lord, *from* "The Oak," 450
Tense. *See* Verbs.
Tests
reviewing for, 534–535
taking, 536–537
Thank-you notes, 404–405
Their, there, they're, 128–129
Thesaurus, 555–574
using, 4–5, 13, 23, 31, 41, 47, 63, 89, 105, 119, 171
Thinking skills
analogies, 538–539
cause and effect, 426–427
classifying information, 420–421
comparison and contrast, 430–431
critical listening, 486–487
drawing conclusions, 426–427
fact and opinion, 350–351
Time order, in paragraphs, 320–321
Title page of a book, xv–xvi
Titles
abbreviation of, 224–225
capitalization of, 224–225, 232–233, 236
with italics, 256–257
for people, 224–225, 236
with quotation marks, 252–253, 262, 264, 265
underlining, 256–257
To, at, 132–133
To, too, two, 128–129
Topic, selecting and narrowing, 308–309

Topic sentence, 306–307, 310–311
Transitional words and phrases, 324–325
Transitive verbs, 93, 95
Tsuda, Margaret, "Hard Questions," 74

Underlining titles, 256–257
Unity, 318–319
Usage
  adjectives, 156–157, 158–159, 160–161,
    166–167, 168–169
  comparison of, 158–159, 160–161
  adverbs, 162–163, 164–165, 166–167,
    168–169
  comparison of, 162–163
  at, to, 132–133
  be, 182–185, 202–203
  beside, besides, 132–133
  between, among, 132–133
  different from, 132–133
  do, 182–185, 202–203
  double negatives, 164–165, 173
  good, well, 168–169, 170, 171, 172
  have, 182–185, 202–203
  homophones, 127, 128–129
  in, into, 132–133
  its, it's, 130–131
  leave, let, 192–193
  lie, lay, 194–195, 196, 218
  most, almost, 168–169, 170, 171, 172
  nouns
    possessive, 140–141, 142
    singular and plural, 136–137, 138–139,
      142
    special plural forms, 138–139
  prepositions, 132–133
  preview of, 126–127
  pronouns
    avoiding errors, 150–151
    cases of, 146–147
    choosing correct, 146–147
    indefinite, rules for, 150–151
    interrogative, rules for, 150–151
    reflexive, rules for, 150–151
  real, really, 168–169, 170, 171, 172
  rise, raise, 194–195, 196, 218
  review of, 154–155, 172–173, 196–197,
    214–215, 216–219

set, sit, 192–193, 196, 218
subject-verb agreement, 200–201,
  202–203, 204–205, 206–207,
  208–209, 210–211, 212, 214, 215, 218
  with compound subjects, 206–207
  with indefinite pronouns, 210–211
  in inverted sentences, 208–209
sure, surely, 168–169, 170, 172
their, there, they're, 128–129
to, too, two, 128–129
verbs
  irregular, 186–189
    See also Verbs.
  principal parts, 176–177
  tenses, 178–179, 180, 181, 197
who, whom, 150–151
whose, who's, 130–131
your, you're, 130–131

Verb phrase, 38–39, 40–41, 48, 49
Verbals
  definition of, 98–99
  gerunds, 100–101, 104, 106, 107, 124, 125
  infinitives, 102–103, 104, 106, 107, 124,
    125
  kinds of, 98
  participles
    as adjectives, 98–99, 107, 124
    as main verbs, 98
    past, 98–99, 104, 106
    present, 98–99, 104, 106, 125
Verbs
  action, 36–37, 40–41, 48, 49, 70
  agreement with subject, 200–201,
    202–203, 204–205, 206–207,
    208–209, 210–211, 212, 214, 215, 218
  be, 182–185, 202–203
  compound, 86–87, 107, 121, 125
  conjugation, 179
  definition of, 3, 36
  direct object of, 90–91, 106, 107, 123, 125
  do, 182–185, 202–203
  future perfect tense, 178–179
  future tense, 178–179
  have, 182–185, 202–203
  helping, 38–39, 40, 49, 70

indirect object of, 96–97, 107, 123, 125
infinitive, 102–103
intransitive, 93, 95
invisible action, 36–37, 40–41, 48, 49, 70
irregular, 176–177, 188–189, 190–191, 196
  become, 186–189
  begin, 186–189
  bite, 186–189
  blow, 186–189
  catch, 186–189
  draw, 186–189
  drink, 186–189
  drive, 186–189
  eat, 186–189
  fall, 186–189
  fly, 186–189
  get, 186–189
  give, 186–189
  go, 186–189
  grow, 186–189
  know, 186–189
  ride, 186–189
  ring, 186–189
  say, 186–189
  see, 186–189
  shake, 186–189
  sing, 186–189
  sink, 186–189
  steal, 186–189
  swim, 186–189
  take, 186–189
  teach, 186–189
  think, 186–189
  throw, 186–189
  wear, 186–189
  write, 186–189
linking, 92–93, 95, 107
main, 38–39, 40, 49, 70
past participles, 98–99, 176–177
past perfect tense, 178–179
past tense, 178–179
present participles, 98–99, 176–177
present perfect tense, 178–179
present tense, 178–179
principal parts of, 176–177
review of, 48–49, 196–197
as simple predicates, 82–83, 88, 95, 106, 123

spelling of, 176–177, 200–201
state-of-being, 36–37, 40, 48, 49, 70
tenses, 178–179, 180–181, 197
transitive, 93, 95
used as different parts of speech. *See*
  Verbals.
using in writing, 41, 191, 213
visible action, 36–37, 40–41, 48, 49, 70
Vocabulary
connotation, 524–525
definition of, 512
denotation, 524–525
history of English, 514–517
how to study, 512–513
prefixes, 522–523
suffixes, 522–523
using context clues, 526–529

Well, good, 168–169, 170, 171, 172
Who, whom, 150–151
Whose, who's, 130–131
Word order in sentences, 84–85, 124
Writers at Work
Carnegie, Andrew, 327
Carson, Rachel, 343
Sears, Richard, 303
Wilder, Laura Ingalls, 289
Writer's Checklist, 340
Writing
audience for, 294–295, 296–297,
  298–299, 300, 301, 302
basics of, 270–271
basics preview, 272–273
book reports, 508–509
business letters, 406–407
character sketch, 364–367
choosing form for, 298–299, 300, 301,
  302
comparison/contrast paragraph,
  430–431
consumer report, 432–435
descriptive paragraph, 362–363, 369
dialogue, 374–375
editing. *See* Writing process.
explanatory paragraph, 312–313
fact paragraph, 314–315
friendly letters, 402–403

590

invitations, 404–405
letter of opinion, 410–413
media review, 422–425
mystery story, 386–389
narrative paragraph, 372–373, 380–381
news story, 354–357
paragraphs
  checklist, 323
  comparison/contrast, 430–431
  descriptive, 362–363, 369
  explanatory, 312–313 '
  fact, 314–315
  narrative, 372–373
  organizational patterns, 320–322
  persuasive, 316–317
  unity, 318–319
persuasive paragraph, 316–317
preview of, 344–345
prewriting. *See* Writing process.
proofreading. *See* Writing process.
publishing. *See* Writing process.
report, 506–507
revising. *See* Writing process.

sentences, 276–277, 278–279, 280–281,
  282–283, 288
  revising, 284–285, 286–287
social notes, 404–405
survey summary, 398–401, 415
thank-you notes, 404–405
tone and voice, 296–297
Writing process
  checklist, 340
  editing, 338, 342, 389, 401
  photo essay, 330–335
  prewriting, 330–331, 336–337, 386–387
    methods of, 336–337, 398–399
  proofreading, 334, 339, 389, 401
  publishing, 335, 339, 389, 401
  revising, 333–334, 338, 388–389,
    400–401
  stages of, 336–339
  writing. *See* Writing.
Wylie, Elinor, "Velvet Shoes," 156

You **(understood),** 84–85
Your, you're, 130–131